QUECHUA SPANISH ENGLISH Dictionary

QUECHUA SPANISH ENGLISH Dictionary

A Trilingual Reference

Odi Gonzales
Christine Mladic Janney
Emily Fjaellen Thompson

Hippocrene Books, Inc.
New York

For information, address:
HIPPOCRENE BOOKS, INC.
171 Madison Avenue
New York, NY 10016
www.hippocrenebooks.com

Library of Congress Cataloging-in-Publication Data

Names: Gonzales, Odi, 1962-, author. | Mladic Janney, Christine, author. Thompson, Emily Fjaellen, author.
Title: Quechua-Spanish-English dictionary / Odi Gonzales, Christine Mladic Janney, Emily Fjaellen Thompson.
Description: New York, NY : Hippocrene Books, Inc., [2018]
Identifiers: LCCN 2017038881| ISBN 9780781813549 (softcover) | ISBN 0781813549 (softcover)
Subjects: LCSH: English language--Dictionaries--Quechua. | Spanish language--Dictionaries--Quechua. | Quechua language--Dictionaries--English | Quechua language--Dictionaries--Spanish.
Classification: LCC PM6306 .G57 2017 | DDC 498/.323361--dc23
LC record available at https://lccn.loc.gov/2017038881

Printed in the United States of America.

CONTENTS

ACKNOWLEDGEMENTS / AGRADECIMIENTOS

A mis padres, que me enseñaron los saberes básicos, esenciales en el habla Quechua, no en la lengua de las frases hechas y la retórica. A mis estudiantes de New York University que con sus consultas y comentarios enriquecen mi runasimi en cada salón de clase.

— *Odi Gonzales*

This project is the outcome of collaborations and connections that span many years and places. We sincerely thank the many Quechua and Kichwa speakers both in Peru and the United States who so graciously helped us learn their languages and invited us to experience cultural practices despite our fumblings and mistakes, in particular: Juan Reymundo Vega, Nilda Bendezu Flores, Regina Tupacyupanqui Arredondo, Edith Zeballos, Benita Paredes Cusi, Ruth Yabar Challco, Elva Ambía and the Quechua Collective of New York, and Charlie Uruchima and Kichwa Hatari Radio. We are grateful to the Center for Latin American and Caribbean Studies at New York University for supporting us during our Quechua language studies, and for sponsoring the Quechua outreach efforts of our student group. We would like to thank the members of that student group, the Runasimi Outreach Committee, whose energy and dedication continue to inspire us. For years, our families and friends have generously tolerated our lengthy Skype meetings with whispers and tiptoes. Christine thanks her family for their love and humor, and Eathan Janney for shoulder massages and moral support. Emily thanks Sandy Thompson and Bonnie Richardson for putting her on that plane ten years ago despite her best efforts to convince them otherwise. Although it's impossible to list the many people who have inspired and encouraged us over the years, this project is dedicated to all of you.

— *Christine Mladic Janney and*
Emily Fjaellen Thompson

As a group, we would like to thank Hippocrene Books for accepting our project, and publisher and editorial director Priti Gress for helping us bring it to fruition with clarity and kindness.

ENGLISH INTRODUCTION

Since pre-Columbian times, the Quechua language, or Runasimi,[1] has spread and diversified throughout the Andean region of South America. There are currently an estimated 10 million Quechua speakers throughout Bolivia, Ecuador, and Peru, and in certain regions of Argentina, Colombia, and Chile.[2] Today, Quechua is understood as a language family that has many varieties; some of them are mutually intelligible, others are not.

Most scholars believe that members of the Inka[3] culture used a variety of Quechua as their lingua franca, while other languages were spoken by multilingual ethnic groups in the same time period. Due to prolonged coexistence, Quechua and other languages (Aymara, Pukina, etc) influenced one another, and the results are reflected in many of the words in this dictionary. In 1532, shortly after Spain's arrival to the New World, the Spanish priests Domingo de Santo Tomás and Diego González Holguín studied Quechua with the intention of evangelizing local populations, and were the first to write a Quechua

[1] Literally, *Runasimi* is translated as *the speech of humans*, which is how speakers refer to the language. "Quechua" was the name assigned by the Spanish priest Domingo de Santo Tomás, the first grammarian of the Andean language. It comes from *qheswa*, which refers to a geographic area.

[2] This number does not include Quechua speakers who have immigrated to the U.S., Europe, or other places of the world, whose numbers remain unknown.

[3] "Inca" is the most commonly used spelling in English and Spanish, due to how it was written by the first Spanish chroniclers. We made the decision to use "Inka", as it follows the sounds and patterns of normalized Cusqueñan Quechua.

grammar and bilingual Quechua-Spanish dictionaries.[4] It wasn't until the twentieth century that scholars and linguists began to pay sustained attention to the study of Quechua, turning to its phonological, morphological, lexicological, and semantic aspects. Two independent studies, carried out by Gary Parker and Alfredo Torero, have proposed that Quechua languages and dialects can be organized into two branches, each with its own subdivided varieties. Although not universally accepted, this classification system still persists today.[5]

The Quechua that we present here is that which is spoken in the Cusco region of Peru, the Cusco-Collao variety, which is understood as a variant of Southern Peruvian Quechua. To the best of our knowledge, it is the first Quechua-English-Spanish dictionary published in the United States.

Fixing Spoken Language into Written Form

Creating a dictionary can be a rather abstract scholarly project, presenting language as a list of terms with minimal mention of contexts of use. A dictionary can neither register all of the impulses found within living languages, nor avoid the collision of two irreducible codes: orality and writing. Current evidence shows that Quechua was fixed into written form by Spanish priests in the 16th century. While the documents they created are valuable resources, because they were created with the intention of subordinating and converting Quechua speakers, their analysis must not be separated from this contentious motive.

Developing this dictionary was a challenge for many reasons, not the least of which comes from Quechua's agglutinative

---

[4] See Domingo de Santo Tomás: *Grammatica o arte de la lengua general de los indios de los reynos del Peru* (Valladolid, 1560); *Lexicón o vocabulario de la lengua general de los indios del Peru llamada Quichua* (Valladolid, 1560). Diego González Holguín: *Gramática y arte nueva de la lengua general de todo el Peru llamada lengua qquichua o lengua del inca* (1607); *Vocabulario de la lengua general de todo el Peru llamada lengua qquichua o lengua del inca* (1608).

[5] For more information, we refer you to the work of Bruce Mannheim, Peter Landerman, and Rodolfo Cerrón Palomino, listed in the bibliography.

character. This means that a series of suffixes can be attached to root words to create new, long words, each with its own elaborate and precise meaning. For example, the verb *akllay* is defined as *choose*, and is related to the following terms: *akllachiy → make choose; akllakuy → choose for oneself; akllaysiy → help choose*. In some cases, translations that may appear to be synonyms are not, but the distinction may have been too detailed to include. For example, the word *dusk* is translated as *ch'isinyay, rasphiyay,* and *tutayay*. While at first glance these may appear as synonyms, they actually each refer to different and distinct moments in the process of nightfall.

After nearly six centuries of coexistence, it is not surprising that Quechua and Spanish languages as spoken in the Andean region have many links and interdependencies. There is some convergence in pronunciation as well as some similarities in orthography; for example, *tuta → night* is pronounced and written the same in Quechua and Spanish.

Quechua was written down by Spaniards using the Roman alphabet. The Quechua words in this dictionary follow the standard of Cusqueñan Quechua, using 5 vowels (A, E, I, O, U), 2 semivowels (W, Y), and 24 consonants (CH, CHH, CH', H, K, KH, K', L, LL, M, N, Ñ, P, PH, P', Q, QH, Q', R, S, SH, T, TH, T'), but without using these Roman alphabet letters: B, C, F, G, J, V, X, and Z.[6] Unlike Spanish, some Quechua consonants display their own inflections. For example, glottal stops are represented with an apostrophe: *t'ika*; aspirated sounds are represented with either "h" or "hh": *phuyu, chhachu*.

The translations in this dictionary offer an approximate idea of the words and concepts presented, and cannot communicate their full complexity and richness. Despite these limitations,

[6] There are generally two ways of writing in Quechua, one that uses five vowels (A, E, I, O, U) and one that uses three (A, I, U). We have chosen the pentavocalic way because it is what Professor Gonzales knows as a bilingual Spanish/ Cusqueñan Quechua speaker, and what is most familiar to his students. We respect trivocalic Quechua. However, even though it is used in vast areas of the Andes, it is neither the only nor the representative form of Quechua; there are other monolingual varieties as well as other mixed forms of Quechua.

our hope is that this dictionary can be a tool to facilitate and encourage increased use of Quechua, and we recommend that students use it as a resource alongside a class or more in-depth independent study.

Writing and Resignification

Dictionaries (Domingo de Santo Tomás, 1560; Anónimo, 1586; Diego González Holguín, 1607), catechist texts (*Doctrina Christiana y catecismo para Instrucción de indios*, 1584), and compilations (*Manuscrito de Huarochirí*, 1598/1608?) made by Spanish priests with bilingual assistants during the evangelization process are the earliest known written examples of Quechua using the Roman alphabet. In many cases the transcriptions might not have been faithful to native dictation because they were interpreted from Spanish-speakers' points of view. These first dictionaries, while fundamental and invaluable documents, also recorded the manipulations perpetrated at the semantic level during evangelization, where Quechua words had one meaning before conquest and another after. This was very common with terms related to faith and various Andean cultural notions, for example:

Quechua: Pre-Hispanic Meaning → Post-Evangelization Meaning

supay: shadow → demon
saqra: mischievous → devil
hucha: failure to follow through → sin
yana: black *(color)* → ethnicity[7]

Fortunately, communities of Quechua speakers, themselves a living dictionary, often maintain and reinforce pre-Columbian meanings through language use. At the same time, however,

[7] One example of this change can be seen in *Lexicón o Vocabulario de la lengua general de los indios del Peru, llamada Quichua* by Domingo de Santo Thomas. Although most Quechua speakers use the term *yana* exclusively to refer to the color black, the Dominican dictionary includes the following contentious entry, which uses *yana* to refer to ethnicity: "negro yana runa; negra de guinea yana guarme" (1560: 79).

historical meanings have been severely impacted by language contact and language change, whether that be with Spanish, English, or many other languages. In this dictionary we tried to represent pre-Hispanic meanings as well as those given in the process of evangelization and afterwards; we seldom opt for neologisms, such as *hanaq pacha → heaven.*

Likewise, there are meanings that are encoded in different words and depend on contextual use, which we note when possible, for example:

amaru: serpent *(ritual)*
mach'aqway: snake *(common animal)*

pikchay: chew coca *(ceremonial)*
hallpay: chew coca *(everyday)*

Question marks, exclamation points, and other conventions of writing are dispensable in written Quechua, for example, interrogation requires the suffix *-chu*. We have applied these signs to Quechua words for pedagogical purposes only. The gender of the speaker, on the other hand, is often decisive in Quechua. There can be different adjectives and nouns for each sex, as well as for human beings and objects, for example:

tura: brother *(of a woman)*
wayqe: brother *(of a man)*

ñaña: sister *(of a woman)*
pana: sister *(of a man)*

wayna: young man, boy
sipas: young woman, girl

machu: old man
mawk'a: used, old *(thing)*

In some cases, when the Quechua word does not specify gender, it is used for both sexes, and when necessary we clarify in the English and Spanish entries. Occasionally, entries may only appear for one gender because in some cases the Spanish likely replaced the original Quechua word:

kaka: uncle *(maternal)*
waylaka: disinterested *(woman)*, unorganized *(woman)*
ikma: widow *(woman)*

Andean Cultural Contexts, Suffixes, and Clarifications

Due to cultural and contextual differences, and because Quechua has a tendency toward concrete actions, some ideas or Andean concepts are very difficult to translate to Spanish or English, and vice versa. Such is the case of the spatial/temporal concept *pacha*, which in Quechua captures both *time* and *space*. According to Andean thought, everything transpires within this duality. But it is also equivalent to *earth* in the planetary and cosmogonic sense. The term *pacha* is further developed by the following modifiers: *hananpacha* → *world above* (space); *kunanpacha* → *right now* (time). In the cosmogonic sense we have, for example, the expression *mamapacha* → *mother earth.*[8] In our dictionary, we chose the translations *timespace, land*, even though we recognize that these few words do not fully express the more complex Andean concepts.

The basic Quechua verb form is the singular imperative, but for pedagogical reasons, and because of its coexistence with Spanish, we have translated Quechua verbs to match the infinitive form of Spanish and English:

llank'ay: work! *(imperative)* *v.* work *(infinitive)*
lloqsiy: leave! *(imperative)* *v.* leave *(infinitive)*

Abstract terms and concepts are not commonly found in Quechua. For example, there is no Quechua word for the verb *to like*, perhaps because it is not commonly understood as a verb of action. However, Quechua speakers have incorporated

[8] There is a general tendency to write *pachamama: mother earth*, which reveals a Spanish influence; in the Quechua structure it is actually *mamapacha*, like *mamakilla: mother moon*, and *mamaqocha: mother lake*.

the Spanish word for *to like* → *gustar*, and conjugate it following Quechua grammar rules.

There are no verbs related to the operation of machines and technology. Runasimi (speech of humans) was configured from the perspective of the human being, not the machine. Perhaps in the future, speakers will create new terms for these situations.

There are many verbs and nouns that are shared with animals, or that come from the animal kingdom:

thunkuy: tying the legs *(of an animal)*; tie down *(human)*
phaka: crotch, groin *(both human and animal)*

In other cases the root is similarly applied to both human and animal, but the difference is marked by a suffix, for example:

wachay: give birth *(animal)*
wachakuy: give birth *(human)*

There are verb forms whose suffixes (*-sqa*, *-paku*, for example) denote temporality. Participles like *machasqa* → *drunk* (in the moment/temporary) are different from *machaq* → *drunk* (someone who is a drunk, or always drunk). Similarly, the suffix *-paku* alludes to temporary work in *llank'apakuy* but, depending on the verb, carries various temporal connotations. The suffix *-ri* marks the course of time in the execution of an action: *illariy* → *dawn arrives* (does not happen suddenly).[9] Likewise, the suffix *-ya* denotes a process, something that occurs over time: *machuyay* → *grow old (man)*. The words referring to time, *ch'isi* → *night, last night; tuta* → *night; tutantin* → *all night; watantin* → *all year round,* etc., carry inflections and suffixes from the particular Andean way of measuring time.

Adding the suffix *-chi* creates a causative verb that indicates that someone or something causes or facilitates the action of

---

[9] The suffix *-ri* also serves the function of attenuating an imperative.

another, for example: *llank'achiy → make work, waqachiy → make cry,* and *miyuchiy → command to poison.*

The suffix *-ysi* varies according to the verb that it accompanies, for example: *llank'aysiy → to help to work* or *to collaborate with work; mihuysiy → to take advantage of* or *to take food from another*. In the same way, the suffix *-rpariy* denotes both an intention and a lack of intention, determined by the context: *kunparpariy → to tear down something with/without intention.*

We have also included colloquial expressions such as *akakutirpa → stingy,* or *one who takes back what they give.*[10]

There are derivative verbs that carry a literal and a figurative meaning: *akanayay → have the urge to defecate* (literal); *become bothered* (figurative).

Paronyms do not abound, but they do exist, for example: *chayay → arrive; cook completely.*

The suffix *-masi* denotes a link marked by the word it is attached to, for example: *llank'aqmasi → colleague; wasimasi → neighbor.*

Due to the inherent structure of dictionaries, for some terms—such as agents or participles—we have had to make some translations that might seem oversimplified or awkward. In several cases we found Quechua words leant themselves to a more direct translation in Spanish *or* English, but not both. For example, we could only translate the word *qhellichaq* literally into English as *person who dirties*, but were able to make a more direct translation for *takiq → singer* (literally *person who sings*). In other instances we included both the literal and con-

[10] Literally "person who vomits his/her feces."

temporary translations. *Qhawana,* which literally refers to an *observatory*, or *the place through or from which one watches*, we translated as *lookout point*, as well as the more common contemporary equivalent of *window*. Further, the word *tupuq* → *measurer*, when viewed from Spanish and English, could mean the person who measures or the tool with which one measures, however Quechua considers the term *measurer* to signify only the person, not the tool. Although subtleties like these are not explicit, it is our hope that highlighting certain instances here will be helpful.

Adjectives dealing with quantity (*askha, ancha, ñisu, sinchi,* etc.) become adverbs when they bear the mark *-ta: askhata, anchata, ñisuta, sinchita*. Onomatopoeic verbs are common, such as *ch'allchay,* which conveys the action of persistent rain. There are many patronymics of Andean mythology (*waka, awki, apu, etc.*) that we define generically as "Andean deity" although each is distinct and specific. Listing their unique attributes and nature would be too much for this project. Adjectives or verbs that concern humans note (*man*) or (*woman*) where necessary. When words repeat themselves, such as in *hanku hanku,* they take on a new meaning of their own; in this case, *hanku hanku* means *undercooked*, even though its literal translation would be *raw raw*.

A FEW NOTES ON THE FORMAT OF THIS DICTIONARY

While the Quechua-English-Spanish word list gives each entry its own line, the English-Quechua and Spanish-Quechua word lists group related entries together in an effort to make the lists more user-friendly. Readers should note that not all grouped entries share a common Quechua root. We have included parenthetical notes to offer additional information when necessary. When there are no parenthetical notes, the word can be used more generally. In some cases, the parenthetical note appears before the part of speech, and therefore applies to all following grouped entries. In other cases, the parenthetical notes only apply to a single entry within a larger group of translations. Some parenthetical notes differentiate a generic term from more specific types. For example, *taki* is *song* in general, while *haylli* and *wayno* are two Andean varieties of songs:

> **song** *n.* taki; *(Andean varieties)* haylli, wayno
> **die** *v.* wañuy, *(person)* wañupuy
> **build** (*with mud*) *v.* llut'ay; **help build** llut'aysiy; **make build** llut'achiy
> **beat** *v.* (*heart*) phatatatay, *(fight)* maqay; **help beat** *(fight)* maqaysiy; **let oneself be beat** *(fight)* maqachikuy

Due to Quechua's agglutinative character, prepositions are not free morphemes, which means that they are not free-standing words like they are in English or Spanish. Instead, they are added as suffixes to other words. Sometimes their meanings vary depending on use. Some have fairly direct translations from English and are more straightforward. For example, *-paq* translates as *for*, and *-wan* as *with,* thus *alqopaq* → *for the dog* and *alqowan* → *with the dog*. The suffix *-pi* translates as *in* for both time and space, thus you have *wasipi* → *in the house* and *tutapi* → *in the night*. Other prepositional suffixes are more complicated. For example, *-manta* could mean *from*, *about*, or *pertaining to*, depending on the context, and *-kama* could mean *towards* or *until* for both time and space. There are many more prepositions that have complex meanings and uses, but their use in Quechua is better understood through grammatical study, and therefore have not been included in this dictionary.

We hope that these glimpses into the language will help provide an access point for students and speakers, and serve as an aide for learners of all levels.

A NOTE FROM THE AUTHORS — A PROFESSOR AND HIS STUDENTS

The idea of writing this trilingual dictionary emerged in the classrooms of New York University, where Peruvian professor and native Cusqueñan Quechua-speaker Odi Gonzales teaches. Professor Gonzales has devoted his life to the study of Andean language and thought as a researcher, poet, and translator (Smithsonian National Museum of American Indian, National Geographic Television, and National Foreign Language Center at the University of Maryland College Park, Washington, DC). Graduate students Christine Mladic Janney and Emily Fjaellen Thompson completed New York University's Quechua program under the direction of Professor Gonzales, during which time they traveled to Cusco for Quechua language immersion coursework. Both have spent extended time living and working throughout the Andean region, and as we complete this project, Christine is returning from fieldwork in Peru for her doctoral dissertation research in Anthropology.

During the teaching/learning process of the Quechua language, we realized that we lacked a dictionary containing the most commonly used words, and felt inspired to do something about it. But also, this dictionary is a response to the requests of Quechua-speaking communities in the United States and Peru, for whom Quechua language materials are just as scarce. For these reasons we came together to work on this project that has taken more than six years to complete as a team; in the case of Professor Gonzales, it is his life's work. We present this dictionary as a product driven by our own passion and ideas, despite its shortcomings. We have tried to elaborate a dictionary from the perspective of a native speaker and his students, using the Quechua courses and the philological investigations and translations made and published by the professor. We use Cusqueñan Quechua because Professor Gonzales is a native speaker of this variety, and it is what his students learn, speak, and write.

Finally, dear reader, we offer you this dictionary with both enthusiasm and humility, and with our apologies for any errors that escaped our notice, or for omissions due to our own limitations. As we do in our classroom, let us remove the barrier between teacher and student and practice the Andean concept of reciprocity in which no one knows everything and no one knows nothing: everything is shared. In Quechua, the verbs *to teach* and *to learn* are the same word: *yachay*. The forms are differentiated because *to learn* is always conjugated in the progressive; learning is a process that never ends: we are all always learning.

Tukuy sonqoykuwan.

— Odi Gonzales, Christine Mladic Janney,
and Emily Fjaellen Thompson

INTRODUCCIÓN EN ESPAÑOL

Desde épocas precolombinas, el quechua, o runasimi[1] se ha difundido y se ha diversificado por los Andes de Sudamérica. Actualmente, hay alrededor de diez millones de hablantes a lo largo de Bolivia, Ecuador y Perú, así como en ciertas regiones de Argentina, Colombia y Chile.[2] Hoy en día, el quechua forma parte de una familia lingüística que tiene muchas variedades; algunas de ellas son mutuamente inteligibles y otras no lo son.

La mayoría de investigadores piensa que la cultura inka[3] utilizó una variante del quechua como lingua franca, sobre otras lenguas y variantes que eran habladas por grupos étnicos multilingües en el mismo período. Esta coexistencia prolongada del quechua con otras lenguas (aymara, pukina, etc.) generó una influencia que se mantiene hasta hoy y que se refleja en muchas de las palabras quechuas de este diccionario. Poco después de la llegada de España al Nuevo Mundo en 1532, los sacerdotes españoles Domingo de Santo Tomás y Diego González Holguín estudiaron el quechua con la intención de evangelizar a las poblaciones indígenas. Ellos fueron los primeros en redactar un texto de gramática quechua y los primeros diccionarios

---

[1] Literalmente, runasimi es equivalente a "el habla de la gente", y así la llama la comunidad de hablantes. "Quechua" es el nombre asignado por el sacerdote español Domingo de Santo Tomás, el primer gramático del idioma andino. Proviene de qheswa que refiere un nivel geográfico.

[2] Esta cifra no incluye a los quechuahablantes migrantes en los Estados Unidos, Europa u otros lugares, cuyo número es desconocido.

[3] "Inca" es la transcripción más usada en español e inglés. Proviene del oído y la escritura de los primeros cronistas. Nos sentimos más cómodos transcribiéndola tal como se la percibe desde el oído andino, "inka," y porque, finalmente, todas las entradas quechuas están escritas en el quechua normalizado cusqueño.

bilingües (quechua-español).[4] No fue sino hasta el siglo XX que académicos y lingüistas comenzaron a prestar una sostenida atención al estudio del quechua, investigando sus aspectos fonológicos, morfológicos, lexicológicos y semánticos. Los estudios realizados por Gary Parker y Alfredo Torero proponen que las lenguas y dialectos quechuas se organicen en dos ramas, cada una con sus propias variedades subdivididas. A pesar de no ser totalmente aceptado, este sistema de clasificación persiste hasta hoy.[5]

El quechua que presentamos aquí es el que se habla en la región de Cusco, Perú, o Cusco-Collao, que se entiende como una variante del quechua sureño del Perú. Al parecer, este diccionario Quechua-Español-Inglés es el primero que se publica en los Estados Unidos.

Fijación de la oralidad en la escritura

Redactar un diccionario puede ser un proyecto académico meramente abstracto al presentar una lista de términos con mínima mención de los contextos de uso. Un diccionario no puede registrar todos los impulsos que conlleva un idioma vivo, ni puede evitar la colisión de dos códigos irreductibles: la oralidad y la escritura. El quechua fue fijado en la escritura por los sacerdotes españoles durante el siglo XVI con la intención de evangelizar y convertir a los pueblos andinos; por esta razón, al margen de sus invalorables contribuciones, estos diccionarios quechuas conllevan—en algunas de sus definiciones—una motivación contenciosa.

La elaboración de este diccionario fue un verdadero reto,

---

[4] Ver Domingo de Santo Tomás: *Grammatica o arte de la lengua general de los indios de los reynos del Peru* (Valladolid, 1560); *Lexicon o vocabulario de la lengua general de los indios del Peru, llamada Quichua* (Valladolid, 1560). Diego González Holguín: *Gramática y arte nueva de la lengua general de todo el Peru llamada lengua qquichua o lengua del inca (1607); Vocabulario de la lengua general de todo el Peru llamada lengua qquichua o lengua del inca (1608).*

[5] Para mayor información, consultar en la bibliografía adjunta la obra de Bruce Mannheim, Peter Landerman y Rodolfo Cerrón Palomino.

entre otras razones, por el carácter aglutinante del quechua, lo que significa que una palabra puede llevar muchos sufijos que denotan matices semánticos únicos y precisos. Por ejemplo, el verbo *akllay* se define como *escoger*, y está relacionado con los siguientes términos: *akllachiy* → *hacer escoger*; *akllakuy* → *escoger para uno mismo*; *akllaysiy* → *ayudar a escoger*. De la misma forma, algunas preposiciones del inglés y el español van adicionadas como sufijos en el quechua, lo que marca una diferencia a nivel estructural. Por ejemplo, el sufijo *-kama* equivale a *hasta*; *-wan,* a *con;* y *–manta,* a *de (procedencia).* Estas formas no están incluidas en las entradas del diccionario porque no son morfemas independientes en quechua. En algunos casos, cuando nuestro diccionario presenta traducciones que pueden parecer sinónimos equivalentes, no los son. Por ejemplo, la palabra *anochecer* se traduce como *ch'isinyay, rasphiyay* o *tutayay*. Aunque a primera vista pueden parecer sinónimos, en realidad cada una refiere a momentos distintos del proceso del anochecer.

Después de casi seis siglos de convivencia, el quechua y el español de la región andina mantienen muchos vínculos e interdependencias. Hay cierta convergencia en la pronunciación, así como algunas similitudes en la ortografía; por ejemplo, *tuta* → *noche* se pronuncia y se escribe lo mismo en quechua que en español. Como se sabe, el quechua fue escrito por los españoles usando el alfabeto latino. La escritura quechua de este diccionario utiliza 5 vocales (A, E, I, O, U), 2 semivocales (W, Y) y 24 consonantes (CH, CHH, CH', H, K, KH, K, L, LL, M, N, Ñ, P, PH, P', Q, QH, Q', R, S, SH, T, TH, T'), que prescinden de B, C, F, G, J, V y Z.[6] A diferencia del español,

[6] Hay dos teorías que promueven la escritura quechua: usando cinco vocales (A, E, I, O, U) o tres (A, I, U). Hemos elegido el quechua pentavocálico porque el profesor Gonzales es un hablante bilingüe de español/quechua cusqueño y porque es la variante que mejor hablamos todos los autores. Respetamos, por supuesto, el quechua trivocálico, y aunque sea hablado en vastas regiones de los Andes, no puede ser tomada esta modalidad como única y representativa; eso sería excluir a las otras variantes monolingües que no usan el modo trivocálico, así como a los grupos de dicciones mixtas, igualmente quechua-hablantes.

algunas consonantes quechuas muestran sus propias inflexiones, por ejemplo, las palabras glotalizadas representadas por un apóstrofe, como *t'ika*, o los sonidos aspirados que llevan las consonantes "h" o "hh", como *phuyu, chhachu.*

Las traducciones en este diccionario ofrecen una idea aproximada de las palabras y conceptos presentados, y no pueden comunicar su complejidad y riqueza total. A pesar de estas limitaciones, esperamos que este diccionario sea una herramienta para facilitar y fomentar el uso del quechua. Recomendamos que los estudiantes lo usen como un recurso junto con una clase o un estudio independiente más profundo.

Escritura y resemantización

Durante el proceso de evangelización, los primeros diccionarios (Domingo de Santo Tomás, 1560; Anónimo, 1586; Diego González Holguín, 1607), textos catequísticos (*Doctrina Christiana y catecismo para Instrucción de indios*, 1584) y recopilaciones (*Manuscrito de Huarochirí*, 1598/1608?) realizados por sacerdotes españoles con asistentes bilingües fijaron por primera vez en la escritura las palabras quechuas; en muchos casos las transcripciones no son fieles a la dicción nativa porque la transcripción está basada en el oído español. Por otro lado, los primeros diccionarios, si bien documentos primigenios e invalorables, registraron también las manipulaciones a nivel semántico perpetradas durante el proceso de evangelización, en el que palabras quechuas que antes de la Conquista tenían un significado, después de la misma aparecen con otro. Esto fue muy común con los términos relacionados con la fe y algunas categorías culturales andinas. He aquí algunos casos de resemantización:

Quechua: Significado prehispánico → Postevangelización

supay: sombrear, ensombrecer → demonio
saqra: hiperactivo/a, travieso/a → diablo
hucha: incumplimiento a un acuerdo → pecado
yana: negro *(color)* → referente étnico[7]

[7] Un ejemplo de esta alteración puede verse en *Lexicón o Vocabulario de la lengua general de los indios del Perú, llamada Quichua de Domingo de Santo*

Afortunadamente, la comunidad de quechuahablantes, ese gran diccionario vivo, aún conserva muchos de los significados precolombinos. Sin embargo, los significados históricos se han visto gravemente afectados por el contacto lingüístico con el español, el inglés u otros idiomas. Este diccionario intenta registrar el significado prehispánico y el que le adjudicaron en el proceso de evangelización y después; pocas veces se optó por los neologismos, tales como *hanaq pacha → cielo.*

Asimismo, hay palabras que teniendo un mismo significado rigen en el ámbito cotidiano y ritual, el cual lo remarcamos:

amaru: serpiente *(ritual)*
mach'aqway: serpiente, culebra *(animal común)*

pikchay: masticar coca *(ceremonial)*
hallpay: masticar coca *(cotidiano)*

Los signos de interrogación, de admiración y otras convenciones de la escritura son prescindibles en el quechua; la interrogación lo marca un sufijo (*-chu*) no el tono de voz; hemos aplicado estos signos a las palabras quechuas sólo por razones pedagógicas. El género del hablante, por otro lado, es determinante en el quechua: hay adjetivos y sustantivos diferentes para cada sexo, así como para el ser humano y los objetos, por ejemplo:

tura: hermano *(de la mujer)*
wayqe: hermano *(del hombre)*

ñaña: hermana *(de la mujer)*
pana: hermana *(del hombre)*

wayna: joven *(hombre)*
sipas: joven *(mujer)*

machu: viejo, anciano *(hombre)*
mawk'a: antiguo/a *(cosa)*

Tomás. Desde antes de la Conquista y hasta ahora, en la comunidad de hablantes se usa el término *yana* para referir exclusivamente el color, pero el diccionario del dominico registra esta controvertida definición en la que *yana* se refiere a la etnicidad: "negro yana runa; negra de guinea yana guarme" (1560: 79).

En algunos casos, cuando la palabra quechua no remarca el género, indica que se usa para ambos sexos; su equivalente en español o inglés lo especifica. En algunos casos, ciertas entradas registran un solo género. Es el caso, por ejemplo, de tío (lado materno); sus pares contrarios acaso fueron sustituidos por el avance del español.

kaka: tío *(materno)*
waylaka: descomedida *(mujer)*, desorganizada *(mujer)*
ikma: viuda

Las categorías culturales andinas, los sufijos y las declinaciones

Debido a las diferencias culturales, a la diferencia de códigos, y porque el quechua es una lengua con tendencia a las acciones concretas, algunos conceptos o categorías andinas son harto difíciles de plasmar en español o inglés, y viceversa. Es el caso de la categoría espacio/temporal *pacha,* que en quechua alberga *tiempo* y *espacio,* dualidad en la que, según el pensamiento andino, discurre todo. Pero también equivale a *tierra*, en el sentido planetario y cosmogónico. El término espacial *pacha* se diferencia del de tiempo por los modificadores que le preceden: *hanaq pacha → mundo de arriba* (espacio); *kunan pacha → ahora mismo* (tiempo). En cambio en el sentido cosmogónico se tiene, por ejemplo, la expresión *mamapacha → tierra madre.*[8] En nuestro diccionario, optamos por las traducciones *tiempo/espacio; tierra,* aunque reconocemos que vertidas así no expresan cabalmente su sentido.

La forma básica de los verbos en quechua es el imperativo singular, pero por razones pedagógicas y comparativas con el español —la lengua de convivencia— los tradujimos como si fueran infinitivos, igual que en español y en inglés:

---

[8] Hay una tendencia generalizada a escribir *pachamama: madre tierra* con influjo del español; en la estructura quechua es *mamapacha* como lo son *mamakilla: luna madre, mamaqocha: lago madre.*

llank'ay: ¡trabaja! *(imperativo)* *v.* trabajar *(infinitivo)*
lloqsiy: ¡sal! *(imperativo)* *v.* salir *(infinitivo)*

Tal como en el inglés, el quechua sólo tiene una palabra para el pronombre de segunda persona; es decir, no hay diferencia entre el *tú* informal y el *usted* formal, ya que ambos son expresados por la misma palabra *qan* en el quechua.

El verbo *kay* en quechua equivale a *ser/estar* en español; *estar* se diferencia de *ser* en quechua únicamente porque va en progresivo (*-sha*), que denota una temporalidad. Por ejemplo, ***Estoy*** *feliz* se puede traducir como *Kusisqa* ***kashani***.

El quechua no es muy proclive a manejar conceptos ni términos abstractos. Las abstracciones no abundan; no existe, por ejemplo, el verbo "gustar", quizá por no ser propiamente un verbo de acción, pero los quechuahablantes lo tomaron del español y lo conjugan como si fuera una palabra quechua.

No hay verbos relacionados con el accionar de las máquinas y la tecnología; el Runasimi (habla de la gente) fue configurado desde la perspectiva del ser humano, no de la máquina. Tal vez en el futuro, los hablantes crearán nuevos términos para estas situaciones.

Hay una gran cantidad de verbos y sustantivos que se comparten con los animales, o que provienen del reino animal:

thunkuy: atar las patas *(de un animal)*; maniatar, encadenar *(humano)*
phaka: entrepierna, ingle *(animal y humano)*

En otros casos el radical es el mismo para ambos; la diferencia lo marca un sufijo, por ejemplo:

wachay: parir *(animal)*
wacha<u>ku</u>y: dar a luz *(humano)*

Hay formas verbales cuyos sufijos (*–sqa, -paku,* por ejemplo) denotan una temporalidad. Los participios del tipo *machasqa → ebrio*, que es distinto de *machaq → borracho* (consuetudinario). El sufijo *–paku* alude al trabajo temporal en *llank'apakuy* pero, dependiendo del verbo, lleva diversas connotaciones. El sufijo *–ri* marca el transcurso del tiempo en la ejecución de una acción: *illariy → amanecer, llegar la luz del día* (no ocurre repentinamente).[9] Igualmente el sufijo *–ya* denota un proceso, algo que ocurre en el tiempo: *machuyay → envejecer (hombre)*. Los vocablos que refieren al tiempo *ch'isi → noche/ anoche; tuta → noche; tutantin → toda la noche; watantin → todo el año*, etc. llevan inflexiones y sufijos provenientes de la particular manera andina de medir el tiempo.

Al añadir el sufijo *-chi* se obtiene un verbo causativo que indica que alguien o algo causa o facilita la acción del sujeto. Por ejemplo, *llank'achiy → hacer trabajar*, *waqachiy → hacer llorar*, and *miyuchiy → mandar a envenenar.*

El sufijo *-ysi* varía de acuerdo al verbo que acompaña. Por ejemplo, en *llank'aysiy → ayudar a trabajar, colaborar en el trabajo*; en *mihuysiy → aprovechar o usufructuar de la comida de otro*. Del mismo modo, el sufijo *–rpariy* denota una intención o falta de intención, determinada por el contexto: *kunparpariy → derribar algo con/sin intención.*

Las expresiones coloquiales forman parte también de este diccionario: *akakutirpa → se le dice a quien exige que le devuelvan lo que obsequió.*[10]
Hay verbos derivativos que llevan un significado literal y otro connotativo: *akanayay → tener deseos de defecar* (literal); *estar molesto* (connotativo).

---

[9] El sufijo *–ri* también cumple la función de atenuar un imperativo.

[10] Literalmente "el que vomita sus heces".

Los parónimos no abundan mucho, pero los hay, como: *chayay* → *arribar, llegar*; *cocer, cocinarse totalmente.*

El sufijo *–masi* denota un vínculo marcado por la palabra en la que va: *llank'aqmasi* → *colega*; *wasimasi* → *vecino/a.*

Debido a la estructura interna de los diccionarios, algunos términos, como ciertos agentivos o participios, tuvimos que convertirlos al español o al inglés de un modo que parecen barbarismos. Por ejemplo, el vocablo *qhellichaq,* que literalmente sería *el/la que ensucia*, lo tradujimos como *ensuciador/a*; *takiq* → *el/la que canta* como *cantor/a.* En otros casos, el español nos permitió equivalentes más viables como *preguntón* para *tapupakuq*, no *preguntador*. No en pocos casos tuvimos que actualizar el significado originario de algunos términos, como *qhawana,* que literalmente refiere un observatorio, el sitio por donde o desde el cual uno atisba u observa; junto a esta definición registramos su equivalente actualizado: *ventana.* En el término *tupuq* → *medidor* confluyen el hombre y la máquina; desde luego que el quechua sólo registra como *medidor* a la persona que mide, no al medidor de luz, un caso en el que la máquina desplaza al hombre.

Los adjetivos de cantidad *askha, ancha, ñisu*, *sinchi*, etc. devienen en adverbios cuando llevan la marca *–ta*: *askhata, anchata, ñisuta, sinchita.* Los verbos onomatopéyicos son comunes, por ejemplo *ch'allchay,* que registra la acción de llover persistentemente. Hay muchos patronímicos de la mitología andina (*waka, awki, apu*, etc) que definimos genéricamente como *deidad andina* aunque cada uno es distinto y específico; enumerar sus atributos e índole sería complicado. Los adjetivos o verbos que conciernen a seres humanos llevan el género en paréntesis (*hombre*) o (*mujer*) cuando es necesario. Cuando las palabras se repiten, como *hanku hanku,* toman un nuevo significado; en este caso, *hanku hanku* significa *a medio cocer* aunque su traducción literal sería *crudo crudo.*

ALGUNAS NOTAS ACERCA DEL FORMATO DE ESTE DICCIONARIO

Mientras que la lista de palabras de la sección Quechua-Inglés-Español le da a cada entrada su propio renglón, la sección Inglés-Quechua y Español-Quechua trata de agrupar entradas que están relacionadas con el fin de que las listas sean más fáciles de leer. Los usuarios deben notar que no todas las entradas agrupadas comparten una raíz quechua común. Para precisar su alcance semántico hemos incluido notas con información adicional en paréntesis. Cuando no hay notas en paréntesis es porque la palabra puede definirse de modo más general. En algunos casos, las notas en paréntesis aparecen antes de la locución, y por lo tanto se aplican a todas las entradas agrupadas que aparecen a continuación. En otros casos, las notas en paréntesis solo se aplican a una sola entrada dentro de un grupo más grande de traducciones. Algunas notas en paréntesis son para diferenciar lo general de lo específico. Por ejemplo, *taki* es una canción en general, mientras que *haylli* y *wayno* son dos tipos de canciones andinas:

> **flor** *s.* t'ika; *(variedades andinas)* phallcha, sirwana
> **morir** *v.* wañuy; *(persona)* wañupuy
> **sacar del agua** *(algo)* *v.* llaphch'ay; **ayudar a sacar del agua** llaphch'aysiy
> **contado/a** *adj.* *(historias)* willasqa; *(cantidad)* yupasqa

Debido al carácter aglutinante del quechua, las preposiciones no son morfemas autónomas; es decir, no conllevan un significado independiente como en español o inglés. Las preposiciones quechuas van añadidas a las palabras-referentes como sufijos. En algunos casos sus significados varían de acuerdo al uso y contexto. Unas veces tienen equivalentes muy próximos en español e inglés. Por ejemplo, *–paq* y *–wan* equivalen en su traducción a las preposiciones *para* y *con*, respectivamente: *alqopaq*: *para el perro*, *alqowan*: *con el perro*. El sufijo *–pi* en sus traducción es equivalente a la preposición *en* (implica tiempo y espacio): *wasipi*: *en la casa*; *tutapi*: *en la noche*. Otros sufijos-preposicionales cumplen funciones que se van diversificando de acuerdo al contexto. Por ejemplo *–manta* puede referir *lugar de procedencia o pertenencia (de)*, *alusión (acerca de, sobre),* y *–kama* puede equivaler a las preposiciones *hacia* o *hasta* (ambos engloban tiempo y espacio). Hay, desde luego, muchas otras preposiciones que conllevan funciones y usos más complejos para cuyo análisis se requiere de categorías gramaticales y lexicográficas que exceden a este diccionario.

Esperamos que estas notas sobre el idioma ofrezcan a los estudiantes y a los hablantes un punto de entrada, y que sean una herramienta útil para quienes están aprendiendo el idioma, sin importar su nivel.

UNA NOTA DE LOS AUTORES — UN PROFESOR Y SUS ESTUDIANTES

La idea de redactar este diccionario trilingüe surgió en las aulas de New York University, donde enseña el profesor peruano, nativo hablante del quechua cusqueño, Odi Gonzales. El profesor Gonzales ha dedicado toda su vida al estudio de la lengua y el pensamiento andino como investigador, poeta y traductor (Smithsonian National Museum of American Indian, National Geographic Television y National Foreign Language Center de University of Maryland College Park, Washington DC). Christine Mladic Janney y Emily Fjaellen Thompson, estudiantes de posgrado, realizaron estudios de quechua con el profesor Gonzales en New York University durante cuatro semestres. Ellas viajaron a Cusco para ampliar sus estudios de quechua y realizar trabajos de campo en la región andina. Christine acaba de regresar de Perú donde realizó su trabajo de campo para la investigación de su tesis doctoral en antropología.

En el proceso enseñanza/aprendizaje de la lengua quechua, nos dimos cuenta de que carecíamos de un diccionario que contenga las palabras más usadas para comunicarnos y enriquecer nuestro aprendizaje. Pero este diccionario también fue pensado para satisfacer el pedido de las comunidades quechuahablantes de Estados Unidos y Perú, para quienes los materiales quechuas son igualmente escasos. Fue así que nos unimos en este proyecto que llevó algo más de seis años como equipo, pero que en el caso del profesor Gonzales lleva toda una vida. Así, elaboramos este diccionario inducidos por nuestras propias ideas, necesidades y carencias. Hemos redactado este diccionario desde la perspectiva de un nativo hablante y sus estudiantes, basándonos en los cursos de quechua y en las investigaciones filológicas y las traducciones realizadas y publicadas por el profesor. Utilizamos el quechua pentavocálico cusqueño porque el profesor Gonzales es nativo hablante de esta variante, y sus estudiantes aprendieron, hablan y escriben esta variante.

Finalmente, amigo lector, queremos ofrecerle este diccionario con humildad y fervor, anticipándole nuestras disculpas por algún error que no advertimos, o por los vacíos propios de nuestras limitaciones. Como en nuestro salón de clase, eliminemos la barrera entre quien enseña y quienes aprenden; practiquemos la categoría andina de la reciprocidad donde no hay una persona que lo sabe todo ni una que no sabe nada: todo es compartido. En quechua, los verbos *enseñar* y *aprender* son la misma palabra: *yachay*. Se les diferencia porque *aprender* va siempre en la forma progresiva: el aprendizaje es un proceso que nunca termina: todos aprendemos siempre.

Tukuy sonqoykuwan.

— Odi Gonzales, Christine Mladic Janney,
y Emily Fjaellen Thompson

BIBLIOGRAPHY / BIBLIOGRAFÍA

ACADEMIA MAYOR DE LA LENGUA QUECHUA. *Diccionario Quechua-Español-Quechua*. Cusco: Gobierno regional del Cusco, 2005. Versión electrónica: http://lengamer.org/admin/language_folders/quechuadecusco/user_uploaded_files/links/File/AMLQuechua-Dic.pdf

ANÓNIMO. *Arte y vocabulario en la lengua general del Peru, llamada Quichua, y en la lengua Española*. El mas copioso y elegante que hasta agora se ha impreso. Lima. En los Reyes. Imprenta de Antonio Ricardo 1586. Versión electrónica: https://dl.wdl.org/13769/service/13769.pdf

CERRÓN PALOMINO, Rodolfo. *Lingüística quechua*. Cusco: Centro de estudios rurales andinos Bartolomé de las Casas, 1987.

——. *Quechumara. Estructuras paralelas del quechua y del aimara*. La Paz: Plural editores, 2008.

DIOSES Y HOMBRES DE HUAROCHIRÍ. Traducción de José María Arguedas. México: Siglo Veintiuno editores, 1975.

——. Narración Quechua recogida por Francisco deÁvila (1598?/ 1608). Traducción de José María Arguedas. Lima: Ediciones Universidad Antonio Ruiz de Montoya, 2007.

DOCTRINA CHRISTIANA *y catecismo para instrvcción de los indios*. 1584. Edición facsimilar. Español, quechua, aymara. Lima: PetroPerú ([1584] 1984).

GONZALES, Odi. *Runasimi. Lengua y Cultura Quechua*. Vol. I-II-III-IV. New York: Center for Latin American and Caribbean Studies CLACS, New York University, 20015

——. "Juicio oral. Los entuertos del Quijote en la versión Quechua". *Desde el sur*. Revista de Ciencias Sociales y Humanas de la Universidad Científica del Sur. Lima, vol. 7. No. 2 (20015). Versión electrónica: http://revistas.cientifica.edu.pe/index.php?journal=desdeelsur&page=article&op=view&path%5B%5D=130

——. "Corrupción y arbitrariedades en la enseñanza del Quechua". *STLILLA*, Kellogg Institute, University of Notre Dame, 2012. Versión electrónica: https://kellogg.nd.edu/STLILLA/proceedings/Gonzales_Odi.pdf

——. *Elegía Apu Inka Atawallpaman. Primer documento de la resistencia Inka (siglo XVI)*. Lima: Center for Latin American and Caribbean Studies CLACS-NYU, UNMSM, Facultad de Letras y Ciencias Humanas, Pakarina editores, 2014.

——. *El condenado: peregrinaje y expiación entre dos mundos. Voz y memoria quechua en la configuración de la novela Los ríos profundos.* Lima: Universidad Nacional Mayor de San Marcos, Facultad de Letras y Ciencias Humanas, 2013.

GONZÁLEZ HOLGUÍN, Diego. *Vocabulario de la lengua de todo el Perú, llamada lengua Qquichua o del Inca.* Lima: Editorial de la Universidad Nacional Mayor de San Marcos, ([1607] 1989).

——. *Gramatica y arte nueva de la lengua general de todo el Peru llamada lengua Qquichua o lengua del inca.* Lima 1607; Génova 1842.

LANDERMAN, Peter."Glottalization and aspiration in Quechua and Aymara, reconsidered. *Languages in the Andes.* Compilación de Peter Cole, Gabriella Hermon y Mario Daniel Martin. LAS: Newark, Delaware, 1994. pp. 332-378.

LIRA, Jorge A; MEJIA HUAMAN, Mario. *Diccionario Quechua-Castellano.* Lima: Editorial Universitaria, Universidad Ricardo Palma, 2008.

MANNHEIM, Bruce. *The language of the Inka since the European invasion.* Austin: University of Texas Press, 1991.

PARKER, Gary. "La clasificación genética de los dialectos quechuas". Lima: Revista del Museo Nacional. Vol. XXXII, pp. 241-252.

ROWE, John. "Sound patterns in three inca dialects". IJAL 16, 1950. pp.137-148.

SANTO TOMÁS, Domingo de. *Lexicon o Vocabulario de la lengua general del Peru.* Lima: Edición facimilar del Instituto de Historia. Prólogo de Raúl Porras Barrenechea, ([1560]-1951).

——. *Lexicón, o Vocabulario de la lengua General del Peru,* 1561. Edición y comentarios de Jan Szeminski. Lima: Ediciones Santo Oficio, 2006.

——. *Lexicon o Vocabulario de la lengua general de los indios del Peru, llamada Quichua,1560.* Versión electrónica: https://archive.org/stream/lexiconovocabula00domi#page/n173/mode/2up

——. *Grammatica o arte de la lengua general de los indios de los reynos del Peru.* (Valladolid,1560). Transliteración y estudio de Rodolfo Cerrón-Palomino.Madrid: Ediciones de cultura hispánica, Agencia española de cooperación internacional, 1994.

TORERO, Alfredo. "Los dialectos quechuas". Lima: Anales científicos de la Universidad Agraria. Vol. II. No. 4, 1964. págs. 446-478.

Abbreviations for parts of speech

adj.	adjective
adv.	adverb
conj.	conjunction
ind. art.	indefinite article
imp.	imperative
interj.	interjection
inter.	interrogative
n.	noun
num.	number
prep.	preposition
pron.	pronoun
v.	verb

Abreviaturas de la locución

adj.	adjetivo
adv.	adverbio
art. indef.	articulo indefinido
conj.	conjunción
imp.	imperativo
interj.	interjección
inter.	interrogativo
num.	número
prep.	preposición
pron.	pronombre
s.	sustantivo
v.	verbo

QUECHUA ENGLISH SPANISH

Quechua Alphabetical Order:
A, CH, CHH, CH', E, H, I, K, K', L, LL, M, N, Ñ, O, P, PH, P', Q, QH, Q', R, S, T, TH, T', U, W, Y

A

achachaw *interj.* oh no! || *interj.* ¡qué problema!
achakaw *interj.* ouch! || *interj.* ¡qué dolor!
achalaw *interj.* how beautiful! || *interj.* ¡qué hermoso/a!
achhi *n.* sneeze || *s.* estornudo
achhiq *n.* sneezer || *s.* estornudador/a
achhiy *v.* sneeze || *v.* estornudar
achhuchiy *v.* scoot, make move || *v.* hacer mover, apartar
achhupayay *v.* keep moving closer, pester || *v.* acercar constantamente, asediar
achhuy *v.* approach || *v.* asomar
achhuykuy *v.* get closer, bring closer || *v.* acercarse, aproximarse
achura *n.* ration || *s.* ración
achurachiq *n.* person who makes distribute || *s.* el/la que hace repartir
achurachiy *v.* make distribute || *v.* hacer repartir
achurakuy *v.* take one's ration || *v.* tomar uno/a su ración
achuraq *n.* rationer, distributor || *s.* racionador/a
achuray *v.* ration, distribute || *v.* racionar, repartir
achuraysiy *v.* help distribute || *v.* ayudar a repartir
aka *n.* excrement || *s.* excremento
akachiy *v.* make defecate; defeat categorically || *v.* hacer defecar; vencer categóricamente
akakallaw *interj.* how sad!, what a pity! || *interj.* ¡qué pena!
akakutirpa *adj.* stingy || *adj.* tacaño/a
akanayay *v.* have the urge to defecate; get in a bad mood || *v.* tener deseos de defecar; ponerse de mal humor
akasapa *adj.* useless || *adj.* inútil
akatanqa *n.* beetle || *s.* escarabajo
akay *v.* defecate || *v.* defecar
akha *n.* chicha *(corn beer)* || *s.* chicha
aklla *n.* chosen woman in Inkan times || *s.* mujer escogida en tiempos del inka
akllachiy *v.* make choose || *v.* hacer escoger
akllakuy *v.* choose for oneself || *v.* escoger para sí
akllaq *n.* chooser || *s.* escogedor/a

akllasqa *adj.* chosen, selected || *adj.* escogido/a, seleccionado/a
akllay *v.* choose, select || *v.* escoger, seleccionar
akllaysiy *v.* help choose, help select || *v.* ayudar a escoger, ayudar a seleccionar
akna *adv.* like this || *adv.* así, de esta manera
akullichiy *v.* make chew coca leaves || *v.* hacer masticar hoja de coca
akulliq *n.* chewer of coca leaves || *s.* masticador/a de hoja de coca
akulliy *v.* chew coca leaves || *v.* masticar hoja de coca
alalaw *interj.* how cold! || *interj.* ¡qué frío!
allachiy *v.* make harvest *(from the ground)*, make dig || *v.* hacer recoger frutos *(de debajo de la tierra)*, hacer escarbar
allachu *n.* rake, digging tool || *s.* rastrillo, herramienta para escarbar
allana *n.* rake, digging tool || *s.* rastrillo, herramienta para escarbar
allapayay *v.* harvest *(from the ground)* again and again, dig repeatedly || *v.* recoger frutos *(de debajo de la tierra)* una y otra vez, escarbar una y otra vez
allaq *n.* harvester *(from the ground)*, digger || *s.* recogedor/a de frutos *(de debajo de la tierra)*, escarbador/a
allasqua *adj.* harvested *(from the ground)* || *adj.* recogido/a *(de debajo de la tierra)*
allay *v.* harvest *(from the ground)*, dig || *v.* recoger frutos *(de debajo de la tierra)*, escarbar
allaysiy *v.* help harvest *(from the ground)*, help dig || *v.* ayudar a recoger frutos *(de debajo de la tierra)*, ayudar a escarbar
allichachiy *v.* get *(something)* fixed || *v.* hacer arreglar *(algo)*
allichallamanta *adv.* carefully || *adv.* con mucho cuidado
allichaq *n.* repairperson || *s.* arreglador/a
allichasqa *adj.* fixed, repaired || *adj.* arreglado/a, reparado/a
allichay *v.* fix, repair || *v.* arreglar
allillamanta *adv.* little by little || *adv.* poco a poco
allin *adj.* good || *adj.* bueno/a
allinchay *v.* improve || *v.* mejorar
allinta *adv.* well || *adv.* bien, de buena manera
allinyay *v.* heal, get better || *v.* sanar, mejorarse
allipunachiq *n.* person who makes others reconcile, mediator || *v.* el/la que hace reconciliar
allipunachiy *v.* make two people reconcile || *v.* hacer que dos personas se reconcilien

allipunakuy *v.* reconcile mutually || *v.* reconciliarse mutuamente
alliyachiy *v.* make heal, make someone get better || *v.* hacer sanar
alliyaq *n.* person who gets better || *s.* la persona que se mejora
alliyay *v.* heal, get better || *v.* sanar, mejorarse
allpa *n.* soil, terrain, earth, ground || *s.* tierra, terreno, suelo
allpachay *v.* cover with soil || *v.* cubrir con tierra
allpamanta *adj.* made from soil || *adj.* hecho de tierra
allpanay *v.* remove soil || *v.* quitar la tierra
allpasapa *adj.* dusty and dirty || *adj.* terroso con mucho polvo
allpayachiy *v.* grind || *v.* pulverizar
allpayapuy *v.* turn into soil, turn into dust || *v.* convertirse en tierra, convertirse en polvo
allpayasqa *adj.* reduced to dust || *adj.* reducido/a a polvo
allpayoq *n.* landowner || *s.* terrateniente, el/la que posee tierras
allwichiy *v.* make warp threads || *v.* hacer urdir hilos
allwina *n.* loom || *s.* telar
allwiq *n.* person who warps threads || *s.* persona que urde hilos
allwisqa *adj.* warped *(threads)* || *adj.* urdido/a *(hilos),* entretejido/a *(hilos)*
allwiy *v.* warp threads *(literal)*; weave a plot *(figurative)* || *v.* urdir hilos *(literal)*; conspirar *(figurado)*
allwiysiy *v.* help warp threads || *v.* ayudar a urdir hilos
alqo *n.* dog || *s.* perro
alqochay *v.* scorn, humiliate || *v.* menospreciar, humillar
ama *adv.* do not *(prohibitive)* || *adv.* no *(prohibitivo)*
amaña *adv.* not anymore || *adv.* ya no
amapuni *adv.* no way || *adv.* de ninguna manera
amaraq *adv.* not yet || *adv.* aún no, todavía no
amaru *n.* serpent *(ritual)* || *s.* serpiente *(ritual)*
amisqa *adj.* bored with *(food),* sick of *(food)* || *adj.* hastiado/a, empalagado/a
amiy *v.* become bored with *(food)*, get sick of *(food)* || *v.* hastiar, empalagar
amu *adj.* mute || *adj.* mudo/a
amuyay *v.* become mute || *v.* enmudecer
ana *n.* birth mark || *s.* lunar
ananay *interj.* what suffering! || *interj.* ¡qué sufrimiento!
anaq *adj.* hard, resistant || *adj.* duro/a, resistente
ancha *adj.* a lot, many, very || *adj.* mucho/a, harto/a, muy
anchata *adv.* very, a lot || *adv.* muy, mucho/a

anchhiq *n.* sobber, sigher || *s.* sollozante, suspirante
anchhiy *v.* sob, sigh || *v.* sollozar, suspirar
anchhiykachay *v.* sob constantly, sigh constantly || *v.* sollozar constantemente, suspirar constantemente
anka *n.* eagle || *s.* águila
ankalli *n.* rebel • *adj.* rebellious || *s.* rebelde • *adj.* rebelde
anqas *adj.* blue || *adj.* azul
anqasllay *v.* turn blue || *v.* tornarse azul
anqosay *v.* toast *(celebrate)* || *v.* brindar
antara *n.* pan flute || *s.* zampoña
anyachiq *n.* person who makes scold, person who makes berate || *s.* el/la que hace regañar, el/la que hace reprochar
anyachiy *v.* make scold, make berate || *v.* hacer regañar, hacer reprochar
anyakuy *v.* scold oneself, berate oneself || *v.* regañarse, reprocharse
anyanakuy *v.* quarrel, argue || *v.* regañarse mutuamente, reprocharse mutuamente
anyapakuy *v.* scold oneself again and again, berate oneself again and again || *v.* regañarse insistentemente, reprocharse insistentemente
anyapayay *v.* scold again and again, berate again and again || *v.* regañar continuamente, reprochar continuamente
anyaq *n.* scolder, berater || *s.* regañador/a, reprochador/a
anyay *v.* scold, berate || *v.* regañar, reprochar
añaku *adj.* useless || *adj.* inútil
añañaw *interj.* how beautiful! || *interj.* ¡qué hermoso/a!
añas *n.* skunk || *s.* zorrino, zorrillo
añu *n.* tuber *(Andean variety)* || *s.* tubérculo *(variedad andina)*
apachiy *v.* send || *v.* enviar
apakachay *v.* bring *(something)* from one place to another || *v.* llevar de un lugar a otro *(algo)*
apakamuy *v.* find and take *(something)* for oneself || *v.* tomar y llevárselo *(algo)*
apakapuy *v.* recover and take one's belongings || *v.* recuperar uno sus pertenencias y llevárselas
apaq *n.* person who brings || *s.* el/la que lleva
apasanka *n.* spider || *s.* araña
apay *v.* bring, guide || *v.* llevar, guiar
api *adj.* wet, humid || *adj.* mojado/a, húmedo/a

apichay *v.* wet || *v.* mojar
apiyay *v.* get wet || *v.* mojarse
apu *n.* Andean deity || *s.* deidad andina
apuchasqa *adj.* venerated, honored || *adj.* venerado/a, honrado/a
apuchay *v.* venerate, honor || *v.* venerar, honrar
apusonqo *adj.* conceited, arrogant || *adj.* engreído/a, arrogante
aqo *n.* sand || *s.* arena
aqochinchay *n.* meteorite || *s.* aerolito
aqopampa *n.* beach || *s.* playa
aqosapa *adj.* sandy || *adj.* arenoso/a
aqoyraki *n.* misfortune || *s.* desgracia
aqtonayay *v.* have the urge to vomit, be about to vomit || *v.* tener deseos de vomitar, estar a punto de vomitar
aqtopayay *v.* vomit constantly || *v.* vomitar constantemente
aqtoy *v.* vomit || *v.* vomitar
areq *n.* volcano || *s.* volcán
arí *adv.* yes || *adv.* sí
armakuy *v.* bathe oneself, take a bath || *v.* bañarse
armasqa *adj.* bathed || *adj.* bañado/a
armay *v.* bathe || *v.* bañar
arpana *n.* place of offering || *s.* lugar de ofrendas
arpaq *n.* person who gives offering || *s.* oferente
arpay *v.* give offering || *v.* ofrendar
arpha *n.* twilight || *s.* penumbra
arphayay *v.* turn dark || *v.* tornarse oscuro/a
arwichiy *v.* make entangle || *v.* hacer enredar
arwipayay *v.* entangle again and again || *v.* enredar una y otra vez
arwisqa *adj.* entangled || *adj.* enredado/a
arwiy *v.* entangle || *v.* enredar
arwiysiy *v.* help entangle || *v.* ayudar a enredar
as *adj.* few || *adj.* poco/a
asichinakuy *v.* make one another laugh || *v.* provocarse risa unos a otros
asichiy *v.* make laugh || *v.* hacer reír
asikuy *v.* laugh || *v.* reírse
asina *adj.* laughable || *adj.* risible
asipayay *v.* laugh at pain of others || *v.* reírse del dolor de otros
asiq *n.* laugher || *s.* reidor/a
asirikuy *v.* smile to oneself || *v.* sonreírse
asiriy *v.* smile || *v.* sonreír

asiy *v.* laugh || *v.* reír
asiykachay *v.* laugh continuously || *v.* reírse continuamente
askha *adj.* a lot of, many, very || *adj.* mucho/a, bastante, muy
askhata *adv.* a lot || *adv.* mucho, bastante
askhayachiy *v.* increase || *v.* incrementar, aumentar
aslla *adj.* a few || *adj.* escaso
asllallamanta *adv.* little by little || *adv.* poco a poco
asllayachiy *v.* decrease || *v.* disminuir
asnachiq *n.* person who causes bad smell || *s.* el/la que hace heder
asnachiy *v.* make stink || *v.* hacer heder
asnaq *n.* stinky person/thing • *adj.* stinky || *s.* el/la/lo que hiede • *adj.* apestoso/a
asnay *v.* stink • *n.* stench || *v.* heder • *s.* hedor
asta *adv.* a little || *adv.* poco
astachiy *v.* make transport || *v.* hacer trasladar
astakuq *n.* person who relocates || *s.* el/la que se muda
astakuy *v.* relocate || *v.* mudarse, trasladarse
astana *n.* temporary storage || *s.* depósito provisional
astapayay *v.* transport constantly || *v.* trasladar constantemente
astaq *n.* mover || *s.* el/la que traslada
astawan *adv.* even more || *adv.* aún más
astay *v.* transport || *v.* trasladar
astaysiy *v.* help transport || *v.* ayudar a trasladar
aswan *adj.* more • *adv.* rather || *adj.* más • *adv.* más bien
aswanta *adv.* even more || *adv.* aún más
atakaw *interj.* how scary! || *interj.* ¡qué miedo!
atataw *interj.* how disgusting! || *interj.* ¡qué desagradable!
atinalla *adj.* doable || *adj.* factible
atipachikuy *v.* let oneself be defeated, let oneself be dominated || *v.* dejarse vencer, dejarse dominar
atipakuq *adj.* stubborn, persistent || *adj.* porfiado/a, persistente
atipakuy *v.* strive, persist || *v.* porfiar, persistir
atipanakuy *v.* compete, dispute || *v.* competir, disputar
atipaq *n.* victor, dominator || *s.* vencedor/a, dominador/a
atipasqa *adj.* defeated, dominated || *adj.* vencido/a, dominado/a
atipay *v.* defeat, dominate || *v.* vencer, dominar
atiy *v.* be able to || *v.* poder
atiylla *adj.* doable || *adj.* factible
atoq *n.* fox || *s.* zorro
atoqrayay *v.* set a trap *(like a fox)* || *v.* asechar *(como un zorro)*

awachiy *v.* make weave || *v.* hacer tejer
awana *n.* weaving place; weaving tool || *s.* lugar donde se teje; instrumento para tejer
awaq *n.* weaver || *s.* tejedor/a
awasqa *adj.* woven || *adj.* tejido/a
away *v.* weave || *v.* tejer
awaysiy *v.* help weave || *v.* ayudar a tejer
awki *n.* Andean deity || *s.* deidad andina
awqa *n.* enemy, rival || *s.* enemigo/a, rival
awqanachiy *v.* make enemies || *v.* hacer enemistar
awqanakuy *v.* fight || *v.* luchar
aya *n.* corpse || *s.* cadáver
aycha *n.* flesh, meat || *s.* carne
aycharay *v.* remove flesh || *v.* descarnar
aychasapa *adj.* fleshy || *adj.* carnoso/a
ayllu *n.* community, family || *s.* comunidad, familia
aylluchakuy *v.* become family || *v.* emparentarse
aymura *n.* harvest season || *s.* periodo de cosecha
aymuray *v.* harvest || *v.* cosechar
ayni *n.* reciprocity in work || *s.* reciprocidad en el trabajo
aypay *v.* catch up, reach || *v.* alcanzar, lograr
aypaysiy *v.* help catch up, help reach || *v.* ayudar a alcanzar, ayudar a lograr
ayqechiy *v.* make escape, help run away || *v.* hacer escapar, ayudar a huir
ayqepayay *v.* escape constantly || *v.* huir constantemente
ayqeq *n.* fugitive || *s.* fugitivo
ayqey *v.* escape, run away || *v.* huir
aysay *v.* pull, drag || *v.* jalar, arrastrar
aysaysiy *v.* help pull, help drag || *v.* ayudar a jalar, ayudar a arrastrar

CH

chaka *n.* leg; bridge || *s.* pierna; puente
chakachay *v.* hang a bridge, build a bridge || *v.* tender un puente
chakachikuy *v.* choke on || *v.* atragantarse
chakan *n.* haunch || *s.* pernil
chakanay *v.* place crossbeams || *v.* colocar travesaños
chakannay *v.* amputate leg || *v.* amputar la pierna
chakapa *n.* beam, crossbeam || *s.* viga, travesaño
chakapay *v.* raise a beam || *v.* colocar una viga
chakarayay *v.* plug up || *v.* atascarse
chakatasqa *adj.* affixed in the form of a cross || *adj.* fijado/a en forma de cruz
chakatay *v.* affix in the form of a cross || *v.* fijar en forma de cruz
chakchaku *adj.* nosy || *adj.* entrometido/a
chakchay *v.* chew coca leaves; skip *(step)* || *v.* masticar hoja de coca; trotar con brincos
chaki *n.* foot, paw || *s.* pie, pata
chakichay *v.* attach supports || *v.* colocar soportes a las cosas
chakinnay *v.* mutilate foot || *v.* mutilar el pie
chakisapa *adj.* big-footed || *adj.* de pies grandes
chakisenqa *n.* shin || *s.* canilla
chakitaklla *n.* footplow || *s.* tirapié, herramienta de labranza
chakra *n.* field *(agricultural)*, farming land || *s.* sembrío, labrantío
chakrayoq *n.* landowner || *s.* poseedor/a de tierras
chaku *n.* capture of animals among many people *(ritual)* || *s.* captura de animales entre muchas personas *(ritual)*
chakuy *v.* capture a live animal || *v.* atrapar a un animal vivo
challpuq *n.* person who submerges || *s.* el/la que sumerge
challpusqa *adj.* submerged || *adj.* sumergido/a
challpuy *v.* submerge || *v.* sumergir
challpuykachay *v.* submerge repeatedly || *v.* sumergir una y otra vez
challwa *n.* fish || *s.* pez, pescado
challwaq *n.* fisherman || *s.* pescador/a
challwawanka *n.* siren, mermaid || *s.* sirena
challway *v.* fish || *v.* pescar

chanaku *n.* youngest son || *s.* el menor de los hijos
chani *n.* value || *s.* valoración
chanin *adj.* fair, true || *adj.* justo/a, verdad
chaninchaq *n.* evaluator || *s.* valorador/a
chaninchay *v.* value || *v.* valorar
chanqasqa *adj.* tossed, thrown || *adj.* lanzado/a, arrojado/a
chanqay *v.* toss, throw || *v.* lanzar, arrojar
chanqaykachay *v.* toss things carelessly, throw things carelessly || *v.* lanzar cosas sin freno, arrojar cosas sin freno
chanrara *n.* cowbell || *s.* cencerro
chanraraay *v.* reverberate *(cowbells)* || *v.* resonar el cencerro
chapusqa *adj.* soaked, steeped || *adj.* remojado/a
chapuy *v.* soak, steep || *v.* remojar
chapuykachay *v.* soak repeatedly, steep repeatedly || *v.* remojar una y otra vez
chaqmachiy *v.* make plow || *v.* hacer barbechar
chaqmay *v.* plow || *v.* barbechar
chaqmaysiy *v.* help plow || *v.* ayudar a barbechar
chaqnay *v.* tie hands || *v.* maniatar
chaqrusqa *adj.* stirred, mixed || *adj.* revuelto/a, mezclado/a
chaqruy *v.* stir, mix || *v.* revolver, mezclar
chaskichikuq *n.* person who is welcomed; person who lets their belongings be taken || *s.* acogido/a; persona que se deja despojar sus pertenencias
chaskichikuy *v.* let oneself be stripped of belongings || *v.* dejarse despojar de las pertenencias
chaskikuq *n.* person who receives for oneself || *s.* el/la que recibe para sí
chaskiq *n.* recipient, host/hostess || *s.* recibiente, acogedor/a
chaskisqa *adj.* received, welcomed || *adj.* recibido/a, acogido/a
chaskiy *v.* receive, welcome || *v.* recibir, acoger
chatu *n.* pitcher || *s.* cántaro
chawpi *n.* center, middle || *s.* centro, medio
chawpichaq *n.* person who puts in center, person who puts in middle || *s.* el/la que centra *(algo)*
chawpichay *v.* center || *v.* centrar *(algo)*
chawpinakuy *v.* intervene || *v.* interponerse
chawpinay *v.* center || *v.* centrar *(algo)*
chawpinchakuy *v.* intervene || *v.* interponerse
chay *adj.* that • *pron.* that || *adj.* esa/ese • *pron.* ésa/ése, éso

chayhina *adv.* like that || *adv.* así, de esa manera
chayasqa *adj.* cooked || *adj.* cocinado/a
chayay *v.* arrive; cook completely || *v.* llegar; cocer
chaycha *pron.* that little thing || *pron.* esita *(diminutivo)*, esito *(diminutivo)*
chaychá *adv.* maybe, perhaps || *adv.* tal vez, quizás
chaylla *adv.* that's it || *adv.* nada más
chayman *adv.* towards there || *adv.* hacia allí
chaymanta *conj.* after that || *conj.* después de eso
chaymantapacha *conj.* from then on || *conj.* desde entonces
chayneqpi *adv.* near there || *adv.* cerca de allí
chayninta *adv.* over there || *adv.* por allí
chaypacha *adv.* that time || *adv.* esa vez
chaypi *adv.* there || *adv.* allí
chayqa *conj.* then, and then || *conj.* entonces, y entonces
chayraq *adv.* recently || *adv.* recién
chayrí *inter.* and then? || *inter.* ¿y entonces?
cheqaq *adj.* true || *adj.* cierto/a, verdadero/a
cheqaqchay *v.* verify || *v.* verificar
cheqnikuy *v.* detest || *v.* detestar
cheqninakuy *v.* hate one another || *v.* odiarse mutuamente
cheqnisqa *adj.* hated || *adj.* odiado/a
cheqniy *v.* hate || *v.* odiar
chichuyay *v.* gestate || *v.* gestar *(procreación)*
chikachay *v.* decrease, reduce || *v.* disminuir, apocar
chikchi *n.* hail || *s.* granizo
chikchiy *v.* hail || *v.* granizar
chikllusqa *adj.* selected || *adj.* seleccionado/a
chiklluy *v.* select || *v.* seleccionar
chilu *n.* whistle || *s.* silbato
china *n.* female • *adj.* female || *s.* hembra • *adj.* hembra
chinkachiy *v.* lose, misplace || *v.* extraviar, hacer perder
chinkakuy *v.* get lost || *v.* perderse, extraviarse
chinkasqa *adj.* lost || *adj.* perdido/a
chinkay *v.* get diverted, get lost || *v.* desviarse, perderse
chinpa *adv.* across from || *adv.* enfrente de
chinpachiq *n.* person who helps cross || *s.* el/la que ayuda a cruzar
chinpachiy *v.* help cross || *v.* ayudar a cruzar
chinpay *v.* cross, ford *(a river)* || *v.* cruzar, vadear

chinru *adj.* leaning to the side || *adj.* ladeado/a
chipchiy *n.* shine • *v.* shine || *s.* brillo • *v.* brillar
chirapa *n.* drizzle during sunshine || *s.* llovizna con sol
chirapay *v.* drizzle during sunshine || *v.* lloviznar mientras brilla el sol
chiri *adj.* cold || *adj.* frío/a
chiriy *v.* be cold || *v.* hacer frío
chiriyachiy *v.* cool down || *v.* hacer enfriar
chiriyasqa *adj.* cooled down || *adj.* enfriado/a
chiriyay *v.* become cold || *v.* enfriar
chirmaq *n.* person/thing that causes harm || *s.* el/la/lo que causa daño
chirmasqa *adj.* harmed || *adj.* dañado/a
chirmay *v.* harm || *v.* dañar
chita *n.* lamb || *s.* cría de oveja
chiway *v.* mate *(birds)* || *v.* aparearse *(aves)*
chiwchi *n.* chick || *s.* pichón de ave
chiwchiyay *v.* hatch *(chick)* || *v.* devenir en pichón de ave
choqasqa *adj.* launched roughly, thrown roughly || *adj.* lanzado/a bruscamente, arrojado/a bruscamente
choqay *v.* launch roughly, throw roughly || *v.* lanzar bruscamente, arrojar bruscamente
choqchi *adj.* scrawny, weak || *adj.* enclenque, esmirriado/a
choqchiyay *v.* lose weight, slim down || *v.* enflaquecer
choqe *n.* gold mine || *s.* mina de oro
choqllo *n.* fresh ear of corn || *s.* choclo, maíz fresco
chuchu *adj.* hard || *adj.* duro/a
chuchuyay *v.* harden || *v.* ponerse duro
chukcha *n.* hair *(head)* || *s.* cabello
chukchasapa *adj.* hairy *(head)* • *n.* person with a lot of head hair || *adj.* con mucho cabello • *s.* persona con mucho cabello
chukchuchiy *v.* make tremble, shake something || *v.* hacer temblar, sacudir
chukchuq *n.* trembling person/thing || *s.* el/la/lo que tiembla
chukchuy *v.* tremble, shudder || *v.* temblar, estremecerse
chuku *n.* hat, cap || *s.* sombrero, gorro
chukuchakuy *v.* put on hat || *v.* ponerse el sombrero, ponerse el gorro
chullusqa *adj.* dissolved || *adj.* disuelto/a, remojado/a
chulluy *v.* dissolve || *v.* disolver, remojar

chunka *num.* ten || *num.* diez
chunkachay *v.* group by tens || *v.* agrupar por decenas
chunkay *v.* group by tens || *v.* agrupar por decenas
chunpi *n.* woven sash, woven belt || *s.* faja tejida, correa tejida
chunpiy *v.* swaddle a baby || *v.* fajar un bebé
chunu *adj.* small-eared, with mutilated ear || *adj.* de oreja pequeña, de oreja mutilada
chupa *n.* tail || *s.* cola
chupi *n.* hearty soup; vagina || *s.* caldo sustancioso; vagina
chupiy *v.* stew || *v.* guisar
churakuy *v.* put on; position oneself || *v.* ponerse; situarse
churana *n.* place to put things momentarily || *s.* lugar donde se pone momentáneamente *(algo)*
churasqa *adj.* put, placed || *adj.* puesto/a, colocado/a
churay *v.* put, place || *v.* poner, colocar
churchu *adj.* one-eyed || *adj.* tuerto/a
churchuyay *v.* become one-eyed || *v.* devenir en tuerto/a
churi *n.* son of father || *s.* hijo varón del padre
churichasqa *n.* adopted son || *s.* hijo adoptivo
churisapa *n.* man with many sons • *adj.* with many sons *(man)* || *s.* hombre con muchos hijos varones • *adj.* con muchos hijos varones *(hombre)*
churiyaq *n.* progenitor || *s.* engendrador/a
churiyasqa *adj.* conceived *(procreation)* || *adj.* engendrado/a
churiyay *v.* procreate || *v.* engendrar, procrear
churpuy *v.* place pot on stove || *v.* asentar la olla en el fogón
chusi *n.* blanket || *s.* manta
chutachiy *v.* make stretch, make pull || *v.* hacer estirar, hacer jalar
chutapakuy *v.* pull forcefully || *v.* jalar esforzadamente
chutaq *n.* person who stretches, person who pulls || *s.* el/la que estira, el/la que jala
chutarayay *v.* lie down || *v.* yacer
chutarikuy *v.* stretch out || *v.* estirarse, desperezarse
chutasqa *adj.* stretched || *adj.* estirado/a
chutay *v.* pull, stretch || *v.* jalar, estirar
chutaysiy *v.* help pull || *v.* ayudar a jalar
chuwi *n.* bean *(Andean variety)* || *s.* frijol *(variedad andina)*

CHH

chhachu *adj.* ragged || *adj.* harapiento/a, desharrapado/a
chhachuy *v.* wear out clothing until ragged || *v.* desgastar la ropa hasta deshilachar
chhakchay *v.* expel air || *v.* ventosear
chhalla *n.* dry cornstalks || *s.* tallos resecos de maíz
chhallakuy *v.* gather dry cornstalks || *v.* recolectar los tallos resecos de maíz
chhallayay *v.* lose weight, lighten in weight || *v.* bajar de peso, aligerar
chhallchay *v.* action of water boiling || *v.* acción del agua hirviendo
chhallmay *v.* dekernel || *v.* desgranarse
chhallusqa *adj.* shattered || *adj.* quebrantado/a
chhalluy *v.* shatter || *v.* quebrantar
chhanqa *adj.* grainy || *adj.* granuloso/a
chhaphchiq *n.* shaker || *s.* sacudidor/a
chhaphchiy *v.* shake || *v.* sacudir
chhaphchiykachay *v.* shake constantly || *v.* sacudir constantemente
chhaphchiysiy *v.* help shake || *v.* ayudar a sacudir
chhaplla *adj.* lightweight || *adj.* liviano/a
chhapu *n.* thin root, loose thread || *s.* raicilla, hilacha
chhasay *v.* expel air noisily || *v.* expeler aire con ruido seco
chhayna *adv.* like that, in that way || *adv.* así, de esa manera
chhillpa *n.* splinter || *s.* astilla de madera
chhillpanay *v.* remove splinters from wood || *v.* desastillar
chhillpay *v.* splinter || *v.* astillar
chhuchuy *v.* sneak || *v.* reptar
chhulla *n.* frost || *s.* escarcha
chhullasqa *adj.* frosted || *adj.* escarchado/a
chhullay *v.* frost || *v.* escarchar
chhulli *n.* cold *(illness)* || *s.* gripe
chhullmichiy *v.* make collapse || *v.* hacer colapsar
chhullmisqa *adj.* collapsed || *adj.* desparramado/a
chhullmiy *v.* collapse || *v.* colapsar

CH'

ch'achachiy *v.* cause deprivation || *v.* causar una privación
ch'achaq *n.* starved person, deprived person || *s.* el/la que padece una privación
ch'achay *v.* starve, deprive || *v.* padecer una privación
ch'achu *adj.* swindling • *n.* debtor || *adj.* moroso/a • *s.* deudor/a
ch'achuy *v.* swindle, not pay a debt || *v.* estafar, no pagar una deuda
ch'ak *n.* radiance • *adj.* radiant || *s.* resplandor • *adj.* radiante
ch'aka *adj.* hoarse || *adj.* afónico/a, ronco/a
ch'akayachiy *v.* cause hoarseness || *v.* ocasionar afonía
ch'akayapuy *v.* become hoarse for life || *v.* enronquecer de por vida
ch'akayay *v.* become hoarse || *v.* enronquecer
ch'aki *adj.* dry || *adj.* seco/a
ch'akipa *n.* refreshment || *s.* refresco
ch'akisonqo *adj.* sober *(not drunk)* || *adj.* sobrio/a *(no ebrio/a)*
ch'akisqa *adj.* dried out || *adj.* desecado/a
ch'akiy *v.* dry; be thirsty • *n.* thirst || *v.* secar; tener sed • *s.* sed
ch'aku *n.* furry dog || *s.* perro peludo
ch'allapayay *v.* sprinkle repeatedly *(ritual)* || *v.* asperjar repetidamente *(ritual)*
ch'allaq *n.* person who sprinkles *(ritual)* || *s.* asperjador/a *(ritual)*
ch'allasqa *adj.* sprinkled *(ritual)* || *adj.* asperjado/a *(ritual)*
ch'allay *v.* sprinkle *(ritual)* || *v.* asperjar *(ritual)*
ch'allchay *v.* rain heavily || *v.* llover persistentemente
ch'alqe *adj.* limp || *adj.* gaunt, flácido/a
ch'alqey *v.* mummify || *v.* disecar, momificar
ch'alqeyay *v.* become gaunt || *v.* ponerse flácido/a
ch'amillku *n.* small pot || *s.* olla pequeña
ch'anpa *n.* earthen clump with grass || *s.* terrón con césped
ch'anpaq *n.* person who digs up earthen clumps with grass || *s.* sacador/a de terrones con césped
ch'anpay *v.* dig up earthen clumps with grass || *v.* sacar terrones con césped
ch'antaq *n.* person who makes bouquets, person who gathers flowers || *s.* el/la que hace ramilletes

ch'antay *v.* make bouquets, gather flowers || *v.* hacer ramilletes
ch'antiy *v.* hammer; prick || *v.* clavar; pinchar
ch'aphra *n.* branch; fallen leaves || *s.* rama; hojarasca
ch'aphrachakuy *v.* cover oneself with branches, cover oneself with fallen leaves || *v.* cubrirse con ramas, cubirse con hojarasca
ch'apu *adj.* bearded || *adj.* barbado
ch'aqcha *n.* river crossing || *s.* vado de un río
ch'aqchusqa *adj.* wet || *adj.* humedecido/a, regado/a
ch'aqchuy *v.* wet the floor || *v.* humedecer el piso
ch'aqeq *n.* thrower, tosser || *s.* lanzador/a, arrojador/a
ch'aqesqa *adj.* thrown, tossed || *adj.* lanzado/a, arrojado/a
ch'aqey *v.* throw, toss || *v.* lanzar, arrojar
ch'aqeysiy *v.* help throw, help toss || *v.* ayudar a lanzar, ayudar a arrojar
ch'aqla *n.* slap || *s.* bofetada
ch'aqlachikuy *v.* let oneself be slapped || *v.* dejarse abofetear
ch'aqlanakuy *v.* slap one another || *v.* abofetearse mutuamente
ch'aqlapayay *v.* slap repeatedly || *v.* abofetear reiteradamente
ch'aqlaq *n.* slapper || *s.* abofeteador/a
ch'aqlay *v.* slap || *v.* abofetear
ch'aran *adj.* damp || *adj.* húmedo/a
ch'aranchay *v.* dampen || *v.* humedecer
ch'arki *n.* jerky, dried meat || *s.* cecina
ch'arkichiq *n.* person who makes jerky || *s.* acecinador/a
ch'arkichiy *v.* make jerky || *v.* acecinar
ch'arkisqa *adj.* dried *(meat)* || *adj.* resecado/a *(carne)*
ch'arkiyay *v.* dry out *(meat)*; become too skinny || *v.* resecarse *(carne)*; enflaquecer demasiado
ch'arwasqa *adj.* wrung out || *adj.* exprimido/a *(algo mojado)*
ch'arway *v.* wring out || *v.* exprimir *(algo mojado)*
ch'arwaysiy *v.* help wring out || *v.* ayudar a exprimir *(algo mojado)*
ch'arwichiy *v.* make entangle || *v.* hacer enredar
ch'arwipayay *v.* entangle again and again || *v.* enredar una y otra vez
ch'arwiy *v.* entangle, confuse || *v.* enredar, confundir
ch'arwiysiy *v.* help entangle || *v.* ayudar a enredar
ch'aska *n.* star || *s.* estrella
ch'askayay *v.* become radiant || *v.* ponerse radiante
ch'aspasqa *adj.* stolen || *adj.* sustraído/a
ch'aspaq *n.* thief || *s.* sustraedor/a

ch’aspay *v.* steal || *v.* sustraer
ch’aspaysiy *v.* help steal || *v.* ayudar a sustraer
ch’asti *adj.* skilled || *adj.* hábil
ch’atasqa *adj.* bound || *adj.* enlazado/a
ch’atay *v.* bind || *v.* enlazar
ch’ataysiy *v.* help bind || *v.* ayudar a enlazar
ch’awaq *n.* person who milks || *s.* ordeñador/a
ch’awasqa *adj.* milked || *adj.* ordeñado/a
ch’away *v.* milk || *v.* ordeñar
ch’awaysiy *v.* help milk || *v.* ayudar a ordeñar
ch’awisqa *adj.* crumpled || *adj.* ajado/a
ch’awiy *v.* become crumpled || *v.* ajarse
ch’ayña *n.* goldfinch || *s.* jilguero
ch’eqchi *adj.* black and white spotted || *adj.* jaspeado/a de blanco y negro
ch’eqchiyay *v.* turn black and white spotted || *v.* jaspearse en blanco y negro
ch’eqe *adj.* dispersed, sparse || *adj.* disperso/a, esparcido/a
ch’eqesqa *adj.* dispersed, sparse || *adj.* dispersado/a, esparcido/a
ch’eqechiy *v.* disperse, scatter || *v.* dispersar, esparcir
ch’eqlla *n.* frog || *s.* rana
ch’eqollo *n.* nightingale || *s.* ruiseñor
ch’eqta *n.* parcel of land || *s.* parcela
ch’eqtachiy *v.* order to chop || *v.* mandar a talar
ch’eqtay *v.* chop || *v.* talar
ch’eqtaysiy *v.* help chop || *v.* ayudar a talar
ch’ichi *n.* sprout, bud || *s.* retoño, brote
ch’ichiy *v.* sprout, bud || *v.* retoñar, brotar
ch’ikway *v.* spray || *v.* chisguetear
ch’ila *adj.* hard; consistent || *adj.* duro/a; consistente
ch’illiku *n.* cricket || *s.* grillo
ch’illmipayay *v.* wink repeatedly || *v.* guiñar reiteradamente
ch’illmiy *v.* wink, blink || *v.* parpadear, pestañear
ch’illu *adj.* blackest black || *adj.* negrísimo/a
ch’illuchay *v.* dye dark black || *v.* teñir de negrísimo
ch’illuyasqa *adj.* dyed dark black || *adj.* teñido/a de negrísimo
ch’illuyay *v.* turn dark black || *v.* tornarse negrísimo/a
ch’in *adj.* silent • *n.* silence || *adj.* silencioso/a • *s.* silencio
ch’inlla *adv.* silently || *adv.* silenciosamente
ch’inyay *v.* become silent || *v.* callar

ch'iñi *adj.* tiny || *adj.* diminuto/a
ch'ipasqa *adj.* attached || *adj.* adherido/a
ch'ipusqa *adj.* wrinkled, folded || *adj.* fruncido/a, plegado/a
ch'ipuy *v.* wrinkle, fold || *v.* fruncir, plegar
ch'irchi *n.* crybaby || *s.* niño/a llorón/a
ch'irchiykachay *v.* whine || *v.* lloriquear
ch'isi *n.* night • *adv.* last night || *s.* noche • *adv.* anoche
ch'isinyay *v.* become night || *v.* anochecer
ch'isiyaq *adv.* all day || *adv.* todo el día
ch'isiyay *v.* end the day || *v.* finalizar el día
ch'ita *adj.* runaway || *adj.* cimarrón
ch'itakuy *v.* evade || *v.* evadirse
ch'iti *adj.* clever, intelligent || *adj.* ingenioso/a, inteligente
ch'itilla *adv.* cleverly || *adv.* ingeniosamente
ch'iwkay *v.* spray || *v.* chisguetear
ch'iya *n.* nit || *s.* liendre
ch'iyaq *n.* nit remover || *s.* sacador/a de liendres
ch'iyasapa *adj.* infested with nits || *adj.* liendroso/a
ch'olqe *adj.* gaunt, loose || *adj.* flácido/a, suelto/a
ch'olqeyay *v.* become gaunt, become loose || *v.* tornarse flácido/a, tornarse suelto/a
ch'onqaq *n.* person who sucks || *s.* chupador/a
ch'onqay *v.* suck, suckle || *v.* chupar, succionar
ch'onqaykachay *v.* suck incessantly || *v.* chupar incesantemente
ch'oqmi *n.* fist || *s.* puño
ch'oqñi *n.* eye discharge • *adj.* bleary-eyed || *s.* lagaña • *adj.* lagañoso/a
ch'oqñiyay *v.* become bleary-eyed || *v.* tornarse lagañoso/a
ch'oqo *adj.* cross-eyed || *adj.* bizco
ch'oseq *n.* owl || *s.* búho
ch'ukasqa *adj.* sewn roughly || *adj.* cosido/a toscamente
ch'ukay *v.* sew roughly || *v.* coser toscamente
ch'ukaysiy *v.* help sew roughly || *v.* ayudar a coser toscamente
ch'ukchu *n.* little person *(male)* || *s.* enano
ch'uklla *n.* hut || *s.* choza
ch'ukllachiy *v.* order to build a hut || *v.* hacer construir una choza
ch'ukllaq *n.* builder of huts || *s.* constructor/a de chozas
ch'ukllay *v.* build a hut || *v.* construir una choza
ch'ullachakuy *v.* exclude oneself || *v.* excluirse
ch'ullalla *adj.* just one || *adj.* solo uno/a

ch'ullan *adj.* unmatched, unpaired || *adj.* impar, sin par
ch'ullayay *v.* become one || *v.* reducirse a uno/a
ch'ullpa *n.* prehispanic tomb || *s.* tumba prehispánica
ch'ullpi *n.* corn with small kernels || *s.* maíz de grano pequeño
ch'ullu *n.* Andean hat || *s.* gorro andino
ch'umasqa *adj.* strained || *adj.* colado/a
ch'umay *v.* strain || *v.* colar
ch'unchu *n.* jungle inhabitant || *s.* habitante de la selva
ch'unchul *n.* intestine || *s.* intestino
ch'unku *adj.* crowded, gathered || *adj.* apiñado/a, aglutinado/a
ch'unkunakuy *v.* crowd together, gather || *v.* apiñarse, aglomerarse
ch'unpi *adj.* brown || *adj.* marrón, castaño
ch'unpichasqa *adj.* dyed brown || *adj.* teñido/a de marrón, teñido/a de castaño
ch'unpichay *v.* dye brown || *v.* teñir de marrón, teñir de castaño/a
ch'unpiyay *v.* turn brown || *v.* tornarse marrón, tornarse castaño/a
ch'uñu *n.* dehydrated potato || *s.* papa deshidratada
ch'upa *n.* calf *(anatomical)* || *s.* pantorrilla
ch'upu *n.* tumor, abscess || *s.* tumor, absceso
ch'uru *n.* shell || *s.* concha del molusco
ch'usa *n.* absence, distance || *s.* ausencia, alejamiento
ch'usaq *adj.* empty • *n.* absentee || *adj.* vacío/a • *s.* el/la que se ausenta
ch'usaqyachiy *v.* empty, vacate, make disappear || *v.* vaciar, hacer desaparecer
ch'usaqyapuy *v.* disappear forever || *v.* desaparecer para siempre
ch'usaqyasqa *adj.* disappeared, emptied || *adj.* desaparecido/a, vaciado/a
ch'usaqyay *v.* disappear || *v.* desaparecer
ch'usay *v.* leave, travel || *v.* ausentarse, viajar
ch'uspa *n.* bag || *s.* bolso
ch'uspi *n.* fly || *s.* mosca
ch'utichiy *v.* order to skin; order to strip *(belongings)* || *v.* mandar a desollar; mandar a despojar
ch'utikuy *v.* undress || *v.* desvestirse
ch'utiy *v.* skin; strip *(belongings)* || *v.* desollar; despojar
ch'utu *n.* thick lips || *s.* labios gruesos
ch'uya *adj.* clear, clean || *adj.* diáfano/a, limpio/a
ch'uyanay *v.* rinse || *v.* enjuagar
ch'uyayachiy *v.* purify || *v.* purificar, depurar

ch'uychu *adj.* drenched || *adj.* empapado/a de agua
ch'uychuy *v.* gush, flow *(water)* || *v.* chorrear, fluir agua
ch'uymay *v.* empty completely of liquid || *v.* vaciar un líquido totalmente

E

enqa *n.* amulet of stone || *s.* amuleto de piedra
enqaychu *n.* amulet of stone || *s.* amuleto de piedra
enqhepakuy *v.* get in a bad mood constantly || *v.* ponerse de mal humor constantemente
enqhey *v.* get in a bad mood || *v.* ponerse de mal humor
eqeqo *n.* Andean doll for good luck || *s.* muñeco andino para la buena suerte
eqhasqa *adj.* scraped || *adj.* rasgado/a
eqhay *v.* scrape || *v.* rasgar
eqo *adj.* sickly || *adj.* esmirriado/a
eqosqa *adj.* malnourished || *adj.* malnutrido/a
era *n.* place to winnow grain || *s.* lugar donde se ventean los granos
eray *v.* winnow grain || *v.* ventear los granos
erqe *n.* child, kid || *s.* niño/a
erqechay *v.* pamper; adopt || *v.* mimar; adoptar
erqekachay *v.* behave like a child || *v.* portarse como un/a niño/a
erqeyay *v.* feel like a child || *v.* sentirse como un/a niño/a

H

hach'iq *n.* person who scatters; sneezer || *s.* esparcidor/a; estornudador/a
hach'iy *v.* scatter; sneeze || *v.* esparcir; estornudar
hach'iykachay *v.* scatter everywhere || *v.* esparcir por todos lados
hach'iysiy *v.* help scatter || *v.* ayudar a esparcir
hach'u *n.* chewed pulp || *s.* bocado masticado
hach'u hach'u *adj.* half-chewed || *adj.* masticado a medias
hach'uy *v.* spit out chewed pulp || *v.* esputar el bocado masticado
hakllu *adj.* stuttering • *n.* stutterer || *adj.* tartamudo/a • *s.* tartamudo/a
haklluykachay *v.* stutter, stammer || *v.* tartamudear
haku *interj.* let's go! || *interj.* ¡vamos!
hakuchis *interj.* let's go! || *interj.* ¡vamos!
hak'akllu *n.* bird *(Andean variety)* || *s.* pájaro *(variedad andina)*
hak'u *n.* flour • *adj.* floury || *s.* harina • *adj.* harinoso/a
hak'uchaq *n.* person who dusts with flour || *s.* polvoreador/a con harina
hak'uchay *v.* dust with flour || *v.* polvorear con harina
hak'uchiq *n.* grinder || *s.* moledor/a
hak'uchiy *v.* grind || *v.* moler
hak'usqa *adj.* dusted with flour || *adj.* polvoreado/a con harina
hak'uy hak'uy *adj.* very floury || *adj.* muy harinoso/a
hallaka *adj.* featherless || *adj.* sin plumas
hallmachiy *v.* make unearth || *v.* mandar a aporcar
hallmana *n.* Andean agricultural tool || *s.* herramienta andina de agricultura
hallmaq *n.* person who unearths || *s.* aporcador/a
hallmasqa *adj.* unearthed || *adj.* aporcado/a
hallmay *v.* unearth || *v.* aporcar
hallmaysiy *v.* help unearth || *v.* ayudar a aporcar
hallmu *adj.* dull, blunt || *adj.* desgastado/a, romo
hallpa *n.* work break || *s.* pausa en el trabajo
hallpay *v.* chew coca leaves || *v.* masticar la hoja de coca
hallp'iq *n.* scratcher || *s.* rasguñador/a
hallp'iy *v.* scratch || *v.* rasguñar
hamak'u *n.* tick *(insect)* || *s.* garrapata

hamanq'ay *n.* white lily || *s.* lirio blanco
hamanq'ayay *v.* become white like a lily || *v.* ponerse blanco como el lirio
hampuy *v.* return || *v.* volver, retornar
hamut'a *n.* intellect || *s.* intelecto
hamut'aq *n.* intellectual || *s.* intelectual
hanan *adv.* above || *adv.* arriba
hanaq *prep.* on top || *prep.* encima
hanaqpacha *n.* upper level; sky || *s.* nivel superior; cielo
hanch'uy *v.* nibble || *v.* mordisquear
hanku *adj.* raw || *adj.* crudo/a
hanku hanku *adj.* undercooked || *adj.* a medio cocer
hank'a *n.* toasted grain or beans || *s.* grano tostado
hank'ana *n.* Andean pot for toasting || *s.* vasija andina para tostar
hank'aq *n.* toaster of grains or beans || *s.* el/la que tuesta granos
hank'arpa *adj.* horizontal || *adj.* horizontal
hank'arpamanta *adv.* face up || *adv.* boca arriba
hank'ay *v.* toast grains or beans || *v.* tostar granos
hank'u *n.* *(anatomical)* nerve, tendon || *s.* nervio, tendón
hanllarayay *v.* be stupefied || *v.* atolondrarse
hanllariy *v.* yawn || *v.* bostezar
hanllay *v.* open one's mouth || *v.* abrir la boca
hanllaykachay *v.* open and close one's mouth repeatedly || *v.* abrir y cerrar la boca constantamente
hanllu *adj.* toothless || *adj.* desdentado/a
hanlluy *v.* babble || *v.* balbucir
hanp'atu *n.* toad || *s.* sapo
hanpi *n.* medicine, remedy || *s.* medicina, remedio
hanpichikuy *v.* let oneself be cured by someone || *v.* hacerse curar
hanpichiy *v.* make cure || *v.* hacer curar
hanpikuy *v.* cure oneself || *v.* curarse
hanpiq *n.* doctor, healer || *s.* médico/a, curandero/a
hanpisqa *adj.* cured || *adj.* curado/a
hanpiy *v.* cure || *v.* curar
hanpiysiy *v.* help cure || *v.* ayudar a curar
hanrayay *v.* be engrossed || *v.* abstraerse
hanuk'achiy *v.* make wean || *v.* hacer destetar
hanuk'asqa *adj.* weaned || *adj.* destetado/a
hanuk'ay *v.* wean || *v.* destetar
hap'ichikuy *v.* let oneself be captured, get caught || *v.* dejarse capturar, ser pillado/a

hap'ichiy *v.* burn || *v.* encender
hap'ina *n.* handle || *s.* asa
hap'inalla *adj.* easy to capture || *adj.* fácil de capturar
hap'irayay *v.* hold *(something)* for a while || *v.* asir *(algo)* prolongadamente
hap'iy *v.* grab, capture, catch || *v.* agarrar, capturar
haphlla *adj.* rude || *adj.* descortés
hapht'a *n.* handful || *s.* puñado
hapht'ay *v.* pick up by handfuls || *v.* recoger en puñados
hapht'aykachay *v.* pick up by handfuls constantly || *v.* recoger en puñados constantemente
hapht'aysiy *v.* help pick up by handfuls || *v.* ayudar a recoger en puñados
haqey *v.* disregard || *v.* prescindir
haqhay *adj.* that *(far)* • *pron.* that *(far)* || *adj.* aquel, aquella • *pron.* aquél, aquélla, aquello
harawi *n.* poem || *s.* poema
harchi *adj.* skinny, thin || *adj.* flaquísimo/a
hark'ana *n.* obstruction || *s.* obstrucción
hark'apayay *v.* obstruct || *v.* obstruir
hark'ay *v.* intercept, detain || *v.* interceptar, detener
hark'aysiy *v.* help intercept, help detain || *v.* ayudar a interceptar, ayudar a detener
harwiq *n.* stirrer || *s.* revolvedor/a
harwisqa *adj.* stirred *(grains)* || *adj.* revuelto *(granos)*
harwiy *v.* stir grains || *v.* revolver granos
hasp'ichiy *v.* make dig || *v.* hacer escarbar
hasp'ina *n.* digging tool || *s.* herramienta para escarbar
hasp'iq *n.* digger || *s.* escarbador/a
hasp'iy *v.* dig || *v.* escarbar
hasp'iysiy *v.* help dig || *v.* ayudar a escarbar
hasut'i *n.* whip || *s.* látigo
hatarichiy *v.* erect || *v.* erigir
hatariy *v.* get up || *v.* levantarse
hatun *adj.* big, tall || *adj.* grande
hatunchay *v.* enlarge, expand || *v.* agrandar, expandir
hatunkaray *adj.* enormous || *adj.* enorme
hatunyay *v.* grow || *v.* crecer, desarrollarse
hat'ay *v.* kick someone out || *v.* expulsar a alguien
hat'upa *n.* corn smut • *adj.* clumsy || *s.* mazorca con hongo • *adj.* torpe

hawa *prep.* outside || *prep.* afuera
haway *n.* grandchild || *s.* nieto/a
hawaychuri *n.* stepson || *s.* entenado
hawisqa *adj.* smeared || *adj.* ungido/a
hawiy *v.* smear || *v.* ungir
haya *adj.* spicy || *adj.* picante
hayaqe *n.* bile || *s.* hiel
hayk'a *inter.* how much?, how many? || *inter.* ¿cuánto/a?, ¿cuántos/as?
hayk'aq *inter. adv.* when? || *inter. adv.* ¿cuándo?
haykuchiy *v.* put away; let in || *v.* encajar; permitir entrar
haykuna *n.* entrance || *s.* entrada
haykuy *v.* enter || *v.* entrar
haylli *n.* poem, song *(Andean variety)* || *s.* poema, canción *(variedad andina)*
haymay *v.* collaborate, help || *v.* colaborar, ayudar
hayt'a *n.* kick; foot of the bed || *s.* patada; parte de la cama donde van los pies
hayt'achiy *v.* make kick || *v.* hacer patear
hayt'anakuy *v.* kick one another || *v.* patearse mutuamente
hayt'arikuy *v.* stretch one's legs || *v.* estirar las piernas
hayt'asqa *adj.* kicked || *adj.* pateado/a
hayt'ay *v.* kick || *v.* patear
hayt'aykachay *v.* kick and stomp || *v.* patalear
hayt'aysiy *v.* help kick || *v.* ayudar a patear
haywanakuy *v.* exchange || *v.* intercambiar
haywapakuy *v.* try to reach with hands || *v.* intentar alcanzar con las manos
haywapayay *v.* reach with hands repeatedly || *v.* alcanzar con las manos reiteradamente
haywarikuy *v.* offer || *v.* ofrendar
hayway *v.* hand over || *v.* pasar con la mano
hich'apayay *v.* spill again and again || *v.* derramar una y otra vez
hich'asqa *adj.* spilled || *adj.* derramado/a
hich'ay *v.* spill || *v.* derramar
hich'aysiy *v.* help spill || *v.* ayudar a derramar
hik'i *n.* hiccup || *s.* hipo
hik'ipakuy *v.* sob || *v.* sollozar
hik'iy *v.* hiccup || *v.* hipar
hillu *n.* candy || *s.* golosina
hina *adv.* like || *adv.* como

hinaspa *conj.* and then || *conj.* y entonces
hink'iy *v.* tiptoe || *v.* caminar de puntillas
hisp'achiy *v.* make urinate || *v.* hacer orinar
hisp'ana *n.* urinal, bathroom || *s.* urinario, baño
hisp'anayay *v.* have the urge to urinate || *v.* tener deseos de orinar
hisp'apakuy *v.* urinate constantly || *v.* orinar constantemente
hisp'ay *v.* urinate • *n.* urine || *v.* orinar • *s.* orina
hoq *adj.* other, another || *adj.* otro/a
hoqarinalla *adj.* easy to raise, easy to pick up || *adj.* fácil de recoger, fácil de alzar
hoqariy *v.* raise, pick up || *v.* recoger, alzar
hoqariysiy *v.* help raise, help pick up || *v.* ayudar a recoger, ayudar a alzar
hoqmanta *adv.* again || *adv.* otra vez, de nuevo
hoqniraq *adj.* different || *adj.* diferente
hoqniraqta *adv.* differently || *adv.* diferentemente
hoq'o *adj.* damp || *adj.* húmedo/a
hoq'oyllo *n.* tadpole || *s.* renacuajo
horqochikuy *v.* let *(something)* be taken from you, let *(something)* be removed from you || *v.* dejarse extraer *(algo)*
horqoq *n.* person who takes out || *s.* sacador/a, el/la que extrae
horqosqa *adj.* taken out, removed || *adj.* extraído/a
horqoy *v.* take out, remove || *v.* sacar, extraer
hucha *n.* failure to follow through; sin || *s.* incumplimiento; pecado
huchallikuy *v.* sin || *v.* pecar
huchasapa *n.* person who never follows through; sinner || *s.* el/la que incumple mucho; pecador/a
huchay *v.* fail to follow through || *v.* incumplir
huchayoq *n.* defaulter; sinner || *s.* incumplidor/a; pecador/a
huch'uy *adj.* small, little || *adj.* pequeño/a
huch'uyllaña *adj.* tiny || *adj.* minúsculo/a
huch'uyniraq *adj.* smallish || *adj.* más o menos pequeño
huch'uyyachiy *v.* reduce || *v.* reducir
huk *num.* one • *ind. art.* a/an || *num.* uno/a • *art. indet.* un/a
huklla *adv.* only one || *adv.* solamente uno/a
hukllanay *v.* separate || *v.* desunir
hukllasqa *adj.* unified || *adj.* unificado/a
hukllay *v.* unify || *v.* unificar
huk'i *n.* angle || *s.* ángulo
huk'ucha *n.* mouse || *s.* ratón

hunp'i *n.* sweat || *s.* sudor
hunp'ichiy *v.* make sweat || *v.* hacer sudar
hunp'iq *n.* person who sweats || *s.* sudador/a
hunp'isqa *adj.* sweaty || *adj.* sudado/a
hunp'iy *v.* sweat || *v.* sudar
hunt'a *adj.* complete, full || *adj.* completo/a, lleno/a
hunt'asqa *adj.* completed, filled || *adj.* completado/a, llenado/a
hunt'ay *v.* complete, fill || *v.* completar, llenar
huñunakuy *v.* get together || *v.* reunirse
huñuq *n.* person who gathers together || *s.* agrupador/a
huñuy *v.* gather together || *v.* agrupar
huñuysiy *v.* help gather together || *v.* ayudar a agrupar
hurk'ay *v.* come to an agreement || *v.* acordar
husk'ay *v.* scatter seeds || *v.* esparcir semillas
husk'aysiy *v.* help scatter seeds || *v.* ayudar a esparcir semillas
husut'a *n.* sandal || *s.* sandalia
hut'u *adj.* infested *(grains)* || *adj.* infestado/a *(granos)*
hut'uy *v.* dampen until infested *(grains)* || *v.* humedecer hasta infestar *(granos)*
hut'uyay *v.* become infested *(grains)*, become spoiled *(grains)* || *v.* infestarse *(granos)*, corroerse *(granos)*

I

icha *conj.* or • *adv.* perhaps || *conj.* o • *adv.* acaso
ichapas *adv.* could be || *adv.* puede ser que
ichaqa *conj.* but || *conj.* pero
ichhu *n.* hay || *s.* paja
ichhuna *n.* sickle || *s.* segadera
ichhupanpa *n.* brush *(plant)* || *s.* pajonal
ichhuy *v.* reap hay || *v.* segar la paja
ichiy *v.* walk with small steps || *v.* caminar con pasos cortos
ikma *n.* widow *(woman)* || *s.* viuda
ikmayay *v.* become widowed *(woman)* || *v.* enviudar *(mujer)*
illapa *n.* lightning || *s.* relámpago
illapay *v.* flash || *v.* relampaguear
illaq *adj.* radiant || *adj.* radiante
illariy *n.* dawn • *v.* dawn || *s.* amanecer • *v.* amanecer
ima *inter.* what? • *conj.* and || *inter.* ¿qué? • *conj.* y
ima rayku *inter.* why? || *inter.* ¿por qué razón?
imamanta *inter.* for what reason? || *inter.* ¿a causa de qué?
imapaq *inter.* for what? || *inter.* ¿para qué?
inchis *n.* peanut || *s.* maní
inkill *n.* garden || *s.* jardín
inkillpata *n.* garden terrace || *s.* andén florido
inti *n.* sun || *s.* sol
intiyay *v.* lose track of time; become afternoon || *v.* dejarse ganar por las horas del día, hacerse tarde
ipa *n.* paternal aunt || *s.* tía paterna
iphu *n.* drizzle || *s.* llovizna
iphuy *v.* drizzle || *v.* lloviznar
irpasqa *adj.* marked || *adj.* marcado/a
irpay *v.* mark || *v.* marcar
isanka *n.* basket || *s.* canasta
iskay *num.* two || *num.* dos
iskaychay *v.* divide in two; duplicate || *v.* dividir en dos; duplicar
iskayllu *adj.* disloyal || *adj.* desleal
iskayyay *v.* doubt, vacillate || *v.* dudar, vacilar
isma *n.* manure || *s.* estiércol

ismu *adj.* rotten || *adj.* podrido/a
ismusqa *adj.* rotten || *adj.* podrido/a
ismuy *v.* rot || *v.* pudrir
isqon *num.* nine || *num.* nueve
itha *n.* mite || *s.* ácaro

K

kachariy *v.* drop, let fall || *v.* soltar, dejar caer
kacharpariy *v.* drop suddenly || *v.* soltar repentinamente
kachay *v.* order someone to do something || *v.* ordenar a hacer algo
kachi *n.* salt || *s.* sal
kachisapa *adj.* salty || *adj.* salado/a
kachiyay *v.* salt || *v.* salar
kachun *n.* cucumber || *s.* pepino
kaka *n.* maternal uncle || *s.* tío materno
kakallaw *interj.* how sad!, what a pity! || *interj.* ¡qué pena!
kallchay *v.* harvest corn • *n.* corn harvest || *v.* segar maíz • *s.* siega de maíz
kallpa *n.* strength || *s.* fuerza
kallpachakuy *v.* become strong || *v.* fortalecerse
kallpachay *v.* strengthen || *v.* fortalecer
kallpasapa *adj.* strong || *adj.* fuerte
kamachi *n.* rule || *s.* mandato
kamachiq *n.* ruler || *s.* mandatario
kamachiy *v.* rule || *v.* mandar
kamaq *n.* creator || *s.* creador/a
kamasqa *adj.* created || *adj.* creado/a
kamay *v.* create || *v.* crear
kanasqa *adj.* burnt || *adj.* quemado/a
kanay *v.* burn || *v.* quemar
kancha *n.* corral || *s.* corral
kaniy *v.* bite || *v.* morder
kanka *n.* roasted meat || *s.* carne asada
kankay *v.* roast meat || *v.* asar carne
kaqniyoq *n.* owner, proprietor || *s.* dueño/a, propietario/a
karu *adv.* far • *adj.* far || *adv.* lejos • *adj.* lejano/a
karunchakuy *v.* distance oneself || *v.* alejarse
karunchay *v.* move away || *v.* alejar
kasukuq *adj.* obedient || *adj.* obediente
kasuy *v.* obey || *v.* obedecer
kaw kaw *n.* fish eggs, roe || *s.* huevecillos de los peces

kawitu *n.* wooden platform || *s.* tarima
kawsaq *adj.* alive || *adj.* viviente
kawsaqmasi *n.* life partner || *s.* conviviente
kawsarichiy *v.* animate || *v.* reanimar
kawsariy *v.* revive || *v.* revivir
kawsay *v.* exist || *v.* existir
kawsay *n.* life, existence || *s.* vida, existencia
kay[1] *adj.* this • *pron.* this || *adj.* este, esta • *pron.* éste, ésta, esto
kay[2] *v.* be, have || *v.* ser, tener
kayhina *adv.* like this || *adv.* así, de esta manera
kaycha *pron.* this little thing || *pron.* estito/a *(diminutivo)*
kayman *adv.* towards here || *adv.* hacia aquí
kayneqpi *adv.* near here || *adv.* cerca de aquí
kayninta *adv.* over here || *adv.* por aquí
kaypi *adv.* here || *adv.* aquí
kicharayaq *adj.* ajar || *adj.* entreabierto/a
kichariy *v.* open slowly; open suddenly || *v.* abrir lentamente; abrir súbitamente
kichasqa *adj.* open || *adj.* abierto/a
kichay *v.* open || *v.* abrir
kikin *adj.* same, identical || *adj.* mismo/a, idéntico/a
killa *n.* moon, month || *s.* luna, mes
kinra *n.* side || *s.* lado, costado
kinranpa *adj.* leaning to one side || *adj.* inclinado/a a un costado
kinranpamanta *adv.* leaning to one side || *adv.* inclinado/a a un costado
kinray *v.* go to one side, lean to one side || *v.* ir hacia un costado, ladearse
kinsa *num.* three || *num.* tres
kinwa *n.* quinoa, Andean grain || *s.* quinua, grano andino
kirkiy *v.* tiptoe || *v.* caminar de puntillas
kirpa *n.* cover || *s.* tapa
kirpay *v.* cover || *v.* tapar
kiru *n.* tooth || *s.* diente
kisa *n.* nettle || *s.* ortiga
kiska *n.* thorn || *s.* espina
kiskasapa *adj.* thorny, prickly || *adj.* espinoso/a
kisma *n.* uterus || *s.* útero
kuchuna *n.* knife || *s.* cuchillo
kuchuy *v.* cut || *v.* cortar

kuka *n.* coca || *s.* coca
kukuchi *n.* phantom, ghost || *s.* fantasma, aparecido/a
kukuli *n.* Andean variety of bird || *s.* variedad de ave andina
kukupin *n.* liver || *s.* hígado
kullachiy *v.* tickle someone || *v.* hacer cosquillas a alguien
kulli *adj.* purple || *adj.* morado/a
kunachallan *adv.* immediately || *adv.* inmediatamente
kunan *adv.* today, now || *adv.* hoy, ahora
kunanllaraq *adv.* recently || *adv.* recientemente
kunanpacha *adv.* right now, immediately || *adv.* ahora mismo, inmediatamente
kunka *n.* neck; voice || *s.* cuello; voz
kunparpariy *v.* knock down with or without intention || *v.* derribar con o sin intención
kunpasqa *adj.* knocked down || *adj.* derribado/a
kunpay *v.* knock down || *v.* derribar
kuntur *n.* condor || *s.* cóndor
kuraq *adj.* older || *adj.* mayor *(edad)*
kurku *n.* tree trunk || *s.* tronco de árbol
kuru *n.* worm || *s.* gusano
kusa *interj.* how nice! || *interj.* ¡qué bueno/a!
kusay *v.* roast tubers || *v.* asar tubérculos
kusi *n.* happiness || *s.* alegría
kusikuy *v.* be happy || *v.* alegrarse
kusisqa *adj.* happy || *adj.* alegre
kuska *adj.* together, united || *adj.* junto, unido/a
kuskalla *adv.* jointly || *adv.* juntamente
kuskan *n.* half || *s.* mitad
kuskiy *v.* plow || *v.* barbechar
kusma *n.* tunic || *s.* túnica
kutama *n.* sack || *s.* talego
kutana *n.* mortar and pestle || *s.* mortero y piedra plana para moler
kutasqa *adj.* ground *(crushed)* || *adj.* molido/a
kutay *v.* grind || *v.* moler
kutaysiy *v.* help grind || *v.* ayudar a moler
kuti *n.* time *(frequency)* || *s.* vez *(frecuencia)*
kuti kuti *adv.* repeatedly || *adv.* repetidamente
kutichiy *v.* return, respond || *v.* devolver, responder
kutipakuy *v.* persist; object || *v.* porfiar; objetar
kutipay *v.* do again || *v.* hacer de nuevo

kutiriy *v.* go back slowly, turn slowly || *v.* retroceder, girar lentamente
kutirpay *v.* regurgitate || *v.* regurgitar
kutit'ikra *adv.* there and back • *adj.* round-trip || *adv.* ida y vuelta • *adj.* ida y vuelta
kutiy *v.* return || *v.* regresar
kututu *n.* guinea pig *(male)*; breeding male || *s.* cuy macho; macho reproductor
kuyuchiy *v.* make move, rock || *v.* hacer mover, mecer
kuyuriy *v.* retreat, move over || *v.* retirarse, desplazarse
kuyuy *v.* move oneself || *v.* moverse

KH

khacha *adj.* dirty || *adj.* sucio/a
khachusqa *adj.* nibbled || *adj.* mordisqueado/a
khachuy *v.* bite, nibble || *v.* morder, mordisquear
khaka *adj.* clustered • *n.* duck *(male)* || *adj.* enracimado/a • *s.* pato macho
khakay *v.* break off a piece || *v.* desgajar
khakuy *v.* pick *(fruit)* || *v.* desprender *(frutos)*
khallachiy *v.* make cut open || *v.* hacer sajar
khallaq *n.* cutter || *s.* sajador/a
khallasqa *adj.* cut open || *adj.* sajado/a
khallay *v.* cut open || *v.* sajar
khallaysiy *v.* help cut open || *v.* ayudar a sajar
khallka *adj.* pebbly || *adj.* pedregoso/a
khallkachay *v.* cover a path with gravel || *v.* cubrir con cascajo una vía
khallkanay *v.* remove gravel from path || *v.* quitar el cascajo de una vía
khallpay *v.* splinter, chip || *v.* astillar, desportillar
khamuchiy *v.* make bite off a big piece || *v.* hacer dentellear
khamusqa *adj.* bitten off || *adj.* dentelleado/a
khamuy *v.* bite off a big piece || *v.* dentellear
khanka *adj.* filthy || *adj.* mugriento/a
khapay *v.* burp || *v.* eructar
khapuchiy *v.* make drill hole|| *v.* hacer perforar
khapusqa *adj.* drilled *(hole)* || *adj.* perforado/a
khapuy *v.* drill hole || *v.* perforar
khapuysiy *v.* help drill hole || *v.* ayudar a perforar
kharka *adj.* dirty *(skin)* || *adj.* sucio/a *(piel)*
kharkachakuy *v.* get dirty *(skin)* || *v.* enmugrecerse *(piel)*
kharkannay *v.* clean one's dirty skin || *v.* limpiar la suciedad de la piel
khasay *v.* burp || *v.* eructar
khaskaq *n.* gnawer || *s.* roedor/a
khaskasqa *adj.* gnawed || *adj.* roído/a
khaskay *v.* gnaw || *v.* roer

khastuy *v.* chew on || *v.* roer
khatatachiy *v.* make shiver, make tremble || *v.* hacer tiritar, hacer temblar
khatatay *v.* shiver, tremble || *v.* tiritar, temblar
khayna *adv.* like this || *adv.* así
khiki *n.* pimple, acne || *s.* grano, acné
khikisapa *adj.* pimply || *adj.* graniento *(piel)*
khipu *n.* bundle, knot || *s.* envoltorio, nudo
khipuchiy *v.* make knot || *v.* hacer anudar
khipupayay *v.* knot constantly || *v.* anudar constantemente
khipusqa *adj.* knotted || *adj.* anudado/a
khipuy *v.* knot || *v.* anudar
khipuysiy *v.* help knot || *v.* ayudar a anudar
khitu *adj.* clumsy *(while walking)* || *adj.* torpe *(al andar)*
khuchi *n.* pig || *s.* cerdo
khullu *adj.* small || *adj.* menudo/a, pequeño/a
khutu *adj.* frigid || *adj.* gélido/a
khutuy *v.* freeze || *v.* helar
khutuyay *v.* become frigid || *v.* ponerse gélido/a
khuyapayaq *n.* person who pities || *s.* el/la que se compadece
khuyapayay *v.* pity || *v.* compadecerse
khuyay khuyay *adv.* sadly || *adv.* tristemente
khuyuq *n.* whistler || *s.* silbador/a
khuyuy *v.* whistle || *v.* silbar

K'

k'acha *adj.* elegant || *adj.* elegante
k'achallikuy *v.* dress up || *v.* vestirse bien
k'achanpa *adj.* inclined, leaning || *adj.* ladeado/a, inclinado/a
k'achanpachiy *v.* position something sideways || *v.* colocar en posición lateral *(algo)*
k'achanpakuy *v.* be tilted, be leaning || *v.* ladearse, inclinarse
k'achanpamanta *adv.* sideways || *adv.* de costado *(posición)*
k'achanpay *v.* put *(something)* sideways || *v.* poner de costado *(algo)*
k'achay k'achay *adv.* elegantly || *adv.* elegantemente
k'achayay *v.* make oneself elegant || *v.* ponerse elegante
k'akara *n.* crest, plume || *s.* cresta, penacho
k'aki *n.* jaw, chin || *s.* quijada, mentón
k'aklla *n.* cheek; thorn || *s.* pómulo; espina
k'akra *n.* pottery, ceramics || *s.* tiesto, vasija, cerámica
k'aku *adj.* nasal || *adj.* gangoso/a
k'alla *n.* small parrot || *s.* loro pequeño
k'allallallay *n.* parrot squawk || *s.* sonido emitido por los loros
k'allanpa *n.* mushroom || *s.* hongo
k'ami *n.* insult || *s.* insulto
k'aminakuy *v.* insult one another || *v.* insultarse mutuamente
k'amipayay *v.* insult repeatedly || *v.* insultar reiteradamente
k'amiq *n.* person who insults || *s.* insultador/a
k'amiy *v.* insult || *v.* insultar
k'analla *n.* Andean pot for toasting || *s.* vasija andina para tostar
k'ancha *n.* light || *s.* luz
k'anchaq *adj.* shiny, burning || *adj.* luminoso/a, ardiente
k'anchay *v.* illuminate || *v.* iluminar
k'anchay k'anchay *adj.* luminescent, resplendent || *adj.* muy luminoso/a, resplandeciente
k'anka *n.* rooster || *s.* gallo
k'antiy *v.* warp threads || *v.* urdir hilos
k'apak *adj.* exact, precise || *adj.* exacto/a, preciso/a
k'apaklla *adv.* exactly || *adv.* exactamente
k'aphtisqa *adj.* chipped || *adj.* desportillado/a
k'aphtiy *v.* chip || *v.* desportillar

k'araq *n.* stinging wound || *s.* herida que pica, herida que escuece
k'aray *n.* burning sensation, irritation || *s.* picor, irritación
k'aray *v.* sting *(a wound)* || *v.* picar *(una herida)*, escocer
k'arpa *n.* ceramic shards || *s.* pedazos rotos de tiestos
k'arpi *adj.* scrawny || *adj.* enjuto/a, enclenque
k'askachiq *n.* person who adheres, person who pastes || *s.* el/la que adhiere, el/la que pega
k'askasqa *adj.* adhered, pasted || *adj.* adherido/a, pegado/a
k'askay *v.* adhere, paste || *v.* adherir, pegar
k'aski *adj.* arrogant || *adj.* arrogante
k'askiy k'askiy *adv.* arrogantly || *adv.* arrogantemente
k'aspi *n.* log || *s.* palo
k'asu *adj.* scrawny || *adj.* enjuto/a
k'awtiy *v.* chew something tough || *v.* mascotear; masticar sin llegar a triturar
k'ayra *n.* frog || *s.* rana
k'ayrapin *n.* pancreas || *s.* páncreas
k'ayu *n.* dried grains or beans || *s.* granos secos
k'ichi *n.* small man || *s.* hombre pequeño
k'iki *adj.* dense || *adj.* tupido/a
k'ikllu *n.* street • *adj.* narrow || *s.* callejuela • *adj.* estrecho/a
k'ikuy *v.* menstruate • *n.* menstruation || *v.* menstruar • *s.* menstruación
k'illichu *n.* Andean hawk || *s.* cernícalo andino
k'illinsa *n.* charcoal || *s.* carbón
k'iñasqa *adj.* split open || *adj.* hendido/a
k'iñay *v.* split open || *v.* hender
k'inllay *v.* bat eyelashes || *v.* parpadear
k'inti *n.* attachment || *s.* adjunto
k'intisqa *adj.* attached || *adj.* adjuntado/a
k'intiy *v.* attach || *v.* adjuntar
k'intu *n.* bunch of coca leaves || *s.* ramillete de hojas de coca
k'intuq *n.* preparer of coca leaves *(ritual)* || *s.* el/la que prepara las hojas coca *(ritual)*
k'intuy *v.* prepare coca leaves *(ritual)* || *v.* preparar hojas de coca *(ritual)*
k'iphta *n.* fragment, piece || *s.* fragmento, pedazo
k'iphtay *v.* fragment, break into pieces || *v.* fragmentar, despedazar
k'ipi *n.* cringe from bitter taste || *s.* amargor en los dientes
k'ir *n.* creak || *s.* chirrido

k'irachiy *v.* make recline || *v.* hacer recostar
k'irana *n.* furniture for reclining || *s.* lecho
k'irasqa *adj.* reclined || *adj.* recostado/a
k'iraw *n.* crib || *s.* cuna
k'iray *v.* recline, lean back on || *v.* recostar, inclinarse
k'iri *n.* wound • *adj.* wounded || *s.* herida • *adj.* herido/a
k'iriy *v.* injure || *v.* herir
k'irku *adj.* dried out || *adj.* reseco/a
k'iski *adj.* narrow • *n.* dried mucous || *adj.* estrecho/a • *s.* moco seco
k'iskiy *v.* squeeze || *v.* apretujar
k'iskiyay *v.* squeeze in || *v.* apretujarse
k'ispa *n.* brown || *s.* castaño
k'isuy *v.* remove || *v.* extraer
k'ita *adj.* untamed, social outcast || *adj.* cimarrón, paria
k'itakuy *v.* run away || *v.* evadirse
k'uchu *n.* corner *(interior)* || *s.* rincón
k'uchunay *v.* put in corner || *v.* arrinconar
k'uchunchay *v.* put in corner || *v.* arrinconar
k'uku *adj.* unripe *(fruit)* || *adj.* inmaduro *(fruto)*
k'ullpi *n.* wooden splinter || *s.* astilla de madera
k'ullu *n.* log • *adj.* indolent || *s.* madero • *adj.* indolente
k'ulluyapuy *v.* become indolent || *v.* volverse indolente
k'umillu *n.* servant || *s.* sirviente
k'umu *adj.* downcast || *adj.* cabizbajo
k'umuchiy *v.* make bow || *v.* hacer agachar
k'umuy *v.* bow down || *v.* agacharse
k'umuykachay *v.* swallow one's pride || *v.* humillarse
k'unu *n.* pat on the back || *s.* palmada en la espalda
k'unuy *v.* pat on the back || *v.* palmear en la espalda
k'upa *adj.* curly || *adj.* crespo/a
k'urpa *n.* clod || *s.* terrón
k'usillu *n.* monkey || *s.* mono
k'usillukuy *v.* imitate a monkey || *v.* imitar al mono
k'uskiy *v.* search through, rummage || *v.* rebuscar, hurgar
k'uspa *adj.* curly || *adj.* crespo/a
k'utuy *v.* grind up with teeth || *v.* triturar con los dientes
k'uychi *n.* rainbow || *s.* arco iris
k'uyka *n.* earthworm || *s.* lombriz
k'uyuy *v.* roll up || *v.* enrollar

L

lachiwa *n.* honey || *s.* miel
lachiwana *n.* hive || *s.* panal
lakawiti *n.* pumpkin || *s.* calabaza
lamuku *adj.* crazed • *n.* crazy person || *adj.* alocado/a • *s.* alocado/a
lanq'e *n.* sandal || *s.* sandalia
laphapay *v.* flutter || *v.* ondear
laphara *n.* banner || *s.* banderola
lapht'anakuy *v.* insult one another || *v.* injuriarse mutuamente
lapht'ay *v.* lap up || *v.* beber a lengüetazos
laqha *adj.* dark || *adj.* oscuro/a
laqhayay *v.* become dark || *v.* oscurecer
laqla *n.* chatterbox • *adj.* chatty || *s.* hablador/a • *adj.* hablador/a
laqlay *v.* boast || *v.* alardear
laqmu *adj.* toothless || *adj.* desdentado/a
laq'achiy *v.* make trip and fall || *v.* hacer tropezar y caer
laq'akuy *v.* trip and fall || *v.* tropezarse y caerse
laq'asqa *adj.* plastered || *adj.* emplastado/a
laq'ay *v.* plaster || *v.* emplastar
laq'aysiy *v.* help plaster || *v.* ayudar a emplastar
laq'o *n.* joke, trick || *s.* burla, engaño
laq'osqa *adj.* tricked || *adj.* engañado/a
laq'oy *v.* joke, trick || *v.* burlar, engañar
last'ay *v.* laminate || *v.* laminar
lawa *n.* thick soup || *s.* sopa densa
lawq'ay *v.* lick all over || *v.* lengüetear
layqa *n.* witch; witchcraft || *s.* brujo/a; brujería
layqachiy *v.* make bewitch || *v.* hacer embrujar
layqasqa *adj.* bewitched || *adj.* embrujado/a
layqay *v.* bewitch || *v.* embrujar
lerq'o *adj.* cross-eyed || *adj.* bizco
lerq'oyay *v.* cross one's eyes, become cross-eyed || *v.* bizquear, volverse bizco
lirpuy *v.* reflect || *v.* reflejar
lonq'o *n.* sphere • *adj.* spherical || *s.* esfera • *adj.* esférico
loqhe *adj.* deranged || *adj.* trastornado/a

loqloy *v.* slurp || *v.* sorber
loqt'o *adj.* deaf || *adj.* sordo/a
lulunakuy *v.* caress one another || *v.* acariciarse mutuamente
luluy *v.* pamper, caress || *v.* mimar, acariciar
lunp'u *n.* sphere || *s.* esfera
luychu *n.* deer || *s.* venado

LL

llachi *n.* desire, illusion || *s.* anhelo, ilusión
llachi llachi *adv.* delusionally || *adv.* ilusoriamente
llachichiy *v.* make delude || *v.* hacer ilusionar
llaki *n.* sadness, pity || *s.* tristeza, pena
llakichiy *v.* cause sadness || *v.* causar pena
llakikuy *v.* become sad || *v.* entristecerse
llakilla *adv.* sadly || *adv.* tristemente
llakipakuy *v.* get upset continuously || *v.* afligirse continuamente
llakipayay *v.* console || *v.* condolerse
llakisqa *adj.* sad, upset || *adj.* triste, afligido/a
llalli llalli *adv.* triumphantly || *adv.* triunfantemente
llalliq *n.* victor, winner || *s.* vencedor/a, triunfador/a
llalliy *v.* win, triumph || *v.* vencer, triunfar
llama *n.* llama || *s.* llama
llamayoq *n.* llama owner || *s.* llamero
llamikuy *v.* feel *(oneself)* || *v.* palparse
llaminakuy *v.* feel one another, touch one another || *v.* palparse mutuamente, tocarse mutuamente
llaminalla *adv.* palpable || *adv.* palpable
llamipayay *v.* touch repeatedly, feel repeatedly || *v.* tocar reiteradamente, palpar reiteradamente
llamiy *v.* touch, feel || *v.* palpar, tocar
llamiykuy *v.* touch softly, feel softly || *v.* tocar suavamente, palpar suavamente
llankhuy *v.* grope || *v.* manosear
llank'achiy *v.* make work || *v.* hacer trabajar
llank'ana *n.* work, chore || *s.* trabajo, tarea
llank'apakuq *n.* day laborer || *s.* jornalero
llank'apakuy *v.* work temporarily || *v.* trabajar temporalmente
llank'aq *n.* worker || *s.* trabajador/a
llank'ay *v.* work || *v.* trabajar
llank'aysiy *v.* help work || *v.* ayudar a trabajar
llank'i *adj.* creamy, smooth || *adj.* mantecoso/a, blando/a
llank'iyay *v.* become creamy, become smooth || *v.* ponerse mantecoso/a, ponerse blando/a

llanllariy *v.* sprout again || *v.* retoñar
llanllasqa *adj.* revived || *adj.* reverdecido/a
llanllay *v.* revive || *v.* reverdecer
llanp'u *adj.* soft || *adj.* suave
llanp'ullaña *adj.* very soft || *adj.* suavísimo
llanp'una *n.* sheet || *s.* sábana
llanp'uyariy *v.* become soft || *v.* ponerse suave
llanthu *n.* shadow || *s.* sombra
llanthuna *n.* parasol || *s.* quitasol, sombrilla
llanthunakuy *v.* shade one another || *v.* hacerse sombra mutuamente
llanthurikuy *v.* go into shade || *v.* ponerse en la sombra
llanthuy *v.* shade || *v.* sombrear
llant'a *n.* firewood || *s.* leña
llant'achay *v.* make firewood || *v.* hacer leña
llant'aq *n.* woodcutter || *s.* leñador/a
llapa *adj.* all || *adj.* todo/a, todos/as
llapan *adj.* all || *adj.* todo/a, todos/as
llapanta *adv.* all, completely || *adv.* todo, completamente
llaphch'apayay *v.* remove from water again and again || *v.* sacar del agua una y otra vez *(algo)*
llaphch'ay *v.* remove from water || *v.* sacar del agua *(algo)*
llaphch'aysiy *v.* help remove from water || *v.* ayudar a sacar del agua *(algo)*
llaphlla *adj.* weak, lightweight || *adj.* tenue, liviano/a
llaphllayay *v.* become weak, become lightweight || *v.* ponerse tenue, ponerse liviano/a
llaphsa *adj.* weak, lightweight || *adj.* tenue, liviano/a
llaphsayay *v.* become weak, become lightweight || *v.* ponerse tenue, ponerse liviano/a
llap'i *n.* nightmare || *s.* pesadilla
llaqllachiy *v.* make plane *(wood)* || *v.* hacer cepillar *(madera)*
llaqllana *n.* planing tool *(wood)* || *s.* herramienta para cepillar *(madera)*
llaqllasqa *adj.* planed *(wood)* || *adj.* cepillado/a *(madera)*
llaqllay *v.* plane *(wood)* || *v.* cepillar *(madera)*
llaqllaysiy *v.* help plane *(wood)* || *v.* ayudar a cepillar *(madera)*
llaqolla *n.* cloak || *s.* manto
llaqta *n.* country; town || *s.* país; pueblo
llaqtachakuy *v.* colonize, occupy a territory || *v.* colonizar, ocupar un territorio

llaqtamasi *n.* fellow countryperson || *s.* paisano
llaqwachikuy *v.* let oneself be licked || *v.* dejarse lamer
llaqwakuy *v.* lick one's lips || *v.* lamerse
llaqwanakuy *v.* lick one another || *v.* lamerse mutuamente
llaqwapakuy *v.* lick one's lips again and again || *v.* relamerse
llaqwapayay *v.* lick repeatedly || *v.* relamer
llaqwaq *n.* licker || *s.* lamedor/a
llaqwasqa *adj.* licked || *adj.* lamido/a
llaqway *v.* lick || *v.* lamer
llasa *adj.* heavy || *adj.* pesado/a, pesante
llasallaña *adj.* very heavy || *adj.* muy pesado/a, muy pesante
llasaq *adj.* a lot || *adj.* bastante
llasay *v.* overload || *v.* sobrepesar
llasayachiy *v.* make heavier || *v.* hacer más pesado/a
llat'anay *v.* strip off || *v.* despojar
llat'asqa *adj.* uncovered || *adj.* descubierto/a
llat'ay *v.* uncover || *v.* descorrer, desplegar
llawsa *n.* drool || *s.* baba
llawsasuru *adj.* drooling • *n.* drooler || *adj.* babeante • *s.* babeante
llawsay *v.* drool || *v.* babear
llawt'u *n.* emblem || *s.* insignia
lleqmasqa *adj.* overflowing || *adj.* rebasado/a
lleqmay *v.* overflow || *v.* rebasar
lliklla *n.* blanket || *s.* manta
llik'i *adj.* broken || *adj.* roto/a
llik'isimi *adj.* tactless || *adj.* indiscreto/a
llik'iy *v.* unstitch, rip || *v.* descoser, desgarrar
llilliy *v.* ooze || *v.* rezumar
llinp'asqa *adj.* full, fulfilled || *adj.* colmado/a
llinp'ay *v.* fill, fulfill || *v.* llenar, colmar
llipch'iy *v.* pinch || *v.* pellizcar
lliphch'a *n.* quinoa leaf || *s.* hoja de quinua
lliphlliy *v.* shine brightly || *v.* relumbrar, resplandecer
lliphlliyay *v.* become dazzling, become resplendent || *v.* ponerse relumbrante, ponerse resplandeciente
lliw *adj.* all || *adj.* todo/a, todos/as
lloqe *n.* tree *(Andean variety)* || *s.* árbol *(variedad andina)*
lloqhachiy *v.* make crawl || *v.* hacer gatear
lloqhaq *n.* creeper, crawler || *v.* reptador/a, gateador/a
lloqhay *v.* creep, crawl || *v.* reptar, gatear

lloqlla *n.* flood || *s.* aluvión
lloqllo *adj.* rotten *(egg)* || *adj.* podrido *(huevo)*
lloqsichiy *v.* make leave || *v.* hacer salir
lloqsipayay *v.* leave again and again || *v.* salir una y otra vez
lloqsiy *v.* leave || *v.* salir
lloq'e *adj.* left *(opposite of right)*; left-handed || *adj.* izquierdo/a; zurdo/a
lloq'enchu *adj.* left-handed || *adj.* zurdo/a
lloq'eyay *v.* become left-handed || *v.* devenir en zurdo/a
lluch'a *n.* gums || *s.* encías
lluch'isqa *adj.* flayed, skinned || *adj.* desollado/a, despellejado/a
lluch'iy *v.* flay, skin || *v.* desollar, despellejar
llukusqa *adj.* trapped in a net || *adj.* atrapado/a con una red
llukuy *v.* trap with net || *v.* atrapar con una red
lluk'i *n.* armpit || *s.* axila
lluk'iy *v.* carry in armpit || *v.* llevar en el sobaco
llulla *n.* lie • *adj.* liar || *s.* mentira • *adj.* mentiroso/a
llullakuy *v.* lie *(deceive)* || *v.* mentir
llullay llullay *adv.* falsely || *adv.* falsamente
llullu *adj.* unripe *(fruit)* || *adj.* inmaduro *(fruto)*
llunch'iy *v.* rub, smear || *v.* ungir, embadurnar
llunk'u *n.* licker; flatterer || *s.* lamedor/a; adulador/a
llunk'uy *v.* lick; flatter || *v.* lamer; adular
llunp'a *adj.* pure • *s.* purity || *adj.* puro/a • *s.* pureza
llusikuy *v.* spread on oneself, smear on oneself || *v.* untarse
llusinakuy *v.* spread on one another, smear on one another || *v.* untarse mutuamente
llusipayay *v.* spread on again and again, smear on again and again || *v.* untar una y otra vez
llusisqa *adj.* spread, smeared || *adj.* untado/a
llusiy *v.* spread on, smear on || *v.* untar
llusiysiy *v.* help spread on, help smear on || *v.* ayudar a untar
lluskha *adj.* slippery || *adj.* resbaloso/a
lluskhachiy *v.* make slip || *v.* hacer resbalar
lluskhay *v.* slip || *v.* resbalar
llusp'iy *v.* drip || *v.* escurrir
llust'i *adj.* bare || *adj.* pelado/a
llust'iy *v.* flay, skin || *v.* desollar, despellejar
lluthu *n.* partridge || *s.* perdiz
llut'achiy *v.* make build *(with mud)* || *v.* hacer erigir *(con barro)*

llut'ay *v.* build *(with mud)* || *v.* erigir *(con barro)*
llut'aysiy *v.* help build *(with mud)* || *v.* ayudar a erigir *(con barro)*
lluy *adj.* all || *adj.* todo/a, todos/as
lluyta *adv.* all, completely || *adv.* todo, completamente

M

machachiy *v.* get someone drunk || *v.* hacer embriagar, hacer emborrachar
machaq *n.* drunk • *adj.* drunk || *s.* borracho/a • *adj.* borracho/a
machasqa *adj.* inebriated, drunk || *adj.* embriagado/a, emborrachado/a
machay *v.* inebriate, get drunk || *v.* embriagarse, emborracharse
machaysiy *v.* get drunk with || *v.* acompañar a embriagarse
machu *n.* old man || *s.* viejo, anciano *(hombre)*
machula *n.* old man *(affectionate)* || *s.* viejito *(hombre)*
machullaña *adj.* very old *(man)* || *adj.* muy viejo *(hombre)*
machusqa *n.* sickness, illness || *s.* enfermedad, mal
machuyachiy *v.* make grow old *(man)* || *v.* hacer envejecer *(hombre)*
machuyasqa *adj.* elderly *(man)*, aged *(man)*; deteriorated *(health)* || *adj.* envejecido *(hombre)*; decaído *(salud)*
machuyay *v.* grow old *(man)* || *v.* envejecer *(hombre)*
mach'aqway *n.* snake || *s.* culebra
mach'ay *n.* cave, cavern || *s.* cueva, caverna
maki *n.* hand || *s.* mano
makiyoq *n.* thief || *s.* ladrón
mak'a *n.* arm || *s.* brazo
mak'allinakuy *v.* hug one another || *v.* abrazarse mutuamente
mak'alliy *v.* hug || *v.* abrazar
mak'as *n.* large ceramic jug || *s.* jarrón grande de cerámica
mallichiy *v.* make taste || *v.* hacer degustar
malliy *v.* taste || *v.* degustar
mallki *n.* small tree || *s.* árbol pequeño
mallmay *v.* flatten || *v.* aplanar
malqo *n.* chick *(animal)* || *s.* pichón de ave
malta *adj.* medium || *adj.* mediano
mama *n.* mother || *s.* madre
mamaku *n.* old woman *(affectionate)* || *s.* viejita
mamapacha *n.* mother earth || *s.* madre tierra, tierra madre
mamaqocha *n.* sea, ocean || *s.* mar, océano
mamaruk'ana *n.* thumb || *s.* dedo pulgar

mana *adv.* no, not || *adv.* no
mana allin *adj.* bad || *adj.* mal
manakaw *interj.* no! || *interj.* ¡no!
mananchay *v.* reject || *v.* negar
manapaschá *adv.* maybe not || *adv.* tal vez no
manapuni *adv.* no way || *adv.* de ninguna manera
manaraq *adv.* not yet || *adv.* todavía no
manchachiy *v.* scare, shock || *v.* asustar
manchakuy *v.* fear || *v.* temer
manchali *adj.* timid, scared || *adj.* tímido/a, asustadizo/a
manchana *adj.* fearsome, scary || *adj.* temible
mancharichiy *v.* cause fear || *v.* causar susto
mancharikuy *v.* be scared || *v.* asustarse
mancharisqa *adj.* shocked || *adj.* asustado/a
manchay *v.* frighten • *n.* fear • *adj.* very || *v.* asustar • *s.* susto • *adj.* muy
manka *n.* pot, pan || *s.* olla
manti *adj.* soft || *adj.* suave
mant'achiy *v.* make smooth || *v.* hacer tender
mant'apayay *v.* smooth out again and again || *v.* tender una y otra vez
mant'asqa *adj.* smoothed out || *adj.* tendido/a
mant'ay *v.* smooth out || *v.* tender
mant'aysiy *v.* help smooth out || *v.* ayudar a tender
manu *n.* debt || *s.* deuda
manuchay *v.* charge, accuse || *v.* cobrar, imputar
manukuy *v.* borrow money || *v.* prestarse dinero
manuq *n.* moneylender • *adj.* moneylending || *s.* prestamista • *adj.* prestamista
manuy *v.* lend money || *v.* prestar dinero
manuyay *v.* make a debtor || *v.* hacerse deudor
mañakuy *v.* ask for || *v.* pedir
mañarikuy *v.* beg || *v.* implorar
mañasqa *adj.* lent || *adj.* prestado/a
mañay *v.* lend || *v.* prestar
map'a *adj.* dirty || *adj.* sucio/a
map'ay *v.* dirty || *v.* ensuciar
maqachikuy *v.* let oneself be beat || *v.* dejarse golpear
maqanakuy *v.* beat one another || *v.* pelearse
maqapayay *v.* beat constantly || *v.* golpear constantemente
maqaq *n.* beater || *s.* golpeador/a

maqay *v.* beat || *v.* golpear
maqaysiy *v.* help beat || *v.* ayudar a golpear
maqchhichiy *v.* make wash || *v.* hacer lavar
maqchhikuy *v.* wash oneself || *v.* lavarse
maqchhipayay *v.* wash again and again || *v.* lavar una y otra vez
maqchhiy *v.* wash || *v.* lavar
maqchhiysiy *v.* help wash || *v.* ayudar a lavar
maqlla *adj.* stingy || *adj.* tacaño/a
maqt'a *n.* young man, boy || *s.* joven *(hombre)*, muchacho
maq'a *adj.* rancid || *adj.* rancio/a
maq'ayay *v.* become rancid || *v.* ponerse rancio/a
maran *n.* mortar || *s.* piedra plana para moler
marka *n.* area, territory || *s.* perímetro, territorio
marq'a *n.* arm || *s.* brazo
marq'achikuy *v.* let oneself be carried in arms || *v.* dejarse llevar en brazos
marq'aq *n.* godparent of baptized child; person who carries in arms || *s.* padrino/madrina de niño/a bautizado/a; el/la que lleva en brazos
marq'asqa *n.* godchild in baptism • *adj.* carried *(in arms)* || *s.* ahijado/a de bautizo • *adj.* llevado/a *(en brazos)*
marq'ay *v.* carry in arms || *v.* llevar en brazos
masapayay *v.* expose to sun continuously || *v.* exponer al sol continuamente
masasqa *adj.* exposed to sun || *adj.* expuesto al sol
masay *v.* expose to sun || *v.* exponer al sol
masaykachay *v.* expose to sun again and again || *v.* exponer al sol una y otra vez
maskhaq *n.* person who searches || *s.* buscador/a
maskhasqa *adj.* searched for, solicited || *adj.* buscado/a, solicitado/a
maskhay *v.* search || *v.* buscar
maskhaykachay *v.* search for again and again || *v.* rebuscar
maskhaysiy *v.* help search || *v.* ayudar a buscar
mast'achiy *v.* make smooth || *v.* hacer tender
mast'apayay *v.* smooth out repeatedly || *v.* tender una y otra vez
mast'ariy *v.* spread, extend || *v.* difundir, extender
mast'asqa *adj.* smoothed out || *adj.* tendido/a
mast'ay *v.* smooth out || *v.* tender
mast'aysiy *v.* help smooth out || *v.* ayudar a tender
masu *n.* vampire; bat || *s.* vampiro; murciélago

maswa *n.* tuber *(Andean variety)* || *s.* tubérculo *(variedad andina)*
mat'ay *v.* carve meat || *v.* filetear la carne
mat'i *adj.* tight • *n.* forehead || *adj.* apretado/a • *s.* frente
mat'ina *n.* belt, sash || *s.* correa, faja
mat'ipayay *v.* tighten again and again, adjust again and again || *v.* apretar una y otra vez, ajustar una y otra vez
mat'isqa *adj.* tight || *adj.* apretado/a
mat'iy *v.* tighten, adjust || *v.* apretar, ajustar
mat'iy mat'iy *adv.* tightly || *adv.* apretadamente
maway *n.* first harvest *(potato)* || *s.* primera cosecha *(papa)*
mawk'a *adj.* used, old *(thing)* || *adj.* usado/a, antiguo/a *(cosa)*
mayllikuy *v.* wash oneself || *v.* lavarse
mayllisqa *adj.* washed || *adj.* lavado/a
maylliy *v.* wash || *v.* lavar
maylliysiy *v.* help wash || *v.* ayudar a lavar
mayman *inter.* to where? || *inter.* ¿hacia dónde?
maymanta *inter.* from where? || *inter.* ¿de dónde?
mayninpi *adv.* sometimes || *adv.* a veces, de vez en cuando
maypi *inter.* where? || *inter.* ¿en dónde?, ¿dónde?
mayqen *inter.* which? || *inter.* ¿cuál?
mayt'usqa *adj.* rolled and tied up || *adj.* enrollado/a y liado/a
mayt'uy v. roll and tie up || *v.* enrollar y liar
mayt'uykachay *v.* rolled and tied up again and again || *v.* enrollar y liar una y otra vez
mayt'uysiy *v.* help roll and tie up || *v.* ayudar a enrollar y liar
mayu *n.* river || *s.* río
maywisqa *adj.* stirred || *adj.* revuelto
maywiy *v.* stir || *v.* revolver
maywiysiy *v.* help stir || *v.* ayudar a revolver
melq'osqa *adj.* gulped || *adj.* engullido/a
melq'oy *v.* gulp || *v.* engullir
michi *n.* cat || *s.* gato
michina *n.* pasture || *s.* pastura
michipakuy *v.* herd another's flock || *v.* pastorear el ganado ajeno
michiq *n.* shepherd || *s.* pastor *(de animales)*
michiy *v.* herd || *v.* pastorear
michiysiy *v.* help herd || *v.* ayudar a pastorear
mich'a *adj.* stingy || *adj.* tacaño/a
mich'uchiy *v.* make intermingle || *v.* hacer entremezclar, hacer entreverar

mich'usqa *adj.* intermingled || *adj.* entreverado/a
mich'uy *v.* intermingle || *v.* entremezclar, entreverar
mihuchiy *v.* feed || *v.* alimentar
mihuna *n.* food || *s.* comida
mihunayay *v.* have the urge to eat || *v.* tener deseos de comer
mihupayay *v.* eat constantly || *v.* comer constantemente
mihuq *n.* eater || *s.* el/la que come
mihusqa *adj.* eaten || *adj.* comido
mihuy *v.* eat || *v.* comer
millachiy *v.* cause disgust || *v.* causar asco
millakuy *v.* be disgusted || *v.* tener asco
millay *adj.* unpleasant, ugly, disgusting || *adj.* desagradable, feo/a, asqueroso/a
millay millay *adv.* disagreeably || *adv.* desagradablemente
millma *n.* wool || *s.* lana
millmachay *v.* cover with wool || *v.* cubrir con lana
millmasapa *adj.* wooly || *adj.* lanudo/a
millp'uchiy *v.* make gulp, make swallow || *v.* hacer engullir, hacer tragar
millp'unakuy *v.* offend one another || *v.* injuriarse
millp'upakuy *v.* swallow saliva || *v.* tragar saliva
millp'upayay *v.* gulp again and again, swallow again and again || *v.* engullir una y otra vez, tragar una y otra vez
millp'usqa *adj.* gulped, swallowed || *adj.* engullido/a, tragado/a
millp'uti *n.* esophagus || *s.* esófago
millp'uy *v.* gulp, swallow || *v.* engullir, tragar
minchha *n.* day after tomorrow || *s.* pasado mañana
mink'a *n.* system of mutual help, system of communal work || *s.* sistema de ayuda mutua, sistema de trabajo comunal
mink'akuq *n.* person who summons for communal work || *v.* convocador/a para un trabajo comunal
mink'asqa *adj.* summoned for communal work || *adj.* convocado/a para un trabajo comunal
mink'ay *v.* summon for communal work || *v.* convocar para un trabajo comunal
minupayay *v.* mix again || *v.* remezclar
minusqa *adj.* mixed || *adj.* mezclado/a
minuy *v.* mix || *v.* mezclar
minuysiy *v.* help mix || *v.* ayudar a mezclar
mirachiq *n.* person who makes reproduce || *s.* el/la que hace reproducir

mirachiy *v.* make reproduce || *v.* hacer reproducir
miray *v.* reproduce || *v.* reproducirse
miskha *n.* first harvest *(corn)* || *s.* primera cosecha *(maíz)*
misk'akuy *v.* trip over || *v.* tropezarse
misk'i *adj.* sweet || *adj.* dulce
misk'ichiy *v.* sweeten || *v.* endulzar
misk'illaña *adj.* very sweet || *adj.* muy dulce
mitma *n.* occupier, colonist || *s.* ocupante, colono/a
mitmay *v.* occupy a territory, colonize || *v.* ocupar un territorio, colonizar
mit'a *n.* season, time period || *s.* estación, periodo de tiempo
miyu *n.* venom || *s.* veneno
miyuchiy *v.* command to poison || *v.* mandar a envenenar
miyusqa *adj.* poisoned || *adj.* envenenado/a
miyuy *v.* poison || *v.* envenenar
moqch'ikuy *v.* rinse out one's mouth || *v.* enjuagarse la boca
moqo *n.* knee; hill || *s.* rodilla; colina
moraya *n.* white dehydrated potato || *s.* chuño blanco
morq'a *n.* blunt knife || *s.* cuchillo desafilado
mosoq *adj.* new *(thing)* || *adj.* nuevo/a *(cosa)*
mosoqchaq *n.* restorer, renovator || *s.* restaurador/a, renovador/a
mosoqchay *v.* restore, renovate || *v.* restaurar, renovar
mosoqllaña *adj.* very new || *adj.* muy nuevo/a
mosqhokuy *v.* dream || *v.* soñar
mosqhopakuy *v.* dream fitfully || *v.* soñar y sobresaltarse
mosqhoy *n.* dream, daydream || *s.* sueño, ensueño
mosqhoychay *v.* appear in dreams || *v.* aparecer en sueños
mot'e *n.* boiled corn || *s.* maíz hervido
muchuchiy *v.* cause deprivation || *v.* causar privación
muchuy *v.* deprive oneself • *n.* famine || *v.* privarse • *s.* hambruna
muchhasqa *adj.* dekerneled *(corn)* || *adj.* desgranado *(maíz)*
muchhay *v.* dekernel *(corn)* || *v.* desgranar *(maíz)*
muchhaysiy *v.* help dekernel *(corn)* || *v.* ayudar a desgranar *(maíz)*
much'achikuy *v.* let oneself be kissed || *v.* dejarse besar
much'anakuy *v.* kiss one another || *v.* besarse mutuamente
much'apayaq *n.* person who kisses all over || *s.* besuqueador/a
much'apayay *v.* kiss all over || *v.* besuquear
much'aq *n.* kisser || *s.* besador/a
much'asqa *adj.* kissed || *adj.* besado/a
much'ay *v.* kiss || *v.* besar

much'aykachay *v.* kiss indiscriminately || *v.* besar indistintamente
much'u *n.* nape || *s.* nuca
muhu *n.* seed || *s.* semilla
muhuchaq *n.* selector of seeds || *s.* seleccionador/a de semillas
muhuchay *v.* select seeds || *v.* seleccionar las semillas
mukisqa *adj.* suffocated, asphyxiated || *adj.* sofocado/a, asfixiado/a
mukiy *v.* suffocate, asphyxiate || *v.* sofocar, asfixiar
mulla *n.* nephew || *s.* sobrino
mullkhuq *n.* fondler || *s.* manoseador/a
mullkhusqa *adj.* fondled || *adj.* manoseado/a
mullkhuy *v.* fondle || *v.* manosear
mullmusqa *adj.* dissolved in one's mouth || *adj.* disuelto en la boca
mullmuy *v.* dissolve in one's mouth || *v.* disolver en la boca
mullpha *adj.* decayed || *adj.* carcomido/a
mullphayay *v.* decay || *v.* carcomerse
mullu *n.* coral || *s.* coral
munakuy *v.* love || *v.* querer *(afecto)*
munanakuy *v.* love one another || *v.* quererse mutuamente
munapayay *v.* pretend || *v.* pretender
munasqa *adj.* beloved || *adj.* querido/a
munay *adj.* cute, agreeable, nice || *adj.* lindo/a, agradable
munay *v.* want, desire || *v.* querer, desear
munay munaylla *adv.* voluntarily || *adv.* voluntariamente
muskhichiy *v.* make smell || *v.* hacer oler
muskhinakuy *v.* smell one another || *v.* olfatearse mutuamente
muskhipakuy *v.* smell from a distance || *v.* olfatear a distancia
muskhipayay *v.* smell constantly || *v.* olfatear constantemente
muskhiy *v.* smell || *v.* oler
muspha muspha *adv.* deliriously || *adv.* delirantemente
musphapayay *v.* talk while dreaming constantly || *v.* delirar constantemente
musphaq *adj.* delirious || *adj.* delirante
musphay *v.* talk while dreaming || *v.* delirar
mutk'a *n.* pestle || *s.* mortero
mut'u *adj.* cut off, amputated || *adj.* cercenado/a, mutilado/a
mut'uchikuy *v.* allow one's limb to be amputated || *v.* hacerse cercenar, hacerse mutilar
mut'uy *v.* cut off, amputate || *v.* cercenar, mutilar
muya *n.* orchard || *s.* frutal

muyu *n.* circle • *adj.* round || *s.* círculo • *adj.* redondo/a
muyuchasqa *adj.* rounded || *adj.* redondeado/a
muyuchiy *v.* make spin, make go in circles || *v.* hacer dar vueltas
muyupayay *v.* encircle || *v.* rondar
muyuy *v.* spin, go in circles || *v.* girar, dar vueltas
muyuykachay *v.* creep around || *v.* asediar

N

nak'achiy *v.* make slaughter || *v.* hacer degollar
nak'achu *n.* executioner, slaughterer || *s.* degollador/a, matarife
nak'ana *n.* knife for slaughter || *s.* cuchillo para degollar
nak'aq *n.* executioner, slaughterer || *s.* degollador/a, matarife
nak'asqa *adj.* slaughtered, sacrificed *(animal)* || *adj.* degollado/a, sacrificado/a *(animal)*
nak'ay *v.* slaughter, sacrifice *(animal)* || *v.* degollar, sacrificar *(animal)*
nanachiy *v.* cause pain || *v.* causar dolor
nanapayay *v.* hurt constantly || *v.* doler constantemente
nanaq *n.* wound || *s.* herida
nanay *n.* pain • *v.* hurt || *s.* dolor • *v.* doler
napaykunakuy *v.* greet each other || *v.* saludarse mutuamente
napaykuy *v.* greet || *v.* saludar
neqninta *adv.* around || *adv.* alrededor
nina *n.* fire || *s.* fuego
ninachay *v.* light a fire || *v.* encender el fuego
ninakuy *v.* reply to one another || *v.* replicarse mutuamente
niy *v.* say || *v.* decir
nuna *n.* soul, spirit || *s.* alma, espíritu

Ñ

ñakapakuy *v.* curse continuously, reproach oneself continuously || *v.* maldecir continuamente, recriminarse continuamente
ñakaq *n.* person who curses another, slanderer || *s.* maldecidor/a
ñakasqa *adj.* cursed || *adj.* maldecido/a
ñakay *v.* curse another || *v.* maldecir
ñak'a *n.* affliction, hardship || *s.* padecimiento, penuria
ñak'arichiy *v.* torment, make suffer || *v.* atormentar, hacer padecer
ñak'ariy *v.* suffer || *v.* padecer, sufrir
ñak'ay *adv.* hardly, barely || *adv.* apenas
ñak'ayllaña *adv.* painfully || *adv.* penosamente
ñan *n.* way, path || *s.* vía, camino
ñaña *n.* sister *(of a woman)* || *s.* hermana *(de mujer)*
ñañu *adj.* worn out *(thing)* || *adj.* delgado/a *(cosa)*
ñañuyasqa *adj.* worn down || *adj.* adelgazado/a *(cosas)*
ñapu *adj.* soft || *adj.* blando/a
ñapuy *v.* soften || *v.* ablandar
ñapuyay *v.* become soft || *v.* ablandarse
ñaqch'a *n.* comb, brush || *s.* peine
ñaqch'akuy *v.* comb one's hair, brush one's hair || *v.* peinarse
ñaqch'apakuy *v.* comb one's hair again and again, brush one's hair again and again || *v.* peinarse una y otra vez
ñaqch'apayay *v.* comb again and again, brush again and again || *v.* peinar una y otra vez
ñaqch'asqa *adj.* combed, brushed || *adj.* peinado/a
ñaqch'ay *v.* comb, brush *(hair)* || *v.* peinar
ñaqch'aysiy *v.* help comb, help brush *(hair)* || *v.* ayudar a peinar
ñaqha *adv.* earlier || *adv.* hace un momento
ñawi *n.* eye || *s.* ojo
ñawi qara *n.* eyelid || *s.* párpado
ñawi ruru *n.* pupil || *s.* pupila
ñawpa *adj.* old *(person)* || *adj.* antiguo/a *(persona)*
ñawpaq *adj.* previous || *adj.* previo, anterior
ñawpaqta *adv.* previously || *adj.* previamente, anteriormente
ñawpariy *v.* precede || *v.* anteceder
ñawpay *v.* anticipate || *v.* anticiparse

ñawsa *adj.* blind • *n.* blind person || *adj.* ciego • *s.* invidente
ñawsayay *v.* become blind || *v.* volverse ciego/a
ñisu *adj.* too much || *adj.* demasiado/a, mucho/a
ñisuta *adv.* a lot, too || *adv.* demasiado/a, mucho/a
ñit'ichiy *v.* make compress || *v.* hacer comprimir
ñit'ipayay *v.* compress again and again || *v.* comprimir una y otra vez
ñit'isqa *adj.* compressed || *adj.* comprimido/a
ñit'iy *v.* compress || *v.* comprimir
ñit'iysiy *v.* help compress || *v.* ayudar a comprimir
ñoqa *pron.* I || *pron.* yo
ñoqanchis *pron.* we *(inclusive)* || *pron.* nosotros *(inclusivo)*
ñoqayku *pron.* we *(exclusive)* || *pron.* nosotros *(exclusivo)*
ñosqhon *n.* brain || *s.* seso
ñukñu *n.* milk || *s.* leche
ñukñuy *v.* milk || *v.* ordeñar
ñuñu *n.* breast, nipple || *s.* seno, pezón
ñuñupakuy *v.* nurse from another mother || *v.* lactar la leche de madre ajena
ñuñuq *n.* nursing baby, breastfeeding mother || *s.* lactante, madre que da de lactar
ñuñuy *v.* nurse, breastfeed || *v.* mamar, dar leche de pecho
ñup'usqa *adj.* compressed || *adj.* comprimido/a
ñup'uy *v.* compress || *v.* comprimir
ñupu *n.* fontanel || *s.* fontanela
ñuskhu *adj.* clumsy, slow || *adj.* torpe, lento/a
ñuskhu ñuskhulla *adv.* clumsily, slowly || *adv.* torpemente, lentamente
ñusñuy *v.* sniffle || *v.* resonar por la nariz al respirar
ñust'a *n.* Inkan princess || *s.* princesa inka
ñut'u *adj.* ground, crushed || *adj.* triturado/a, molido/a
ñut'uy *v.* grind, crush || *v.* triturar, moler

O

onqokuq *n.* expectant mother || *s.* gestante
onqokuy *v.* be pregnant || *v.* estar embarazada
onqoli *adj.* sickly, fragile *(person)* || *adj.* enfermizo/a, frágil *(persona)*
onqopayay *v.* get sick frequently || *v.* enfermarse frecuentemente
onqoq *adj.* sick; pregnant || *adj.* enfermo/a; embarazada
onqoy *n.* sickness, illness • *v.* get sick || *s.* enfermedad, mal • *v.* enfermar
opa *adj.* naïve, silly • *n.* idiot || *adj.* bobo/a, tonto/a • *s.* idiota
opayachiy *v.* drive crazy || *v.* causar idiotez
opayay *v.* become an idiot || *v.* devenir en idiota
oqa *n.* tuber *(Andean variety)* || *s.* tubérculo *(variedad andina)*
oqarayay *v.* fool around || *v.* tontear
oqe *adj.* gray || *adj.* gris
oqeyay *v.* turn gray || *v.* tornarse gris
oqhe *adj.* gray || *adj.* gris
oqheyay *v.* turn gray || *v.* tornarse gris
oqllay *v.* warm up with body heat, incubate || *v.* calentar con el calor del cuerpo, empollar
oqochiy *v.* make gobble, make gulp || *v.* hacer engullir, hacer tragar
oqocho *adj.* short and chubby *(man)* || *adj.* rechoncho *(hombre)*
oqopayay *v.* gobble again and again, gulp again and again || *v.* engullir una y otra vez, tragar una y otra vez
oqosqa *adj.* gobbled, gulped || *adj.* engullido/a, tragado/a
oqoy *v.* gobble, gulp || *v.* engullir, tragar
orqo *n.* male; mountain || *s.* macho; montaña
osqo *adj.* timid, shy || *adj.* tímido/a, huraño/a
osqollo *n.* mountain lion || *s.* gato montés
osqoyay *v.* become timid, become shy || *v.* volverse tímido/a, volverse huraño/a
otaq *conj.* or || *conj.* o

P

pacha *n.* timespace; Earth || *s.* tiempo-espacio; Tierra
pacha illariy *n.* dawn || *s.* madrugada
pacha phuyu *n.* fog || *s.* neblina
pachakuyuy *n.* earthquake || *s.* terremoto
pachaq *num.* one hundred || *num.* cien
pachaqchay *v.* group by hundreds || *v.* agrupar por cientos
pachas *n.* plaster || *s.* yeso
pachiy *v.* sit *(used with children)* || *v.* sentarse *(expresión coloquial para niño/as)*
pakachiy *v.* make hide || *v.* mandar a esconder
pakakuna *n.* hiding place || *s.* escondite
pakakuy *v.* hide oneself || *v.* esconderse
pakalla *adv.* stealthily || *adv.* ocultamente
pakanakuy *v.* cover up for one another || *v.* encubrirse mutuamente
pakasqa *adj.* hidden, covered up || *adj.* escondido/a, encubierto/a
pakay *v.* hide, cover up || *v.* ocultar, encubrir
pakaysiy *v.* help hide, help cover || *v.* ayudar a ocultar, ayudar a cubrir
pallachiy *v.* order to harvest *(above ground)*, order to pick produce || *v.* mandar a cosechar *(sobre la tierra)*, mandar a recoger frutos *(sobre la tierra)*
pallapakuq *n.* collector of remains || *s.* recolector/a de restos
pallapay *v.* collect remains || *v.* recolectar restos
pallaq *n.* harvester *(above ground)* || *s.* recogedor/a de frutos *(sobre la tierra)*,
pallasqa *adj.* harvested *(above ground)*, picked || *adj.* cosechado/a *(sobre la tierra)*, recogido/a *(sobre la tierra)*
pallay *v.* harvest *(above ground)*, pick || *v.* cosechar *(sobre la tierra)*, recoger *(sobre la tierra)*
pallaysiy *v.* help harvest *(above ground)*, help pick || *v.* ayudar a cosechar *(sobre la tierra)*, ayudar a recoger *(sobre la tierra)*
paltasqa *adj.* overloaded || *adj.* sobrecargado/a
paltay *v.* overload || *v.* sobrecargar
pana *n.* sister *(of male)* || *s.* hermana *(de varón)*
panpa *n.* flat field, plain || *s.* campo, planicie
panpachay *v.* level out; forgive || *v.* nivelar; perdonar
pantachiy *v.* cause to make a mistake || *v.* hacer equivocar

pantaq *n.* person who goes the wrong way; adulterer || *s.* el/la que va en sentido equivocado; adúltero/a
pantasqa *adj.* mistaken || *adj.* equivocado/a
pantay *v.* go the wrong way; commit adultery || *v.* ir en sentido equivocado; cometer adulterio
pantaylla *adv.* mistakenly || *adv.* equivocadamente
panti *adj.* lilac || *adj.* lila
paña *adj.* right *(opposite of left)* || *adj.* derecha
papa *n.* potato || *s.* papa
paqarichiq *n.* creator, person who makes appear || *s.* creador/a, el/la que hace surgir
paqarichiy *v.* create, make appear || *v.* crear, hacer surgir
paqarin *n.* tomorrow || *s.* mañana *(día de mañana)*
paqariy *v.* be born; wake up in the morning || *v.* nacer, amanecer
paqocha *n.* alpaca || *s.* alpaca
paqta *adv.* maybe, perhaps || *adv.* tal vez, quizás
paqtataq *interj.* beware of ... || *interj.* cuidado con ..., cuidado que ...
para *n.* rain || *s.* lluvia
parachiy *v.* cause rain || *v.* causar lluvia
paranayay *v.* be about to rain || *v.* estar a punto de llover
paraq *adj.* rainy || *adj.* lluvioso/a
paray *v.* rain || *v.* llover
paraykachay *v.* rain constantly || *v.* llover constantemente
pariwana *n.* flamingo *(bird)* || *s.* flamenco *(ave)*
paruchiy *v.* brown in fire || *v.* hacer dorar a fuego
parusqa *adj.* browned || *adj.* dorado/a
paruy *v.* brown in fire || *v.* dorar a fuego
pasaq *adj.* frequent || *adj.* frecuente
pasaqlla *adv.* frequently || *adv.* frecuentemente
paskachiy *v.* make untie || *v.* hacer desatar
paskaq *n.* person who unties || *s.* desatador/a
paskasqa *adj.* untied || *adj.* desatado/a
paskay *v.* untie, let loose || *v.* desatar, soltar
pata *adv.* on top • *n.* top part || *adv.* encima • *s.* parte alta
patan *n.* edge || *s.* borde, orilla
pataray *v.* fold, crease || *v.* doblar, plegar
pay *pron.* he, she || *pron.* el, ella
paya *n.* old woman || *s.* vieja *(mujer)*, anciana *(mujer)*
payallaña *adj.* very old *(woman)* || *adj.* muy vieja *(mujer)*
payayachiy *v.* make grow old *(woman)* || *v.* hacer envejecer *(mujer)*

payayasqa *adj.* elderly *(woman)*, aged *(woman)* || *adj.* envejecida *(mujer)*
payayay *v.* grow old *(woman)* || *v.* envejecer *(mujer)*
paykuna *pron.* they || *pron.* ellos, ellas
perqa *n.* wall || *s.* pared, muro
perqaq *n.* builder of walls || *s.* constructor/a de muros
perqasqa *adj.* walled || *adj.* amurallado/a
perqay *v.* build a wall || *v.* levantar un muro, construir un muro
pi *inter.* who? || *inter.* ¿quién?
pichachiy *v.* make sweep || *v.* hacer barrer
pichakuy *v.* clean oneself || *v.* limpiarse
pichana *n.* broom || *s.* escoba
pichapayay *v.* sweep continuously || *v.* barrer continuamente
pichaq *n.* sweeper || *s.* barredor/a
pichasqa *adj.* swept || *adj.* barrido/a
pichay *v.* sweep || *v.* barrer
pichaysiy *v.* help sweep || *v.* ayudar a barrer
pichinku *n.* sparrow || *s.* gorrión
pikchay *v.* chew coca leaves || *v.* masticar la hoja de coca
pikchu *n.* mountaintop, triangular hill || *s.* cima de una montaña, cerro de forma triangular
piki *n.* flea || *s.* pulga
pikiy *v.* deflea || *v.* espulgar
pillpintu *n.* butterfly || *s.* mariposa
pin *inter.* who? || *inter.* ¿quién?
pinchinkuru *n.* firefly || *s.* luciérnaga
pinkuyllu *n.* flute || *s.* flauta
pipu *adj.* dense, thick || *adj.* denso/a, espeso/a
pirwasqa *adj.* piled || *adj.* arrumado/a
pirway *v.* pile || *v.* arrumar
pirwaysiy *v.* help pile || *v.* ayudar a arrumar
pisi *adj.* a little, scarce || *adj.* poco/a, escaso
pisi pisimanta *adv.* little by little || *adv.* poco a poco
pisichay *v.* underestimate, reduce || *v.* menospreciar, reducir
pisichiy *v.* make smaller || *v.* hacer reducir
pisipasqa *adj.* weakened || *adj.* debilitado/a
pisipay *v.* become weak || *v.* debilitarse
pisiy *v.* lack || *v.* escasear
piskita *n.* handkerchief || *s.* pañuelo
pisqa *num.* five || *num.* cinco

pitay *v.* smoke || *v.* fumar
pitu *n.* flute || *s.* flauta
pituchakuy *v.* beg with hands || *v.* implorar con las manos
poqochiy *v.* make ripe, make ferment || *v.* hacer madurar, hacer fermentar
poqosqa *adj.* ripe, fermented || *adj.* maduro/a, fermentado/a
poqoy *v.* ripen, ferment || *v.* madurar, fermentar
puchu *n.* leftover || *s.* sobrante, remanente
puchuy *v.* be left over || *v.* sobrar
puka *adj.* red || *adj.* rojo
pukayay *v.* redden || *v.* enrojecer
pukllachiy *v.* make play, entertain || *v.* hacer jugar, entretener
pukllana *n.* toy, playground || *s.* juguete, patio de juegos
pukllanayay *v.* have the desire to play || *v.* tener deseos de jugar
pukllapayay *v.* play constantly || *v.* jugar constantemente
pukllaq *adj.* playful • *n.* player || *adj.* juguetón/a • *s.* jugador/a
pukllay *v.* play • *n.* game || *v.* jugar • *s.* juego
pukuchu *n.* mask || *s.* máscara
pukyu *n.* fountain || *s.* manantial
pullurki *n.* eyebrow || *s.* ceja
punkisqa *adj.* swollen || *adj.* hinchado/a
punkiy *v.* swell up || *v.* hincharse
punku *n.* door, exit || *s.* puerta, salida
punkuchay *v.* break out of || *v.* abrir una salida
puñuna *n.* bed; bedroom || *s.* cama; dormitorio
puñunayay *v.* have the desire to sleep, be about to fall asleep || *v.* tener deseos de dormir, estar a punto de dormir
puñupakuy *v.* sleep in another's house || *v.* dormir en casa ajena
puñupayay *v.* doze || *v.* dormitar
puñusqa *adj.* asleep || *adj.* dormido/a
puñuy *v.* sleep || *v.* dormir
puñuysiy *v.* accompany to sleep, keep vigil over someone sleeping || *v.* acompañar a dormir, velar el sueño de otro/a
puputi *n.* belly button || *s.* ombligo
purichiy *v.* help walk || *v.* ayudar a caminar
purikuy *v.* stroll || *v.* pasear
puriq *n.* walker, traveller || *s.* caminante, viajero/a
puriy *v.* walk, travel || *v.* caminar, viajar
purun *adj.* wild, uninhabited || *adj.* silvestre, inhabitado/a
pusachiy *v.* make take someone, make guide someone || *v.* hacer llevar a alguien, hacer guiar a alguien

pusaq *num.* eight • *n.* guide || *num.* ocho • *n.* guía
pusay *v.* take someone, guide someone || *v.* llevar a alguien, guiar a alguien
puska *n.* spindle || *s.* huso
puskaq *n.* spinner || *s.* hilandero/a
puskasqa *adj.* spun || *adj.* hilado/a
puskay *v.* spin || *v.* hilar
puskaysiy *v.* help spin || *v.* ayudar a hilar
pututu *n.* conch shell || *s.* concha marina
puyllu *n.* tassle || *s.* borla de lana
puytu *n.* rhombus || *s.* rombo

PH

phaka *n.* groin || *s.* entrepierna
phakachakuy *v.* mount || *v.* montar
phakallichiy *v.* make mount || *v.* hacer montar
phakallikuq *n.* person who mounts || *s.* montador/a
phakallikuy *v.* hide *(something)* between one's legs, mount oneself on something || *v.* proteger entre las piernas *(algo)*, montarse sobre algo
phakmi *n.* fraction, fragment || *s.* fracción, fragmento
phakmisqa *adj.* fractioned, fragmented || *adj.* fraccionado/a, fragmentado/a
phakmiy *v.* divide into fractions, fragment || *v.* fraccionar, fragmentar
phaksa *n.* potbelly • *adj.* potbellied || *s.* barrigón • *adj.* barrigón
phalalalay *v.* flap || *v.* aletear
phallay *v.* illuminate; give birth *(animal)* || *v.* alumbrar; parir *(animal)*
phallcha *n.* flower *(Andean variety)* || *s.* flor *(variedad andina)*
phallu *adj.* inclined, slanted || *adj.* ladeado/a, sesgado/a
phanchiy *v.* blossom || *v.* abrirse una flor
phapallu *n.* hoof || *s.* pezuña
phaqcha *n.* waterfall || *s.* cascada
phar *n.* sound of wings flapping at moment of flight || *s.* sonido de alas al momento de emprender vuelo
phararaas *v.* flap || *v.* aletear
pharpa *n.* wing || *s.* ala
phasi *adj.* cooked with steam || *adj.* cocido/a al vapor
phasiy *v.* cook with steam || *v.* cocer al vapor
phaski *adj.* dried out, air-dried || *adj.* oreado/a
phaskichikuy *v.* air out until dry || *v.* airearse hasta secarse
phaskiq *adj.* can be dried out, can be air dried || *adj.* oreable
phaskiy *v.* dry out, air dry || *v.* orear
phaskiyachiy *v.* make dry out || *v.* hacer airear
phaspa *adj.* scaly || *adj.* escamoso/a
phaspayay *v.* become scaly || *v.* escamarse
phatachiy *v.* make pop || *v.* hacer reventar
phataq *adj.* poppable, burstable || *adj.* que revienta

phatasqa *adj.* popped *(corn or wheat)* || *adj.* reventado *(maíz o trigo)*
phatatatay *v.* beat *(heart)*, pulse || *v.* latir *(corazón)*, pulsar
phatay *v.* pop, burst || *v.* reventar, estallar
phatu *adj.* wide || *adj.* grueso/a
phatuchay *v.* widen || *v.* engrosar
phawachiq *n.* person who makes run || *v.* el/la que hace correr
phawachiy *v.* make run, let escape || *v.* hacer correr, dejar escapar
phawakachay *v.* run around || *v.* corretear
phawanayay *v.* have the desire to run || *v.* tener deseos de correr
phawaq *n.* runner || *s.* corredor/a
phaway *v.* run; fly || *v.* correr; volar
phawaylla *adv.* quickly || *adv.* aprisa
phiña *adj.* irritable || *adj.* iracundo
phiñaq *n.* reprimander || *s.* reprendedor/a
phiñasqa *adj.* angry || *adj.* enojado/a
phiñay *v.* reprimand || *v.* reprender
phiwi *n.* first born || *s.* primogénito/a
phosoqo *n.* foam || *s.* espuma
phuchu *n.* calf *(baby cow)* || *s.* ternero
phukuchiy *v.* make blow *(person)* || *v.* hacer soplar
phukupakuy *v.* huff and puff || *v.* resoplar
phukupayay *v.* blow again and again || *v.* soplar una y otra vez
phukuq *n.* blower *(person)* || *s.* soplador/a
phukusqa *adj.* blown *(person)* || *adj.* soplado/a
phukuy *v.* blow *(person)* || *v.* soplar
phukuysiy *v.* help blow *(person)* || *v.* ayudar a soplar
phullpuy *v.* flow || *v.* manar
phuru *n.* feather || *s.* pluma
phurullikuy *v.* cover oneself with feathers || *v.* cubrirse con plumas
phurunaq *n.* person who plucks || *s.* desplumador/a
phurunay *v.* pluck || *v.* desplumar
phuspu *n.* boiled fava beans || *s.* habas hervidas
phuspuy *v.* boil fava beans || *v.* hervir habas
phuturiy *v.* sprout slowly || *v.* brotar lentamente
phutusqa *adj.* sprouted || *adj.* brotado/a
phutuy *v.* sprout || *v.* brotar
phuyu *n.* cloud • *adj.* cloudy || *s.* nube • *adj.* nublado/a
phuyuy *v.* cloud || *v.* nublar

P'

p'acha *n.* clothing || *s.* ropa
p'achachiy *v.* help dress || *v.* ayudar a vestir
p'achakuy *v.* get dressed || *v.* vestirse
p'achasqa *adj.* dressed || *adj.* vestido/a
p'achay *v.* dress || *v.* vestir
p'akichiy *v.* command to break || *v.* mandar a romper
p'akina *adj.* fragile *(thing)* || *adj.* frágil *(cosa)*
p'akisqa *adj.* broken || *adj.* roto/a
p'akiy *v.* break || *v.* romper
p'akiysiy *v.* help break || *v.* ayudar a romper
p'alta *adj.* flattened || *adj.* aplanado/a
p'altachiy *v.* flatten || *v.* aplanar
p'anachiy *v.* command to hit with stick || *v.* mandar a apalear
p'anana *n.* stick for hitting || *s.* palo para golpear
p'ananakuy *v.* hit one another with stick || *v.* apalearse mutuamente
p'anapakuy *v.* defend oneself with stick || *v.* defenderse dando palazos
p'anay *v.* hit with stick || *v.* apalear
p'anaysiy *v.* help hit with stick || *v.* ayudar a apalear
p'anpachikuy *v.* let oneself be covered with soil || *v.* dejarse cubrir con tierra
p'anpachiy *v.* make bury || *v.* hacer enterrar
p'anpana *n.* grave || *s.* sepulcro
p'anpaq *n.* burier || *s.* enterrador/a
p'anpay *v.* bury || *v.* enterrar
p'anra *adj.* dimwitted || *adj.* lerdo
p'anrayay *v.* become dimwitted || *v.* ponerse lerdo/a
p'aqla *adj.* bald || *adj.* pelado/a, calvo/a
p'aqlayay *v.* become bald || *v.* volverse pelado/a, volverse calvo/a
p'aqo *adj.* blonde, golden || *adj.* rubio/a, dorado/a
p'aqoyay *v.* turn blonde, become golden || *v.* tornarse rubio/a, volverse dorado/a
p'asña *n.* young woman, girl || *s.* joven *(mujer)*, muchacha
p'atanakuy *v.* bite one another || *v.* dentellearse mutuamente
p'atasqa *adj.* bitten off || *adj.* dentelleado/a
p'atay *v.* bite off a big piece || *v.* dentellear

p'enqachiy *v.* embarrass another || *v.* hacer avergonzar
p'enqakuq *n.* person who is ashamed, person who gets embarrassed || *s.* el/la que se averguenza
p'enqakuy *v.* be ashamed, be embarrassed || *v.* avergonzarse
p'enqali *adj.* blushing, timid || *adj.* avergonzado/a, tímido/a
p'enqasqa *adj.* ashamed, embarrassed || *adj.* avergonzado/a
p'enqay *n.* shame, embarrassment || *s.* vergüenza, bochorno
p'esqoyllo *n.* spinning top || *s.* trompo
p'isaqa *n.* partridge || *s.* perdiz
p'istuchikuy *v.* let oneself be bundled up || *v.* dejarse abrigar
p'istuchiy *v.* make bundle up || *v.* hacer abrigar
p'istukuy *v.* bundle oneself up || *v.* abrigarse
p'istuna *n.* coat, shawl || *s.* abrigo, chalina
p'istuy *v.* bundle up || *v.* abrigar
p'itaq *n.* jumper || *s.* saltador/a
p'itay *v.* jump || *v.* saltar
p'itakachaq *v.* skipper || *v.* saltarín
p'itaykachay *v.* skip *(step)* || *v.* brincotear
p'itayuy *v.* jump down || *v.* saltar hacia abajo
p'iti *adj.* very narrow || *adj.* muy angosto/a
p'itichiy *v.* make tear off a string || *v.* hacer arrancar un hilo
p'itiy *v.* tear off a string || *v.* arrancar un hilo
p'olqo *adj.* stretched out *(thing)* • *n.* woven booty || *adj.* holgado/a *(cosa)* • *s.* calzado tejido
p'onqo *adj.* deep • *n.* puddle || *adj.* hondo • *s.* charco
p'onqochakuy *v.* pool || *v.* empozarse
p'oqasqa *adj.* squeezed || *adj.* estrujado/a
p'oqay *v.* squeeze || *v.* estrujar
p'osqo *adj.* bitter, fermented || *adj.* agrio, fermentado/a
p'osqolli *n.* stomach acid || *s.* acidez estomacal
p'osqoy *v.* embitter, ferment || *v.* agriarse, fermentarse
p'ukru *n.* pit, hollow space || *s.* hoyo, cavidad
p'uktu *n.* basket || *s.* canasta
p'uku *n.* plate, bowl || *s.* plato, pocillo
p'unchay *n.* day || *s.* día
p'unchaynintin *adv.* all day || *adv.* todo el día
p'unchayyay *v.* become daytime || *v.* hacerse de día
p'unpu *adj.* swollen || *adj.* hinchado/a
p'unpuyay *v.* swell up || *v.* hincharse
p'uyñu *n.* pitcher, jug || *s.* cántaro, jarro
p'uytu *n.* prehispanic tomb || *s.* tumba prehispánica

Q

qacha *n.* dried herbs || *s.* hierbas secadas
qachasqa *adj.* dehydrated by the sun || *adj.* deshidratado/a por el sol
qachay *v.* dry herbs in sun || *v.* secar hierbas al sol
qachipayay *v.* scatter by hand again and again, disperse by hand again and again || *v.* esparcir con la mano una y otra vez, dispersar con la mano una y otra vez
qachisqa *adj.* scattered by hand, dispersed by hand || *adj.* esparcido/a con la mano, dispersado/a con la mano
qachiy *v.* scatter by hand, disperse by hand || *v.* esparcir con la mano, dispersar con la mano
qachiysiy *v.* help scatter by hand, help disperse by hand || *v.* ayudar a esparcir con la mano, ayudar a dispersar con la mano
qallariq *n.* person who starts, beginner || *s.* el/la que comienza, principiante
qallarisqa *adj.* started, begun || *adj.* comenzado, empezado
qallariy *v.* start, begin || *v.* comenzar, empezar
qallu *n.* tongue *(anatomical)* || *s.* lengua *(órgano)*
qalluykachay *v.* stick out tongue || *v.* mostrar la lengua
qan *pron.* you *(singular)* || *pron.* tú
qanchis *num.* seven || *num.* siete
qaparichiy *v.* make yell || *v.* hacer gritar
qapariy *v.* yell || *v.* gritar
qaparqachay *v.* yell continuously || *v.* gritar continuamente
qaparqachanakuy *v.* yell at one another || *v.* gritarse mutuamente
qaqa *n.* rock • *adj.* crowded || *s.* roca • *adj.* apretujado/a
qaqapachiy *v.* make fall from cliff || *v.* hacer despeñar, hacer desbarrancar
qaqapana *n.* cliff || *s.* despeñadero, barranco
qaqapay *v.* fall from cliff || *v.* despeñarse, desbarrancarse
qara *n.* leather, skin || *s.* cuero, pellejo
qarachiy *v.* command to serve food || *v.* mandar a servir los alimentos
qaray *v.* serve food || *v.* servir los alimentos
qaraysiy *v.* help serve food || *v.* ayudar a servir los alimentos

qaraywa *n.* lizard || *s.* lagarto
qarpapayay *v.* water constantly, irrigate constantly || *v.* regar constantemente, irrigar constantemente
qarpasqa *adj.* watered, irrigated || *adj.* regado/a, irrigado/a
qarpay *v.* water, irrigate || *v.* regar, irrigar
qarpaysiy *v.* help water, help irrigate || *v.* ayudar a regar, ayudar a irrigar
qarqochiy *v.* make expel, make kick out || *v.* hacer expulsar, hacer despedir de mala manera
qarqosqa *adj.* expelled, kicked out || *adj.* expulsado/a, despedido/a de mala manera
qarqoy *v.* expel, kick out || *v.* expulsar, despedir de mala manera
qarqoysiy *v.* help expel, help kick out || *v.* ayudar a expulsar, ayudar a despedir de mala manera
qasa *n.* frost || *s.* helada
qasasqa *adj.* frozen || *adj.* helado/a
qasay *v.* freeze || *v.* helar
qasi *adj.* calm || *adj.* tranquilo
qasi qasilla *adv.* calmly || *adv.* quietamente, tranquilamente
qasichiy *v.* vacate, empty || *v.* vaciar
qasirayay *v.* do nothing || *v.* estar sin hacer nada
qata *n.* blanket || *s.* frazada
qatakuy *v.* cover oneself with blankets || *v.* cubrirse con frazada
qatanakuy *v.* cover one another with blankets || *v.* cubrirse mutuamente con frazadas
qataq *n.* person who covers with blankets || *s.* el/la que cubre con frazada
qatasqa *adj.* covered with blankets || *v.* cubierto/a con frazada
qatay *n.* son-in-law • *v.* cover with blankets || *s.* yerno • *v.* cubrir con frazada
qati qati *adv.* one behind another || *adv.* uno tras otro
qatikachay *v.* follow, pursue || *v.* perseguir
qatinakuy *v.* follow one another || *v.* perseguirse mutuamente
qatipayay *v.* pursue continuously, follow continuously || *v.* perseguir continuamente
qatiy *v.* follow; herd || *v.* seguir; arrear
qayllalla *adv.* successively || *adv.* sucesivamente
qayna p'unchay *n.* yesterday || *s.* ayer
qayninpa *n.* day before yesterday || *s.* anteayer
qayri *n.* cousin || *s.* primo/a

qaywichiy *v.* make stir || *v.* hacer revolver
qaywina *n.* stirring utensil || *s.* instrumento para revolver
qaywisqa *adj.* stirred *(fluids)* || *adj.* revuelto *(fluidos)*
qaywiy *v.* stir fluids || *v.* revolver fluidos
qaywiykachay *v.* stir fluids with indifference || *v.* revolver fluidos con indiferencia
qaywiysiy *v.* help stir fluids || *v.* ayudar a revolver fluidos
qaywiyuy *v.* stir fluids with intention || *v.* revolver fluidos con mucha voluntad
qechuy *v.* snatch, grab || *v.* arrebatar
qechuykachay *v.* snatch constantly, grab constantly || *v.* arrebatar constantemente
qechuysiy *v.* help snatch, help grab || *v.* ayudar a arrebatar
qella *adj.* lazy, slow || *adj.* perezoso/a, flojo/a
qellwa *n.* gull || *s.* gaviota
qena *n.* flute || *s.* flauta
qepu *n.* thistle, thorn || *s.* abrojo, espina
qepuchiy *v.* prick with thorn || *v.* pinchar con abrojo
qeqochikuy *v.* let oneself be tricked || *v.* dejarse engañar
qeqosqa *adj.* tricked || *adj.* engañado/a
qeqoy *v.* trick || *v.* engañar
qespi *n.* crystal || *s.* cristal
qespichiq *n.* revitalizer || *s.* revitalizador/a
qespichiy *v.* make revitalize || *v.* hacer revitalizar
qespiy *v.* revitalize || *v.* revitalizar
qocha *n.* lake, lagoon || *s.* lago, laguna
qochapata *n.* beach || *s.* playa
qochayuyu *n.* seaweed || *s.* alga marina
qochikuy *v.* ask for, solicit *(something)* || *v.* pedir, solicitar *(algo)*
qochiy *v.* take *(something)* from someone || *v.* quitarle a alguien *(algo)*
qollpa *adj.* salty || *adj.* salado/a
qollwi *n.* big ant || *s.* hormiga grande
qolqe *n.* silver *(mineral)*, money || *s.* plata *(mineral)*, dinero
qolqeyoq *adj.* rich || *adj.* adinerado/a
qonakuy *v.* exchange || *v.* intercambiar
qonqachiy *v.* make forget || *v.* hacer olvidar
qonqana *adj.* forgettable || *adj.* olvidable
qonqasqa *adj.* forgotten, abandoned || *adj.* olvidado/a, abandonado/a
qonqay *v.* forget || *v.* olvidar

qonqaylla *adv.* suddenly || *adv.* repentinamente
qonqor *n.* knee || *s.* rodilla
qonqorikuy *v.* kneel || *v.* arrodillarse
qoq *n.* giver || *s.* dador/a
qora *n.* herb || *s.* hierba
qoray *v.* pick a plant || *v.* desyerbar
qori *n.* gold || *s.* oro
qorpachakuy *v.* stay, lodge || *v.* hospedarse, alojarse
qorpachaq *n.* host/hostess || *s.* hospedador/a
qorpachay *v.* host, accommodate || *v.* hospedar, alojar
qosa *n.* husband || *s.* esposo
qosayoq *adj.* married *(woman)*, with husband || *adj.* casada *(mujer)*, con esposo
qosi *adj.* light blue || *adj.* celeste
qosqa *adj.* given, bestowed || *adj.* dado/a, otorgado/a
qowi *n.* guinea pig || *s.* cuy
qoy *v.* give || *v.* dar
qoya *n.* queen || *s.* reina
qoyllur *n.* star || *s.* estrella
qoywiy *v.* whistle || *v.* silbar

QH

qhachun *n.* daughter-in-law || *s.* nuera
qhali *adj.* healthy || *adj.* sano/a
qhaliyachiq *n.* healer || *s.* curador/a
qhaliyachiy *v.* make healthy, cure || *v.* hacer sanar, curar
qhaliyasqa *adj.* cured || *adj.* curado/a
qhaliyay *v.* become healthy little by little || *v.* sanar poco a poco
qhanra *n.* filth || *s.* suciedad
qhanra qhanra *adj.* filthy || *adj.* sucio/a
qhanray *v.* get filthy || *v.* ensuciar
qhapaq *adj.* powerful, respected || *adj.* poderoso/a, apreciado/a
qhapchi *adj.* elegant, fine || *adj.* elegante, fino/a
qhaphchiykachaq *adj.* presumptuous || *adj.* presuntuoso/a
qhaphra *adj.* fragile *(thing)*, breakable || *adj.* frágil *(cosa)*, quebradizo/a
qhaqllin *n.* jaw bone || *s.* mandíbula
qhaqya *n.* thunder || *s.* trueno
qhari *n.* male, man || *s.* varón, hombre
qhari wawa *n.* son *(of mother)* || *s.* hijo *(de madre)*
qharichakuy *v.* get the nerve || *v.* envalentonarse
qharincha *n.* manly woman || *s.* ahombrada
qhariyay *v.* become a man || *v.* devenir en adulto *(hombre)*
qhasqa *adj.* rough || *adj.* áspero
qhasqo *n.* chest || *s.* pecho
qhasqo tullu *n.* sternum || *s.* esternón
qhasusqa *adj.* torn *(fabric)* || *adj.* roto/a *(tela)*
qhasuy *v.* tear *(fabric)* || *v.* romper *(tela)*
qhasuykachay *v.* tear again and again *(fabric)* || *v.* romper una y otra vez *(tela)*
qhaswa *n.* Andean carnaval dance || *s.* danza andina de carnaval
qhata *n.* slope, mountainside || *s.* ladera
qhatqe *adj.* bitter || *adj* amargo/a
qhatu *n.* market, trading place || *s.* mercado, lugar donde se expende
qhatuq *n.* seller, vendor || *s.* vendedor/a, expendedor/a
qhatuy *v.* sell || *v.* vender, expender

qhatuysiy *v.* help sell || *v.* ayudar a vender, ayudar a expender
qhawachiy *v.* show || *v.* mostrar
qhawana *n.* lookout point, window || *s.* mirador, ventana
qhawanakuy *v.* look at one another, observe one another || *v.* mirarse mutuamente, observarse mutuamente
qhawapayakuy *v.* look at oneself frequently, observe oneself frequently || *v.* mirarse asiduamente, observarse asiduamente
qhawapayay *v.* look frequently, observe frequently || *v.* mirar asiduamente, observar asiduamente
qhawaq *n.* person who looks, observer || *s.* observador/a
qhawarayay *v.* look indefinitely, observe indefinitely || *v.* mirar indefinidamente, observar indefinidamente
qhaway *v.* look, observe || *v.* mirar, observar
qhayqa *n.* sickness caused by a corpse || *s.* mal causado por el influjo de un cádaver
qhechincha *n.* soot || *s.* hollín
qhechiphra *n.* eyelash || *s.* pestaña
qhelli *n.* filth • *adj.* dirty || *s.* mugre • *adj.* sucio/a
qhellichakuy *v.* become dirty || *v.* ensuciarse
qhellichaq *n.* person who dirties || *s.* ensuciador/a
qhellichasqa *adj.* dirtied || *adj.* ensuciado/a
qhellichay *v.* get dirty || *v.* ensuciar
qhencha *n.* fatality • *adj.* fatal || *s.* fatalidad • *adj.* fatal
qhepa *prep.* behind • *adv.* after || *prep.* atrás • *adv.* tras
qhepachiy *v.* retain || *v.* retener
qhepakuy *v.* stay || *v.* quedarse
qhepanchay *v.* postpone || *v.* posponer
qhepay *v.* stay, remain || *v.* quedarse, permanecer
qhetupayay *v.* scrape again and again || *v.* raspar una y otra vez
qhetuy *v.* scrape || *v.* raspar
qhetuykachay *v.* scrape insistently || *v.* raspar insistentemente
qholla *adj.* unripe; tender || *adj.* inmaduro; tierno
qhoña *n.* mucus || *s.* moco
qhoqa *adj.* discolored, faded || *adj.* descolorido/a, desteñido/a
qhoqayay *v.* become discolored, become faded || *v.* descolorarse, desteñirse
qhorqoq *n.* snorer || *s.* roncador/a
qhorqoy *v.* snore || *v.* roncar
qhoruchiy *v.* command to mutilate || *v.* mandar a mutilar
qhorusqa *adj.* mutilated || *adj.* mutilado/a

qhoruy *v.* mutilate || *v.* mutilar
qhospay *v.* roll around || *v.* revolcarse
qhoto *n.* phlegm || *s.* esputo
qhotoy *v.* cough up || *v.* esputar

Q'

q'achu *n.* grass || *s.* pasto
q'ala *adj.* naked || *adj.* desnudo
q'alachakuy *v.* undress oneself || *v.* desnudarse
q'alachay *v.* undress; strip belongings from another || *v.* desnudar; despojar de las pertenencias
q'alachikuy *v.* let oneself be undressed || *v.* dejarse desnudar
q'alachiq *n.* person who makes undress; person who makes strip belongings from another || *s.* desnudador/a; el/la que hace despojar de las pertenencias
q'alalla *adj.* naked; without means || *adj.* desnudo/a; sin recursos
q'alata *adv.* totally || *adv.* totalmente
q'alayasqa *adj.* impoverished || *adj.* empobrecido/a
q'alayay *v.* end up naked; impoverish || *v.* terminar desnudo/a; empobrecer
q'allachiy *v.* make slice || *v.* hacer rebanar
q'allasqa *adj.* sliced || *adj.* rebanado/a
q'allay *v.* slice || *v.* rebanar
q'allpay *v.* uncover; lift up a woman's skirt || *v.* descubrir lo que está cubierto; levantar la falda a una mujer
q'apachikuy *v.* perfume oneself || *v.* perfumarse
q'apachisqa *adj.* perfumed || *adj.* perfumado/a
q'apachiy *v.* perfume || *v.* perfumar
q'aparishaq *adj.* fragrant || *adj.* fragante
q'apay *v.* emit a good smell || *v.* exhalar buen olor
q'aphñisqa *adj.* dented || *adj.* abollado/a
q'aphñu q'aphñu *adj.* dented || *adj.* abollado/a
q'aphñuy *v.* dent || *v.* abollar
q'apichiy *v.* command to squeeze || *v.* mandar a estrujar
q'apisqa *adj.* squeezed || *adj.* estrujado/a
q'apiy *v.* squeeze || *v.* estrujar
q'apiykachay *v.* squeeze constantly || *v.* estrujar constantemente
q'ara *adj.* bald, naked || *adj.* pelado/a, desnudo/a
q'aray *v.* remove hair *(body)*; undress || *v.* pelar; desnudar
q'arayay *v.* become bald; undress oneself || *v.* pelarse; desnudarse
q'asa *n.* mountain pass || *s.* paso entre dos montañas

q'asasqa *adj.* chipped || *adj.* desportillado/a
q'asay *v.* chip || *v.* desportillar
q'aspasqa *adj.* singed || *adj.* chamuscado/a
q'aspay *v.* singe || *v.* chamuscar
q'asuchiy *v.* command to hit with stick || *v.* mandar a apalear
q'asuna *n.* stick for hitting || *s.* palo para golpear
q'asunakuy *v.* hit one another with stick || *v.* apalearse mutuamente
q'asupakuy *v.* defend oneself with stick || *v.* defenderse dando palazos
q'asuy *v.* hit with stick || *v.* apalear
q'asuysiy *v.* help hit with stick || *v.* ayudar a apalear
q'ata *adj.* murky || *adj.* turbio/a
q'atachakuy *v.* become murky || *v.* enturbiarse
q'atachay *v.* make murky || *v.* enturbiar
q'atayay *v.* become murky little by little || *v.* volverse turbio poco a poco
q'awa *n.* manure || *s.* bosta, estiércol
q'awachiy *v.* command to collect manure || *v.* mandar a recolectar bosta
q'away *v.* collect manure || *v.* recolectar bosta
q'awaysiy *v.* help collect manure || *v.* ayudar a recolectar bosta
q'awti *adj.* skinny || *adj.* flacuchento/a
q'ayma *adj.* bland || *adj.* insípido/a
q'aytu *n.* wool thread || *s.* hilo de lana
q'ea *n.* puss || *s.* pus
q'eanay *v.* remove puss || *v.* sacar pus
q'echa *n.* diarrhea || *s.* diarrea
q'echanayay *v.* have diarrhea || *v.* estar con diarrea
q'ello *adj.* yellow || *adj.* amarillo/a
q'ellochay *v.* yellow || *v.* amarillear
q'elloyay *v.* turn yellow || *v.* tornarse amarillo/a
q'emichiy *v.* make brace || *v.* hacer apuntalar
q'emina *n.* object for bracing || *s.* objeto para apuntalar
q'emipakuy *v.* support oneself on something or someone || *v.* apoyarse en algo o alguien
q'emisqa *adj.* braced || *adj.* apuntalado/a
q'emiy *v.* brace, uphold || *v.* apuntalar, sostener
q'enpichiy *v.* make fold || *v.* hacer doblar, hacer plegar
q'enpisqa *adj.* folded || *adj.* doblado/a *adj.* plegado/a
q'enpiy *v.* fold || *v.* doblar, plegar

q'enqo *n.* zigzag, curve || *s.* zigzag, curva
q'ente *n.* hummingbird || *s.* picaflor
q'eperina *n.* cloth for carrying on back || *s.* tela para cargar en la espalda
q'epi *n.* cargo, bundle || *s.* carga, bulto
q'epichakuy *v.* ready oneself to travel || *v.* alistarse para viajar
q'epichay *v.* prepare cargo || *v.* preparar la carga
q'epichiy *v.* make carry on back || *v.* hacer cargar en la espalda
q'epina *adj.* possible to be carried on back || *adj.* posible de ser cargado/a en la espalda
q'epiq *n.* carrier || *s.* cargador/a
q'episqa *adj.* carried *(on back)* || *adj.* cargado/a *(en la espalda)*
q'epiy *v.* carry on back || *v.* cargar en la espalda
q'epiysiy *v.* help carry on back || *v.* ayudar a cargar en la espalda
q'ero *n.* cup || *s.* vaso
q'esa *n.* nest || *s.* nido
q'esachakuy *v.* build a nest; occupy another's place || *v.* construir un nido; ocupar un lugar ajeno
q'estisqa *adj.* shrunken *(thing)* || *adj.* encogido/a *(cosa)*
q'estiy *v.* shrink *(thing)* || *v.* encogerse *(cosa)*
q'eswa *n.* rope || *s.* soga
q'ewi q'ewi *adj.* very twisted || *adj.* retorcido/a
q'ewichiy *v.* make twist || *v.* hacer torcer
q'ewisqa *adj.* twisted || *adj.* torcido/a
q'ewiy *v.* twist || *v.* torcer
q'ewiysiy *v.* help twist || *v.* ayudar a torcer
q'ochachiy *v.* heat in sun || *v.* insolar
q'ochasqa *adj.* heated in sun || *adj.* insolado/a
q'ocho q'ocho *adv.* happily || *adv.* alegremente
q'omer *adj.* green || *adj.* verde
q'omerchay *v.* turn green || *v.* tornarse verde
q'omeryay *v.* turn green again || *v.* reverdecer
q'oncha *n.* stove, fireplace || *s.* fogón
q'onchachay *v.* build a stove || *v.* construir un fogón
q'oñi *adj.* hot, warm || *adj.* caliente, cálido/a
q'oñichiy *v.* heat up, make warm || *v.* calentar
q'oñikuy *v.* get warm || *v.* calentarse
q'oñiy *v.* heat || *v.* calentar
q'opa *n.* dried leaves; garbage || *s.* hojas secas; basura
q'opanay *v.* clean up dried leaves; clean up garbage || *v.* recoger las hojas secas; recoger la basura

q'osñi *n.* smoke || *s.* humo
q'osñichiy *v.* make smoke || *v.* hacer humear
q'osti *adj.* fast • *adv.* rapidly || *adj.* rápido/a • *adv.* rápidamente
q'otochikuy *v.* let oneself be tricked || *v.* dejarse engañar
q'otosqa *adj.* gulped; tricked || *adj.* engullido; engañado/a
q'otoy *v.* gulp; trick || *v.* engullir; engañar
q'oyo *n.* bruise || *s.* moretón
q'oyosqa *adj.* bruised || *adj.* amoretado/a

R

rachinakuy *v.* scratch one another || *v.* rascarse mutuamente
rachinayakuy *v.* have the urge to scratch oneself || *v.* tener deseos de rascarse
rachipayay *v.* scratch again and again || *v.* rascar una y otra vez
rachiy *v.* scratch || *v.* rascar
rakhu *adj.* thick || *adj.* grueso
rakhuyay *v.* thicken || *v.* engrosar
rakichiy *v.* make distribute || *v.* hacer distribuir
rakinakuy *v.* distribute mutually || *v.* distribuirse mutuamente
rakiq *n.* distributor || *s.* distribuidor/a
rakisqa *adj.* distributed || *adj.* distribuido/a
rakiy *v.* distribute || *v.* distribuir
rakiysiy *v.* help distribute || *v.* ayudar a repartir
rakrapu *n.* glutton || *s.* glotón
rakraq *n.* glutton || *s.* glotón
rakrasqa *adj.* swallowed || *adj.* tragado/a
rakray *v.* swallow || *v.* tragar
rank'usqa *adj.* entwined, braided || *adj.* enredado/a, trenzado/a
rank'uy *v.* entwine, braid || *v.* enredar *v.* trenzar
ranpay *v.* take someone || *v.* llevar a alguien
ranpaysiy *v.* help take someone || *v.* ayudar a llevar a alguien
rantichiy *v.* make buy, command to buy || *v.* hacer comprar, mandar a comprar
rantinayay *v.* have the urge to buy || *v.* tener deseos de comprar
rantiq *n.* buyer || *s.* comprador/a
rantisqa *adj.* bought || *adj.* comprado/a
rantiy *v.* replace, buy || *v.* reemplazar, comprar
raphi *n.* leaf || *s.* hoja
raphra *n.* wing || *s.* ala
raqra *adj.* cracked • *n.* crack || *adj.* rajado/a • *s.* rajadura
raqray *v.* get cracked || *v.* rajarse
rasphiyay *v.* become night || *v.* anochecer
ratasqa *adj.* wrapped around || *adj.* enrollado/a
ratay *v.* wrap around || *v.* enrollarse
rawi *adj.* messy || *adj.* desordenado/a

rawiy *v.* mess up || *v.* desordenar
rawiysiy *v.* mess up together || *v.* colaborar en desordenar
rawraq *adj.* burning || *adj.* ardiente
rawrachiy *v.* make burn || *v.* hacer arder
rawrasqa *adj.* burnt || *adj.* ardido/a
rawray *v.* burn || *v.* arder
rawraykachay *v.* burn with difficulty || *v.* arder con dificultad
raymi *n.* massive party || *s.* fiesta masiva
reqsichikuy *v.* introduce oneself || *v.* hacerse conocer, presentarse
reqsichiy *v.* make know, make familiar with || *v.* hacer conocer
reqsikuy *v.* recognize || *v.* reconocer
reqsinakuy *v.* get to know one another || *v.* conocerse mutuamente
reqsinayay *v.* have the urge to know, have the urge to be familiar with || *v.* tener deseos de conocer
reqsisqa *adj.* known • *n.* acquaintance || *adj.* conocido/a • *s.* conocido/a
reqsiy *v.* know, be familiar with || *v.* conocer
rikch'akuy *v.* resemble someone, look like someone || *v.* parecerse a alguien
rikch'anayay *v.* be about to wake up || *v.* estar a punto de despertar
rikch'apakuy *v.* wake up every so often || *v.* despertarse a cada rato
rikch'ay *v.* wake up || *v.* despertar
rikhurichiy *v.* make appear || *v.* hacer aparecer
rikhuriy *v.* appear || *v.* aparecer
riki *adv.* clearly yes, of course || *adv.* claro que sí, por supuesto
rikra *n.* shoulder || *s.* hombro
rikraq *n.* person who carries on shoulders || *s.* el/la que lleva en hombros
rikray *v.* carry on shoulders || *v.* llevar en hombros
rikuchikuy *v.* let oneself be seen || *v.* dejarse ver
rikuchiy *v.* make see || *v.* hacer ver
rikunakuy *v.* see one another || *v.* verse mutuamente
rikunalla *adj.* visible || *adj.* visible
rikusqa *adj.* seen || *adj.* visto
rikuy *v.* see || *v.* ver
rimachiy *v.* make talk, make speak || *v.* hacer hablar
rimakachay *v.* talk for talking's sake, speak for the sake of it || *v.* hablar por hablar
rimanakuy *v.* talk to one another, speak to one another || *v.* hablarse mutuamente

rimanayay *v.* have the urge to talk, have the urge to speak || *v.* tener deseos de hablar
rimapakuy *v.* talk to one's self, speak to one's self || *v.* hablar para sí
rimapayay *v.* talk constantly, speak constantly || *v.* hablar constantemente
rimaq *n.* talker, speaker || *s.* hablante
rimay *v.* talk, speak || *v.* hablar
rimaysikuy *v.* participate in a conversation without being invited || *v.* participar en una conversación sin ser invitado/a
rinri *n.* ear || *s.* oreja
rinrinay *v.* cut off ear || *v.* desorejar
ripuy *v.* return || *v.* irse
rit'i *n.* snow || *s.* nieve
rit'iy *v.* snow || *v.* nevar
riy *v.* go || *v.* ir
roqt'o *adj.* deaf • *n.* deaf person || *adj.* sordo/a • *s.* sordo/a
roqt'oyay *v.* become deaf || *v.* ensordecer
rumi *n.* stone, rock || *s.* piedra
rumu *n.* yuca || *s.* yuca
runa *n.* individual, person || *s.* individuo, persona
runayay *v.* recover *(health)* || *v.* restablecerse *(salud)*
runtu *n.* egg || *s.* huevo
rupha *adj.* hot || *adj.* caliente
ruphachiy *v.* make burn || *v.* hacer quemar
ruphapakuy *v.* suffocate from heat || *v.* sofocarse de calor
ruphasqa *adj.* burned || *adj.* quemado/a
ruphay *n.* heat from sun • *v.* burn || *s.* calor del sol • *v.* quemar
ruphayay *v.* heat in sun || *v.* solear
ruru *n.* fruit, seed || *s.* fruto, semilla
ruruchiy *v.* make bear fruit || *v.* hacer frutecer
ruruy *v.* bear fruit || *v.* frutecer
rutuchikuy *v.* let one's hair be cut *(head)* || *v.* dejarse cortar el cabello
rutuchiy *v.* make cut hair *(head)*; make reap || *v.* hacer cortar el cabello; hacer segar
rutuy *v.* cut hair *(head)*; reap || *v.* cortar el cabello; segar
rutuysiy *v.* help reap || *v.* ayudar a segar
ruwachiy *v.* command to make, command to do || *v.* mandar a hacer

ruwana *n.* task || *s.* tarea
ruwanayay *v.* have the urge to do something || *v.* tener deseos de hacer algo
ruwasqa *adj.* made, done || *adj.* hecho
ruway *v.* make, do || *v.* hacer
ruwaysiy *v.* help make, help do || *v.* ayudar a hacer

S

sach'a *n.* tree with many branches || *s.* árbol frondoso
sach'a sach'a *n.* forest || *s.* bosque
saksasqa *adj.* satisfied, satiated || *adj.* satisfecho/a, saciado/a
saksay *v.* become satisfied, become satiated || *v.* satisfacerse, saciarse
salqa *adj.* wild, unfriendly || *adj.* salvaje, arisco
salqa uywa *n.* wild animal || *s.* animal salvaje
salqayay *v.* become wild || *v.* volverse salvaje
samachiy *v.* make rest || *v.* hacer descansar
samana *n.* resting place || *s.* lugar de descanso
samanayay *v.* have the urge to rest || *v.* tener deseos de descansar
samasqa *adj.* rested || *adj.* descansado/a
samay *n.* breath || *s.* aliento
samay *v.* rest; breathe || *v.* descansar; respirar
saminchay *v.* revere || *v.* reverenciar
sani *adj.* purple || *adj.* morado/a
saniyay *v.* turn purple || *v.* volverse morado/a
sankha *n.* abyss, deep hole || *s.* abismo, hoyo profundo
sanp'a *adj.* docile || *adj.* manso/a
sanp'ayay *v.* become docile || *v.* volverse manso/a
sansa *n.* ember || *s.* brasa
sansachay *v.* put over embers || *v.* poner sobre las brasas
sapa *adj.* only || *adj.* único/a
sapanchasqa *adj.* excluded || *adj.* excluido/a
sapanchay *v.* exclude || *v.* excluir
sapanka *adj.* each one || *adj.* cada uno/a
sapaq *adj.* particular, distinct || *adj.* particular, distinto/a
saphi *n.* root || *s.* raíz
saphinay *v.* uproot || *v.* desenraízar
saphiy *v.* take root || *v.* enraízar
saphsa *adj.* ragged • *n.* person in rags || *adj.* harapiento/a • *s.* harapo
saphsachay *v.* become ragged || *v.* convertir en harapos
saqechikuy *v.* be left behind, be abandoned || *v.* hacerse dejar atrás, hacerse abandonar

saqekuy *v.* leave in someone's care || *v.* dejar al cuidado de alguien
saqesqa *adj.* abandoned || *adj.* abandonado/a
saqey *v.* leave behind, abandon || *v.* dejar, abandonar
saqma *n.* fist || *s.* puño
saqmachikuy *v.* let oneself be punched || *v.* dejarse puñetear
saqmachiy *v.* make punch *(someone)* || *v.* hacer golpear con el puño
saqmanakuy *v.* punch one another || *v.* puñetearse mutuamente
saqmapayay *v.* punch constantly || *v.* puñetear constantemente
saqmasqa *adj.* punched || *adj.* golpeado/a con el puño
saqmay *v.* punch || *v.* puñetear
saqmaykachay *v.* punch repeatedly || *v.* dar puñetazos repetidamente
saqra *adj.* mischievous || *adj.* travieso/a
saqrayay *v.* become mischievous || *v.* volverse travieso/a
saqraykachay *v.* make mischief || *v.* hacer travesuras
saqtachiy *v.* make crush, make pound || *v.* hacer machucar
saqtana *n.* crushing tool, pounding tool || *s.* instrumento para machucar
saqtasqa *adj.* crushed, pounded || *adj.* machucado/a
saqtay *v.* crush, pound || *v.* machucar
saqtaysiy *v.* help crush, help pound || *v.* ayudar a machucar
sara *n.* corn || *s.* maíz
saruchasqa *adj.* humiliated || *adj.* humillado/a
saruchay *v.* humiliate || *v.* menospreciar, humillar
saruchikuy *v.* get stepped on, let oneself be humiliated || *v.* hacerse pisar, dejarse humillar
sarunakuy *v.* step on one another repeatedly || *v.* pisotearse mutuamente
saruq *n.* person who steps on || *s.* el/la que pisa
sarusqa *adj.* stepped on || *adj.* pisado/a
saruy *v.* step on || *v.* pisar
saruykachay *v.* step on again and again || *v.* pisotear
sasa *adj.* difficult || *adj.* difícil
sasachay *v.* make difficult || *v.* dificultar
sasay sasay *adv.* with difficulty || *adv.* dificilmente
sasi *n.* fast || *s.* ayuno
sasichiy *v.* make fast *(not eat)* || *v.* hacer ayunar
sasiy *v.* fast || *v.* ayunar
sat'ina *n.* pointed object || *s.* objeto punzante
sat'ipakuy *v.* meddle || *v.* meterse porfiadamente

sat'irayay *v.* stay too long || *v.* permancer sin salir
sat'isqa *adj.* nailed, pricked || *adj.* clavado, punzado
sat'iy *v.* nail, prick || *v.* clavar, punzar
sawna *n.* pillow; headboard || *s.* almohada; cabecera de la cama
sawnakuy *v.* put head on pillow || *v.* poner la cabeza sobre la almohada
sayachiy *v.* detain, stand up || *v.* detener, poner de pie
sayana *n.* stopping place, stop || *s.* posada, paradero
sayanayay *v.* have the urge to stand up || *v.* tener deseos de estar parado/a
sayanpa *adj.* vertical, on foot || *adj.* vertical, de pie
sayanpamanta *adv.* vertically • *adj.* on foot || *adv.* verticalmente • *adj.* de pie
sayapakuy *v.* defend another || *v.* defender a alguien
sayarayay *v.* remain standing || *v.* permanecer parado/a
sayarisqa *adj.* arisen, erect || *adj.* levantado/a, erguido/a
sayariy *v.* get up || *v.* levantarse
sayay *n.* size • *v.* be on foot || *s.* tamaño • *v.* estar de pie
sayk'uchiy *v.* tire out || *v.* causar cansancio
sayk'usqa *adj.* tired, exhausted || *adj.* cansado/a, agotado/a
sayk'uy *v.* tire, be exhausted || *v.* cansarse, agotarse
sayk'uylla *adv.* wearily || *adv.* cansadamente
saynata *n.* mask || *s.* máscara
sayri *n.* tobacco plant || *s.* planta de tabaco
senq'ay *v.* sniff up, snort || *v.* sorber por la nariz, inhalar por la nariz
senqa *n.* nose || *s.* nariz
seqachinakuy *v.* yell at one another || *v.* discutir
seqachiy *v.* make climb || *v.* hacer subir
seqana *n.* steps || *s.* gradería
seqanayay *v.* have the urge to climb || *v.* tener deseos de subir
seqapakuy *v.* try to climb || *v.* intentar subir
seqapayay *v.* climb again and again || *v.* subir una y otra vez
seqay *v.* climb || *v.* subir
seqaysiy *v.* help climb || *v.* ayudar a subir
seqra *n.* diarrhea || *s.* diarrea
seqray *v.* have diarrhea *(literal)*; evacuate quickly *(figurative)* || *v.* tener diarrea *(literal)*; evacuar raudamente *(figurado)*
seqsichiy *v.* cause stinging || *v.* causar escozor
seqsiy *v.* sting || *v.* escocer

seq'ochiy *v.* command to strangle || *v.* mandar a estrangular
seq'oq *n.* strangler || *s.* estrangulador/a
seq'osqa *adj.* strangled || *adj.* estrangulado/a
seq'oy *v.* strangle || *v.* estrangular
seq'oysiy *v.* help strangle || *v.* ayudar a estrangular
sichus *conj.* if || *conj.* si
siki *n.* buttocks, bottom || *s.* trasero, base
siklla *adj.* adorned || *adj.* engalanado/a
sikwachiy *v.* command to whip || *v.* mandar a azotar
sikwana *n.* whip || *s.* azote
sikwanakuy *v.* whip one another || *v.* azotarse mutuamente
sikwaq *n.* person who whips || *s.* azotador/a
sikwasqa *adj.* whipped || *adj.* azotado/a
sikway *v.* whip || *v.* azotar
sikwaykachay *v.* whip constantly and disinterestedly || *v.* azotar constante y desganadamente
sikwaysiy *v.* help whip || *v.* ayudar a azotar
sik'ichiy *v.* command to extract || *v.* mandar a extraer
sik'isqa *adj.* extracted || *adj.* extraído/a
sik'iy *v.* extract || *v.* extraer
sik'iysiy *v.* help extract || *v.* ayudar a extraer
sillkuy *v.* scratch || *v.* rasguñar
sillu *n.* fingernail, claw || *s.* uña, garra
simi *n.* mouth; speech || *s.* boca; habla
siminchasqa *adj.* insinuated || *adj.* insinuado/a
siminchay *v.* insinuate || *v.* insinuar
sinchi *adj.* many || *adj.* mucho/a
sinchita *adv.* very, a lot || *adv.* muy, mucho/a
sinkhasqa *adj.* peeled off with teeth *(husk)* || *adj.* descortezado/a con los dientes *(un tallo)*
sinkhay *v.* peel off with teeth *(husk)* || *v.* descortezar con los dientes *(un tallo)*
sinp'a *n.* braid || *s.* trenza
sinp'achikuy *v.* let one's hair be braided || *v.* dejarse trenzar
sinp'achiy *v.* command to braid || *v.* mandar a trenzar
sinp'anay *v.* unbraid || *v.* destrenzar
sinp'aq *n.* braider || *s.* trenzador/a
sinp'asqa *adj.* braided || *adj.* trenzado/a
sinp'ay *v.* braid || *v.* trenzar
sinp'aysiy *v.* help braid || *v.* ayudar a trenzar

sinriy *v.* line up || *v.* alinear
sipas *n.* young woman, girl || *s.* joven *(mujer)*, muchacha
sipasyay *v.* grow up *(girl)*; rejuvenate *(woman)* || *v.* devenir en joven *(la adolescente)*; rejuvenecer *(la mujer vieja)*
siphsi *n.* drizzle || *s.* llovizna
siphsiq *n.* whisperer || *s.* cuchicheador/a
siphsiy *v.* drizzle; whisper || *v.* lloviznar; cuchichear
sipichiy *v.* command to murder || *v.* mandar a asesinar
sipiq *n.* murderer || *s.* asesino/a
sipisqa *adj.* murdered || *adj.* asesinado/a
sipiy *v.* murder || *v.* asesinar
sipiysiy *v.* help murder || *v.* ayudar a asesinar
sip'usqa *adj.* gathered *(fabric)* || *adj.* fruncido/a *(una tela)*
sip'uy *v.* gather *(fabric)* || *v.* fruncir *(una tela)*
sirachikuy *v.* order to have clothing sewn for someone || *v.* mandar a coser ropa para uno/a
sirana *n.* sewing needle || *s.* aguja para coser
siranay *v.* unstitch || *v.* descoser
siraq *n.* sewer, tailor || *s.* cosedor/a, costurero/a
sirasqa *adj.* sewn || *adj.* cosido/a
siray *v.* sew || *v.* coser
siraysiy *v.* help sew || *v.* ayudar a coser
sirk'a *n.* vein || *s.* vena
sirk'ay *v.* bleed || *v.* sangrar
sirk'ayoq *n.* venous || *s.* venoso/a
sirpaq *n.* traitor || *s.* traidor/a
sirpasqa *adj.* betrayed || *adj.* traicionado/a
sirpay *v.* betray || *v.* traicionar
sirpaylla *adv.* deceptively || *adv.* traicioneramente
sirwana *n.* flower *(Andean variety)* || *s.* flor *(variedad andina)*
sisa *n.* pollen || *s.* polen
sisi *n.* ant || *s.* hormiga
sisiy *v.* fill a place || *v.* colmar un lugar
sisiykuy *v.* congregate || *v.* aglomerarse
sispa *adj.* near, close || *adj.* cerca, próximo
sispay *v.* get closer, approach || *v.* acercarse, aproximarse
sit'i *adj.* scrawny || *s.* esmirriado/a
sit'iyay *v.* become scrawny || *v.* esmirriarse
siwina *n.* whistle || *s.* silbato
siwinayay *v.* have the urge to whistle || *v.* tener deseos de silbar

siwiy *v.* whistle || *v.* silbar
sonqo *n.* heart, center || *s.* corazón, centro
sonqonay *v.* wrap; center || *v.* envolver; centrar
sonqosapa *adj.* generous || *adj.* generoso/a
soqo *n.* gray hair • *adj.* gray-haired || *s.* cana • *adj.* canoso/a
soqonay *v.* pull out gray hairs || *v.* quitar las canas
soqos *n.* reed || *s.* carrizo
soqoyay *v.* become gray-haired || *v.* encanecer
soqta *num.* six || *num.* seis
soqyay *v.* fall and roll || *v.* caer rodando
soq'a *adj.* lethal || *adj.* letal
soq'achiy *v.* command to whip || *v.* mandar a azotar
soq'ana *n.* whip || *s.* azote
soq'anakuy *v.* whip one another || *v.* azotarse mutuamente
soq'apayay *v.* whip again and again || *v.* azotar una y otra vez
soq'aq *n.* person who whips || *s.* azotador/a
soq'asqa *adj.* whipped || *adj.* azotado/a
soq'ay *v.* whip || *v.* azotar
soq'aysiy *v.* help whip || *v.* ayudar a azotar
sorq'an *n.* lung || *s.* pulmón
such'u *adj.* crippled || *adj.* tullido/a
such'uyay *v.* become crippled || *v.* volverse tullido/a
suchi *n.* package, shipment || *s.* encargo, remesa
suchiq *n.* sender, shipper || *s.* encargador/a, remesante
suchisqa *adj.* sent *(thing)* || *adj.* encargado/a *(cosa)*
suchiy *v.* send, ship || *v.* encargar, remesar
sullk'a *adj.* younger || *adj.* menor *(edad)*
sullu *n.* fetus || *s.* feto
sulluchiy *v.* make abort || *v.* hacer abortar
sullusqa *adj.* aborted || *adj.* abortado/a
sulluy *v.* abort || *v.* abortar
sumaq *adj.* exquisite, beautiful, nice || *adj.* exquisito/a, bonito/a, agradable
sumaqlla *adv.* exquisitely, beautifully || *adv.* exquisitamente, bellamente
sumaqta *adv.* exquisitely, beautifully || *adv.* exquisitamente, bellamente
sumaqyay *v.* become exquisite, become beautiful || *v.* volverse exquisito/a, volverse bonito/a
sumaychasqa *adj.* honored, exalted || *adj.* honrado/a, ensalzado/a

sumaychay *v.* honor, exalt || *v.* honrar, ensalzar
suni *adj.* long, elongated || *adj.* largo/a, alargado/a
suniy *v.* elongate || *v.* alargar
sunkha *n.* beard || *s.* barba
sunkhay *v.* graze woman's forehead with beard || *v.* rozar la frente de una mujer con la barbilla
sunkhayay *v.* grow a beard || *v.* crecer la barba
sunkhayoq *adj.* bearded || *adj.* barbado/a
suntur *adj.* circular || *adj.* circular
suntusqa *adj.* stacked || *adj.* amontonado/a
suntuy *v.* stack || *v.* amontonar
supa *n.* shadow || *s.* sombra
supay *v.* shadow || *v.* sombrear
suphu *n.* bristle || *s.* cerda *(pelo grueso)*
suphunay *v.* remove bristles || *v.* quitar las cerdas *(pelo grueso)*
surusqa *adj.* trickled || *adj.* escurrido/a
suruy *v.* trickle || *v.* escurrir
susigo *adv.* slowly, calmly || *adv.* despacio, con calma
suskha *adj.* slippery || *adj.* resbaloso/a
suskhay *v.* slip || *v.* resbalar
suti *n.* name || *s.* nombre
sutichay *v.* name || *v.* nombrar
sutiyay *v.* nickname || *v.* apodar
sut'in *adj.* clear, evident || *adj.* claro, evidente
sut'inchasqa *adj.* clarified || *adj.* esclarecido/a
sut'inchay *v.* clarify || *v.* esclarecer
sut'u *n.* drip, drop || *s.* gota *(líquido)*
sut'uy *v.* drip || *v.* gotear
suwa *n.* thief || *s.* ladrón
suwachikuy *v.* get robbed || *v.* sufrir un robo
suwachiy *v.* make steal, make rob || *v.* mandar a robar
suwasqa *adj.* stolen, robbed || *adj.* robado/a
suway *v.* steal, rob || *v.* robar
suwaysiy *v.* help steal, help rob || *v.* ayudar a robar
suyapayay *v.* wait anxiously || *v.* esperar ansiosamente
suyaq *n.* person who waits || *s.* el/la que espera
suyasqa *adj.* anticipated || *adj.* esperado/a
suyay *v.* wait || *v.* esperar
suysuchiy *v.* command to sift || *v.* mandar a cernir
suysusqa *adj.* sifted || *adj.* cernido/a

suysuy *v.* sift || *v.* cernir
suysuysiy *v.* help sift || *v.* ayudar a cernir
suyt'u *adj.* oval • *n.* snout of certain animals || *adj.* ovalado • *s.* hocico de ciertos animales
suyu *n.* region || *s.* región
suyunchay *v.* demarcate || *v.* demarcar

T

takapayay *v.* hit repeatedly, nail repeatedly || *v.* golpear repetidas veces, clavar repetidas veces
takarayay *v.* wait for a long time *(standing)* || *v.* esperar por mucho tiempo *(parado)*
takay *v.* hit, nail || *v.* golpear, clavar
takaysiy *v.* help hit, help nail || *v.* ayudar a golpear, ayudar a clavar
taki *n.* song || *s.* canción
takillpa *n.* heel || *s.* talón
takinayay *v.* have the urge to sing || *v.* tener deseos de cantar
takipayay *v.* sing constantly || *v.* cantar constantemente
takiq *n.* singer || *s.* cantor
takiy *v.* sing || *v.* cantar
takiykachay *v.* sing softly || *v.* canturrear
takiysiy *v.* sing with others || *v.* acompañar a cantar
taklla *n.* Andean plow || *s.* arado andino
taksa *adj.* medium small || *adj.* mediano casi pequeño
taksayachiy *v.* reduce || *v.* reducir
takyay *v.* put down roots, settle || *v.* arraigar, asentarse
tallisqa *adj.* empty || *adj.* vaciado
talliy *v.* empty out a container || *v.* vaciar un recipiente
talliysiy *v.* help empty out a container || *v.* ayudar a vaciar un recipiente
tanka *n.* wooden post *(medium) (literal)*; small man *(figurative)* • *adj.* short *(man)* || *s.* poste de madera *(mediano) (literal)*; hombre pequeño *(figurado)* • *adj.* menudo *(hombre)*
tankachay *v.* support with stick || *v.* sostener con un palo
tankayllu *n.* horsefly || *s.* tábano
tanpu *n.* inn, lodging || *s.* posada
tanqa tanqa *adv.* rashly || *adv.* atropelladamente
tanqanakuy *v.* push one another || *v.* empujarse mutuamente
tanqay *v.* push, propel || *v.* empujar, impulsar
tantanakuy *v.* get together || *v.* reunirse, congregarse
tantay *v.* put together || *v.* reunir, congregar
taparaku *n.* nocturnal butterfly || *s.* mariposa nocturna

taparasqa *adj.* folded || *adj.* plegado
taparay *v.* fold || *v.* plegar
taparaysiy *v.* help fold || *v.* ayudar a plegar
tapuchiy *v.* make question || *v.* mandar a preguntar
tapukachay *v.* ask about many things, investigate || *v.* preguntar sobre una y otra cosa, indagar una y otra vez
tapukuy *v.* ask oneself || *v.* preguntarse a sí mismo
tapuna *n.* question || *s.* pregunta
tapunakuy *v.* ask one another || *v.* preguntarse mutuamente
tapupakuq *n.* questioner || *s.* preguntón
tapuy *v.* ask about, inquire, question || *v.* preguntar, indagar
taqe *n.* granery; woven container || *s.* granero; recipiente tejido
taqechiy *v.* order to stock products || *v.* mandar a almacenar productos
taqey *v.* stock products || *v.* almacenar productos
taqeysiy *v.* help stock products || *v.* ayudar a almacenar productos
taqrunakuy *v.* mix together || *v.* entremezclarse
taqruq *n.* mixer || *s.* mezclador/a
taqrusqa *adj.* mixed || *adj.* mezclado
taqruy *v.* mix || *v.* mezclar
taqruykachay *v.* mix again and again || *v.* mezclar una y otra vez
taqruysiy *v.* help mix || *v.* ayudar a mezclar
tara *n.* medicinal tree || *s.* árbol medicinal
taripay *v.* catch up || *v.* dar alcance
tarisqa *adj.* found || *adj.* encontrado
tariy *v.* find || *v.* encontrar
tariysiy *v.* help find || *v.* ayudar a encontrar
tarpuchiy *v.* make sow, make plant seeds || *v.* hacer sembrar
tarpuq *n.* sower, seed planter || *s.* sembrador/a
tarpusqa *adj.* sown, planted || *adj.* sembrado/a
tarpuy *v.* sow, plant seeds || *v.* sembrar
tarpuysiy *v.* help sow, help plant seeds || *v.* ayudar a sembrar
taruka *n.* deer || *s.* venado
tarwi *n.* bean *(Andean variety)* || *s.* frijol *(variedad andina)*
tatichiy *v.* interrupt || *v.* interrumpir
tatiy *v.* cease || *v.* cesar
tawa *num.* four || *num.* cuatro
tawachaki *adj.* four-legged || *adj.* cuadrúpedo
tawna *n.* cane || *s.* bastón
tawqa tawqa *adj.* stacked || *adj.* apilado

tawqachiy *v.* make stack || *v.* mandar a apilar
tawqaq *n.* person who stacks || *s.* el/la que apila
tawqasqa *adj.* stacked || *adj.* apilado
tawqay *v.* stack || *v.* apilar
tawqaysiy *v.* help stack || *v.* ayudar a apilar
tayta *n.* patriarch, father || *s.* patriarca, padre
taytachakuy *v.* make a father figure || *v.* hacerse de un padre ajeno
teqni *n.* hip || *s.* cadera
teqnisapa *adj.* large-hipped || *adj.* caderona
teqsi *n.* base || *s.* base
teqsimuyu *n.* universe || *s.* universo
teqsiy *v.* found || *v.* fundar
teqte *n.* sweet corn drink || *s.* refresco dulce de maíz
tikayay *v.* coagulate || *v.* coagularse
tikti *n.* wart || *s.* verruga
tinku *n.* confrontation || *s.* confrontación
tinkuchiy *v.* make confront || *v.* hacer confrontar
tinkunakuy *v.* confront one another || *v.* confrontarse
tinkuy *v.* converge, confront || *v.* confluir, confrontar
tinya *n.* small drum || *s.* tamborcillo
tinyay *v.* beat a drum || *s.* tañer el tambor
tipichiy *v.* make shuck corn || *v.* mandar a deshojar la mazorca de maíz
tipisqa *adj.* shucked *(corn)* || *adj.* deshojado *(mazorca de maíz)*
tipiy *v.* shuck corn || *v.* deshojar la mazorca de maíz
tipiysiy *v.* help shuck corn || *v.* ayudar a deshojar la mazorca de maíz
titi *n.* lead *(metal)* || *s.* plomo
tiwti *adj.* rickety || *adj.* endeble
tiwtiyay *v.* become weak, become skinny || *v.* debilitarse, enflaquecer
tiyachiy *v.* make sit || *v.* hacer sentar
tiyakachay *v.* sit again and again || *v.* sentarse una y otra vez
tiyana *n.* seat, chair || *s.* asiento, silla
tiyanayay *v.* have the urge to sit || *v.* tener deseos de sentarse
tiyapakuy *v.* live in another's house temporarily || *v.* vivir temporalmente en casa ajena
tiyapayay *v.* spend time with someone in their house || *v.* pasar el tiempo con alguien en su casa
tiyarayay *v.* stay seated for a long time || *v.* mantenerse sentado/a por largo tiempo

tiyasqa *adj.* seated || *adj.* sentado/a
tiyay *v.* sit, inhabit || *v.* sentarse, asentarse
tiyaysiy *v.* care for someone in their house || *v.* cuidar a alguien en su casa
tonqor *n.* throat || *s.* garganta
toqti *adj.* rickety || *adj.* endeble
toqton *n.* marrow || *s.* médula
totora *n.* marsh plant || *s.* arbusto ribereño
tuku *n.* owl || *s.* búho
tukuchiy *v.* make finish || *v.* hacer terminar, hacer concluir
tukukuy *v.* be finished, run out of *(something)* || *v.* acabarse, concluir
tukupay *v.* finish one's uncompleted task || *v.* terminar lo que se dejó inconcluso
tukurpariy *v.* finish in a hurry || *v.* terminar de prisa, concluir de prisa
tukusqa *adj.* finished || *adj.* terminado/a, concluido/a
tukuy *v.* finish • *adj.* all || *v.* terminar • *adj.* todo/a, todos/as
tukuysiy *v.* help finish || *v.* ayudar a terminar, ayudar a concluir
tullka *n.* son-in-law || *s.* yerno
tullpuchiy *v.* make dye || *v.* mandar a teñir
tullpuq *n.* dyer || *s.* teñidor/a
tullpusqa *adj.* dyed || *adj.* teñido/a
tullpuy *v.* dye || *v.* teñir
tullpuysiy *v.* help dye || *v.* ayudar a teñir
tullu *n.* bone • *adj.* skinny || *s.* hueso • *adj.* flaco/a
tullusapa *adj.* boney || *adj.* huesudo/a
tulluyachiy *v.* make become skinny || *v.* hacer enflaquecer
tulluyay *v.* become skinny, lose weight || *v.* enflaquecer
tuma *n.* lap *(around)* || *s.* rodeo, vuelta
tumay *v.* circle, walk around || *v.* rodear, caminar alrededor de
tumi *n.* knife *(ritual)* || *s.* cuchilla *(ritual)*
tunki *n.* bird *(Andean variety)* || *s.* pájaro *(variedad andina)*
tunpanakuy *v.* accuse one another, blame one another || *v.* inculparse mutuamente
tunpaq *n.* accuser, person who blames || *s.* inculpador/a
tunpasqa *adj.* accused, blamed || *adj.* inculpado/a
tunpay *v.* accuse, blame || *v.* inculpar
tunta *n.* dehydrated potato || *s.* papa desidratada
tupachiy *v.* put together || *v.* conjuntar
tupaq *n.* person who encounters, person who meets || *s.* el/la que se encuentra con, el/la que converge con

tupay *v.* encounter, meet || *v.* encontrarse *(con)*, converger *(con)*
tupaykuy *v.* touch slightly || *v.* palpar levemente
tupu *n.* brooch || *s.* prendedor
tupuchay *v.* fasten clothes with brooch || *v.* sujetar la ropa con un prendedor
tupuchiy *v.* make measure || *v.* mandar a medir
tupuq *n.* measurer || *s.* medidor/a
tupuy *v.* measure || *v.* medir
tura *n.* brother *(of woman)* || *s.* hermano *(de mujer)*
turachakuy *v.* treat someone like a brother *(woman)* || *v.* tratar a alguien como hermano *(mujer)*
turay *v.* put in balance; stabilize || *v.* estabilizar, contrapesar
tusachiy *v.* make brace, make bear || *v.* hacer apuntalar, hacer sostener
tusaq *n.* person who braces, person who bears || *s.* apuntalador/a, sostenedor/a
tusasqa *adj.* braced || *adj.* apuntalado/a, sostenido/a
tusay *v.* brace, bear || *v.* apuntalar, sostener
tusaysiy *v.* help brace, help bear || *v.* ayudar a apuntalar, ayudar a sostener
tusuchiy *v.* make dance || *v.* hacer bailar
tusunayay *v.* have the urge to dance || *v.* tener deseos de bailar
tusuq *n.* dancer || *s.* bailarín
tusuy *v.* dance || *v.* bailar
tusuysiy *v.* dance with someone || *v.* acompañar a bailar
tuta *n.* night || *s.* noche
tutamanta *adv.* in the morning || *adv.* por la mañana
tutantin *adv.* all night || *adv.* toda la noche
tutapay *v.* get up early || *v.* madrugar
tutayaq *n.* darkness || *s.* oscuridad
tutayay *v.* become night, become dark || *v.* anochecer, oscurecer
tutuy *v.* breastfeed, nurse || *v.* lactar
tuya *n.* skylark || *s.* calandria
tuyrusqa *adj.* marked || *adj.* marcado/a
tuyruy *v.* mark, signal || *v.* marcar, señalizar
tuytuq *adj.* floating • *n.* floater || *adj.* flotante • *s.* flotador
tuytuy *v.* float || *v.* flotar
tuyuy *v.* row || *v.* remar

TH

thak *adv.* calmly • *adj.* calm || *adv.* tranquilamente • *adj.* tranquilo
thaka *adj.* dense, thick *(liquid)* || *adj.* denso/a, espeso/a *(líquido)*
thakayachiy *v.* make thicken *(liquid)* || *v.* hacer espesar *(líquido)*
thakayay *v.* become thickened *(liquid)* || *v.* espesarse *(líquido)*
thallachiy *v.* put face down, make put face down || *v.* colocar en posición boca abajo, mandar a colocar en posición boca abajo
thallanpamanta *adv.* face down || *adv.* boca abajo
thallaq *n.* person who is face down || *s.* el/la que está boca abajo
thaltay *v.* drool || *v.* babear
thamalanku *adj.* untidy, disorderly || *adj.* desarreglado/a, desordenado/a
thanichiy *v.* make alleviate || *v.* hacer aliviar
thaniq *n.* person who alleviates || *s.* el/la que se alivia
thanisqa *adj.* alleviated || *adj.* aliviado/a
thaniy *v.* feel better, become alleviated || *v.* mejorarse, aliviarse
thanpi *adj.* stunned || *adj.* aturdido/a
thanpiy *v.* be stunned || *v.* estar aturdido/a
thanta *adj.* threadbare, worn out *(clothes)* || *adj.* raído/a, desgastado/a por el uso *(ropa)*
thantay *v.* wear out *(clothes)*, deteriorate || *v.* desgastar *(ropa)*, deteriorar
thasnuchiy *v.* make put out fire with water || *v.* hacer apagar el fuego con agua
thasnuy *v.* put out fire with water || *v.* apagar el fuego con agua
thasnuysiy *v.* help put out fire with water || *v.* ayudar a apagar el fuego con agua
thawtiq *n.* person who talks nonsense || *s.* el/la que dice incoherencias
thawtiy *v.* talk nonsense || *v.* desvariar, decir incoherencias
theqtichiy *v.* fry || *v.* freír
theqtisqa *adj.* fried || *adj.* frito/a
thintipayay *v.* guffaw again and again, laugh loudly again and again || *v.* dar risotadas una y otra vez
thintiy *v.* guffaw, laugh loudly || *v.* dar risotadas
thoqachiy *v.* make spit || *v.* mandar a escupir

thoqanakuy *v.* spit on one another || *v.* escupirse mutuamente
thoqanayay *v.* have the urge to spit || *v.* tener deseos de escupir
thoqapayay *v.* spit constantly || *v.* escupir constantamente
thoqasqa *adj.* spit out || *adj.* escupido
thoqay *n.* saliva • *v.* spit || *s.* saliva • *v.* escupir
thukichiy *v.* make doubt || *v.* hacer dudar
thukiq *n.* doubter || *s.* el/la que duda
thukiy *v.* doubt || *v.* dudar
thukiykachay *v.* doubt often || *v.* dudar a menudo
thullkisqa *adj.* fallen over, undone || *adj.* desmoronado/a, deshecho/a
thullkiy *v.* fall over, undo || *v.* desmoronar, deshacer
thultu *adj.* disabled, decrepit || *adj.* incapacitado/a, decrépito/a
thultuyay *v.* become disabled, become decrepit || *v.* devenir en incapacitado/a, devenir en decrépito/a
thunichiy *v.* make collapse, make demolish || *v.* hacer desplomar, hacer derrumbar
thunisqa *adj.* collapsed, demolished || *adj.* desplomado/a, derrumbado/a
thuniy *v.* collapse, demolish || *v.* desplomar, derrumbar
thunkuchiy *v.* make tie down || *v.* mandar a maniatar
thunkuy *v.* tie down || *v.* maniatar
thunkuysiy *v.* help tie down || *v.* ayudar a maniatar
thupasqa *adj.* scraped, grated || *adj.* raspado/a, rallado/a
thupay *v.* scrape, grate || *v.* raspar, rallar
thupaykachay *v.* scrape again and again, grate again and again || *v.* raspar una y otra vez, rallar una y otra vez
thupaysiy *v.* help scrape, help grate || *v.* ayudar a raspar, ayudar a rallar
thuta *n.* moth || *s.* polilla
thutasqa *adj.* moth-eaten || *adj.* apolillado/a
thutay *v.* get eaten by moths || *v.* apolillar
thutuy *v.* mutter, murmur || *v.* mascullar, murmurar

T'

t'akasqa *adj.* scattered || *adj.* diseminado/a
t'akay *v.* scatter || *v.* diseminar
t'anpa *adj.* disheveled || *adj.* desgreñado/a
t'anpachakuy *v.* become disheveled || *v.* desgreñarse
t'anta *n.* bread || *s.* pan
t'antasqa *adj.* consumed || *adj.* consumido/a
t'antay *v.* consume || *v.* consumir
t'aqa *n.* group || *s.* grupo
t'aqachiy *v.* command to separate || *v.* mandar a separar
t'aqapayay *v.* separate again and again || *v.* separar una y otra vez
t'aqasqa *adj.* separated || *adj.* separado/a
t'aqay *v.* separate || *v.* separar
t'aqaysiy *v.* help separate || *v.* ayudar a separar
t'aqllapayay *v.* pat repeatedly || *v.* palmear reiteradamente
t'aqllay *v.* applaud; pat || *v.* aplaudir; palmear
t'aqsachiy *v.* command to wash *(clothes)* || *v.* mandar a lavar *(ropa)*
t'aqsasqa *adj.* washed *(clothes)* || *adj.* lavado/a *(ropa)*
t'aqsay *v.* wash *(clothes)* || *v.* lavar *(ropa)*
t'aqsaysiy *v.* help wash *(clothes)* || *v.* ayudar a lavar *(ropa)*
t'aqwichiy *v.* command to search for || *v.* mandar a rebuscar
t'aqwiq *n.* person who searches for || *s.* rebuscador/a
t'aqwiy *v.* search for || *v.* rebuscar
t'aqwiysiy *v.* help search for || *v.* ayudar a rebuscar
t'asnu *adj.* flattened || *adj.* achatado/a
t'asnuy *v.* flatten || *v.* achatar
t'eqtichiy *v.* fry || *v.* freír
t'eqtisqa *adj.* fried || *adj.* frito/a
t'ika *n.* flower || *s.* flor
t'ikayay *v.* flower || *v.* florecer
t'ikranpamanta *adv.* backward || *adv.* al revés
t'ikray *v.* turn over; translate || *v.* voltear; traducir
t'ikraysiy *v.* help turn over || *v.* ayudar a voltear
t'iksuy *v.* lean, tilt || *v.* inclinar
t'iksuykachay *v.* lean over || *v.* inclinarse
t'ini *n.* puppy || *s.* cachorro

t'inkisqa *adj.* joined || *adj.* juntado/a
t'inkiy *v.* join || *v.* juntar
t'inkiysiy *v.* help join || *v.* ayudar a juntar
t'inpusqa *adj.* boiled || *adj.* hervido/a
t'inpuy *v.* boil || *v.* hervir
t'ipichikuy *v.* let oneself be pinched || *v.* dejarse pellizcar
t'ipinakuy *v.* pinch one another || *v.* pellizcarse mutuamente
t'ipipayay *v.* pinch constantly || *v.* pellizcar constantemente
t'ipiy *v.* pinch || *v.* pellizcar
t'irasqa *adj.* uprooted || *adj.* desenraízado/a
t'iray *v.* uproot || *v.* desenraízar
t'iraysiy *v.* help uproot || *v.* ayudar a desenraizar
t'iyu *n.* sand, sediment || *s.* arena, sedimento
t'ohasqa *adj.* exploded || *adj.* estallado/a, tronado/a
t'ohay *v.* explode || *v.* estallar, tronar
t'oqo *n.* hole || *s.* agujero, hueco
t'oqosqa *adj.* full of holes || *adj.* agujereado/a, ahuecado/a
t'oqsiq *n.* finger pointer || *s.* señalador/a con el dedo
t'oqsiy *v.* point out with finger || *v.* señalar con el dedo
t'oqyasqa *adj.* exploded || *adj.* estallado/a, tronado/a
t'oqyay *v.* explode || *v.* estallar, tronar
t'urpuna *n.* pin || *s.* punzón
t'urpuy *v.* stick, prick || *v.* punzar, hincar
t'uru *n.* mud || *s.* barro
t'uruchasqa *adj.* muddy || *adj.* embarrado/a
t'uruchay *v.* prepare mud || *v.* preparar barro
t'urunay *v.* remove mud || *v.* desembarrar
t'usta *adj.* short *(woman)* || *adj.* menuda *(mujer)*
t'ustu *n.* small woman || *s.* mujer pequeña
t'ustuyay *v.* shrink with age *(woman)* || *v.* empequeñecerse en la vejez *(mujer)*
t'uyuy *v.* row || *v.* remar
t'uyuysiy *v.* help row || *v.* ayudar a remar

U

uchu *n.* pepper || *s.* ají
uchuchay *v.* season, season with pepper || *v.* sazonar, aliñar con ají
uchukuta *n.* hot sauce || *s.* ají molido
uchusapa *adj.* spicy, very seasoned || *adj.* picante, muy sazonado/a
uchha *n.* manure || *s.* estiércol
uchhay *v.* defecate *(livestock)* || *v.* defecar *(ganado)*
uhu *n.* cough || *s.* tos
uhuchiy *v.* make cough || *v.* hacer toser
uhunayay *v.* have the urge to cough || *v.* tener deseos de toser
uhupakuy *v.* cough constantly || *v.* toser constantemente
uhuq *n.* cougher || *s.* el/la que tose
uhuy *v.* cough || *v.* toser
ukhu *prep.* inside • *adj.* interior || *prep.* adentro • *adj.* interior
ukhu *n.* body *(person)* || *s.* cuerpo *(persona)*
ukhuchay *v.* go into || *v.* adentrar, internar
ukhuna *n.* underwear || *s.* ropa interior
ukhunakuy *v.* put on underwear || *v.* ponerse la ropa interior
uksiy *v.* rout around || *v.* hozar
ukuku *n.* bear || *s.* oso
ukyachiy *v.* make drink || *v.* hacer beber
ukyana *n.* drink || *s.* bebida
ukyanayay *v.* have the urge to drink || *v.* tener deseos de beber
ukyaq *n.* drinker || *s.* bebedor/a
ukyarpariy *v.* drink hurriedly || *v.* beber a prisa
ukyay *v.* drink || *v.* beber
ukyaysiy *v.* join in drinking || *v.* sumarse a una libación
ullpu ullpu *adv.* humbly, submissively || *adv.* humildemente, sumisamente
ullu *n.* penis || *s.* pene
ulluku *n.* tuber *(Andean variety)* || *s.* tubérculo *(variedad andina)*
ulthuy *v.* foam at the mouth || *v.* espumajear
uma *n.* head || *s.* cabeza
umala *n.* top; beginning || *s.* cabecera; inicio
umalli *n.* leader || *s.* líder

umalliy *v.* lead || *v.* liderar
umanay *v.* decapitate || *v.* decapitar
umasapa *adj.* big-headed, stubborn || *adj.* cabezón, obstinado/a
umiña *n.* precious stone || *s.* piedra preciosa
umipayay *v.* feed mouth-to-mouth constantly || *v.* dar de comer de boca a boca constantemente
umiq *n.* person who feeds mouth-to-mouth *(like a bird)* || *s.* el/la que da de comer de boca a boca *(como las aves)*
umiy *v.* feed mouth-to-mouth || *v.* dar de comer de boca a boca
umulliy *v.* foretell, predict || *v.* presagiar, predecir
umusqa *adj.* bewitched || *adj.* embrujado/a
umutu *n.* little person *(male)* || *s.* enano
umuy *v.* bewitch || *v.* embrujar
unanchasqa *adj.* marked || *adj.* marcado/a
unanchay *v.* mark, indicate || *v.* marcar
unay *n.* long time, span of time || *s.* mucho tiempo, lapso de tiempo
unay unay *adv.* prolonged || *adv.* prolongadamente
unayachiy *v.* make delay || *v.* hacer demorar
unaymanta *adv.* after a long time || *adv.* después de mucho tiempo
unkaka *n.* opossum; vixen *(animal)* || *s.* zarigüeya; raposa
unku *n.* tunic, shirt || *s.* túnica, camisón
unkucha *n.* tuber *(Andean variety)* || *s.* tubérculo *(variedad andina)*
unkuña *n.* shawl || *s.* chal
unphu *adj.* languid, timid || *adj.* lánguido/a, pusilánime
unphuyay *v.* become languid, become timid || *v.* volverse lánguido/a, volverse pusilánime
unu *n.* water || *s.* agua
unuchasqa *adj.* mixed with water || *adj.* mezclado/a con agua
unuchay *v.* mix with water || *v.* mezclar con agua
ununayay *v.* have the urge to drink water || *v.* tener deseos de beber agua
unuy unuy *adj.* watery || *adj.* aguanoso/a
unuyachisqa *adj.* dissolved, diluted || *adj.* disuelto/a, diluido
unuyachiy *v.* dissolve || *v.* disolver
unuyay *v.* become diluted, become flooded || *v.* diluirse, anegarse
uña *n.* young offspring || *s.* crío/a
upa *n.* mute • *adj.* mute; absentminded || *s.* mudo/a • *adj.* mudo/a; abstraído/a

upallachiy *v.* make silence, make be quiet || *v.* hacer callar
upallay *v.* silence || *v.* callar
upallaspa *adv.* silently || *adv.* calladamente
upallasqa *adj.* silenced || *adj.* callado/a
upayay *v.* become mute; become absentminded || *v.* volverse mudo/a; abstraerse
uphachiy *v.* make wash one's face || *v.* hacer lavar la cara
uphakuy *v.* wash one's face || *v.* lavarse la cara
upi *n.* unfermented juice || *s.* mosto, chicha no fermentada
upichiy *v.* make slurp, make sip || *v.* hacer sorber, hacer libar
upichu *adj.* anemic, yellowish || *adj.* anémico/a, amarillento/a
upiy *v.* slurp, sip || *v.* sorber, libar
ura *prep.* under || *prep.* debajo
uranayay *v.* have the urge to go down || *v.* tener deseos de bajar
urapakuy *v.* go down with difficulty || *v.* bajar con dificultad
urarpariy *v.* go down quickly || *v.* bajar rápidamente
uray *v.* go down • *prep.* below || *v.* bajar • *prep.* abajo
urayasqa *adj.* descended || *adj.* descendido/a
urayay *v.* descend || *v.* descender
uraysiy *v.* help go down || *v.* ayudar a bajar
urilla *adv.* prematurely || *adv.* prematuramente
uriy *v.* anticipate || *v.* anticipar
urmachiy *v.* make fall, drop || *v.* hacer caer, dejar caer
urmasqa *adj.* fallen || *adj.* caído/a
urmay *v.* fall || *v.* caer
urmaykachay *v.* fall over again and again || *v.* caerse una y otra vez
urpi *n.* bird, dove || *s.* pájaro, paloma
urpu *n.* big pot || *s.* vasija grande
uru *n.* spider || *s.* araña
urwa *adj.* sterile, infertile || *adj.* estéril, infértil
usa *n.* louse || *s.* piojo
usachikuy *v.* let oneself be deloused || *v.* dejarse despiojar
usachiy *v.* make delouse || *v.* hacer despiojar
usariy *v.* stop raining || *v.* escampar
usasapa *adj.* lousy || *adj.* piojoso/a
usasqa *adj.* deloused || *adj.* despiojado/a
usay *v.* delouse || *v.* despiojar
uspha *n.* ash || *s.* ceniza
usphachakuy *v.* become dusty with ash || *v.* empolvarse con ceniza

usphachay *v.* cover with ash || *v.* cubrir con ceniza
usphayay *v.* turn to ash || *v.* volverse ceniza
usphu *adj.* depressed, discouraged || *adj.* decaído/a, desalentado/a
usphuchiy *v.* make discouraged || *v.* hacer desalentar
usphuy *v.* become discouraged || *v.* desalentarse
usqhay *adv.* quickly || *adv.* rápidamente, rápido/a
usqhaylla *adv.* quickly || *adv.* rápidamente, rápido/a
usqhayta *adv.* quickly || *adv.* rápidamente, rápido/a
usuchisqa *adj.* wasted, squandered || *adj.* malgastado/a, desperdiciado/a
usuchiy *v.* waste, squander || *v.* malgastar, desperdiciar
usuri *adj.* unhappy || *adj.* infeliz
ususi *n.* daughter *(of father)* || *s.* hija *(del padre)*
usuta *n.* sandal || *s.* sandalia
usuy *v.* roam, squander away || *v.* vagar, malgastarse
uta *n.* mosquito || *s.* mosquito
utha *n.* sickness transmitted by mosquitos || *s.* mal transmitido por mosquitos
uthay *v.* eat away at, corrode || *v.* carcomer, corroer
uti *adj.* sleepy, inept || *adj.* adormecido/a, inepto/a
uti uti *n.* beetle || *s.* escarabajo
utichiq *n.* person/thing that causes sleepiness || *s.* el/la/lo que causa adormecimiento
utichiy *v.* make fall asleep || *v.* hacer adormecer
utiy *v.* be astonished; fall asleep || *v.* pasmarse; adormecer
uturunku *n.* jaguar || *s.* jaguar
utuskuru *n.* caterpillar || *s.* oruga
uwi *adj.* yellow || *adj.* amarillo/a
uya *n.* face || *s.* cara
uyanchay *v.* face, confront || *v.* encarar, confrontar
uyanpa *n.* obverse || *s.* anverso
uyapakuq *n.* eavesdropper || *s.* escuchador/a
uyapakuy *v.* eavesdrop || *v.* escuchar disimuladamente a otros
uyarichikuy *v.* make another listen, make another hear || *v.* hacerse escuchar, hacerse oír
uyarichiy *v.* make listen, make hear || *v.* hacer escuchar, hacer oír
uyarinakuy *v.* listen to one another, hear one another || *v.* escucharse mutuamente, oírse mutuamente

uyariq *n.* listener, person who hears || *s.* el/la que escucha, oyente
uyariy *v.* listen, hear || *v.* escuchar, oír
uyuy *v.* sob || *v.* sollozar
uywa *n.* domesticated animal || *s.* animal doméstico
uywaq *n.* caretaker, person who raises || *s.* criador/a
uywaqe *n.* advisor || *s.* consejero/a
uywasqa *adj.* cared for, raised || *adj.* criado/a
uyway *v.* care for, raise || *v.* criar

W

wachacha *n.* young woman in puberty || *s.* muchacha en edad de concebir
wachachiq *n.* person who helps give birth || *s.* el/la que ayuda en el parto o a parir
wachachiy *v.* help give birth || *v.* ayudar en el parto o a parir
wachakuq *n.* woman who gives birth || *s.* la que da a luz
wachakuy *v.* give birth *(person)* || *v.* dar a luz *(persona)*
wachanayay *v.* be about to give birth || *v.* estar a punto de dar a luz, estar a punto de parir
wachapakuy *v.* give birth frequently *(person)* || *v.* dar a luz continuamente *(persona)*
wachay *v.* give birth *(animal)* || *v.* parir
wachoq *n.* fornicator || *s.* fornicador/a
wachu *n.* furrow *(earth)* || *s.* surco *(tierra)*
wachu wachu *adj.* furrowed || *adj.* ensurcado/a
wachuy *v.* make furrows || *v.* hacer surcos
wachuysiy *v.* help make furrows || *v.* ayudar a hacer surcos
wach'i *n.* dart || *s.* dardo
wach'iy *v.* shine || *v.* brillar, relumbrar
wach'ichiy *v.* make shine || *v.* hacer brillar
waka *n.* Andean deity || *s.* deidad andina
wakcha *n.* orphan • *adj.* poor || *s.* huérfano • *adj.* pobre
wakchayachiy *v.* make poor || *v.* hacer empobrecer
wakchayay *v.* become poor; become orphaned || *v.* empobrecer; devenir en huérfano/a
wakin *adj.* some, leftover || *adj.* algunos/as, sobrante
wakinchay *v.* collect surplus, collect leftovers || *v.* juntar los sobrantes
wakmanta *adv.* again || *adv.* otra vez, de nuevo
waksi *n.* vapor, steam || *s.* vapor
waksichiy *v.* vaporize || *v.* vaporizar
waksiq *n.* that which evaporates || *s.* lo que evapora
waksiy *v.* evaporate || *v.* evaporar
wakta *adj.* feigned || *adj.* fingido/a
wakwachiy *v.* make sprout abundantly || *v.* hacer brotar copiosamente

wakwasqa *adj.* sprouted with abundance || *adj.* brotado/a copiosamente
wakway *v.* sprout abundantly || *v.* brotar copiosamente
wali *n.* skirt || *s.* falda
wallata *n.* Andean goose || *s.* ganso andino
wallpa *n.* chicken, hen, rooster || *s.* gallina, gallo, pollo
wallpa waqay *n.* rooster's crow || *s.* canto del gallo
wallwak'u *n.* armpit || *s.* sobaco
walqachiy *v.* make hang || *v.* hacer pender
walqay *v.* hang *(something)* • *n.* necklace || *v.* pender • *s.* collar
waltha *n.* cloth for swaddling *a* baby || *s.* prenda para envolver un bebé
walthaq *n.* swaddler of a baby || *s.* fajador/a de un bebé
walthasqa *adj.* swaddled *(baby)* || *adj.* fajado/a *(bebé)*
walthay *v.* swaddle a baby || *v.* fajar un bebé
walthaysiy *v.* help swaddle a baby || *v.* ayudar a fajar un bebé
waman *n.* falcon || *s.* halcón
wamantullu *n.* lukewarm || *s.* tibia
wamink'a *n.* soldier *(man)* || *s.* soldado *(hombre)*
wana *n.* punishment || *s.* escarmiento
wanachiy *v.* make punish || *v.* hacer escarmentar
wanay *v.* punish || *v.* escarmentar
wanka *n.* rock, rocky area || *s.* roca, roquedal
wanka wanka *adj.* rocky || *adj.* rocoso/a
wankar *n.* drum || *s.* tambor
wankhi *adj.* inept || *adj.* inepto/a
wank'ichiy *v.* make wrap || *v.* mandar a enfardar
wank'ipayay *v.* wrap again and again || *v.* enfardar una y otra vez
wank'isqa *adj.* wrapped || *adj.* enfardado/a
wank'iysiy *v.* help wrap || *v.* ayudar a enfardar
wank'uchiy *v.* make tie up || *v.* mandar a liar
wank'upayay *v.* tie up again and again || *v.* liar una y otra vez
wank'usqa *adj.* tied up || *adj.* liado/a
wank'uy *v.* tie up || *v.* liar
wank'uysiy *v.* help tie up || *v.* ayudar a liar
wank'iy *v.* wrap || *v.* enfardar
wanlinyay *v.* sway || *v.* bambolearse
wanpal *n.* nursery *(plants)* || *s.* vivero, almácigo
wanphusqa *adj.* punctured || *adj.* perforado/a
wanphuy *v.* make an opening, puncture || *v.* abrir un forado, perforar

wanphuysiy *v.* help puncture || *v.* ayudar a perforar
wanpuru *n.* wooden tub || *s.* batea de madera
wanp'uchiy *v.* make navigate || *v.* mandar a navegar
wanp'uy *v.* navigate || *v.* navegar
wanqhay *v.* lever || *v.* palanquear
wanq'o *adj.* deaf || *adj.* sordo/a
wanq'oyachiy *v.* deafen || *v.* causar sordera
wanq'oyay *v.* become deaf || *v.* volverse sordo/a
wanthi *n.* venereal disease || *s.* enfermedad venérea
wantu *n.* litter *(for carrying)*, bier || *s.* litera, anda
wantuchikuy *v.* let oneself be carried on shoulders || *v.* dejarse llevar en hombros
wantusqa *adj.* carried on shoulders || *adj.* llevado/a en hombros
wantuy *v.* carry on shoulders || *v.* llevar en hombros
wantuykachay *v.* carry carelessly on shoulders || *v.* llevar atropelladamente en hombros
wanu *n.* manure || *s.* abono
wanuchasqa *adj.* fertilized with manure || *adj.* abonado/a
wanuchay *v.* fertilize with manure || *v.* abonar
wanupay *v.* refertilize with manure || *v.* volver a abonar
wanwa *n.* mosquito || *s.* zancudo
wanway *v.* buzz || *v.* zumbar
wañu wañu *adj.* timid || *adj.* pusilánime
wañuchikuy *v.* kill oneself, commit suicide || *v.* matarse, suicidarse
wañuchinakuy *v.* kill one another || *v.* matarse mutuamente
wañuchiq *n.* killer || *s.* matador/a
wañuchisqa *adj.* killed, victimized || *adj.* matado/a, victimado/a
wañuchiy *v.* kill || *v.* matar
wañunayaq *adj.* dying || *adj.* moribundo/a
wañunayay *v.* agonize || *v.* agonizar
wañupuy *v.* die *(person)*, pass away *(person)* || *v.* morir *(persona)*, perecer *(persona)*
wañuq *n.* mortal || *s.* mortal
wañurqoy *v.* die suddenly; covet desperately || *v.* morir repentinamente; codiciar desesperadamente
wañusqa *adj.* dead • *n.* dead || *adj.* fenecido/a • *s.* muerto/a
wañuy *v.* die || *v.* morir, perecer
wap'unayay *v.* have the urge to devour, have the urge to gulp || *v.* tener deseos de devorar, tener deseos de engullir
wap'usqa *adj.* devoured, gulped || *adj.* devorado/a, engullido/a

wap'uy *v.* devour, gulp || *v.* devorar, engullir
waqachiy *v.* make cry || *v.* hacer llorar
waqanayay *v.* have the urge to cry, || *v.* tener deseos de llorar, estar a punto de llorar
waqapakuy *v.* moan, whine || *v.* sollozar, lloriquear
waqapayay *v.* cry again and again || *v.* llorar una y otra vez
waqaq *n.* crier || *s.* llorador/a
waqati *n.* crybaby • *adj.* disgruntled || *s.* llorón/a • *adj.* descontento/a
waqay *v.* cry || *v.* llorar
waqaychachiy *v.* make put away, make save || *v.* hacer guardar, mandar a preservar
waqaychay *v.* put away, save || *v.* guardar, preservar
waqaychaysiy *v.* help put away, help save || *v.* ayudar a guardar, ayudar a preservar
waqaysiy *v.* cry with || *v.* acompanar en el llanto
waqo *n.* jaw || *s.* quijada
waqra *n.* animal horn || *s.* cuerno
waqrachiy *v.* make gore with horns || *v.* hacer cornear
waqranakuy *v.* gore one another with horns || *v.* cornearse mutuamente
waqranay *v.* cut off horns || *v.* cortar los cuernos
waqranayay *v.* have the urge to gore with horns || *v.* tener deseos de cornear
waqrapakuy *v.* defend oneself with horns || *v.* defenderse dando cornadas
waqrasqa *adj.* gored with horns || *adj.* corneado/a
waqray *v.* gore with horns || *v.* cornear
waqsa *n.* fang || *s.* colmillo
waqta *n.* rib, flank || *s.* costilla, flanco
waqtachikuy *v.* let oneself be whipped || *v.* dejarse latiguear
waqtachiy *v.* make whip || *v.* hacer latiguear
waqtana *n.* whip || *s.* látigo
waqtanakuy *v.* whip one another || *v.* latiguearse mutuamante
waqtapayay *v.* whip again and again || *v.* latiguear una y otra vez
waqtaq *n.* person who whips || *s.* latigueador/a
waqtasqa *adj.* whipped || *adj.* latigueado/a
waqtay *v.* whip || *v.* latiguear
waqtaysiy *v.* help whip || *v.* ayudar latiguear
waqwapayay *v.* bark again and again || *v.* ladrar una y otra vez
waqway *v.* bark, shout || *v.* ladrar, vociferar

waqyachiy *v.* make call || *v.* hacer llamar
waqyanakuy *v.* call one another || *v.* llamarse mutuamente
waqyapayay *v.* call again and again || *v.* llamar una y otra vez
waqyarikuy *v.* invoke || *v.* invocar
waqyasqa *adj.* called || *adj.* llamado/a
waqyay *v.* call || *v.* llamar
waq'a *adj.* crazy || *adj.* loco/a
waq'ayachiy *v.* drive crazy || *v.* hacer enloquecer
waq'ayasqa *adj.* crazed || *adj.* alocado/a, enloquecido/a
waq'ayay *v.* go crazy || *v.* enloquecer
wara *n.* pants || *s.* pantalones
warak'a *n.* slingshot || *s.* honda
warak'ay *v.* hit with a slingshot || *v.* hondear
warani *n.* constellation || *s.* constelación
waranqa *num.* thousand || *num.* mil
warku *n.* that which hangs || *s.* lo que cuelga
warkuchiy *v.* make hang || *v.* hacer colgar
warkuna *n.* hanger, hook || *s.* colgador
warkuq *n.* person who hangs something || *s.* el/la que cuelga *(algo)*
warkusqa *adj.* hung, hanged || *adj.* colgado/a
warkuy *v.* hang || *v.* colgar
warkuysiy *v.* help hang || *v.* ayudar a colgar
warma *n.* child, adolescent || *s.* niño/a, púber
warmi *n.* woman || *s.* mujer
warmi wawa *n.* daughter *(of mother)* || *s.* hija *(de la madre)*
warmichakuy *v.* partner with a woman || *v.* formar pareja con una mujer, emparejarse con mujer
warmiyay *v.* become a grown woman || *v.* volverse mujer adulta
wasa *n.* back || *s.* espalda
wasapay *v.* overcome an obstacle || *v.* atravesar una valla
wasi *n.* house, home || *s.* casa, hogar
wasichay *v.* build a house || *v.* construir una casa
wasimasi *n.* neighbor || *s.* vecino/a
waskha *n.* rope || *s.* soga
waskhay *n.* tie with rope || *v.* enlazar con una soga
wata *n.* year || *s.* año
watachiy *v.* make tie || *v.* hacer atar
watana *n.* string for tying || *s.* cuerda para atar
watantin *adv.* all year || *adv.* todo el año

watapayay *v.* tie again and again || *v.* atar una y otra vez
watasqa *adj.* tied || *adj.* atado/a
watay *v.* tie || *v.* atar
wataysiy *v.* help tie || *v.* ayudar a atar
wathiyay *v.* cook potatoes in the ground || *v.* asar papas bajo tierra
watukuq *n.* visitor || *s.* visitante
watukuy *v.* visit || *v.* visitar
watupakuq *n.* foreteller, person who suspects || *s.* presagiador/a, el/la que sospecha
watupakuy *v.* foretell, suspect || *v.* presagiar, sospechar
watuq *n.* guesser || *s.* adivinador/a
watusqa *adj.* guessed || *adj.* adivinado/a
watuy *v.* guess || *v.* adivinar
wat'a *n.* island || *s.* isla
wawa *n.* baby, child || *s.* bebé, hijo/a
wawachakuy *v.* treat someone like a son/daughter || *v.* tratar a alguien como hijo/a
wawachasqa *adj.* pampered || *adj.* mimado/a
wawachay *v.* procreate; pamper || *v.* procrear; mimar
wawsa *n.* semen || *s.* semen
wawsay *v.* ejaculate || *v.* eyacular
waya *adj.* baggy, loose || *adj.* holgado/a, suelto/a
waykay *v.* attack in a group, take on as a group || *v.* atacar entre varios, acometer entre varios
waykilla *n.* attack of individual by group || *s.* ataque en grupo contra uno
wayk'uchiy *v.* make cook || *v.* hacer cocinar
wayk'unayay *v.* have the urge to cook || *v.* tener deseos de cocinar
wayk'uq *n.* cook || *s.* cocinero/a
wayk'usqa *adj.* cooked || *adj.* cocinado/a, cocido/a
wayk'uy *v.* cook || *v.* cocinar
wayk'uysiy *v.* help cook || *v.* ayudar a cocinar
waylaka *adj.* disinterested *(woman)*, unorganized *(woman)* || *adj.* descomedida *(mujer)*, desorganizada *(mujer)*
waylla *n.* pasture || *s.* pastizal
wayllukuy *v.* caress || *v.* acariciar
wayllunakuy *v.* love one another deeply || *v.* amarse mutuamente
waylluq *n.* lover || *s.* amante
wayllusqa *adj.* beloved || *adj.* amado/a
waylluy *v.* love deeply || *v.* amar

wayna *n.* young man, boy || *s.* joven *(hombre)*, muchacho
waynayay *v.* rejuvenate *(man)*, become a young man || *v.* rejuvenecer *(el hombre viejo)*, devenir joven *(hombre)*
wayno *n.* song *(Andean variety)* || *s.* canción *(variedad andina)*
wayqe *n.* brother *(of male)* || *s.* hermano *(de varón)*
wayra *n.* wind || *s.* viento
wayrachiy *v.* ventilate || *v.* ventilar
wayrari *n.* breeze || *s.* brisa
wayrasqa *n.* sickness caused by an ill wind || *s.* mal causado por el mal viento
wayray *v.* blow *(wind)* || *v.* ventear, soplar el viento
wayronqo *n.* bee, wasp || *s.* abeja, moscardón
wayta *n.* bouquet || *s.* ramo
wayt'aq *n.* swimmer || *s.* nadador/a
wayt'ay *v.* swim || *v.* nadar
wayt'aykachay *v.* splash around || *v.* chapotear
wayuy *v.* bear fruit abundantly || *v.* frutecer abundantemente
waywachiy *v.* make decrease, make diminish || *v.* hacer mermar, hacer disminuir
waywasqa *adj.* decreased, diminished || *adj.* mermado/a, disminuido/a
wayway *v.* decrease, diminish || *v.* mermar, disminuir
welq'achiy *v.* make rummage || *v.* hacer hurgar
welq'ana *n.* rummaging tool || *s.* instrumento para hurgar
welq'aq *n.* rummager || *s.* hurgador/a
welq'ay *v.* rummage || *v.* hurgar
welq'aysiy *v.* help rummage || *v.* ayudar a hurgar
weqe *n.* tear *(eye)* || *s.* lágrima
weqechiy *v.* make tear up *(eye)* || *v.* hacer lagrimear
weqey *v.* tear up *(eye)* || *v.* lagrimear
weqo *adj.* twisted, bent || *adj.* torcido/a, curvado/a
weqochiy *v.* make twist, make bend || *v.* hacer torcer, hacer curvar
weqokuy *v.* become twisted || *v.* torcerse, curvarse
weqoy *v.* twist, bend || *v.* torcer, curvar
weqoysiy *v.* help twist, help bend || *v.* ayudar a torcer, ayudar a curvar
weqru *adj.* crooked || *adj.* chueco/a, arqueado/a
weqruy *v.* arch || *v.* arquear
weq'ana *n.* stirring utensil; digging tool || *s.* instrumento para remover; instrumento para escarbar

weq'aq *n.* stirrer; digger || *s.* removedor/a; escarbador/a
weq'asqa *adj.* stirred, dug up || *adj.* removido/a, escarbado/a
weq'ay *v.* stir; dig up || *v.* remover; escarbar
weq'aysiy *v.* help stir; help dig up || *v.* ayudar a remover; ayudar a escarbar
weq'achiy *v.* make stir; make dig up || *v.* hacer remover; hacer escarbar
werp'a *n.* lower lip || *s.* labio inferior
wesq'achiy *v.* make close || *v.* hacer cerrar
wesq'akapuy *v.* close permanently || *v.* cerrarse difinitivamente
wesq'aq *n.* closer || *s.* el/la que cierra
wesq'arayay *v.* stay permanently closed || *v.* mantenerse cerrado/a permanentemente
wesq'asqa *adj.* closed || *adj.* cerrado/a
wesq'ay *v.* close || *v.* cerrar
wesq'aysiy *v.* help close || *v.* ayudar a cerrar
wesq'o *adj.* cross-eyed || *adj.* bizco
wesq'oy *v.* cross one's eyes || *v.* bizcar
wesq'oyay *v.* become cross-eyed || *v.* volverse bizco
wesq'oykachay *v.* look cross-eyed || *v.* mirar como bizco
wichachiy *v.* make climb, make ascend || *v.* hacer subir, hacer ascender
wichanayay *v.* have the urge to climb, have the urge to ascend || *v.* tener deseos de subir, tener deseos de ascender
wichapakuy *v.* climb with difficulty, ascend with difficulty || *v.* subir con dificultad, ascender con dificultad
wicharpariy *v.* climb rapidly, ascend rapidly || *v.* subir rápidamente, ascender rápidamente
wichay *v.* climb, ascend || *v.* subir, ascender
wichay *adv.* on top, above || *adv.* encima, arriba
wichaysiy *v.* help climb, help ascend || *v.* ayudar a subir, ayudar a ascender
wich'un *n.* femur || *s.* fémur
wikapachiy *v.* make knock down || *v.* hacer derribar
wikapasqa *adj.* knocked down || *adj.* derribado/a
wikapay *v.* knock down, launch through the air || *v.* derribar, lanzar por los aires
wikch'uchiy *v.* make throw out, make abandon || *v.* hacer botar, hacer abandonar
wikch'unayay *v.* have the urge to throw out, have the urge to abandon || *v.* tener deseos de botar, tener deseos de abandonar

wikch'upakuy *v.* vomit || *v.* vomitar
wikch'uq *n.* person who throws out, person who abandons || *s.* botador/a, el/la que abandona
wikch'usqa *adj.* thrown out, abandoned || *adj.* botado/a, abandonado/a
wikch'uy *v.* throw out, abandon || *v.* botar, abandonar
wikch'uysiy *v.* help throw out || *v.* ayudar a botar
wiksa *n.* stomach, abdomen || *s.* estómago, abdomen
wiksayachiy *v.* impregnate || *v.* preñar
wiksayay *v.* become pregnant || *v.* embarazarse
wiksayoq *adj.* pregnant || *adj.* embarazada
wikuña *n.* vicuña || *s.* vicuña
willachiy *v.* make tell || *v.* mandar a contar *(historias)*, mandar a avisar
willakuy *n.* story, notice || *s.* relato, aviso
willanakuy *v.* tell one another || *v.* contarse mutuamente *(historias)*
willanayay *v.* have the urge to tell || *v.* tener deseos de contar *(historias)*, tener deseos de avisar
willapakuq *n.* gossiper || *s.* chismeador/a
willapakuy *v.* gossip || *v.* chismear
willapayay *v.* tell over and over || *v.* contar reiteradamente *(historias)*, avisar reiteradamente
willaq *n.* teller, narrator || *s.* avisador/a, relator/a
willasqa *adj.* told || *adj.* contado/a *(historias)*, avisado/a
willay *v.* tell || *v.* contar *(historias)*, avisar
willaykachay *v.* disclose, divulge || *v.* propalar, divulgar
willka *adj.* sacred || *adj.* sagrado/a
willpusqa *adj.* discouraged || *adj.* desalentado/a
willu *adj.* unpaired, one-armed || *adj.* impar, de un solo brazo
willuchiy *v.* make mutilate, make amputate || *v.* hacer mutilar, hacer amputar
willullu *n.* orphan || *s.* huérfano/a
willusqa *adj.* mutilated, amputated || *adj.* mutilado/a, amputado/a
willuy *v.* mutilate, amputate || *v.* mutilar, amputar
willuysiy *v.* help mutilate, help amputate || *v.* ayudar a mutilar, ayudar a amputar
wiñachiy *v.* make grow, make develop || *v.* hacer crecer, hacer desarrollar
wiñaqmasi *n.* peer || *s.* contemporáneo/a, coetáneo/a
wiñasqa *adj.* grown, developed || *adj.* crecido/a, desarrollado/a
wiñay *v.* grow, develop || *v.* crecer, desarrollar

wiñaypaq *adv.* forever || *adv.* para siempre
wiphala *n.* banner || *s.* banderola
wira *n.* fat • *adj.* fat || *s.* grasa • *adj.* gordo/a
wirasapa *adj.* fat || *adj.* gordo/a
wirayachiy *v.* make fat || *v.* hacer engordar
wirayay *v.* fatten, gain weight || *v.* engordar
wiru *n.* cornstalks *(fresh)* || *s.* caña de maíz
wisa *n.* soldier *(man)* || *s.* soldado *(hombre)*
wisina *n.* ladle || *s.* cucharón para sacar liquidos
wisiy *v.* ladle || *v.* sacar líquido con cucharón
wisiysiy *v.* help ladle || *v.* ayudar a sacar liquidos con cucharon
wislla *n.* wooden spoon || *s.* cuchara de madera
wisnichiy *v.* make scatter || *v.* hacer desparramar
wisniq *n.* person who scatters || *s.* desparramador/a
wisnisqa *adj.* scattered || *adj.* desparramado/a
wisniy *v.* scatter || *v.* desparramar
wisniykachay *v.* scatter everywhere || *v.* desparramar por todas partes
wisniysiy *v.* help scatter || *v.* ayudar a desparramar
wispa *n.* twin || *s.* gemelo
wiswi *adj.* dirty • *n.* dirt || *adj.* sucio/a • *s.* suciedad
wiswiyay *v.* get dirty || *v.* ensuciarse
witichiy *v.* make err, cause to make a mistake || *v.* hacer errar, hacer equivocar
witisqa *adj.* erred, mistaken || *adj.* errado/a, equivocado/a
witiy *v.* err, make a mistake || *v.* errar, equivocar
wit'uchiy *v.* make amputate, make chop down || *v.* hacer amputar, hacer talar
wit'uq *n.* person who amputates, logger || *s.* amputador/a, talador/a
wit'usqa *adj.* amputated, chopped down || *adj.* amputado/a, talado/a
wit'uy *v.* amputate, chop down || *v.* amputar, talar
wit'uysiy *v.* help amputate, help chop down || *v.* ayudar a amputar, ayudar a talar

Y

yachachinakuy *v.* conspire, scheme together || *v.* conspirar, intrigar
yachachiq *n.* teacher, instructor || *s.* instructor/a, maestro/a
yachachiy *v.* teach || *v.* enseñar
yachakuy *n.* become accustomed || *v.* acostumbrarse
yachanayay *v.* have the urge to learn || *v.* tener deseos de aprender
yachapayaq *n.* mocker || *s.* el/la que remeda con burla
yachapayay *v.* imitate in jest, mock in jest || *v.* remedar con burla, imitar con burla
yachaphuku *n.* mocker || *s.* el/la que remeda con burla
yachaq *n.* knower, knowledgeable person || *s.* sabedor/a, persona con sabiduría
yachasqa *adj.* known || *adj.* conocido/a, sabido
yachay *v.* learn, know || *v.* aprender, saber
yachay *n.* knowledge, wisdom || *s.* conocimiento, saber
yachaykachaq *n.* person who pretends to know || *s.* sabihondo/a
yachaysapa *n.* know-it-all || *s.* sabelotodo
yaku *n.* water || *s.* agua
yalliy *v.* overflow, abound || *v.* rebasar, abundar
yana *adj.* black • *n.* partner || *adj.* negro/a • *s.* pareja
yanachakuy *v.* become blackened, become stained || *v.* ennegrecerse, tiznarse
yanachasqa *adj.* blackened, stained || *adj.* ennegrecido/a, tiznado/a
yanachay *v.* darken; partner || *v.* oscurecer, emparejar
yanallikuq *n.* mourner || *s.* el/la que se enluta
yanallikuy *v.* mourn || *v.* enlutarse
yanallisqa *adj.* mourned || *adj.* enlutado/a
yanamanka *n.* soot, smut || *s.* hollín, tizne
yanapachiy *v.* make help, make serve || *v.* mandar a ayudar, mandar a servir
yanapanakuy *v.* help one another, serve one another || *v.* ayudarse mutuamente, servirse mutuamente
yanapaq *n.* helper, server || *s.* ayudante, servidor/a
yanapay *v.* help, serve || *v.* ayudar, servir

yanayay *v.* become black || *v.* ennegrecer
yanqa *adv.* uselessly, in vain || *adv.* inútilmente, en vano
yanqachay *v.* discard, devalue || *v.* desechar, desestimar
yapa *n.* increase || *s.* aumento
yapa yapa *adv.* repeatedly || *adv.* repetidamente
yapachiy *v.* make add, make increase || *v.* hacer agregar, hacer aumentar
yapamanta *adv.* again || *adv.* de nuevo
yapay *v.* add, increase || *v.* agregar, aumentar
yapuchiy *v.* make plow || *v.* hacer barbechar
yapuq *n.* person who plows || *s.* barbechador/a
yapusqa *adj.* plowed || *adj.* barbechado/a
yapuy *v.* plow || *v.* barbechar
yapuysiy *v.* help plow || *v.* ayudar a barbechar
yaqa *adv.* almost || *adv.* casi
yaqapaschá *interj.* who knows! • *adv.* maybe so || *interj.* ¡quién sabe! • *adv.* tal vez sí
yaqolla *n.* cloak, cape || *s.* manto
yarqasqa *adj.* hungry || *adj.* hambriento/a
yarqay *n.* hunger, famine • *v.* be hungry || *s.* hambre, hambruna • *v.* tener hambre
yarqha *n.* canal || *s.* acequia, canal
yarqhachay *v.* dig a canal || *v.* abrir un canal
yaw *interj.* hey! || *interj.* ¡eh!
yawar *n.* blood || *s.* sangre
yawarchakuy *v.* become bloody || *v.* ensangrentarse
yawarchanakuy *v.* bloody one another || *v.* ensangrentarse mutuamente
yawarchasqa *adj.* bloody || *adj.* ensangrentado/a
yawarmasi *n.* blood relative || *s.* consanguíneo
yawrachiy *v.* make burn || *v.* hacer arder
yawrasqa *adj.* burnt, burned || *adj.* ardido/a
yawray *v.* burn || *v.* arder
yawraykachay *v.* burn with difficulty || *v.* arder con dificultad
yawri *n.* large needle || *s.* aguja grande
yaya *adj.* supreme • *n.* patriarch || *adj.* supremo/a • *s.* patriarca
yukachikuy *v.* let oneself be deceived, let oneself be cheated || *v.* dejarse engañar
yukanakuy *v.* deceive one another, cheat one another || *v.* engañarse mutuamente

yukapayay *v.* deceive constantly, cheat constantly || *v.* engañar constantemente
yukaq *n.* person who deceives, cheater || *s.* el/la que engaña
yukasqa *adj.* deceived, cheated || *adj.* engañado/a
yukay *v.* deceive, cheat || *v.* engañar
yukaysiy *v.* help deceive, help cheat || *v.* ayudar a engañar
yuma *n.* semen || *s.* semen
yumay *v.* ejaculate; conceive *(procreation)* || *v.* eyacular; engendrar
yunka *n.* jungle; valley || *s.* selva; valle
yupa *adj.* many, countable || *adj.* mucho, contable *(cantidad)*
yupachiy *v.* make count, make number || *v.* hacer contar *(cantidad)*, hacer numerar
yupapayay *v.* count again and again || *v.* contar una y otra vez *(cantidad)*
yupaq *n.* accountant, person who numbers || *s.* contador/a *(cantidad)*, numerador/a
yupasqa *adj.* counted, numbered || *adj.* contado/a *(cantidad)*, numerado/a
yupay *v.* count, number || *v.* contar *(cantidad)*, numerar
yupaysiy *v.* help count, help number || *v.* ayudar a contar *(cantidad)*, ayudar a numerar
yupi *n.* footprints, tracks || *s.* huella, rastro
yupichay *v.* follow footprints, follow tracks || *v.* seguir las huellas
yupiy *v.* leave footprints, leave tracks || *v.* hollar
yura *n.* tree without many branches || *s.* árbol sin muchas ramas
yuraq *adj.* white || *adj.* blanco/a
yuraqyachiy *v.* whiten || *v.* emblanquecer
yuraqyay *v.* become white || *v.* blanquear
yuray *v.* grow *(tree)* || *v.* crecer *(árbol)*
yuyachiy *v.* make remember || *v.* hacer recordar
yuyapay *v.* commemorate || *v.* rememorar
yuyaq *n.* person who remembers, thinker || *s.* el/la que recuerda, pensador/a
yuyariy *v.* remember suddenly || *v.* recordar súbitamente
yuyasqa *adj.* remembered, thought about || *adj.* recordado/a, pensado/a
yuyay *v.* remember, think || *v.* recordar, pensar
yuyay *n.* intellect, memory || *s.* intelecto, memoria
yuyaychana *adj.* memorable, unforgettable || *adj.* memorable, inolvidable

yuyayniyoq *adj.* intelligent, sensible || *adj.* inteligente, juicioso/a
yuyaypi *adv.* consciously, intentionally || *adv.* conscientemente, adrede
yuyaysapa *adj.* very intelligent, with good memory || *adj.* inteligentísimo/a, memorioso/a

ENGLISH QUECHUA

A

a / an *ind. art.* huk
a few *adj.* aslla
a little *adj.* pisi • *adv.* asta
a lot *adv.* anchata, askhata, ñisuta, sinchita
a lot of *adj.* ancha, askha, llasaq
abandon *v.* saqey, wikch'uy; **be abandoned** saqechikuy; **have the urge to abandon** wikch'unayay; **make abandon** wikch'uchiy • *n.* **person who abandons** wikch'uq
abandoned *adj.* qonqasqa, saqesqa, wikch'usqa
abdomen *n.* wiksa
able: *v.* **be able to** atiy
abort *v.* sulluy; **make abort** sulluchiy
aborted *adj.* sullusqa
abound *v.* yalliy
above *adv.* hanan, wichay
abscess *n.* ch'upu
absence *n.* ch'usa
absentee *n.* ch'usaq
absentminded *adj.* upa • *v.* **become absentminded** upayay
abyss *n.* sankha
accommodate *v.* qorpachay
accountant *n.* yupaq
accuse *v.* manuchay, tunpay
accuse one another *v.* tunpanakuy
accused *adj.* tunpasqa
accuser *n.* tunpaq
accustomed: *v.* **become accustomed** yachakuy
acne *n.* khiki
acquaintance *n.* reqsisqa
across from *adv.* chinpa
add *v.* yapay; **make add** yapachiy
adhere *v.* k'askay • *n.* **person who adheres** k'askachiq
adhered *adj.* k'askasqa
adjust *v.* mat'iy

adjust again and again *v.* mat'ipayay
adolescent *n.* warma
adopt *v.* erqechay
adopted son *n.* churichasqa
adorned *adj.* siklla
adulterer *n.* pantaq • *v.* **commit adultery** pantay
advisor *n.* uywaqe
affix in the form of a cross *v.* chakatay
affixed in the form of a cross *adj.* chakatasqa
affliction *n.* ñak'a
after *adv.* qhepa
after a long time *adv.* unaymanta
after that *conj.* chaymanta
afternoon: *v.* **become afternoon** intiyay
again *adv.* hoqmanta, wakmanta, yapamanta
aged *adj.* *(woman)* payayasqa; *(man)* machuyasqa
agonize *v.* wañunayay
agreement: *v.* **come to an agreement** hurk'ay
agricultural tool *(Andean) n.* hallmana
air dry *v.* phaskiy
air out until dry *v.* phaskichikuy
air-dried *adj.* phaski; **can be air-dried** phaskiq
ajar *adj.* kicharayaq
alive *adj.* kawsaq
all *adv.* llapanta, lluyta • *adj.* llapa, llapan, lliw, lluy, tukuy
all day *adv.* ch'isiyaq, p'unchaynintin
all night *adv.* tutantin
all year *adv.* watantin
alleviate: *v.* **become alleviated** thaniy; **make alleviate** thanichiy • *n.* **person who alleviates** thaniq
alleviated *adj.* thanisqa
almost *adv.* yaqa
alpaca *n.* paqocha
amputate *v.* mut'uy, willuy, wit'uy; **allow one's limb to be amputated** mut'uchikuy; **help amputate** willuysiy, wit'uysiy; **make amputate** willuchiy, wit'uchiy • *n.* **person who amputates** wit'uq
amputate leg *v.* chakannay
amputated *adj.* mut'u, willusqa, wit'usqa
amulet of stone *n.* enqa, enqaychu

an *ind. art.* huk
and *conj.* ima
and then *conj.* chayqa, hinaspa • *inter.* **and then?** chayrí?
anemic *adj.* upichu
angle *n.* huk'i
angry *adj.* phiñasqa
animal *n. (domesticated)* uywa; *(wild)* salqa uywa
animate *v.* kawsarichiy
ant *n.* sisi; **big ant** qollwi
anticipate *v.* ñawpay, uriy
anticipated *adj.* suyasqa
another *adj.* another
applaud *v.* t'aqllay
appear *v.* rikhuriy; **make appear** paqarichiy, rikhurichiy • *n.* **person who makes appear** paqarichiq
appear in dreams *v.* mosqhoychay
approach *v.* achhuy, sispay
arch *v.* weqruy
area *n.* marka
argue *v.* anyanakuy
arisen *adj.* sayarisqa
arm *n.* mak'a, marq'a
armpit *n.* lluk'i, wallwak'u
around *adv.* neqninta
arrive *v.* chayay
arrogant *adj.* apusonqo, k'aski
arrogantly *adv.* k'askiy k'askiy
ascend *v.* wichay; **have the urge to ascend** wichanayay; **help ascend** wichaysiy; **make ascend** wichachiy
ascend rapidly *v.* wicharpariy
ascend with difficulty *v.* wichapakuy
ash *n.* uspha • *v.* **become dusty with ash** usphachakuy; **cover with ash** usphachay; **turn to ash** usphayay
ashamed *adj.* p'enqasqa • *v.* **be ashamed** p'enqakuy • *n.* **person who is ashamed** p'enqakuq
ask about *v.* tapuy
ask about many things *v.* tapukachay
ask for *v.* mañakuy, qochikuy
ask one another *v.* tapunakuy
ask oneself *v.* tapukuy

asleep *adj.* puñusqa • *v.* **be about to fall asleep** puñunayay; **fall asleep** utiy; **make fall asleep** utichiy
asphyxiate *v.* mukiy
asphyxiated *adj.* mukisqa
astonished: *v.* **be astonished** utiy
attach *v.* k'intiy
attach supports *v.* chakichay
attached *adj.* ch'ipasqa, k'intisqa
attachment *n.* k'inti
attack in a group *v.* waykay
attack on individual by group *n.* waykilla
aunt *(paternal) n.* ipa

B

babble *v.* hanlluy
baby *n.* wawa; **nursing baby** ñuñuq
back *n.* wasa
backward *adv.* t'ikranpamanta
bad *adj.* mana allin
bad mood: *v.* **get in a bad mood** akanayay, enqhey; **get in a bad mood constantly** enqhepakuy
bad smell: *n.* **person who causes bad smell** asnachiq
bag *n.* ch'uspa
baggy *adj.* waya
balance: *v.* **put in balance** turay
bald *adj.* p'aqla, q'ara • *v.* **become bald** p'aqlayay, q'arayay
banner *n.* laphara, wiphala
bare *adj.* llust'i
barely *adv.* ñak'ay
bark *v.* waqway
bark again and again *v.* waqwapayay
base *n.* teqsi
basket *n.* isanka, p'uktu
bat *(animal) n.* masu
bat eyelashes *v.* k'inllay
bathe *v.* armay
bathe oneself *v.* armakuy; **take a bath** armakuy
bathed *adj.* armasqa
bathroom *n.* hisp'ana
be *v.* kay
be able to *v.* atiy
be born *v.* paqariy
beach *n.* aqopampa, qochapata
beam *n.* chakapa • *v.* **raise a beam** chakapay
bean *n. (Andean varieties)* chuwi, tarwi; **toasted beans** hank'a; **toaster of beans** hank'aq • *v.* **toast beans** hank'ay
bear *n. (animal)* ukuku; **person who bears** *(carry)* tusaq • *v. (carry)* tusay; **help bear** *(carry)* tusaysiy; **make bear** *(carry)* tusachiy

bear fruit *v.* ruruy; **make bear fruit** ruruchiy
bear fruit abundantly *v.* wayuy
beard *n.* sunkha • *v.* **grow a beard** sunkhayay
bearded *adj.* ch'apu, sunkhayoq
beat *v.* *(heart)* phatatatay; *(fight)* maqay; **help beat** *(fight)* maqaysiy; **let oneself be beat** *(fight)* maqachikuy
beat constantly *(fight)* *v.* maqapayay
beat a drum *v.* tinyay
beat one another *(fight)* *v.* maqanakuy
beater *(fight)* *n.* maqaq
beautiful *adj.* sumaq • *v.* **become beautiful** sumaqyay • *interj.* **how beautiful!** achalaw, añañaw
beautifully *adv.* sumaqlla, sumaqta
become one *v.* ch'ullayay
bed *n.* puñuna
bedroom *n.* puñuna
bee *n.* wayronqo
beetle *n.* akatanqa, uti uti
beg *v.* mañarikuy
beg with hands *v.* pituchakuy
begin *v.* qallariy
beginner *n.* qallariq
beginning *n.* umala
begun *adj.* qallarisqa
behind *prep.* qhepa
belly button *n.* puputi
beloved *adj.* munasqa, wayllusqa
below *prep.* uray
belt *n.* mat'ina; *(woven)* chunpi
bend *v.* weqoy; **help bend** weqoysiy; **make bend** weqochiy
bent *adj.* weqo
berate *v.* anyay; **make berate** anyachiy • *n.* **person who makes berate** anyachiq
berate again and again *v.* *anyapayay*
berate oneself *v.* anyakuy
berate oneself again and again *v.* anyapakuy
berater *n.* anyaq
bestowed *adj.* qosqa
betray *v.* sirpay
betrayed *adj.* sirpasqa

better: *v.* **get better** allinyay, alliyay
beware of ... *interj.* paqtataq
bewitch *v.* layqay, umuy; **make bewitch** layqachiy
bewitched *adj.* layqasqa, umusqa
bier *n.* wantu
big *adj.* hatun
big-footed *adj.* chakisapa
big-headed *adj.* umasapa
bile *n.* hayaqe
bind *v.* ch'atay; **help bind** ch'ataysiy
bird *(Andean varieties) n.* urpi, hak'akllu, kukuli, tunki • *v.* **mate among birds** chiway
bird that feeds mouth-to-mouth *n.* umiq
birth: *v.* **give birth** *(animal)* phallay, *(animal)* wachay, *(person)* wachakuy; **give birth frequently** *(person)* wachapakuy; **be about to give birth** wachanayay; **help give birth** wachachiy • *n.* **person who helps give birth** wachachiq; **woman who gives birth** wachakuq
birth mark *n.* ana
bite *v.* kaniy, khachuy
bite off a big piece *v.* khamuy, p'atay; **make bite off a big piece** khamuchiy
bite one another *v.* p'atanakuy
bitten-off *adj.* khamusqa, p'atasqa
bitter *adj.* p'osqo, qhatqe
black *adj.* yana; **dyed dark black** ch'illuyasqa • *v.* **become black** yanayay; **become blackened** yanachakuy; **dye dark black** ch'illuchay; **turn dark black** ch'illuyay
black and white spotted *adj.* ch'eqchi • *v.* **turn black and white spotted** ch'eqchiyay
blackened *adj.* yanachasqa
blackest black *adj.* ch'illu
blame *v.* tunpay
blame one another *v.* tunpanakuy
blamed *adj.* tunpasqa
bland *adj.* q'ayma
blanket *n.* chusi, lliklla, qata; **person who covers with blankets** qataq • *adj.* **covered with blankets** qatasqa • *v.* **cover with blankets** qatay; **cover one another with blankets** qatanakuy; **cover oneself with blankets** qatakuy

bleed *v.* sirk'ay
bleary-eyed *adj.* ch'oqñi • *v.* **become bleary-eyed** ch'oqñiyay
blind *adj.* ñawsa • *v.* **become blind** ñawsayay
blind person *n.* ñawsa
blink *v.* ch'illmiy
blonde *adj.* p'aqo • *v.* **turn blonde** p'aqoyay
blood *n.* yawar
blood relative *n.* yawarmasi
bloody *adj.* yawarchasqa • *v.* **become bloody** yawarchakuy
bloody one another *v.* yawarchanakuy
blossom *v.* phanchiy
blow *v.* *(wind)* wayray, *(person)* phukuy; **help blow** *(person)* phukuysiy; **make blow** *(person)* phukuchiy
blow again and again *(person)* *v.* phukupayay
blower *(person)* *n.* phukuq
blown *(person)* *adj.* phukusqa
blue *adj.* anqas; **light blue** qosi • *v.* **turn blue** anqasllay
blunt *adj.* hallmu
blunt knife *n.* morq'a
blushing *adj.* p'enqali
boast *v.* laqlay
body *(person)* *n.* ukhu
boil *v.* t'inpuy
boil fava beans *v.* phuspuy
boiled *adj.* t'inpusqa
boiled corn *n.* mot'e
boiled fava beans *n.* phuspu
bone *n.* tullu
boney *adj.* tullusapa
booty *(woven)* *n.* p'olqo
bored with *(food)* *adj.* amisqa • *v.* **become bored with** amiy
born: *v.* **be born** paqariy
borrow money *v.* manukuy
bottom *n.* siki
bought *adj.* rantisqa
bound *adj.* ch'atasqa
bouquet *n.* wayta; **person who makes bouquets** ch'antaq • *v.* **make bouquets** ch'antay
bow down *v.* k'umuy; **make bow down** k'umuchiy
bowl *n.* p'uku

boy *n.* wayna, maqt'a
brace *v.* q'emiy, tusay; **help brace** tusaysiy; **make brace** q'emichiy, tusachiy • *n.* **person who braces** tusaq
braced *adj.* q'emisqa, tusasqa
braid *n.* sinp'a • *v.* rank'uy, sinp'ay; **command to braid** sinp'achiy; **help braid** sinp'aysiy; **let one's hair be braided** sinp'achikuy
braided *adj.* rank'usqa, sinp'asqa
braider *n.* sinp'aq
brain *n.* ñosqhon
branch *n.* ch'aphra • *v.* **cover oneself with branches** ch'aphrachakuy
bread *n.* t'anta
break *v.* p'akiy; **command to break** p'akichiy; **help break** p'akiysiy
break into pieces *v.* k'iphtay
break off a piece *v.* khakay
break out of *v.* punkuchay
breakable *adj.* qhaphra
breast *n.* ñuñu
breastfeed *v.* ñuñuy, tutuy • *n.* **breastfeeding mother** ñuñuq
breath *n.* samay
breathe *v.* samay
breeding male *(animal) n.* kututu
breeze *n.* wayrari
bridge *n.* chaka • *v.* **build a bridge** chakachay; **hang a bridge** chakachay
bring *v.* apay • *n.* **person who brings** apaq
bring closer *v.* achhuykuy
bring something from one place to another *v.* apakachay
bristle *n.* suphu • *v.* **remove bristles** suphunay
broken *adj.* llik'i, p'akisqa
brooch *n.* tupu • *v.* **fasten clothes with brooch** tupuchay
broom *n.* pichana
brother *n.* *(of female)* tura, *(of male)* wayqe • *v.* **treat someone like a brother** *(woman)* turachakuy
brown *n.* k'ispa • *adj.* ch'unpi; **dyed brown** ch'unpichasqa • *v.* **dye brown** ch'unpichay; **turn brown** ch'unpiyay
brown in fire *v.* paruchiy, paruy
browned *adj.* parusqa
bruise *n.* q'oyo
bruised *adj.* q'oyosqa

brush *n.* *(hair)* ñaqch'a; *(plant)* ichhupanpa • *v.* *(hair)* ñaqch'ay; **help brush** *(hair)* ñaqch'aysiy
brush again and again *v.* ñaqch'apayay
brush one's hair *v.* ñaqch'akuy
brush one's hair again and again *v.* ñaqch'apakuy
brushed *adj.* ñaqch'asqa
bud *n.* ch'ichi • *v.* ch'ichiy
build *(with mud)* *v.* llut'ay; **help build** llut'aysiy; **make build** llut'achiy
build a bridge *v.* chakachay
build a house *v.* wasichay
build a hut *v.* ch'ukllay; **order to build a hut** ch'ukllachiy
build a nest *v.* q'esachakuy
build a stove *v.* q'onchachay
build a wall *v.* perqay
builder of huts *n.* ch'ukllaq
builder of walls *n.* perqaq
bundle *n.* khipu, q'epi
bundle up *v.* p'istuy; **let oneself be bundled up** p'istuchikuy; **make bundle up** p'istuchiy
bundle oneself up *v.* p'istukuy
burier *n.* p'anpaq
burn *v.* hap'ichiy, kanay, rawray, ruphay, yawray; **make burn** yawrachiy, rawrachiy, ruphachiy
burn with difficulty *v.* rawraykachay, yawraykachay
burned *adj.* ruphasqa, yawrasqa
burning *adj.* k'anchaq, rawraq
burning sensation *n.* k'aray
burnt *adj.* kanasqa, rawrasqa, yawrasqa
burp *v.* khapay, khasay
burst *v.* phatay
burstable *adj.* phataq
bury *v.* p'anpay; **make bury** p'anpachiy
but *conj.* ichaqa
butterfly *n.* pillpintu; **nocturnal butterfly** taparaku
buttocks *n.* siki
buy *v.* rantiy; **command to buy** rantichiy; **have the urge to buy** rantinayay; **make buy** rantichiy
buyer *n.* rantiq
buzz *v.* wanway

C

calf *n. (baby cow)* phuchu; *(anatomical)* ch'upa
call *v.* waqyay; **make call** waqyachiy
call again and again *v.* waqyapayay
call one another *v.* waqyanakuy
called *adj.* waqyasqa
calm *adj.* qasi, thak
calmly *adv.* qasi qasilla, susigo, thak
canal *n.* yarqha • *v.* **dig a canal** yarqhachay
candy *n.* hillu
cane *n.* tawna
cape *n.* yaqolla
capture *v.* hap'iy; **let oneself be captured** hap'ichikuy • *adj.* **easy to capture** hap'inalla
capture a live animal *v.* chakuy
capture of animals among many people *(ritual) n.* chaku
care for *v.* uyway
care for someone in their house *v.* tiyaysiy
cared-for *adj.* uywasqa
carefully *adv.* allichallamanta
caregiver *n.* uywaq
caress *v.* wayllukuy, luluy
caress one another *v.* lulunakuy
cargo *n.* q'epi • *v.* **prepare cargo** q'epichay
carried in arms *adj.* marq'asqa
carried on back *adj.* q'episqa
carried on shoulders *adj.* wantusqa
carrier *n.* q'epiq
carry carelessly on shoulders *v.* wantuykachay
carry in armpit *v.* lluk'iy
carry in arms *v.* marq'ay; **let oneself be carried in arms** marq'achikuy • *n.* **person who carries in arms** marq'aq
carry on back *v.* q'epiy; **help carry on back** q'epiysiy; **make carry on back** q'epichiy • *adj.* **possible to be carried on back** q'epina
carry on shoulders *v.* rikray, wantuy; **let oneself be carried on**

shoulders wantuchikuy • *n.* **person who carries on shoulders** rikraq
carve meat *v.* mat'ay
cat *n.* michi
catch *v.* hap'iy
catch up *v.* aypay, taripay; **help catch up** aypaysiy
caterpillar *n.* utuskuru
cave *n.* mach'ay
cavern *n.* mach'ay
cease *v.* tatiy
center *n.* chawpi, sonqo; **person who puts in center** chawpichaq • *v.* sonqonay; **put in center** chawpichay, chawpinay
ceramic shards *n.* k'arpa
ceramics *n.* k'akra
chair *n.* tiyana
charcoal *n.* k'illinsa
charge *v.* manuchay
chatterbox *n.* laqla
chatty *adj.* laqla
cheat *v.* yukay; **help cheat** yukaysiy; **let oneself be cheated** yukachikuy
cheat constantly *v.* yukapayay
cheat one another *v.* yukanakuy
cheated *adj.* yukasqa
cheater *n.* yukaq
cheek *n.* k'aklla
chest *n.* qhasqo
chew coca leaves *v.* akulliy, hallpay, pikchay, chakchay; **make chew coca leaves** akullichiy
chew on *v.* khastuy
chew something tough *v.* k'awtiy
chewed pulp *n.* hach'u
chicha *(corn beer) n.* akha
chick *n.* chiwchi, malqo
chicken *n.* wallpa
child *n.* erqe, warma, wawa • *v.* **behave like a child** erqekachay; **feel like a child** erqeyay
chin *n.* k'aki
chip *v.* k'aphtiy, khallpay, q'asay
chipped *adj.* k'aphtisqa, q'asasqa

choke on *v.* chakachikuy
choose *v.* akllay; **help choose** akllaysiy; **make choose** akllachiy
choose for oneself *v.* akllakuy
chooser *n.* akllaq
chop *v.* ch'eqtay; **help chop** ch'eqtaysiy; **order to chop** ch'eqtachiy
chop down *v.* wit'uy; **help chop down** wit'uysiy; **make chop down** wit'uchiy
chopped down *adj.* wit'usqa
chore *n.* llank'ana
chosen *adj.* akllasqa
chosen woman in Inkan times *n.* aklla
circle *n.* muyu • *v.* tumay; **go in circles** muyuy; **make go in circles** muyuchiy
circular *adj.* suntur
clarified *adj.* sut'inchasqa
clarify *v.* sut'inchay
claw *n.* sillu
clean *adj.* ch'uya
clean one's dirty skin *v.* kharkannay
clean oneself *v.* pichakuy
clean up dried leaves *v.* q'opanay
clean up garbage *v.* q'opanay
clear *adj.* ch'uya, sut'in
clearly yes *adv.* riki
clever *adj.* ch'iti
cleverly *adv.* ch'itilla
cliff *n.* qaqapana
climb *v.* seqay, wichay; **have the urge to climb** seqanayay, wichanayay; **help climb** seqaysiy, wichaysiy; **make climb** seqachiy, wichachiy; **try to climb** seqapakuy
climb again and again *v.* seqapayay
climb rapidly *v.* wicharpariy
climb with difficulty *v.* wichapakuy
cloak *n.* llaqolla, yaqolla
clod *n.* k'urpa
close[1] *(nearby) adj.* sispa • *v.* **bring closer** achhuykuy; **get closer** achhuykuy, sispay; **keep moving closer** achhupayay
close[2] *(shut) v.* wesq'ay; **help close** wesq'aysiy; **make close** wesq'achiy • *n.* **closer** wesq'aq
close permanently *v.* wesq'akapuy; **stay permanently closed** wesq'arayay

closed *adj.* wesq'asqa
cloth for carrying on back *n.* q'eperina
cloth for swaddling a baby *n.* waltha
clothing *n.* p'acha • *v.* **order to have clothing sewn for someone** sirachikuy
cloud *n.* phuyu • *v.* phuyuy
cloudy *adj.* phuyu
clumsily *adv.* ñuskhu ñuskhulla
clumsy *adj.* hat'upa, ñuskhu
clumsy while walking *adj.* khitu
clustered *adj.* khaka
coagulate *v.* tikayay
coat *n.* p'istuna
coca leaves *n.* kuka; **bunch of coca leaves** k'intu; **chewer of coca leaves** akulliq; **preparer of coca leaves** *(ritual)* k'intuq • *v.* **chew coca leaves** akulliy, hallpay, pikchay, chakchay; **make chew coca leaves** akullichiy; **prepare coca leaves** *(ritual)* k'intuy
cold[1] *(temperature) adj.* chiri • *interj.* **how cold!** alalaw • *v.* **be cold** chiriy; **become cold** chiriyay
cold[2] *n.* *(illness)* chhulli
collaborate *v.* haymay
collaborate to mess up *v.* rawiysiy
collapse *v.* chhullmiy, thuniy; **make collapse** chhullmichiy, thunichiy
collapsed *adj.* chhullmisqa, thunisqa
collect leftovers *v.* wakinchay
collect manure *v.* q'away; **command to collect manure** q'awachiy; **help collect manure** q'awaysiy; **refertilize with manure** wanupay
collect surplus *v.* wakinchay
collect what remains *v.* pallapay
collector of remains *n.* pallapakuq
colonist *n.* mitma
colonize *v.* llaqtachakuy, mitmay
comb *n.* ñaqch'a • *v.* ñaqch'ay; **help comb** ñaqch'aysiy
comb again and again *v.* ñaqch'apayay
comb one's hair *v.* ñaqch'akuy
comb one's hair again and again *v.* ñaqch'apakuy
combed *adj.* ñaqch'asqa
come to an agreement *v.* hurk'ay
commemorate *v.* yuyapay

commit adultery *v.* pantay
commit suicide *v.* wañuchikuy
communal work: *n.* **system of communal work** mink'a; **person who summons for communal work** mink'akuq • *adj.* **summoned for communal work** mink'asqa • *v.* **summon for communal work** mink'ay
community *n.* ayllu
compete *v.* atipanakuy
complete *adj.* hunt'a • *v.* hunt'ay
completed *adj.* hunt'asqa
completely *adv.* llapanta, lluyta
compress *v.* ñit'iy, ñup'uy; **help compress** ñit'iysiy; **make compress** ñit'ichiy
compress again and again *v.* ñit'ipayay
compressed *adj.* ñit'isqa, ñup'usqa
conceited *adj.* apusonqo
conceive *(procreation) v.* yumay
conceived *(procreation) adj.* churiyasqa
conch shell *n.* pututu
condor *n.* kuntur
confront *v.* tinkuy, uyanchay; **make confront** tinkuchiy
confront one another *v.* tinkunakuy
confrontation *n.* tinku
confuse *v.* ch'arwiy
congregate *v.* sisiykuy
consciously *adv.* yuyaypi
consistent *adj.* ch'ila
console *v.* llakipayay
conspire *v.* yachachinakuy
constellation *n.* warani
consume *v.* t'antay
consumed *adj.* t'antasqa
container *(woven) n.* taqe
converge *v.* tinkuy
cook *n.* wayk'uq • *v.* wayk'uy; **have the urge to cook** wayk'unayay; **help cook** wayk'uysiy; **make cook** wayk'uchiy
cook completely *v.* chayay
cook potatoes in the ground *v.* wathiyay
cooked *adj.* chayasqa, wayk'usqa
cool down *v.* chiriyachiy

cooled down *adj.* chiriyasqa
coral *n.* mullu
corn *n.* sara; **boiled corn** mot'e; **fresh ear of corn** choqllo; **sweet corn drink** teqte
corn harvest *n.* kallchay; **first corn harvest** miskha • *v.* **harvest corn** kallchay
corn smut *n.* hat'upa
corn with small kernels *n.* ch'ullpi
corner *(interior) n.* k'uchu • *v.* **put in corner** k'uchunay, k'uchunchay
cornstalk *n.* wiru; **dry cornstalks** chhalla • *v.* **gather dry cornstalks** chhallakuy
corpse *n.* aya
corral *n.* kancha
corrode *v.* uthay
cough *n.* uhu • *v.* uhuy; **have the urge to cough** uhunayay; **make cough** uhuchiy
cough constantly *v.* uhupakuy
cough up *v.* qhotoy
cougher *n.* uhuq
could be *adv.* ichapas
count *v.* yupay; **help count** yupaysiy; **make count** yupachiy • *n.* **person who counts** yupaq
count again and again *v.* yupapayay
countable *adj.* yupa
counted *adj.* yupasqa
country *n.* llaqta
countryperson: *n.* **fellow countryperson** llaqtamasi
cousin *n.* qayri
cover *n.* kirpa • *v.* kirpay; **help cover** pakaysiy
cover a path with gravel *v.* khallkachay
cover oneself with fallen leaves *v.* ch'aphrachakuy
cover oneself with feathers *v.* phurullikuy
cover up *v.* pakay
cover up for one another *v.* pakanakuy
cover with ash *v.* usphachay
cover with blankets *v.* *qatay*
cover with soil *v.* allpachay; **let oneself be covered with soil** p'anpachikuy
cover with wool v. millmachay
covered up *adj.* pakasqa

covet desperately *v.* wañurqoy
cowbell *n.* chanrara • *v.* **reverberate** *(cowbells)* chanrararay
crack *n.* raqra
cracked *adj.* raqra • *v.* **get cracked** raqray
crawl *v.* lloqhay; **make crawl** lloqhachiy
crawler *n.* lloqhaq
crazed *adj.* lamuku, waq'ayasqa
crazy *adj.* waq'a • *v.* **go crazy** waq'ayay
crazy person *n.* lamuku
creak *n.* k'ir
creamy *adj.* llank'i • *v.* **become creamy** llank'iyay
crease *v.* pataray
create *v.* kamay, paqarichiy
created *adj.* kamasqa
creator *n.* kamaq, paqarichiq
creep *v.* lloqhay
creep around *v.* muyuykachay
creeper *n.* lloqhaq
crest *n.* k'akara
crib *n.* k'iraw
cricket *n.* ch'illiku
crier *n.* waqaq
cringe from bitter taste *n.* k'ipi
crippled *adj.* such'u • *v.* **become crippled** such'uyay
crooked *adj.* weqru
cross *v.* chinpay; **help cross** chinpachiy • *n.* **person who helps cross** chinpachiq
cross one's eyes *v.* lerq'oyay, wesq'oy
crossbeam *n.* chakapa • *v.* **place crossbeams** chakanay
cross-eyed *adj.* ch'oqo, lerq'o, wesq'o • *v.* **become cross-eyed** lerq'oyay, wesq'oyay; **look cross-eyed** wesq'oykachay
crowd together *v.* ch'unkunakuy
crowded *adj.* ch'unku, qaqa
crumpled *adj.* ch'awisqa • *v.* **become crumpled** ch'awiy
crush *v.* ñut'uy, saqtay; **help crush** saqtaysiy; **make crush** saqtachiy
crushed *adj.* ñut'u, saqtasqa
crushing tool *n.* saqtana
cry *v.* waqay; **be about to cry** waqanayay; **have the urge to cry** waqanayay; **make cry** waqachiy

cry again and again *v.* waqapayay
cry with *v.* waqaysiy
crybaby *n.* ch'irchi, waqati
crystal *n.* qespi
cucumber *n.* kachun
cup *n.* q'ero
cure *v.* hanpiy, qhaliyachiy; **help cure** hanpiysiy; **let oneself be cured by someone** hanpichikuy; **make cure** hanpichiy
cure oneself *v.* hanpikuy
cured *adj.* hanpisqa, qhaliyasqa
curly *adj.* k'upa, k'uspa
curse another *v.* ñakay • *n.* **person who curses another** ñakaq
curse continuously *v.* ñakapakuy
cursed *adj.* ñakasqa
curve *n.* q'enqo
cut *v.* kuchuy
cut hair *(head) v.* rutuy; **let one's hair be cut** rutuchikuy; **make cut hair** rutuchiy
cut off *adj.* mut'u • *v.* mut'uy
cut off ear *v.* rinrinay
cut off horns *v.* waqranay
cut open *adj.* khallasqa • *v.* khallay; **help cut open** khallaysiy; **make cut open** khallachiy
cute *adj.* munay
cutter *n.* khallaq

D

damp *adj.* ch'aran, hoq'o
dampen *v.* ch'aranchay
dampen until infested *(grains) v.* hut'uy
dance *n. (Andean carnaval)* qhaswa • *v.* tusuy; **have the urge to dance** tusunayay; **make dance** tusuchiy
dance with someone *v.* tusuysiy
dancer *n.* tusuq
dark *adj.* laqha • *v.* **become dark** laqhayay, tutayay; **turn dark** arphayay
darken *v.* yanachay
darkness *n.* tutayaq
dart *n.* wach'i
daughter *n. (of father)* ususi; *(of mother)* warmi wawa • *v.* **treat someone like a son/daughter** wawachakuy
daughter-in-law *n.* qhachun
dawn *n.* illariy, pacha • *v.* illariy
day *n.* p'unchay • *adv.* **all day** ch'isiyaq, p'unchaynintin • *v.* **become daytime** p'unchayay
day after tomorrow *n.* minchha
day before yesterday *n.* qayninpa
day laborer *n.* llank'apakuq
daydream *n.* mosqhoy
daytime: *v.* **become daytime** p'unchayay
dazzling: *v.* **become dazzling** lliphlliyay
dead *adj.* wañusqa • *n.* wañusqa
deaf *adj.* loqt'o, roqt'o, wanq'o • *v.* **become deaf** roqt'oyay, wanq'oyay
deaf person *n.* roqt'o
deafen *v.* wanq'oyachiy
debt *n.* manu • *v.* **not pay a debt** ch'achuy
debtor *n.* ch'achu • *v.* **make a debtor** manuyay
decapitate *v.* umanay
decay *v.* mullphayay
decayed *adj.* mullpha
deceive *v.* yukay; **help deceive** yukaysiy; **let oneself be deceived** yukachikuy

deceive constantly *v.* yukapayay
deceive one another *v.* yukanakuy
deceived *adj.* yukasqa
deceptively *adv.* sirpaylla
decrease *v.* asllayachiy, chikachay, wayway; **make decrease** waywachiy
decreased *adj.* waywasqa
decrepit *adj.* thultu • *v.* **become decrepit** thultuyay
deep *adj.* p'onqo
deep hole *n.* sankha
deer *n.* luychu, taruka
defeat *v.* atipay; **let oneself be defeated** atipachikuy
defeat categorically *v.* akachiy
defeated *adj.* atipasqa
defecate *v.* akay; *(animal)* uchhay; **have the urge to defecate** akanayay; **make defecate** akachiy
defend another *v.* sayapakuy
defend oneself with horns *v.* waqrapakuy
defend oneself with stick *v.* p'anapakuy, q'asupakuy
defaulter *n.* huchayoq
deflea *v.* pikiy
dehydrated by the sun *adj.* qachasqa
dehydrated potato *n.* ch'uñu, tunta
deity *(Andean) n.* waka, apu, awki
dekernel *v.* chhallmay; *(corn)* muchhay; **help dekernel** *(corn)* muchhaysiy
dekerneled *(corn) adj.* muchhasqa
delay: *v.* **make delay** unayachiy
delirious *adj.* musphaq
deliriously *adv.* muspha muspha
delouse *v.* usay; **let oneself be deloused** usachikuy; **make delouse** usachiy
deloused *adj.* usasqa
delude: *v.* **make delude** llachichiy
delusionally *adv.* llachi llachi
demarcate *v.* suyunchay
demolish *v.* thuniy; **make demolish** thunichiy
demolished *adj.* thunisqa
dense *adj.* k'iki, pipu, thaka
dent *v.* q'aphñuy

dented *adj.* q'aphñisqa, q'aphñu q'aphñu
depressed *adj.* usphu
deprive *v.* ch'achay; **cause deprivation** ch'achachiy, muchuchiy
deprive oneself *v.* muchuy
deprived person *n.* ch'achaq
deranged *adj.* loqhe
descend *v.* urayay
descended *adj.* urayasqa
desire *n.* llachi • *v.* munay
detain *v.* hark'ay, sayachiy; **help detain** hark'aysiy
deteriorate *v.* thantay
deteriorated *(health) adj.* machuyasqa
detest *v.* cheqnikuy
devalue *v.* yanqachay
develop *v.* wiñay; **make develop** wiñachiy
developed *adj.* wiñasqa
devour *v.* wap'uy; **have the urge to devour** wap'unayay
devoured *adj.* wap'usqa
diarrhea *n.* q'echa, seqra • *v.* **have diarrhea** q'echanayay, seqray
die *v.* wañuy; *(person)* wañupuy
die suddenly *v.* wañurqoy
different *adj.* hoqniraq
differently *adv.* hoqniraqta
difficult *adj.* sasa • *v.* **make difficult** sasachay • *adv.* **with difficulty** sasay sasay
dig *v.* allay, hasp'iy; **help dig** allaysiy, hasp'iysiy; **make dig** allachiy, hasp'ichiy
dig a canal *v.* yarqhachay
dig repeatedly *v.* allapayay
dig up *v.* weq'ay; **help dig up** weq'aysiy; **make dig up** weq'achiy
dig up earthen clumps with grass *v.* ch'anpay • *n.* **person who digs up earthen clumps with grass** ch'anpaq
digger *n.* allaq, hasp'iq, weq'aq
digging tool *n.* hasp'ina, allana, allachu, weq'ana
diluted *adj.* unuyachisqa • *v.* **become diluted** unuyay
diminish *v.* wayway; **make diminish** waywachiy
diminished *adj.* waywasqa
dimwitted *adj.* p'anra • *v.* **become dimwitted** p'anrayay
dirt *n.* wiswi
dirtied *adj.* qhellichasqa

dirty *adj.* khacha, map'a, qhelli, wiswi; *(skin)* kharka; **dusty and dirty** allpasapa • *v.* map'ay; **become dirty** qhellichakuy; **get dirty** qhellichay, wiswiyay • *n.* **person who dirties** qhellichaq
dirty one's skin *v.* kharkachakuy
disabled *adj.* thultu • *v.* **become disabled** thultuyay
disagreeably *adv.* millay millay
disappear *v.* ch'usaqyay; **make disappear** ch'usaqyachiy
disappear forever *v.* ch'usaqyapuy
disappeared *adj.* ch'usaqyasqa
discard *v.* yanqachay
disclose *v.* willaykachay
discolored *adj.* qhoqa • *v.* **become discolored** qhoqayay
discouraged *adj.* usphu, willpusqa • *v.* **become discouraged** usphuy; **make discouraged** usphuchiy
disgruntled *adj.* waqati
disgusting *adj.* millay • *interj.* **how disgusting!** atataw • *v.* **be disgusted** millakuy; **cause disgust** millachiy
disheveled *adj.* t'anpa • *v.* **become disheveled** t'anpachakuy
disinterested *(woman) adj.* waylaka
disloyal *adj.* iskayllu
disorderly *adj.* thamalanku
disperse *v.* ch'eqechiy
disperse by hand *v.* qachiy; **help disperse by hand** qachiysiy
disperse by hand again and again *v.* qachipayay
dispersed *adj.* ch'eqe, ch'eqesqa
dispersed by hand *adj.* qachisqa
dispute *v.* atipanakuy
disregard *v.* haqey
dissolve *v.* chulluy, unuyachiy
dissolve in one's mouth *v.* mullmuy
dissolved *adj.* chullusqa, unuyachisqa
dissolved in one's mouth *adj.* mullmusqa
distance *n.* ch'usa
distance oneself *v.* karunchakuy
distinct *adj.* sapaq
distribute *v.* achuray, rakiy; **help distribute** achuraysiy, rakiysiy; **make distribute** achurachiy, rakichiy • *n.* **person who makes distribute** achurachiq
distribute mutually *v.* rakinakuy
distributed *adj.* rakisqa

distributor *n.* achuraq, rakiq
diverted: *v.* **get diverted** chinkay
divide in two *v.* iskaychay
divide into fractions *v.* phakmiy
divulge *v.* willaykachay
do *v.* ruway; **command to do** ruwachiy; **have the urge to do** ruwanayay; **help do** ruwaysiy
do again *v.* kutipay
do not *(prohibitive) adv.* ama
do nothing *v.* qasirayay
doable *adj.* atinalla, atiylla
docile *adj.* sanp'a • *v.* **become docile** sanp'ayay
doctor *n.* hanpiq
dog *n.* alqo; **furry dog** ch'aku
doll for good luck *(Andean) n.* eqeqo
domesticated animal *n.* uywa
dominate *v.* atipay; **let oneself be dominated** atipachikuy
dominated *adj.* atipasqa
dominator *n.* atipaq
done *adj.* ruwasqa
door *n.* punku
doubt *v.* iskayyay, thukiy; **make doubt** thukichiy
doubt often *v.* thukiykachay
doubter *n.* thukiq
dove *n.* urpi
downcast *adj.* k'umu
doze *v.* puñupayay
drag *v.* aysay; **help drag** aysaysiy
dream *n.* mosqhoy • *v.* mosqhokuy; **appear in dreams** mosqhoychay; **talk constantly while dreaming** musphapayay; **talk while dreaming** musphay
dream fitfully *v.* mosqhopakuy
drenched *adj.* ch'uychu
dress *v.* p'achay; **help dress** p'achachiy
dress up *v.* k'achallikuy
dressed *adj.* p'achasqa • *v.* **get dressed** p'achakuy
dried *(meat) adj.* ch'arkisqa
dried grains or beans *n.* k'ayu
dried herbs *n.* qacha
dried leaves *n.* q'opa

dried meat *n.* ch'arki
dried mucous *n.* k'iski
dried-out *adj.* ch'akisqa, k'irku, phaski
drill hole *v.* khapuy; **help drill hole** khapuysiy; **make drill hole** khapuchiy
drilled *(hole) adj.* khapusqa
drink *n.* ukyana • *v.* ukyay; **have the urge to drink** ukyanayay; **have the urge to drink water** ununayay; **join in drinking** ukyaysiy; **make drink** ukyachiy
drink hurriedly *v.* ukyarpariy
drinker *n.* ukyaq
drip *v.* llusp'iy, sut'uy • *n.* sut'u
drive crazy *v.* opayachiy, waq'ayachiy
drizzle *n.* iphu, siphsi • *v.* iphuy, siphsiy
drizzle during sunshine *n.* chirapa • *v.* chirapay
drool *n.* llawsa • *v.* llawsay, thaltay
drooler *n.* llawsasuru
drooling *adj.* llawsasuru
drop *v.* kachariy, urmachiy • *n.* sut'u
drop suddenly *v.* kacharpariy
drum *n.* wankar, *(small)* tinya • *v.* **beat a drum** tinyay
drunk *n.* machaq • *adj.* machasqa, machaq • *v.* **get drunk** machay; **get drunk with** machaysiy; **get someone drunk** machachiy
dry *adj.* ch'aki • *v.* ch'akiy
dry herbs in sun *v.* qachay
dry out *v.* phaskiy, *(meat)* ch'arkiyay; **make dry out** phaskiyachiy • *adj.* **can be dried out** phaskiq
duck *(male) n.* khaka
dug up *adj.* weq'asqa
dull *adj.* hallmu
duplicate *v.* iskaychay
dust: *v.* **turn into dust** allpayapuy • *adj.* **reduced to dust** allpayasqa
dust with flour *v.* hak'uchay • *n.* **person who dusts with flour** hak'uchaq
dusted with flour *adj.* hak'usqa
dusty: *v.* **become dusty with ash** usphachakuy
dusty and dirty *adj.* allpasapa
dye *v.* tullpuy; **help dye** tullpuysiy; **make dye** tullpuchiy
dye brown *v.* ch'unpichay
dye dark black *v.* ch'illuchay

dyed *adj.* tullpusqa
dyed brown *adj.* ch'unpichasqa
dyed dark black *adj.* ch'illuyasqa
dyer *n.* tullpuq
dying *adj.* wañunayaq

E

each one *adj.* sapanka
eagle *n.* anka
ear *n.* rinri • *adj.* **small-eared** chunu; **with mutilated ear** chunu • *v.* **cut off ear** rinrinay
earlier *adv.* ñaqha
Earth *(planet) n.* pacha
earthen clump with grass *n.* ch'anpa; **person who digs up earthen clumps with grass** ch'anpaq • *v* **dig up earthen clumps with grass** ch'anpay
earthquake *n.* pachakuyuy
earthworm *n.* k'uyka
easy to capture *adj.* hap'inalla
easy to pick up *adj.* hoqarinalla
easy to raise *adj.* hoqarinalla
eat *v.* mihuy; **have the urge to eat** mihunayay
eat away *v.* uthay
eat constantly *v.* mihupayay
eaten *adj.* mihusqa
eater *n.* mihuq
eavesdrop *v.* uyapakuy
eavesdropper *n.* uyapakuq
edge *n.* patan
egg *n.* runtu
eight *num.* pusaq
ejaculate *v.* wawsay, yumay
elderly *adj.* *(woman)* payayasqa, *(man)* machuyasqa
elegant *adj.* k'acha, qhapchi • *v.* **make oneself elegant** k'achayay
elegantly *adv.* k'achay k'achay
elongate *v.* suniy
elongated *adj.* suni
embarrass another *v.* p'enqachiy
embarrassed *adj.* p'enqasqa • *v.* **be embarrassed** p'enqakuy • *n.* **person who gets embarrassed** p'enqakuq
embarrassment *n.* p'enqay
ember *n.* sansa • *v.* **put over embers** sansachay

embitter *v.* p'osqoy
emblem *n.* llawt'u
emit a good smell *v.* q'apay
emptied *adj.* ch'usaqyasqa
empty *adj.* ch'usaq, tallisqa • *v.* ch'usaqyachiy, qasichiy
empty completely of liquid *v.* ch'uymay
empty out a container *v.* talliy; **help empty out a container** talliysiy
encircle *v.* muyupayay
encounter *v.* tupay • *n.* **person who encounters** tupaq
end the day *v.* ch'isiyay
enemy *n.* awqa
engrossed: *v.* **be engrossed** hanrayay
enlarge *v.* hatunchay
enormous *adj.* hatunkaray
entangle *v.* arwiy, ch'arwiy; **help entangle** arwiysiy, ch'arwiysiy; **make entangle** arwichiy, ch'arwichiy
entangle again and again *v.* arwipayay, ch'arwipayay
entangled *adj.* arwisqa
enter *v.* haykuy
entertain *v.* pukllachiy
entrance *n.* haykuna
entwine *v.* rank'uy
entwined *adj.* rank'usqa
erect *v.* hatarichiy • *adj.* sayarisqa
err *v.* witiy; **make err** witichiy
erred *adj.* witisqa
escape *v.* ayqey; **let escape** phawachiy; **make escape** ayqechiy
escape constantly *v.* ayqepayay
esophagus *n.* millp'uti
evacuate quickly *v.* seqray
evade *v.* ch'itakuy
evaluater *n.* chaninchaq
evaporate *v.* waksiy • *n.* **that which evaporates** waksiq
even more *adv.* astawan, aswanta
everyone *pron.* llapan • *adj.* lliw
evident *adj.* sut'in
exact *adj.* k'apak
exactly *adv.* k'apaklla
exalt *v.* sumaychay

exalted *adj.* sumaychasqa
exchange *v.* haywanakuy, qonakuy
exclude *v.* sapanchay
exclude oneself *v.* ch'ullachakuy
excluded *adj.* sapanchasqa
excrement *n.* aka
executioner *n.* nak'achu, nak'aq
exhausted *adj.* sayk'usqa
exist *v.* kawsay
existence *n.* kawsay
exit *n.* punku
expand *v.* hatunchay
expectant mother *n.* onqokuq
expel *v.* qarqoy; **help expel** qarqoysiy; **make expel** qarqochiy
expel air *v.* chhakchay
expel air noisily *v.* chhasay
expelled *adj.* qarqosqa
explode *v.* t'oqyay, t'ohay
exploded *adj.* t'oqyasqa, t'ohasqa
expose to sun *v.* masay
expose to sun again and again *v.* masaykachay
expose to sun continuously *v.* masapayay
exposed to sun *adj.* masasqa
exquisite *adj.* sumaq • *v.* **become exquisite** sumaqyay
exquisitely *adv.* sumaqlla, sumaqta
extend *v.* mast'ariy
extract *v.* sik'iy; **command to extract** sik'ichiy; **help extract** sik'iysiy
extracted *adj.* sik'isqa
eye *n.* ñawi
eye discharge *n.* ch'oqñi
eyebrow *n.* pullurki
eyelash *n.* qhechiphra
eyelid *n.* ñawi qara

F

face *n.* uya • *v.* uyanchay
face down *adv.* thallanpamanta • *v.* **make put face down** thallachiy; **put face down** thallachiy • *n.* **person who is face down** thallaq
face up *adv.* hank'arpamanta
faded *adj.* qhoqa • *v.* **become faded** qhoqayay
fail to follow through *v.* huchay
failure to follow through *n.* hucha
fair *adj.* chanin
falcon *n.* waman
fall *v.* urmay; **let fall** kachariy; **make fall** urmachiy
fall and roll *v.* soqyay
fall asleep *v.* utiy; **be about to fall asleep** puñunayay; **make fall asleep** utichiy
fall from cliff *v.* qaqapay; **make fall from cliff** qaqapachiy
fall over *v.* thullkiy
fall over again and again *v.* urmaykachay
fallen *adj.* urmasqa
fallen leaves *n.* ch'aphra • *v.* **cover oneself with fallen leaves** ch'aphrachakuy
fallen over *adj.* thullkisqa
falsely *adv.* llullay llullay
familiar with: *v.* **be familiar with** reqsiy; **have the urge to be familiar with** reqsinayay; **make familiar with** reqsichiy
family *n.* ayllu • *v.* **become family** aylluchakuy
famine *n.* muchuy, yarqay
fang *n.* waqsa
far *adv.* karu • *adj.* karu
farming land *n.* chakra
fast *adj.* *(speed)* q'osti • *n.* *(not eat)* sasi • *v.* *(not eat)* sasiy; **make fast** *(not eat)* sasichiy
fat *adj.* wira, wirasapa • *n.* wira • *v.* **make fat** wirayachiy
fatal *adj.* qhencha
fatality *n.* qhencha
father *n.* tayta • *v.* **make a father figure** taytachakuy

fatten *v.* wirayay
fava beans: *n.* **boiled fava beans** phuspu • *v.* **boil fava beans** phuspuy
fear *n.* manchay • *v.* manchakuy; **cause fear** mancharichiy
fearsome *adj.* manchana
feather *n.* phuru • *v.* **cover oneself with feathers** phurullikuy
featherless *adj.* hallaka
feed *v.* mihuchiy
feed mouth-to-mouth *v.* umiy • *n.* *(like a bird)* **person who feeds mouth-to-mouth** umiq
feed mouth-to-mouth constantly *v.* umipayay
feel *v.* llamiy
feel better *v.* thaniy
feel like a child *v.* erqeyay
feel oneself *v.* llamikuy
feel one another *v.* llaminakuy
feel repeatedly *v.* llamipayay
feel softly *v.* llamiykuy
feigned *adj.* wakta
fellow countryperson *n.* llaqtamasi
female *n.* china
femur *n.* wich'un
ferment *v.* poqoy, p'osqoy; **make ferment** poqochiy
fermented *adj.* p'osqo, poqosqa
fertilize with manure *v.* wanuchay
fertilized with manure *adj.* wanuchasqa
fetus *n.* sullu
few *adj.* as; **a few** aslla
field *(agricultural)* *n.* chakra
fight *v.* awqanakuy
fill *v.* hunt'ay, llinp'ay
fill a place *v.* sisiy
filled *adj.* hunt'asqa
filth *n.* qhanra, qhelli
filthy *adj.* khanka, qhanra qhanra • *v.* **get filthy** qhanray
find *v.* tariy; **help find** tariysiy
find and take for something oneself *v.* apakamuy
fine *adj.* qhapchi
fingernail *n.* sillu
finger-pointer *n.* t'oqsiq

finish *v.* tukuy; **help finish** tukuysiy; **make finish** tukuchiy
finish in a hurry *v.* tukurpariy
finish one's uncompleted task *v.* tukupay
finished *adj.* tukusqa • *v.* **be finished** tukukuy
fire *n.* nina • *v.* **help put out fire with water** thasnuysiy; **light a fire** ninachay; **make put out fire with water** thasnuchiy; **put out fire with water** thasnuy
firefly *n.* pinchinkuru
fireplace *n.* q'oncha
firewood *n.* llant'a • *v.* **make firewood** llant'achay
first born *n.* phiwi
first harvest *n.* *(corn)* miskha; *(potato)* maway
fish *n.* challwa • *v.* challway
fish eggs *n.* kaw kaw
fisherman *n.* challwaq
fist *n.* ch'oqmi, saqma
five *num.* pisqa
fix *v.* allichay; **get something fixed** allichachiy
fixed *adj.* allichasqa
flamingo *(bird)* *n.* pariwana
flank *n.* waqta
flap *v.* phalalalay, phararaeray
flash *v.* illapay
flat field *n.* panpa
flatten *v.* mallmay, p'altachiy, t'asnuy
flattened *adj.* p'alta, t'asnu
flatter *v.* llunk'uy
flatterer *n.* llunk'u
flute *n.* pitu
flay *v.* lluch'iy, llust'iy
flayed *adj.* lluch'isqa
flea *n.* piki
flesh *n.* aycha • *v.* **remove flesh** aycharay
fleshy *adj.* aychasapa
float *v.* tuytuy
floater *n.* tuytuq
floating *adj.* tuytuq
flood *n.* lloqlla • *v.* **become flooded** unuyay
flour *n.* hak'u; **person who dusts with flour** hak'uchaq • *adj.* **dusted with flour** hak'usqa • *v.* **dust with flour** hak'uchay

floury *adj.* hak'u; **very floury** hak'uy hak'uy
flow *v.* phullpuy; *(water)* ch'uychuy
flower *v.* t'ikayay; **gather flowers** ch'antay • *n.* t'ika; *(Andean varieties)* phallcha, sirwana; **person who gathers flowers** ch'antaq
flute *n.* pinkuyllu, qena
flutter *v.* laphapay
fly *n.* *(insect)* ch'uspi • *v.* *(take flight)* phaway
foam *n.* phosoqo
foam at the mouth *v.* ulthuy
fog *n.* pacha phuyu
fold *v.* ch'ipuy, pataray, q'enpiy, taparay; **help fold** taparaysiy; **make fold** q'enpichiy
folded *adj.* ch'ipusqa, q'enpisqa, taparasqa
follow *v.* qatikachay, qatiy
follow continuously *v.* qatipayay
follow footprints *v.* yupichay
follow one another *v.* qatinakuy
follow tracks *v.* yupichay
follow through: *n.* **person who never follows through** huchasapa
fondle *v.* mullkhuy
fondled *adj.* mullkhusqa
fondler *n.* mullkhuq
fontanel *n.* ñupu
food *n.* mihuna
fool around *v.* oqarayay
foot *n.* chaki • *v.* **be on foot** sayay; **mutilate foot** chakinnay
foot of the bed *n.* hayt'a
footplow *n.* chakitaklla
footprints *n.* yupi • *v.* **follow footprints** yupichay; **leave footprints** yupiy
for what? *inter.* imapaq
for what reason? *inter.* imamanta
ford *(a river)* *v.* chinpay
forehead *n.* mat'i
forest *n.* sach'a sach'a
foretell *v.* umulliy, watupakuy
foreteller *n.* watupakuq
forever *adv.* wiñaypaq
forget *v.* qonqay; **make forget** qonqachiy

forgettable *adj.* qonqana
forgive *v.* panpachay
forgotten *adj.* qonqasqa
fornicator *n.* wachoq
found *v.* teqsiy • *adj.* tarisqa
fountain *n.* pukyu
four *num.* tawa
four-legged *adj.* tawachaki
fox *n.* atoq • *v.* **set trap like a fox** atoqrayay
fraction *n.* phakmi
fractioned *adj.* phakmisqa
fragile *adj.* *(thing)* p'akina, *(thing)* qhaphra, *(person)* onqoli
fragment *v.* k'iphtay, phakmiy • *n.* k'iphta, phakmi
fragmented *adj.* phakmisqa
fragrant *adj.* q'aparishaq
freeze *v.* khutuy, qasay
frequent *adj.* pasaq
frequently *adv.* pasaqlla
fried *adj.* theqtisqa, t'eqtisqa
frighten *v.* manchay
frigid *adj.* khutu • *v.* **become frigid** khutuyay
frog *n.* ch'eqlla, k'ayra
from then on *conj.* chaymantapacha
from where? *inter.* maymanta
frost *v.* chhullay • *n.* chhulla, qasa
frosted *adj.* chhullasqa
frozen *adj.* qasasqa
fruit *n.* ruru
fry *v.* theqtichiy, t'eqtichiy
fugitive *n.* ayqeq
fulfill *v.* llinp'ay
fulfilled *adj.* llinp'asqa
full *adj.* hunt'a, llinp'asqa
full of holes *adj.* t'oqosqa
furniture for reclining *n.* k'irana
furrow *(earth)* *n.* wachu • *v.* **help make furrows** wachuysiy; **make furrows** wachuy
furrowed *adj.* wachu wachu
furry dog *n.* ch'aku

G

gain weight *v.* wirayay
game *n.* pukllay
garbage *n.* q'opa • *v.* **clean up garbage** q'opanay
garden *n.* inkill
garden terrace *n.* inkillpata
gather *v.* ch'unkunakuy; *(fabric)* sip'uy
gather flowers *v.* ch'antay • *n.* **person who gathers flowers** ch'antaq
gather together *v.* huñuy; **help gather together** huñuysiy • *n.* **person who gathers together** huñuq
gathered *adj.* ch'unku; *(fabric)* sip'usqa
gaunt *adj.* ch'alqe, ch'olqe • *v.* **become gaunt** ch'alqeyay, ch'olqeyay
generous *adj.* sonqosapa
gestate *v.* chichuyay
get better *v.* allinyay, alliyay; **make someone get better** alliyachiy • *n.* **person who gets better** alliyaq
ghost *n.* kukuchi
girl *n.* sipas, p'asña
give *v.* qoy
give a toast *v.* anqosay
give birth *v.* *(animal)* phallay, *(animal)* wachay, *(person)* wachakuy; **be about to give birth** wachanayay; **help give birth** wachachiy • *n.* **person who helps give birth** wachachiq; **woman who gives birth** wachakuq
give birth frequently *(person) v.* wachapakuy
give offering *v.* arpay • *n.* **person who gives offering** arpaq
given *adj.* qosqa
giver *n.* qoq
glutton *n.* rakrapu, rakraq
gnaw *v.* khaskay
gnawed *adj.* khaskasqa
gnawer *n.* khaskaq
go *v.* riy
go back slowly *v.* kutiriy
go crazy *v.* waq'ayay

go down *v.* uray; **have the urge to go down** uranayay; **help go down** uraysiy
go down quickly *v.* urarpariy
go down with difficulty *v.* urapakuy
go in circles *v.* muyuy; **make go in circles** muyuchiy
go into *v.* ukhuchay
go the wrong way *v.* pantay • *n.* **person who goes the wrong way** pantaq
go to one side *v.* kinray
gobble *v.* oqoy; **make gobble** oqochiy
gobble again and again *v.* oqopayay
gobbled *adj.* oqosqa
godchild in baptism *n.* marq'asqa
godparent of baptized child *n.* marq'aq
gold *n.* qori
gold mine *n.* choqe
golden *adj.* p'aqo • *v.* **become golden** p'aqoyay
goldfinch *n.* ch'ayña
good *adj.* allin
goose *(Andean) n.* wallata
gore one another with horns *v.* waqranakuy
gore with horns waqray; **have the urge to gore with horns** waqranayay; **make gore with horns** waqrachiy
gored with horns *adj.* waqrasqa
gossip *v.* willapakuy
gossiper *n.* willapakuq
grab *v.* hap'iy, qechuy; **help grab** qechuysiy
grab constantly *v.* qechuykachay
grain *(Andean) n.* kinwa; **toasted grain** hank'a; **toaster of grains** hank'aq • *v.* **toast grains** hank'ay
grainy *adj.* chhanqa
grandchild *n.* haway
granery *n.* taqe
grass *n.* q'achu
grate *v.* thupay; **help grate** thupaysiy
grate again and again *v.* thupaykachay
grated *adj.* thupasqa
grave *n.* p'anpana
gravel: *v.* **cover a path with gravel** khallkachay; **remove gravel from path** khallkanay

gray *adj.* oqe, oqhe • *v.* **turn gray** oqheyay, oqeyay
gray hair *n.* soqo • *v.* **pull out gray hairs** soqonay
gray-haired *adj.* soqo • *v.* **become gray-haired** soqoyay
green *adj.* q'omer • *v.* **turn green** q'omerchay; **turn green again** q'omeryay
greet *v.* napaykuy
greet each other *v.* napaykunakuy
grind *v.* allpayachiy, hak'uchiy, kutay, ñut'uy; **help grind** kutaysiy
grind up with teeth *v.* k'utuy
grinder *n.* hak'uchiq
groin *n.* phaka
grope *v.* llankhuy
ground *adj.* *(crushed)* kutasqa, ñut'u • *n.* *(land)* allpa
group *n.* t'aqa; **attack on individual by group** waykilla • *v.* **take on as a group** waykay; **attack in a group** waykay
group by hundreds *v.* pachaqchay
group by tens *v.* chunkachay, chunkay
grow *v.* wiñay, hatunyay, *(tree)* yuray; **make grow** wiñachiy
grow old *v.* *(man)* machuyay, *(woman)* payayay; **make grow old** *(man)* machuyachiy, *(woman)* payayachiy
grow up *v.* *(boy)* waynayay, *(girl)* sipasyay
grown *adj.* wiñasqa
guess *v.* watuy
guessed *adj.* watusqa
guesser *n.* watuq
guffaw *v.* thintiy
guffaw again and again *v.* thintipayay
guide *v.* apay • *n.* pusaq
guide someone *v.* pusay; **make guide someone** pusachiy
guinea pig *n.* qowi, *(male)* kututu
gull *n.* qellwa
gulp *v.* melq'oy, millp'uy, oqoy, q'otoy, wap'uy; **have the urge to gulp** wap'unayay; **make gulp** millp'uchiy, oqochiy
gulp again and again *v.* millp'upayay, oqopayay
gulped *adj.* melq'osqa, millp'usqa, oqosqa, q'otosqa, wap'usqa
gums *n.* lluch'a
gush *v.* ch'uychuy

H

hail *n.* chikchi • *v.* chikchiy
hair *n.* *(head)* chukcha; **person with a lot of head hair** chukchasapa • *v.* **cut hair** *(head)* rutuy; **let one's hair be cut** *(head)* rutuchikuy; **make cut hair** *(head)* rutuchiy; **remove hair** *(body)* q'aray
hairy *(head) adj.* chukchasapa
half *n.* kuskan
half-chewed *adj.* hach'u hach'u
hammer *v.* ch'antiy
hand *n.* maki
hand over *v.* hayway
handful *n.* hapht'a
handle *n.* hap'ina
hang *v.* warkuy, *(something)* walqay; **hang a bridge** chakachay; **help hang** warkuysiy; **make hang** walqachiy, warkuchiy • *n.* **person who hangs something** warkuq; **that which hangs** warku
hanged *adj.* warkusqa
hanger *n.* warkuna
handkerchief *n.* piskita
happily *adv.* q'ocho q'ocho
happiness *n.* kusi
happy *adj.* kusisqa • *v.* **be happy** kusikuy
hard *adj.* ch'ila, chuchu, anaq
harden *v.* chuchuyay
hardly *adv.* ñak'ay
hardship *n.* ñak'a
harm *v.* chirmay • *n.* **person/thing that causes harm** chirmaq
harmed *adj.* chirmasqa
harvest *v.* aymuray • *n.* **first potato harvest** maway; **first corn harvest** miskha
harvest corn *v.* kallchay • *n.* **corn harvest** kallchay; **first corn harvest** miskha
harvest from above ground *v.* pallay; **help harvest from above ground** pallaysiy; **order to harvest from above ground** pallachiy
harvest from the ground *v.* allay; **help harvest from the ground** allaysiy; **make harvest from the ground** allachiy

harvest from the ground again and again *v.* allapayay
harvest season *n.* aymura
harvested from above ground *adj.* pallasqa
harvested from the ground *adj.* allasqa
harvester *(from the ground) n.* allaq
hat *n.* chuku; *(Andean)* ch'ullu • *v.* **put on hat** chukuchakuy
hate *v.* cheqniy
hate one another *v.* cheqninakuy
hated *adj.* cheqnisqa
haunch *n.* chakan
have *v.* kay
hawk *(Andean) n.* k'illichu
hay *n.* ichhu • *v.* **reap hay** ichhuy
he *pron.* pay
head *n.* uma
head cold *n.* chhulli
headboard *n.* sawna
heal *v.* allinyay, alliyay; **make heal** alliyachiy
healer *n.* hanpiq, qhaliyachiq
healthy *adj.* qhali • *v.* **become healthy little by little** qhaliyay; **make healthy** qhaliyachiy
hear *v.* uyariy; **make another hear** uyarichikuy; **make hear** uyarichiy • *n.* **person who hears** uyariq
hear one another *v.* uyarinakuy
heart *n.* sonqo
heat *v.* q'oñiy
heat from sun *n.* ruphay
heat in sun *v.* q'ochachiy, ruphayay
heat up *v.* q'oñichiy
heated in sun *adj.* q'ochasqa
heavy *adj.* llasa; **very heavy** llasallaña • *v.* **make heavier** llasayachiy
heel *n.* takillpa
help *v.* haymay, yanapay; **make help** yanapachiy
help one another *v.* yanapanakuy • *n.* **system of mutual help** mink'a
helper *n.* yanapaq
hen *n.* wallpa
herbs: *n.* **dried herbs** qacha • *v.* **dry herbs in sun** qachay
herd *v.* michiy, qatiy; **help herd** michiysiy
herd another's flock *v.* michipakuy
here *adv.* kaypi; **near here** kayneqpi; **over here** kayninta; **towards here** kayman

hey! *inter.* yaw
hiccup *n.* hik'i • *v.* hik'iy
hidden *adj.* pakasqa
hide *v.* pakay; **help hide** pakaysiy; **make hide** pakachiy
hide oneself *v.* pakakuy
hide something between one's legs *v.* phakallikuy
hiding place *n.* pakakuna
hill *n.* moqo; **triangular hill** pikchu
hip *n.* teqni
hit *v.* takay; **help hit** takaysiy
hit one another with stick *v.* p'ananakuy, q'asunakuy
hit repeatedly *v.* takapayay
hit with slingshot *v.* warak'ay
hit with stick *v.* p'anay, q'asuy; **command to hit with stick** p'anachiy, q'asuchiy; **help hit with stick** p'anaysiy, q'asuysiy • *n.* **stick for hitting** p'anana, q'asuna
hive *n.* lachiwana
hoarse *adj.* ch'aka • *v.* **become hoarse** ch'akayay; **become hoarse for life** ch'akayapuy; **cause hoarseness** ch'akayachiy
hold something for a while *v.* hap'irayay
hole *n.* t'oqo; **deep hole** sankha • *adj.* **full of holes** t'oqosqa
hollow space *n.* p'ukru
home *n.* wasi
honey *n.* lachiwa
honor *v.* apuchay, sumaychay
honored *adj.* apuchasqa, sumaychasqa
hoof *n.* phapallu
hook *n.* warkuna
horizontal *adj.* hank'arpa
horn *(of animal) n.* waqra • *adj.* **gored with horns** waqrasqa • *v.* **cut off horns** waqranay; **gore one another with horns** waqranakuy; **gore with horns** waqray
horsefly *n.* tankayllu
host *v.* qorpachay • *n.* qorpachaq, chaskiq
hot *adj.* q'oñi, rupha
hot sauce *n.* uchukuta
house *n.* wasi • *v.* **build a house** wasichay; **spend time with someone in their house** tiyapayay
how many? *inter.* hayk'a
how much? *inter.* hayk'a

how nice! *interj.* kusa
huff and puff *v.* phukupakuy
hug *v.* mak'alliy
hug one another *v.* mak'allinakuy
humbly *adv.* ullpu ullpu
humid *adj.* api
humiliate *v.* alqochay, saruchay; **let oneself be humiliated** saruchikuy
humiliated *adj.* saruchasqa
hummingbird *n.* q'ente
hung *adj.* warkusqa
hunger *n.* yarqay
hungry *adj.* yarqasqa • *v.* **be hungry** yarqay
hurt *v.* nanay
hurt constantly *v.* nanapayay
husband *n.* qosa • *adj.* **with husband** qosayoq
hut *n.* ch'uklla; **builder of huts** ch'ukllaq • *v.* **build a hut** ch'ukllay; **order to build a hut** ch'ukllachiy

I

I *pron.* ñoqa
identical *adj.* kikin
idiot *n.* *opa* • *v.* **become an idiot** opayay
if *conj.* sichus
illness *n.* onqoy, machusqa
illuminate *v.* k'anchay, phallay
illusion *n.* llachi
imitate a monkey *v.* k'usillukuy
imitate in jest *v.* yachapayay
immediately *adv.* kunachallan, kunanpacha
impoverish *v.* q'alayay
impoverished *adj.* q'alayasqa
impregnate *v.* wiksayachiy
improve *v.* allinchay
in that way *adv.* chhayna
in the morning *adv.* tutamanta
in vain *adv.* yanqa
inclined *adj.* k'achanpa, phallu
increase *n.* yapa • *v.* askhayachiy, yapay; **make increase** yapachiy
incubate *v.* oqllay
indicate *v.* unanchay
individual *n.* runa
indolent *adj.* k'ullu • *v.* **become indolent** k'ulluyapuy
inebriate *v.* machay
inebriated *adj.* machasqa
inept *adj.* uti, wankhi
infertile *adj.* urwa
infested *(grains) adj.* hut'u • *v.* **become infested** hut'uyay
infested with nits *adj.* ch'iyasapa
inhabit *v.* tiyay
injure *v.* k'iriy
Inkan princess *n.* ñust'a
inn *n.* tanpu
inquire *v.* tapuy
inside *prep.* ukhu

insinuate *v.* siminchay
insinuated *adj.* siminchasqa
instructor *n.* yachachiq
insult *v.* k'amiy • *n.* k'ami; **person who insults** k'amiq
insult one another *v.* k'aminakuy, lapht'anakuy
insult repeatedly *v.* k'amipayay
intellect *n.* hamut'a, yuyay
intellectual *n.* hamut'aq
intelligent *adj.* ch'iti, yuyayniyoq; **very intelligent** yuyaysapa
intentionally *adv.* yuyaypi
intercept *v.* hark'ay; **help intercept** hark'aysiy
interior *adj.* ukhu
intermingle *v.* mich'uy; **make intermingle** mich'uchiy
intermingled *adj.* mich'usqa
interrupt *v.* tatichiy
intervene *v.* chawpinakuy, chawpinchakuy
intestine *n.* ch'unchul
introduce oneself *v.* reqsichikuy
investigate *v.* tapukachay
invoke *v.* waqyarikuy
irrigate *v.* qarpay; **help irrigate** qarpaysiy
irrigate constantly *v.* qarpapayay
irrigated *adj.* qarpasqa
irritable *adj.* phiña
irritation *n.* k'aray
island *n.* wat'a

J

jaguar *n.* uturunku
jaw *n.* k'aki, waqo
jaw bone *n.* qhaqllin
jerky *n.* ch'arki; **person who makes jerky** ch'arkichiq • *v.* **make jerky** ch'arkichiy
join *v.* t'inkiy; **help join** t'inkiysiy
joined *adj.* t'inkisqa
jointly *adv.* kuskalla
joke *n.* laq'o, *v.* laq'oy
jug *n.* p'uyñu; **large ceramic jug** mak'as
juice: *n.* **unfermented juice** upi
jump *v.* p'itay
jump down *v.* p'itayuy
jumper *n.* p'itaq
jungle *n.* yunka
jungle inhabitant *n.* ch'unchu
just one *adj.* ch'ullalla

K

keep moving closer *v.* achhupayay
keep vigil over someone sleeping *v.* puñuysiy
kick *n.* hayt'a • *v.* hayt'ay; **help kick** hayt'aysiy; **make kick** hayt'achiy
kick and stomp *v.* hayt'aykachay
kick one another *v.* hayt'anakuy
kick out *v.* qarqoy; **help kick out** qarqoysiy; **make kick out** qarqochiy
kick someone out *v.* hat'ay
kicked out *adj.* qarqosqa
kid *n.* erqe
kill *v.* wañuchiy
kill one another *v.* wañuchinakuy
kill oneself *v.* wañuchikuy
killed *adj.* wañuchisqa
killer *n.* wañuchiq
kiss *v.* much'ay; **let oneself be kissed** much'achikuy
kiss all over *v.* much'apayay • *n.* **person who kisses all over** much'apayaq
kiss indiscriminately *v.* much'aykachay
kiss one another *v.* much'anakuy
kissed *adj.* much'asqa
kisser *n.* much'aq; **person who kisses all over** much'apayaq
knee *n.* moqo, qonqor
kneel *v.* qonqorikuy
knife *n.* kuchuna, *(ritual)* tumi; **blunt knife** morq'a
knife for slaughter *n.* nak'ana
knock down *v.* kunpay, wikapay; **make knock down** wikapachiy
knock down with or without intention *v.* kunparpariy
knocked down *adj.* kunpasqa, wikapasqa
knot *n.* khipu • *v.* khipuy; **help knot** khipuysiy; **make knot** khipuchiy
knot constantly *v.* khipupayay
knotted *adj.* khipusqa
know *v.* reqsiy, yachay; **have the urge to know** reqsinayay; **make know** reqsichiy

know it all *n.* yachaysapa
knower *n.* yachaq
knowledge *n.* yachay
knowledgeable person *n.* yachaq
known *adj.* reqsisqa, yachasqa

L

lack *v.* pisiy
ladle *n.* wisina • *v.* wisiy; **help ladle** wisiysiy
lagoon *n.* qocha
lake *n.* qocha
lamb *n.* chita
laminate *v.* last'ay
landowner *n.* chakrayoq, allpayoq
languid *adj.* unphu • *v.* **become languid** unphuyay
lap *(around) n.* tuma
lap up *v.* lapht'ay
large-hipped *adj.* teqnisapa
last night *adv.* ch'isi
laugh *v.* asikuy, asiy; **make laugh** asichiy; **make one another laugh** asichinakuy
laugh at pain of others *v.* asipayay
laugh continuously *v.* asiykachay
laugh loudly *v.* thintiy
laugh loudly again and again *v.* thintipayay
laughable *adj.* asina
laugher *n.* asiq
launch roughly *v.* choqay
launch through the air *v.* wikapay
launched roughly *adj.* choqasqa
lazy *adj.* qella
lead *n. (metal)* titi • *v. (show the way)* umalliy
leader *n.* umalli
leaf *n.* raphi; **dried leaves** q'opa; **fallen leaves** ch'aphra • *v.* **cover oneself with fallen leaves** ch'aphrachakuy
lean *v.* t'iksuy
lean back on *v.* k'iray
lean over *v.* t'iksuykachay
lean to one side *v.* kinray
leaning *adj.* k'achanpa • *v.* **be leaning** k'achanpakuy
leaning to one side *adj.* kinranpa • *adv.* kinranpamanta
leaning to the side *adj.* chinru

learn *v.* yachay; **have the urge to learn** yachanayay
leather *n.* qara
leave *v.* ch'usay, lloqsiy; **make leave** lloqsichiy
leave again and again *v.* lloqsipayay
leave behind *v.* saqey
leave in someone's care *v.* saqekuy
left *(opposite of right) adj.* lloq'e
left behind: *v.* **be left behind** saqechikuy
left over: *v.* **be left over** puchuy
left-handed *adj.* lloq'e, lloq'enchu • *v.* **become left-handed** lloq'eyay
leftover *n.* puchu • *adj.* wakin • *v.* **collect leftovers** wakinchay
leg *n.* chaka
lend *v.* mañay
lend money *v.* manuy
lent *adj.* mañasqa
let escape *v.* phawachiy
let fall *v.* kachariy
let in *v.* haykuchiy
let loose *v.* paskay
let something be removed/taken from you *v.* horqochikuy; **let oneself be stripped of belongings** chaskichikuy • *n.* **person who lets their belongings be taken** chaskichikuq
let's go! *interj.* haku, hakuchis
lethal *adj.* soq'a
level out *v.* panpachay
lever *v.* wanqhay
liar *adj.* llulla
lick *v.* llaqway, llunk'uy; **let oneself be licked** llaqwachikuy
lick all over *v.* lawq'ay
lick one another *v.* llaqwanakuy
lick one's lips *v.* llaqwakuy
lick one's lips again and again *v.* llaqwapakuy
lick repeatedly *v.* llaqwapayay
licked *adj.* llaqwasqa
licker *n.* llaqwaq
lie *(deceive) n.* llulla • *v.* llullakuy
lie down *v.* chutarayay
life *n.* kawsay
life partner *n.* kawsaqmasi

light *n.* k'ancha
light a fire *v.* ninachay
lighten in weight *v.* chhallayay
lightning *n.* illapa
lightweight *adj.* chhaplla, llaphlla, llaphsa • *v.* **become lightweight** llaphllayay, llaphsayay
like *adv.* hina
like that *adv.* chayhina, chhayna
like this *adv.* akna, kayhina, khayna
lilac *adj.* panti
lily *(white)* *n.* hamanq'ay
limp *adj.* ch'alqe
line up *v.* sinriy
lion: *n.* **mountain lion** osqollo
lip *n.* *(lower)* werp'a; **thick lips** ch'utu
listen *v.* uyariy; **make another listen** uyarichikuy; **make listen** uyarichiy
listen to one another *v.* uyarinakuy
listener *n.* uyariq
litter *(for carrying)* *n.* wantu
little *adj.* huch'uy; **a little** pisi • *adv.* asta
little by little *adv.* allillamanta, asllallamanta, pisi pisimanta
little person *(male)* *n.* ch'ukchu, umutu
live in another's house temporarily *v.* tiyapakuy
liver *n.* kukupin
lizard *n.* qaraywa
llama *n.* llama
llama owner *n.* llamayoq
lodge *v.* qorpachakuy
lodging *n.* tanpu
log *n.* k'aspi, k'ullu
logger *n.* wit'uq
long *adj.* suni
long time *n.* unay • *adv.* **after a long time** unaymanta
look *v.* qhaway
look at one another *v.* qhawanakuy
look at oneself frequently *v.* qhawapayakuy
look cross-eyed *v.* wesq'oykachay
look frequently *v.* qhawapayay
look indefinitely *v.* qhawarayay

look like someone *v.* rikch'akuy
lookout point *n.* qhawana
loom *n.* allwina
loose *adj.* ch'olqe, waya • *v.* **become loose** ch'olqeyay; **let loose** paskay
loose thread *n.* chhapu
lose *v.* chinkachiy
lose track of time *v.* intiyay
lose weight *v.* chhallayay, choqchiyay, tulluyay
lost *adj.* chinkasqa • *v.* **get lost** chinkakuy, chinkay
louse *n.* usa
lousy *n.* usasapa
love *v.* munakuy
love deeply *v.* waylluy
love one another *v.* munanakuy
love one another deeply *v.* wayllunakuy
lover *n.* waylluq
lukewarm *n.* wamantullu
luminescent *adj.* k'anchay k'anchay
lung *n.* sorq'an

M

made *adj.* ruwasqa
make *v.* ruway; **command to make** ruwachiy; **help make** ruwaysiy
make a mistake *v.* witiy
male *n.* orqo, qhari
malnourished *adj.* eqosqa
man *n.* qhari; **old man** machu, *(affectionate)* machula; **small man** k'ichi, tanka • *v.* **become a man** qhariyay
man with many sons *n.* churisapa
manly woman *n.* qharincha
manure *n.* isma, q'awa, uchha, wanu • *v.* **collect manure** q'away; **fertilize with manure** wanuchay; **help collect manure** q'awaysiy; **refertilize with manure** wanupay • *adj.* **fertilized with manure** wanuchasqa
many *adj.* ancha, askha, sinchi, yupa • *inter.* **how many?** hayk'a
mark *v.* irpay, tuyruy, unanchay
marked *adj.* unanchasqa, irpasqa, tuyrusqa
market *n.* qhatu
married *(woman) adj.* qosayoq
marrow *n.* toqton
marsh plant *n.* totora
mask *n.* pukuchu, saynata
mate among birds *v.* chiway
maybe *adv.* chaychá, paqta
maybe not *adv.* manapaschá
maybe so *adv.* yaqapaschá
measure *v.* tupuy; **make measure** tupuchiy
measurer *n.* tupuq
meat *n.* aycha; **roasted meat** kanka • *v.* **roast meat** kankay
meddle *v.* sat'ipakuy
mediator *n.* allipunachiq
medicinal tree *n.* tara
medicine *n.* hanpi
medium *adj.* malta
medium small *adj.* taksa
meet *v.* tupay • *n.* **person who meets** tupaq

memorable *adj.* yuyaychana
memory *n.* yuyay • *adj.* **with good memory** yuyaysapa
menstruate *v.* k'ikuy
menstruation *n.* k'ikuy
mermaid *n.* challwawanka
mess up *v.* rawiy
messy *adj.* rawi
meteorite *n.* aqochinchay
middle *n.* chawpi; **person who puts in middle** chawpichaq • *v.* **put in middle** chawpichay, chawpinay
milk *n.* ñukñu; **person who milks** ch'awaq • *v.* ch'away, ñukñuy; **help milk** ch'awaysiy
milked *adj.* ch'awasqa
mischief: *v.* **make mischief** saqraykachay
mischievous *adj.* saqra • *v.* **become mischievous** saqrayay
misfortune *n.* aqoyraki
misplace *v.* chinkachiy
mistake: *v.* **cause to make a mistake** pantachiy, witichiy; **make a mistake** witiy
mistaken *adj.* pantasqa, witisqa
mistakenly *adv.* pantaylla
mite *n.* itha
mix *v.* chaqruy, minuy, taqruy; **help mix** minuysiy, taqruysiy
mix again *v.* minupayay
mix again and again *v.* taqruykachay
mix together *v.* taqrunakuy
mix with water *v.* unuchay
mixed *adj.* chaqrusqa, minusqa, taqrusqa
mixed with water *adj.* unuchasqa
mixer *n.* taqruq
moan *v.* waqapakuy
mock in jest *v.* yachapayay
mocker *n.* yachaphuku, yachapayaq
money *n.* qolqe
moneylender *n.* manuq
moneylending *adj.* manuq
monkey *n.* k'usillu • *v.* **imitate a monkey** k'usillukuy
month *n.* killa
moon *n.* killa
more *adj.* aswan • *adv.* **even more** aswanta

morning: *adv.* **in the morning** tutamanta
mortal *n.* wañuq
mortar *n.* maran
mortar and pestle *n.* kutana
mosquito *n.* uta, wanwa; **sickness transmitted by mosquitos** utha
moth *n.* thuta • *v.* **get eaten by moths** thutay
moth-eaten *adj.* thutasqa
mother *n.* mama
mother earth *n.* mamapacha
mount *v.* phakachakuy; **make mount** phakallichiy • *n.* **person who mounts** phakallikuq
mount oneself on something *v.* phakallikuy
mountain *n.* orqo
mountain lion *n.* osqollo
mountain pass *n.* q'asa
mountainside *n.* qhata
mountaintop *n.* pikchu
mourn *v.* yanallikuy
mourned *adj.* yanallisqa
mourner *n.* yanallikuq
mouse *n.* huk'ucha
mouth *n.* simi
move: *v.* **keep moving closer** achhupayay; **make move** achhuchiy, kuyuchiy
move away *v.* karunchay
move oneself *v.* kuyuy
move over *v.* kuyuriy
mover *n.* astaq
much: *adv.* **how much?** hayk'a • *adj.* **too much** ñisu
mucus *n.* qhoña; **dried mucus** k'iski
mud *n.* t'uru • *v.* **build with mud** llut'ay; **help build with mud** llut'aysiy; **make build with mud** llut'achiy; **prepare mud** t'uruchay; **remove mud** t'urunay
muddy *adj.* t'uruchasqa
mummify *v.* ch'alqey
murder *v.* sipiy; **command to murder** sipichiy; **help murder** sipiysiy
murdered *adj.* sipisqa
murderer *n.* sipiq
murky *adj.* q'ata • *v.* **become murky** q'atachakuy; **become murky little by little** q'atayay; **make murky** q'atachay

murmur *v.* thutuy
mushroom *n.* k'allanpa
mute *adj.* amu, upa • *n.* upa • *v.* **become mute** amuyay, upayay
mutilate *v.* qhoruy, willuy, *(foot)* chakinnay; **command to mutilate** qhoruchiy; **help mutilate** willuysiy; **make mutilate** willuchiy
mutilated *adj.* qhorusqa, willusqa
mutter *v.* thutuy

N

nail *v.* sat'iy, takay; **help nail** takaysiy
nail repeatedly *v.* takapayay
nailed *adj.* sat'isqa
naive *adj.* opa
naked *adj.* q'ala, q'alalla, q'ara • *v.* **end up naked** q'alayay
name *n.* suti • *v.* sutichay
nape *n.* much'u
narrator *n.* willaq
narrow *adj.* k'ikllu, k'iski; **very narrow** p'iti
nasal *adj.* k'aku
navigate *v.* wanp'uy; **make navigate** wanp'uchiy
near *adj.* sispa
near here *adv.* kayneqpi
near there *adv.* chayneqpi
neck *n.* kunka
necklace *n.* walqay
needle *n. (large)* yawri; **sewing needle** sirana
neighbor *n.* wasimasi
nephew *n.* mulla
nerve *n. (anatomical)* hank'u • *v.* **get the nerve** qharichakuy
nest *n.* q'esa • *v.* **build a nest** q'esachakuy
nettle *n.* kisa
new *(thing) adj.* mosoq; **very new** mosoqllaña
nibble *v.* hanch'uy, khachuy
nibbled *adj.* khachusqa
nice *adj.* sumaq, munay • *interj.* **how nice!** kusa
nickname *v.* sutiyay
night *n.* tuta, ch'isi; **last night** ch'isi • *adv.* **all night** tutantin • *v.* **become night** ch'isinyay, rasphiyay, tutayay
nightingale *n.* ch'eqollo
nightmare *n.* llap'i
nine *num.* isqon
nipple *n.* ñuñu
nit *n.* ch'iya • *adj.* **infested with nits** ch'iyasapa
nit remover *n.* ch'iyaq

no *adv.* mana • *interj.* manakaw
no way *adv.* amapuni, manapuni
nocturnal butterfly *n.* taparaku
nose *n.* senqa
nosy *adj.* chakchaku
not *adv.* mana
not anymore *adv.* amaña
not yet *adv.* amaraq, manaraq
notice *n.* willakuy
now *adv.* kunan; **right now** kunanpacha
number *v.* yupay; **help number** yupaysiy; **make number** yupachiy
numbered *adj.* yupasqa
nurse *(breastfeed) v.* ñuñuy, tutuy
nurse from another mother *v.* ñuñupakuy
nursery *(for plants) n.* wanpal
nursing baby *n.* ñuñuq

O

obedient *adj.* kasukuq
obey *v.* kasuy
object *v.* kutipakuy
object for bracing *n.* q'emina
observe *v.* qhaway
observe frequently *v.* qhawapayay
observe indefinitely *v.* qhawarayay
observe one another *v.* qhawanakuy
observe oneself frequently *v.* qhawapayakuy
observer *n.* qhawaq
obstruct *v.* hark'apayay
obstruction *n.* hark'ana
obverse *n.* uyanpa
occupier *n.* mitma
occupy a territory *v.* llaqtachakuy, mitmay
occupy another's place *v.* q'esachakuy
ocean *n.* mamaqocha
of course *adv.* riki
offend one another *v.* millp'unakuy
offer *v.* haywarikuy
offering: *n.* **person who gives offering** arpaq; **place of offering** arpana • *v.* **give offering** arpay
offspring: *n.* **young offspring** uña
oh no! *interj.* achachaw
old *adj.* *(person)* ñawpa, *(thing)* mawk'a; **very old** *(man)* machullaña, *(woman)* payallaña
old man *n.* machu, *(affectionate)* machula
old woman *n.* paya, *(affectionate)* mamaku
older *adj.* kuraq
on foot *adj.* sayanpa • *adv.* sayanpamanta • *v.* **be on foot** sayay
on top *adv.* pata, wichay • *prep.* hanaq
one *num.* huk • *v.* **become one** ch'ullayay • *adv.* **just one** ch'ullalla; **only one** huklla
one behind another *adv.* qati qati
one hundred *num.* pachaq

one-armed *adj.* willu
one-eyed *adj.* churchu • *v.* **become one-eyed** churchuyay
only *adj.* sapa
only one *adv.* huklla
ooze *v.* llilliy
open *adj.* kichasqa • *v.* kichay; **make an opening** wanphuy
open and close one's mouth repeatedly *v.* hanllaykachay
open one's mouth *v.* hanllay
open slowly *v.* kichariy
open suddenly *v.* kichariy
opossum *n.* unkaka
or *conj.* icha, otaq
orchard *n.* muya
order someone to do something *v.* kachay
orphan *n.* wakcha, willullu • *v.* **become orphaned** wakchayay
other *adj.* hoq
ouch! *interj.* achakaw
outside *prep.* hawa
oval *adj.* suyt'u
over here *adv.* kayninta
over there *adv.* chayninta
overcome an obstacle *v.* wasapay
overflow *v.* lleqmay, yalliy
overflowing *adj.* lleqmasqa
overload *v.* llasay, paltay
overloaded *adj.* paltasqa
owl *n.* ch'oseq, tuku
owner *n.* kaqniyoq

P

package *n.* suchi
pain *n.* nanay • *v.* **cause pain** nanachiy
painfully *adv.* ñak'ayllaña
palpable *adv.* llaminalla
pamper *v.* erqechay, luluy, wawachay
pampered *adj.* wawachasqa
pan *n.* manka
pan flute *n.* antara
pancreas *n.* k'ayrapin
pants *n.* wara
parasol *n.* llanthuna
parcel of land *n.* ch'eqta
parrot *(small) n.* k'alla
parrot squawk *n.* k'allallallay
particular *adj.* sapaq
partner *n.* yana • *v.* yanachay
partner with a woman *v.* warmichakuy
partridge *n.* lluthu, p'isaqa
party *(massive) n.* raymi
pass away *(person) v.* wañupuy
paste *v.* k'askay • *n.* **person who pastes** k'askachiq
pasted *adj.* k'askasqa
pasture *n.* michina, waylla
pat *v.* t'aqllay
pat on the back *n.* k'unu • *v.* k'unuy
pat repeatedly *v.* t'aqllapayay
path *n.* ñan
patriarch *n.* tayta, yaya
paw *n.* chaki
peanut *n.* inchis
pebbly *adj.* khallka
peel off with teeth *(husk) v.* sinkhay
peeled off with teeth *(husk) adj.* sinkhasqa
peer *n.* wiñaqmasi
penis *n.* ullu

pepper *n.* uchu
perfume *v.* q'apachiy
perfume oneself *v.* q'apachikuy
perfumed *adj.* q'apachisqa
perhaps *adv.* chaychá, icha, paqta
persist *v.* atipakuy, kutipakuy
persistent *adj.* atipakuq
person *n.* runa
person in rags *n.* saphsa
pester *v.* achhupayay
pestle *n.* mutk'a
phantom *n.* kukuchi
phlegm *n.* qhoto
pick *v.* pallay; **help pick** pallaysiy; **order to pick produce** pallachiy
pick a fruit *v.* khakuy
pick an herb *v.* qoray
pick up *v.* hoqariy; **help pick up** hoqariysiy • *adj.* **easy to pick up** hoqarinalla
pick up by handfuls *v.* hapht'ay; **help pick up by handfuls** hapht'aysiy
pick up by handfuls constantly *v.* hapht'aykachay
picked *adj.* pallasqa
piece *n.* k'iphta
pig *n.* khuchi
pile *v.* pirway; **help pile** pirwaysiy
piled *adj.* pirwasqa
pillow *n.* sawna • *v.* **put head on pillow** sawnakuy
pimple *n.* khiki
pimply *adj.* khikisapa
pin *n.* t'urpuna
pinch *v.* llipch'iy, t'ipiy; **let oneself be pinched** t'ipichikuy
pinch constantly *v.* t'ipipayay
pinch one another *v.* t'ipinakuy
pit *n.* p'ukru
pit people against each other *v.* awqanachiy
pitcher *n.* chatu, p'uyñu
pity *v.* khuyapayay • *n.* llaki; **person who pities** khuyapayaq • *interj.* **what a pity!** akakallaw, kakallaw
place *v.* churay

place to put things momentarily *n.* churana
placed *adj.* churasqa
plain *n.* panpa
plane *(wood) v.* llaqllay; **help plane** llaqllaysiy; **make plane** llaqllachiy
planed *(wood) adj.* llaqllasqa
planing tool *(wood) n.* llaqllana
plant *n.* qora • *v.* **pick a plant** qoray
plant seeds *v.* tarpuy; **help plant seeds** tarpuysiy; **make plant seeds** tarpuchiy
planted *adj.* tarpusqa
plaster *n.* pachas • *v.* laq'ay; **help plaster** laq'aysiy
plastered *adj.* laq'asqa
plate *n.* p'uku
platform: *n.* **wooden platform** kawitu
play *v.* pukllay; **have the desire to play** pukllanayay; **make play** pukllachiy
play constantly *v.* pukllapayay
player *n.* pukllaq
playful *adj.* pukllaq
playground *n.* pukllana
plow *n. (Andean)* taklla; **person who plows** yapuq • *v.* chaqmay, kuskiy, yapuy; **help plow** chaqmaysiy, yapuysiy; **make plow** chaqmachiy, yapuchiy
plowed *adj.* yapusqa
pluck *v.* phurunay • *n.* **person who plucks** phurunaq
plug up *v.* chakarayay
plume *n.* k'akara
poem *n.* harawi, haylli
point out with finger *v.* t'oqsiy
pointed object *n.* sat'ina
poison *v.* miyuy; **command to poison** miyuchiy
poisoned *adj.* miyusqa
pollen *n.* sisa
pool *v.* p'onqochakuy
poor *adj.* wakcha • *v.* **become poor** wakchayay; **make poor** wakchayachiy
pop *v.* phatay; **make pop** phatachiy
poppable *adj.* phataq
popped *(corn or wheat) adj.* phatasqa

position oneself *v.* churakuy
position something sideways *v.* k'achanpachiy
post: *n.* **wooden post** *(medium)* tanka
postpone *v.* qhepanchay
pot *n.* manka; **big pot** urpu; **small pot** ch'amillku • *v.* **place pot on stove** churpuy
pot for toasting *(Andean varieties) n.* hank'ana, k'analla
potato *n.* papa; **dehydrated potato** ch'uñu, tunta; **first potato harvest** maway; **white dehydrated potato** moraya • *v.* **cook potatoes in the ground** wathiyay
potbellied *adj.* phaksa
potbelly *n.* phaksa
pottery *n.* k'akra
pound *v.* saqtay; **help pound** saqtaysiy; **make pound** saqtachiy
pounded *adj.* saqtasqa
pounding tool *n.* saqtana
powerful *adj.* qhapaq
precede *v.* ñawpariy
precious stone *n.* umiña
precise *adj.* k'apak
predict *v.* umulliy
pregnant *adj.* onqoq, wiksayoq • *v.* **be pregnant** onqokuy; **become pregnant** wiksayay
prematurely *adv.* urilla
presumptuous *adj.* qhaphchiykachaq
pretend *v.* munapayay • *n.* **person who pretends to know** yachaykachaq
previous *adj.* ñawpaq
previously *adv.* ñawpaqta
prick *v.* ch'antiy, sat'iy, t'urpuy
prick with thorn *v.* qepuchiy
pricked *adj.* sat'isqa
prickly *adj.* kiskasapa
procreate *v.* churiyay, wawachay
produce: *v.* **order to pick produce** pallachiy
progenitor *n.* churiyaq
prolonged *adv.* unay unay
propel *v.* tanqay
proprietor *n.* kaqniyoq
puddle *n.* p'onqo

pull *v.* aysay, chutay; **help pull** aysaysiy, chutaysiy; **make pull** chutachiy • *n.* **person who pulls** chutaq
pull forcefully *v.* chutapakuy
pulse *v.* phatatatay
pumpkin *n.* lakawiti
punch *v.* saqmay; **let oneself be punched** saqmachikuy; **make punch** saqmachiy
punch constantly *v.* saqmapayay
punch one another *v.* saqmanakuy
punch repeatedly *v.* saqmaykachay
punched *adj.* saqmasqa
puncture *v.* wanphuy; **help puncture** wanphuysiy
punctured *adj.* wanphusqa
punish *v.* wanay; **make punish** wanachiy
punishment *n.* wana
pupil *n.* ñawi ruru
puppy *n.* t'ini
pure *adj.* llunp'a
purify *v.* ch'uyayachiy
purity *n.* llunp'a
purple *adj.* kulli, sani • *v.* **turn purple** saniyay
pursue *v.* qatikachay
pursue continuously *v.* qatipayay
push *v.* tanqay
push one another *v.* tanqanakuy
puss *n.* q'ea • *v.* **remove puss** q'eanay
put *adj.* churasqa • *v.* churay • *n.* **place to put things momentarily** churana
put away *v.* haykuchiy, waqaychay; **help put away** waqaychaysiy; **make put away** waqaychachiy
put down *v.* saruchay • **get put down** *v.* saruchikuy
put down roots *v.* takyay
put on *v.* churakuy
put on hat *v.* chukuchakuy
put out fire with water *v.* thasnuy; **help put out fire with water** thasnuysiy; **make put out fire with water** thasnuchiy
put something sideways *v.* k'achanpay
put together *v.* tantay, tupachiy

Q

quarrel *v.* anyanakuy
queen *n.* qoya
question *n.* tapuna • *v.* tapuy; **make question** tapuchiy
questioner *n.* tapupakuq
quick *adj.* usqhay
quickly *adv.* phawaylla, usqhay, usqhaylla, usqhayta
quiet: *v.* **make be quiet** upallachiy
quinoa *n.* kinwa
quinoa leaf *n.* lliphch'a

R

radiance *n.* ch'ak
radiant *adj.* ch'ak, illaq • *v.* **become radiant** ch'askayay
ragged *adj.* chhachu, saphsa • *v.* **become ragged** saphsachay
rain *n.* para • *v.* paray; **be about to rain** paranayay; **cause rain** parachiy; **stop raining** usariy
rain constantly *v.* paraykachay
rain heavily *v.* ch'allchay
rainbow *n.* k'uychi
rainy *adj.* paraq
raise *v.* hoqariy, uyway; **help raise** hoqariysiy • *adj.* **easy to raise** hoqarinalla
raise a beam *v.* chakapay
raise a wall *v.* perqay
raised *adj.* uywasqa
rake *n.* allachu, allana
rancid *adj.* maq'a • *v.* **become rancid** maq'ayay
rapidly *adv.* q'osti
rashly *adv.* tanqa tanqa
rather *adv.* aswan
ration *n.* achura • *v.* achuray; **take one's ration** achurakuy
rationer *n.* achuraq
raw *adj.* hanku
reach *v.* aypay; **help reach** aypaysiy
reach with hands repeatedly *v.* haywapayay; **try to reach with hands** haywapakuy
ready oneself to travel *v.* q'epichakuy
reap *v.* rutuy; **help reap** rutuysiy; **make reap** rutuchiy
reap hay *v.* ichhuy
rebel *n.* ankalli
rebellious *adj.* ankalli
receive *v.* chaskiy • *n.* **person who receives for oneself** chaskikuq
received *adj.* chaskisqa
recently *adv.* chayraq, kunanllaraq
recipient *n.* chaskiq
reciprocity in work *n.* ayni

recline *v.* k'iray; **make recline** k'irachiy
reclined *adj.* k'irasqa
recognize *v.* reqsikuy
reconcile: *v.* **make two people reconcile** allipunachiy; **reconcile mutually** allipunakuy • *n.* **person who makes others reconcile** allipunachiq
recover *(health) v.* runayay
recover and take one's belongings *v.* apakapuy
red *adj.* puka
redden *v.* pukayay
reduce *v.* chikachay, huch'uyyachiy, pisichay, taksayachiy
reduced to dust *adj.* allpayasqa
reed *n.* soqos
refertilize with manure *v.* wanupay
reflect *v.* lirpuy
refreshment *n.* ch'akipa
region *n.* suyu
regurgitate *v.* kutirpay
reject *v.* mananchay
rejuvenate *v. (man)* waynayay, *(woman)* sipasyay
relocate *v.* astakuy • *n.* **person who relocates** astakuq
remain *v.* qhepay; **collect what remains** pallapay • *n.* **collector of remains** pallapakuq
remain standing *v.* sayarayay
remedy *n.* hanpi
remember *v.* yuyay; **make remember** yuyachiy • *n.* **person who remembers** yuyaq
remember suddenly *v.* yuyariy
remembered *adj.* yuyasqa
remove *v.* horqoy, k'isuy
remove bristles *v.* suphunay
remove flesh *v.* aycharay
remove from water *v.* llaphch'ay
remove from water again and again *v.* llaphch'apayay
remove gravel from path *v.* khallkanay
remove hair *v.* q'aray
remove mud *v.* t'urunay
remove puss *v.* q'eanay
remove soil *v.* allpanay
remove splinters from wood *v.* chhillpanay

removed *adj.* horqosqa • *v.* **let something be removed from you** horqochikuy
renovate *v.* mosoqchay
renovator *n.* mosoqchaq
repair *v.* allichay
repaired *adj.* allichasqa
repairperson *n.* allichaq
repeatedly *adv.* kuti kuti, yapa yapa
replace *v.* rantiy
reply to one another *v.* ninakuy
reprimand *v.* phiñay
reprimander *n.* phiñaq
reproach oneself continuously *v.* ñakapakuy
reproduce *v.* miray; **make reproduce** mirachiy • *n.* **person who makes reproduce** mirachiq
resemble someone *v.* rikch'akuy
resistant *adj.* anaq
respected *adj.* qhapaq
resplendent *adj.* k'anchay k'anchay • *v.* **become resplendent** lliphlliyay
respond *v.* kutichiy
rest *v.* samay; **have the urge to rest** samanayay; **make rest** samachiy
rested *adj.* samasqa
resting place *n.* samana
restore *v.* mosoqchay
restorer *n.* mosoqchaq
retain *v.* qhepachiy
retreat *v.* kuyuriy
return *v.* kutichiy, kutiy, ripuy, hampuy
reverberate *(cowbells)* *v.* chanrararay
revere *v.* saminchay
revitalize *v.* qespiy; **make revitalize** qespichiy
revitalizer *n.* qespichiq
revive *v.* kawsariy, llanllay
revived *adj.* llanllasqa
rhombus *n.* puytu
rib *n.* waqta
rich *adj.* qolqeyoq
rickety *adj.* tiwti, toqti

right *(opposite of left) adj.* paña
right now *adv.* kunanpacha
rinse *v.* ch'uyanay
rinse out one's mouth *v.* moqch'ikuy
rip *v.* llik'iy
ripe *adj.* poqosqa • *v.* **make ripe** poqochiy
ripen *v.* poqoy
rival *n.* awqa
river *n.* mayu
river crossing *n.* ch'aqcha
roam *v.* usuy
roast meat *v.* kankay
roast tubers *v.* kusay
roasted meat *n.* kanka
rob *v.* suway; **get robbed** suwachikuy; **help rob** suwaysiy; **make rob** suwachiy
robbed *adj.* suwasqa
rock *v.* kuyuchiy • *n.* qaqa, rumi, wanka
rocky *adj.* wanka wanka
rocky area *n.* wanka
roll around *v.* qhospay
roll up *v.* k'uyuy
roll up and tie *v.* mayt'uy; **help roll up and tie** mayt'uysiy
roll up and tie again and again *v.* mayt'uykachay
rolled up and tied *adj.* mayt'usqa
rooster *n.* k'anka, wallpa
rooster's crow *n.* wallpa waqay
root *n.* saphi; **thin root** chhapu • *v.* **take root** saphiy
rope *n.* q'eswa, waskha
rot *v.* ismuy
rotten *adj.* ismu, ismusqa; *(egg)* lloqllo
rough *adj.* qhasqa
round *adj.* muyu
round trip *adj.* kutit'ikra
rounded *adj.* muyuchasqa
rout around *v.* uksiy
row *v.* t'uyuy, tuyuy; **help row** t'uyuysiy
rub *v.* llunch'iy
rude *adj.* haphlla
rule *n.* kamachi • *v.* kamachiy

ruler *n.* kamachiq
rummage *v.* k'uskiy, welq'ay; **help rummage** welq'aysiy; **make rummage** welq'achiy
rummager *n.* welq'aq
rummaging tool *n.* welq'ana
run *v.* phaway; **have the desire to run** phawanayay; **make run** phawachiy • *n.* **person who makes run** phawachiq
run around *v.* phawakachay
run away *v.* ayqey, k'itakuy; **help run away** ayqechiy
run out of something *v.* tukukuy
runaway *adj.* ch'ita
runner *n.* phawaq

S

sack *n.* kutama
sacred *adj.* willka
sacrifice *(animal) v.* nak'ay
sacrificed *(animal) adj.* nak'asqa
sad *adj.* llakisqa • *v.* **become sad** llakikuy • *interj.* **how sad!** akakallaw, kakallaw
sadly *adv.* khuyay khuyay, llakilla
sadness *n.* llaki • *v.* **cause sadness** llakichiy
saliva *n.* thoqay
salt *n.* kachi • *v.* kachiyay
salty *adj.* kachisapa, qollpa
same *adj.* kikin
sand *n.* aqo, t'iyu
sandal *n.* lanq'e, usuta, husut'a
sandy *adj.* aqosapa
sash *n.* mat'ina, *(woven)* chunpi
satiated *adj.* saksasqa • *v.* **become satiated** saksay
satisfied *adj.* saksasqa • *v.* **become satisfied** saksay
save *v.* waqaychay; **help save** waqaychaysiy; **make save** waqaychachiy
say *v.* niy
scaly *adj.* phaspa • *v.* **become scaly** phaspayay
scarce *adj.* pisi
scare *v.* manchachiy
scared *adj.* manchali • *v.* **be scared** mancharikuy
scarf *n.* p'istuna
scary *adj.* manchana • *interj.* **how scary!** atakaw
scatter *v.* ch'eqechiy, hach'iy, t'akay, wisniy; **help scatter** hach'iysiy, wisniysiy; **make scatter** wisnichiy • *n.* **person who scatters** hach'iq, wisniq
scatter by hand *v.* qachiy; **help scatter by hand** qachiysiy
scatter by hand again and again *v.* qachipayay
scatter everywhere *v.* hach'iykachay, wisniykachay
scatter seeds *v.* husk'ay; **help scatter seeds** husk'aysiy
scattered *adj.* t'akasqa, wisnisqa

scattered by hand *adj.* qachisqa
scheme together *v.* yachachinakuy
scold *v.* anyay; **make scold** anyachiy • *n.* **person who makes scold** anyachiq
scold again and again *v.* anyapayay
scold oneself *v.* anyakuy
scold oneself again and again *v.* anyapakuy
scolder *n.* anyaq
scoot *v.* achhuchiy
scorn *v.* alqochay
scrape *v.* eqhay, qhetuy, thupay; **help scrape** thupaysiy
scrape again and again *v.* qhetupayay, thupaykachay
scrape insistently *v.* qhetuykachay
scraped *adj.* eqhasqa, thupasqa
scratch *v.* hallp'iy, rachiy, sillkuy; **have the urge to scratch oneself** rachinayakuy
scratch again and again *v.* rachipayay
scratch one another *v.* rachinakuy
scratcher *n.* hallp'iq
scrawny *adj.* choqchi, k'arpi, k'asu, sit'i • *v.* **become scrawny** sit'iyay
sea *n.* mamaqocha
search *v.* maskhay; **help search** maskhaysiy • *n.* **person who searches** maskhaq
search for *v.* t'aqwiy; **command to search for** t'aqwichiy; **help search for** t'aqwiysiy • *n.* **person who searches for** t'aqwiq
search for again and again *v.* maskhaykachay
search through *v.* k'uskiy
searched for *adj.* maskhasqa
season *n.* *(time)* mit'a; **harvest season** aymura • *v.* *(flavor)* uchuchay • *adj.* **very seasoned** uchusapa
season with pepper *v.* uchuchay
seat *n.* tiyana
seated *adj.* tiyasqa
seaweed *n.* qochayuyu
sediment *n.* t'iyu
see *v.* rikuy; **let oneself be seen** rikuchikuy; **make see** rikuchiy
see one another *v.* rikunakuy
seed *n.* muhu, ruru; **selector of seeds** muhuchaq • *v.* **scatter seeds** husk'ay; **help scatter seeds** husk'aysiy; **select seeds** muhuchay

seed planter *n.* tarpuq
seen *adj.* rikusqa • *v.* **let oneself be seen** rikuchikuy
select *v.* akllay, chiklluy; **help select** akllaysiy
select seeds *v.* muhuchay
selected *adj.* akllasqa, chikllusqa
sell *v.* qhatuy; **help sell** qhatuysiy
seller *n.* qhatuq
semen *n.* wawsa, yuma
send *v.* apachiy, suchiy
sender *n.* suchiq
sensible *adj.* yuyayniyoq
sent *(thing) adj.* suchisqa
separate *v.* hukllanay, t'aqay; **command to separate** t'aqachiy; **help separate** t'aqaysiy
separate again and again *v.* t'aqapayay
separated *adj.* t'aqasqa
serpent *(ritual) n.* amaru
servant *n.* k'umillu
serve *v.* yanapay; **make serve** yanapachiy
serve food *v.* qaray; **command to serve food** qarachiy; **help serve food** qaraysiy
serve one another *v.* yanapanakuy
server *n.* yanapaq
set trap *(like a fox) v.* atoqrayay
settle *v.* takyay
seven *num.* qanchis
sew *v.* siray; **help sew** siraysiy; **order to have clothing sewn for someone** sirachikuy
sew roughly *v.* ch'ukay; **help sew roughly** ch'ukaysiy
sewer *n.* siraq
sewing needle *n.* sirana; **large sewing needle** yawri
sewn *adj.* sirasqa
sewn roughly *adj.* ch'ukasqa
shade *v.* llanthuy; **go into shade** llanthurikuy
shade one another *v.* llanthunakuy
shadow *n.* llanthu, supa • *v.* supay
shake *v.* chhaphchiy; **help shake** chhaphchiysiy
shake constantly *v.* chhaphchiykachay
shake something *v.* chukchuchiy
shaker *n.* chhaphchiq

shame *n.* p'enqali
shatter *v.* chhalluy
shattered *adj.* chhallusqa
shawl *n.* unkuña
she *pron.* pay
sheet *n.* llanp'una
shell *n.* ch'uru; **conch shell** pututu
shepherd *n.* michiq
shin *n.* chakisenqa
shine *n.* chipchiy • *v.* chipchiy, wach'iy; **make shine** wach'ichiy
shine brightly *v.* lliphlliy
shiny *adj.* k'anchaq
ship *v.* suchiy
shipment *n.* suchi
shipper *n.* suchiq
shirt *n.* unku
shiver *v.* khatatay; **make shiver** khatatachiy
shock *v.* manchachiy
shocked *adj.* mancharisqa
short *adj.* *(man)* tanka, *(woman)* t'usta
short and chubby *(man) adj.* oqocho
shoulder *n.* rikra
shout *v.* waqway
show *v.* qhawachiy
shrink *(thing) v.* q'estiy
shrink with age *v.* *(woman)* t'ustuyay
shrunken *(thing) adj.* q'estisqa
shuck *(corn) v.* tipiy; **help shuck** tipiysiy; **make shuck** tipichiy
shucked *(corn) adj.* tipisqa
shudder *v.* chukchuy
shy *adj.* osqo • *v.* **become shy** osqoyay
sick *adj.* onqoq • *v.* **get sick** onqoy; **get sick frequently** onqopayay
sick of *(food) adj.* amisqa • *v.* **get sick of** amiy
sickle *n.* ichhuna
sickly *adj.* eqo, onqoli
sickness *n.* onqoy, machusqa
sickness caused by a corpse *n.* qhayqa
sickness caused by an ill wind *n.* wayrasqa
sickness transmitted by mosquitos *n.* utha
side *n.* kinra

sideways *adv.* k'achanpamanta • *v.* **position something sideways** k'achanpachiy; **put something sideways** k'achanpay
sift *v.* suysuy; **command to sift** suysuchiy; **help sift** suysuysiy
sifted *adj.* suysusqa
sigh *v.* anchhiy
sigh constantly *v.* anchhiykachay
sigher *n.* anchhiq
signal *v.* tuyruy
silence *v.* upallay; **make silence** upallachiy • *n.* ch'in
silenced *adj.* upallasqa
silent *adj.* ch'in • *v.* **become silent** ch'inyay
silently *adv.* upallaspa, ch'inlla
silly *adj.* opa
silver *n.* qolqe
sin *n.* hucha • *v.* huchallikuy
sing *v.* takiy; **have the urge to sing** takinayay
sing constantly *v.* takipayay
sing softly *v.* takiykachay
sing with others *v.* takiysiy
singe *v.* q'aspay
singed *adj.* q'aspasqa
singer *n.* takiq
sinner *n.* huchasapa, huchayoq
sip *v.* upiy; **make sip** upichiy
siren *n.* challwawanka
sit *v.* tiyay, *(used with children)* pachiy; **have the urge to sit** tiyanayay; **make sit** tiyachiy
sit again and again *v.* tiyakachay
six *num.* soqta
size *n.* sayay
skilled *adj.* ch'asti
skin *n.* qara • *v.* lluch'iy, llust'iy, ch'utiy; **order to skin** ch'utichiy
skinned *adj.* lluch'isqa
skinny *adj.* harchi, q'awti, tullu • *v.* **become skinny** tiwtiyay, tulluyay; **become too skinny** ch'arkiyay; **make become skinny** tulluyachiy
skip *(step) v.* chakchay, p'itaykachay
skipper *n.* p'itakachaq
skirt *n.* wali
skunk *n.* añas

sky *n.* hanaqpacha
skylark *n.* tuya
slanderer *n.* ñakaq
slanted *adj.* phallu
slap *n.* ch'aqla • *v.* ch'aqlay; **let oneself be slapped** ch'aqlachikuy
slap one another *v.* ch'aqlanakuy
slap repeatedly *v.* ch'aqlapayay
slapper *n.* ch'aqlaq
slaughter *v.* nak'ay; **make slaughter** nak'achiy
slaughtered *adj.* nak'asqa
slaughterer *n.* nak'achu, nak'aq
sleep *v.* puñuy; **have the desire to sleep** puñunayay
sleep in another's house *v.* puñupakuy
sleepy *adj.* uti • *n.* **person/thing that causes sleepiness** utichiq
slice *v.* q'allay; **make slice** q'allachiy
sliced *adj.* q'allasqa
slim down *v.* choqchiyay
slingshot *n.* warak'a • *v.* **hit with a slingshot** warak'ay
slip *v.* lluskhay, suskhay; **make slip** lluskhachiy
slippery *adj.* lluskha, suskha
slope *n.* qhata
slow *adj.* ñuskhu, qella
slowly *adv.* ñuskhu ñuskhulla, susigo • *v.* **turn slowly** kutiriy
slurp *v.* loqloy, upiy; **make slurp** upichiy
small *adj.* huch'uy, khullu • *v.* **make smaller** pisichiy
smallish *adj.* huch'uyniraq
smear *v.* hawiy, llunch'iy
smear on *v.* llusiy; **help smear on** llusiysiy
smear on again and again *v.* llusipayay
smear on one another *v.* llusinakuy
smear on oneself llusikuy
smeared *adj.* hawisqa, llusisqa
smell *v.* muskhiy; **make smell** muskhichiy
smell constantly *v.* muskhipayay
smell from a distance *v.* muskhipakuy
smell one another *v.* muskhinakuy
smile *v.* asirikuy, asiriy
smoke *n.* q'osñi • *v.* pitay; **make smoke** q'osñichiy
smooth *adj.* llank'i • *v.* **become smooth** llank'iyay; **make smooth** mant'achiy, mast'achiy

smooth out *v.* mant'ay, mast'ay; **help smooth out** mant'aysiy, mast'aysiy
smooth out again and again *v.* mant'apayay
smooth out repeatedly *v.* mast'apayay
smoothed out *adj.* mant'asqa, mast'asqa
smut *n.* yanamanka
snake *n.* mach'aqway
snatch *v.* qechuy; **help snatch** qechuysiy
snatch constantly *v.* qechuykachay
sneak *v.* chhuchuy
sneeze *n.* achhi • *v.* achhiy, hach'iy
sneezer *n.* achhiq, hach'iq
sniff up *v.* senq'ay
sniffle *v.* ñusñuy
snore *v.* qhorqoy
snorer *n.* qhorqoq
snort *v.* senq'ay
snout *(certain animals) n.* suyt'u
snow *n.* rit'i • *v.* rit'iy
soak *v.* chapuy
soak repeatedly *v.* chapuykachay
soaked *adj.* chapusqa
sob *v.* anchhiy, hik'ipakuy, uyuy • *n.* **person who sobs** anchhiq
sob constantly *v.* anchhiykachay
sober *(not drunk) adj.* ch'akisonqo
social outcast *adj.* k'ita
soft *adj.* llanp'u, manti, ñapu; **very soft** llanp'ullaña • *v.* **become soft** llanp'uyariy, ñapuyay
soften *v.* ñapuy
soil *n.* allpa • *v.* **cover with soil** allpachay; **let oneself be covered with soil** p'anpachikuy; **remove soil** allpanay; **turn into soil** allpayapuy • *adj.* **made from soil** allpamanta
soldier *n.* wamink'a, wisa
solicit something *v.* qochikuy
solicited *adj.* maskhasqa
some *adj.* wakin
sometimes *adv.* mayninpi
son *n. (of mother)* qhari wawa, *(of father)* churi; **youngest son** chanaku • *v.* **treat someone like a son/daughter** wawachakuy • *adv.* **with many sons** *(man)* churisapa

son-in-law *n.* qatay, tullka
song *n.* taki, *(Andean varieties)* haylli, wayno
soot *n.* qhechincha, yanamanka
soul *n.* nuna
sound of wings flapping at moment of flight *n.* phar
soup *n. (thick)* lawa, *(hearty)* chupi
sow *v.* tarpuy; **help sow** tarpuysiy; **make sow** tarpuchiy
sower *n.* tarpuq
sown *adj.* tarpusqa
span of time *n.* unay
sparrow *n.* pichinku
sparse *adj.* ch'eqe, ch'eqesqa
speech *n.* simi
speak *v.* rimay
speak for the sake of it *v.* rimakachay
speak constantly *v.* rimapayay
speak to one another *v.* rimanakuy
speak to one's self *v.* rimapakuy
speaker *n.* rimaq
sphere *n.* lonq'o, lunp'u
spherical *adj.* lonq'o
spicy *adj.* haya, uchusapa
spider *n.* apasanka, uru
spill *v.* hich'ay; **help spill** hich'aysiy
spill again and again *v.* hich'apayay
spilled *adj.* hich'asqa
spin *v.* muyuy, puskay; **help spin** puskaysiy; **make spin** muyuchiy
spindle *n.* puska
spinner *n.* puskaq
spinning top *n.* p'esqoyllo
spirit *n.* nuna
spit *v.* thoqay; **have the urge to spit** thoqanayay; **make spit** thoqachiy
spit constantly *v.* thoqapayay
spit on one another *v.* thoqanakuy
spit out *adj.* thoqasqa
spit out chewed pulp *v.* hach'uy
splash around *v.* wayt'aykachay
splinter *n.* chhillpa; **wooden splinter** k'ullpi • *v.* chhillpay, khallpay; **remove splinters from wood** chhillpanay

split open *adj.* k'iñasqa • *v.* k'iñay
spoiled: *v.* **become spoiled** *(grains)* hut'uyay
spoon *(wooden) n.* wislla
spray *v.* ch'ikway, ch'iwkay
spread *adj.* llusisqa • *v.* mast'ariy
spread on *v.* llusiy; **help spread on** llusiysiy
spread on again and again *v.* llusipayay
spread on one another *v.* llusinakuy
spread on oneself *v.* llusikuy
sprinkle *(ritual) v.* ch'allay
sprinkle repeatedly *(ritual) v.* ch'allapayay • *n.* **person who sprinkles** ch'allaq
sprinkled *(ritual) adj.* ch'allasqa
sprout *n.* ch'ichi • *v.* ch'ichiy, phutuy
sprout abundantly *v.* wakway; **make sprout abundantly** wakwachiy
sprout again *v.* llanllariy
sprout slowly *v.* phuturiy
sprouted *adj.* phutusqa
sprouted with abundance *adj.* wakwasqa
spun *adj.* puskasqa
squander *v.* usuchiy
squander away *v.* usuy
squandered *adj.* usuchisqa
squeeze *v.* k'iskiy, p'oqay, q'apiy; **command to squeeze** q'apichiy
squeeze constantly *v.* q'apiykachay
squeeze in *v.* k'iskiyay
squeezed *adj.* p'oqasqa, q'apisqa
stabilize *v.* turay
stack *v.* suntuy, tawqay; **help stack** tawqaysiy; **make stack** tawqachiy • *n.* **person who stacks** tawqaq
stacked *adj.* suntusqa, tawqa tawqa, tawqasqa
stained *adj.* yanachasqa • *v.* **become stained** yanachakuy
stammer *v.* haklluykachay
stand up *v.* sayachiy; **have the urge to stand up** sayanayay; **remain standing** sayarayay
star *n.* ch'aska, qoyllur
start *v.* qallariy
started *adj.* qallarisqa
starve *v.* ch'achay

starved person *n.* ch'achaq
stay *v.* qhepay, qhepakuy, qorpachakuy
stay seated for a long time *v.* tiyarayay
stay too long *v.* sat'irayay
steal *v.* ch'aspay, suway; **help steal** ch'aspaysiy, suwaysiy; **make steal** suwachiy
stealthily *adv.* pakalla
steam *n.* waksi
steam cook *v.* phasiy
steam cooked *adj.* phasi
steep *v.* chapuy
steep repeatedly *v.* chapuykachay
steeped *adj.* chapusqa
stench *n.* asnay
step on *v.* saruy; **get stepped on** saruchikuy • *n.* **person who steps on** saruq
step on again and again *v.* saruykachay
step on one another repeatedly *v.* sarunakuy
stepped on *adj.* sarusqa
steps *n.* seqana
stepson *n.* hawaychuri
sterile *adj.* urwa
sternum *n.* qhasqo tullu
stew *v.* chupiy
stick *v.* t'urpuy
stick for hitting *n.* p'anana, q'asuna • *v.* **help hit with stick** p'anaysiy, q'asuysiy; **hit one another with stick** p'ananakuy, q'asunakuy; **hit with stick** p'anay, q'asuy
stick out tongue *v.* qalluykachay
sting *v.* seqsiy, *(a wound)* k'aray; **cause stinging** seqsichiy
stinging wound *n.* k'araq
stingy *adj.* akakutirpa, maqlla, mich'a
stink *v.* asnay; **make stink** asnachiy • *n.* **person who causes stink** asnachiq
stinky *adj.* asnaq
stinky person/thing *n.* asnaq
stir *v.* chaqruy, maywiy, weq'ay; **help stir** maywiysiy, weq'aysiy; **make stir** qaywichiy, weq'achiy
stir fluids *v.* qaywiy; **help stir fluids** qaywiysiy
stir fluids with indifference *v.* qaywiykachay

stir fluids with intention *v.* qaywiyuy
stir grains *v.* harwiy
stirred *adj.* chaqrusqa, maywisqa, weq'asqa, *(fluids)* qaywisqa, *(grains)* harwisqa
stirrer *n.* harwiq, weq'aq
stirring utensil *n.* weq'ana, qaywina
stock products *v.* taqey; **help stock products** taqeysiy; **order to stock products** taqechiy
stolen *adj.* ch'aspasqa, suwasqa
stomach *n.* wiksa
stomach acid *n.* p'osqolli
stone *n.* rumi
stop *n.* sayana
stopping place *n.* sayana
storage: *v.* **temporary storage** astana
story *n.* willakuy
stove *n.* q'oncha • *v.* **build a stove** q'onchachay; **place pot on stove** churpuy
strain *v.* ch'umay
strained *adj.* ch'umasqa
strangle *v.* seq'oy; **command to strangle** seq'ochiy; **help strangle** seq'oysiy
strangled *adj.* seq'osqa
strangler *n.* seq'oq
street *n.* k'ikllu
strength *n.* kallpa
strengthen *v.* kallpachay
stretch *v.* chutay; **make stretch** chutachiy • *n.* **person who stretches** chutaq
stretch one's legs *v.* hayt'arikuy
stretch out *v.* chutarikuy
stretched *adj.* chutasqa
stretched out *(thing) adj.* p'olqo
string for tying *n.* watana
strip *(belongings) v.* ch'utiy; **order to strip** ch'utiy
strip belongings from another *v.* q'alachay; **let oneself be stripped of belongings** chaskichikuy • *n.* **person who makes strip belongings from another** q'alachiq
strip off *v.* llat'anay
strive *v.* atipakuy

stroll *v.* purikuy
strong *adj.* kallpasapa • *v.* **become strong** kallpachakuy
stubborn *adj.* atipakuq, umasapa
stunned *adj.* thanpi • *v.* **be stunned** thanpiy
stupefied: *v.* **be stupefied** hanllarayay
stutter *v.* haklluykachay
stutterer *n.* hakllu
stuttering *adj.* hakllu
submerge *v.* challpuy • *n.* **person who submerges** challpuq
submerge repeatedly *v.* challpuykachay
submerged *adj.* challpusqa
submissively *adv.* ullpu ullpu
successively *adv.* qayllalla
suck *v.* ch'onqay • *n.* **person who sucks** ch'onqaq
suck incessantly *v.* ch'onqaykachay
suckle *v.* ch'onqay
suddenly *adv.* qonqaylla
suffer *v.* ñak'ariy; **make suffer** ñak'arichiy • *interj.* **what suffering!** ananay
suffocate *v.* mukiy
suffocate from heat *v.* ruphapakuy
suffocated *adj.* mukisqa
suicide: *v.* **commit suicide** wañuchikuy
summon for communal work *v.* mink'ay • *n.* **person who summons for communal work** mink'akuq
summoned for communal work *adj.* mink'asqa
sun *n.* inti; **heat from sun** ruphay • *v.* **expose to sun** masay; **expose to sun again and again** masaykachay; **expose to sun continuously** masapayay; **heat in sun** q'ochachiy, ruphayay • *adj.* **exposed to sun** masasqa
support oneself on something/someone *v.* q'emipakuy
support with stick *v.* tankachay
supreme *adj.* yaya
surplus: *v.* **collect surplus** wakinchay
suspect *v.* watupakuy • *n.* **person who suspects** watupakuq
swaddle a baby *v.* chunpiy, walthay; **help swaddle a baby** walthaysiy • *n.* **cloth for swaddling a baby** waltha
swaddled *(baby) adj.* walthasqa
swaddler of a baby *n.* walthaq
swallow *v.* millp'uy, rakray; **make swallow** millp'uchiy

swallow again and again *v.* millp'upayay
swallow one's pride *v.* k'umuykachay
swallow saliva *v.* millp'upakuy
swallowed *adj.* millp'usqa, rakrasqa
sway *v.* wanlinyay
sweat *v.* hunp'iy; **make sweat** hunp'ichiy • *n.* hunp'i; **person who sweats** hunp'iq
sweaty *adj.* hunp'isqa
sweep *v.* pichay; **help sweep** pichaysiy; **make sweep** pichachiy
sweep continuously *v.* pichapayay
sweeper *n.* pichaq
sweet *adj.* misk'i; **very sweet** misk'illaña
sweeten *v.* misk'ichiy
swell up *v.* p'unpuyay, punkiy
swept *adj.* pichasqa
swim *v.* wayt'ay
swimmer *n.* wayt'aq
swindle *v.* ch'achuy
swindling *adj.* ch'achu
swollen *adj.* punkisqa, p'unpu
system of communal work *n.* mink'a
system of mutual help *n.* mink'a

T

tactless *adj.* llik'isimi
tadpole *n.* hoq'oyllo
tail *n.* chupa
tailor *n.* siraq
take out *v.* horqoy • *n.* **person who takes out** horqoq
take root *v.* saphiy
take someone *v.* pusay, ranpay; **help take someone** ranpaysiy; **make take someone** pusachiy
take something from someone *v.* qochiy
taken out *adj.* horqosqa
talk *v.* rimay; **have the urge to talk** rimanayay; **make talk** rimachiy
talk constantly *v.* rimapayay
talk for talking's sake *v.* rimakachay
talk nonsense *v.* thawtiy • *n.* **person who talks nonsense** thawtiq
talk to one another *v.* rimanakuy
talk to one's self *v.* rimapakuy
talk while dreaming *v.* musphay
talk while dreaming constantly *v.* musphapayay
talker *n.* rimaq
tall *adj.* hatun
task *n.* ruwana
tassle *n.* puyllu
taste *v.* malliy; **make taste** mallichiy
teach *v.* yachachiy
teacher *n.* yachachiq
tear *n.* *(in eye)* weqe • *v.* *(fabric)* qhasuy
tear again and again *(fabric)* *v.* qhasuykachay
tear off a string *v.* p'itiy; **make tear off a string** p'itichiy
tear up *(eye)* *v.* weqey; **make tear up** weqechiy
tell *v.* willay; **have the urge to tell** willanayay; **make tell** willachiy
tell one another *v.* willanakuy
tell over and over *v.* willapayay
temporary storage *n.* astana
ten *num.* chunka
tender *adj.* qholla

tendon *n.* hank'u
terrain *n.* allpa
territory *n.* marka
that *pron.* chay, *(far)* haqhay • *adj.* chay, *(far)* haqhay • *conj.* **after that** chaymanta • *adv.* **like that** chayhina, chhayna
that little thing *pron.* chaycha
that's it *adv.* chaylla
then *conj.* chayqa; **and then** chayqa, hinaspa; **from then on** chaymantapacha • *inter.* **and then?** chayrí?
there *adv.* chaypi; **near there** chayneqpi; **over there** chayninta; **towards there** chayman
there and back *adv.* kutit'ikra
they *pron.* paykuna
thick *adj.* pipu, rakhu; *(liquid)* thaka
thicken *v.* rakhuyay; **become thickened** *(liquid)* thakayay; **make thicken** thakayachiy
thief *n.* makiyoq, suwa, ch'aspaq
thin *adj.* harchi
think *v.* yuyay
thinker *n.* yuyaq
thirst *n.* ch'akiy • *v.* **be thirsty** ch'akiy
this *pron.* kay • *adj.* kay • *adv.* **like this** akna, kayhina, khayna
this little thing *pron.* kaycha
thistle *n.* qepu
thorn *n.* k'aklla, kiska, qepu
thorny *adj.* kiskasapa
thought about *adj.* yuyasqa
thousand *num.* waranqa
thread: *n.* **loose thread** chhapu; **wool thread** q'aytu
threadbare *adj.* thanta
three *num.* kinsa
throat *n.* tonqor
throw *v.* ch'aqey, chanqay; **help throw** ch'aqeysiy
throw roughly *v.* choqay
throw things carelessly *v.* chanqaykachay
throw out *v.* wikch'uy; **have the urge to throw out** wikch'unayay; **help throw out** wikch'uysiy; **make throw out** wikch'uchiy • *n.* **person who throws out** wikch'uq
thrower *n.* ch'aqeq
thrown *adj.* ch'aqesqa, chanqasqa

thrown out *adj.* wikch'usqa
thrown roughly *adj.* choqasqa
thumb *n.* mamaruk'ana
thunder *n.* qhaqya
tick *(insect) n.* hamak'u
tickle someone *v.* kullachiy
tie *v.* watay; **help tie** wataysiy; **make tie** watachiy
tie again and again *v.* watapayay
tie down *v.* thunkuy; **help tie down** thunkuysiy; **make tie down** thunkuchiy
tie hands *v.* chaqnay
tie up *v.* wank'uy; **help tie up** wank'uysiy; **make tie up** wank'uchiy
tie up again and again *v.* wank'upayay
tie with rope *n.* waskhay
tied *adj.* watasqa
tied up *adj.* wank'usqa
tight *adj.* mat'i, mat'isqa
tighten *v.* mat'iy
tighten again and again *v.* mat'ipayay
tightly *adv.* mat'iy mat'iy
tilt *v.* t'iksuy • *v.* **be tilted** k'achanpakuy
time *n. (frequency)* kuti; **long time** unay; **span of time** unay • *adv.* **that time** chaypacha; **after a long time** unaymanta
time period *n.* mit'a
timespace *n.* pacha
timid *adj.* manchali, osqo, p'enqali, unphu, wañu wañu • *v.* **become timid** osqoyay, unphuyay
tiny *adj.* ch'iñi, huch'uyllaña
tiptoe *v.* hink'iy, kirkiy
tire *v.* sayk'uy
tire out *v.* sayk'uchiy
tired *adj.* sayk'usqa
toad *n.* hanp'atu
toast *(celebrate) v.* anqosay
toast grains or beans *v.* hank'ay
toasted grains or beans *n.* hank'a
toaster of grains or beans *n.* hank'aq
tobacco plant *n.* sayri
today *adv.* kunan
together *adj.* kuska

told *adj.* willasqa
tomb *(prehispanic) n.* ch'ullpa, p'uytu
tomorrow *n.* paqarin
tongue *(anatomical) n.* qallu • *v.* **stick out tongue** qalluykachay
too *adv.* ñisuta
too much *adj.* ñisu
tooth *n.* kiru
toothless *adj.* hanllu, laqmu
top *n.* umala
top part *n.* pata
torment *v.* ñak'arichiy
torn *(fabric) adj.* qhasusqa
toss *v.* ch'aqey, chanqay; **help toss** ch'aqeysiy
toss things carelessly *v.* chanqaykachay
tossed *adj.* ch'aqesqa, chanqasqa
tosser *n.* ch'aqeq
totally *adv.* q'alata
touch *v.* llamiy
touch one another *v.* llaminakuy
touch repeatedly *v.* llamipayay
touch slightly *v.* tupaykuy
touch softly *v.* llamiykuy
towards here *adv.* kayman
towards there *adv.* chayman
town *n.* llaqta
toy *n.* pukllana
tracks *n.* yupi • *v.* **follow tracks** yupichay; **leave tracks** yupiy
trading place *n.* qhatu
traitor *n.* sirpaq
translate *v.* t'ikray
transport *v.* astay; **help transport** astaysiy; **make transport** astaysiy
transport constantly *v.* astapayay
trap: *v.* **set trap** *(like a fox)* atoqrayay; **trap with net** llukuy
trapped in a net *adj.* llukusqa
travel *v.* ch'usay, puriy; **ready oneself to travel** q'epichakuy
traveler *n.* puriq
tree *n. (Andean variety)* lloqe, *(small)* mallki
tree trunk *n.* kurku
tree with many branches *n.* sach'a

tree without many branches *n.* yura
tremble *v.* chukchuy, khatatay; **make tremble** chukchuchiy, khatatachiy
trembling person/thing *n.* chukchuq
triangular hill *n.* pikchu
trick *n.* laq'o • *v.* laq'oy, q'otoy, qeqoy; **let oneself be tricked** q'otochikuy, qeqochikuy
tricked *adj.* laq'osqa, q'otosqa, qeqosqa
trickle *v.* suruy
trickled *adj.* surusqa
trip and fall *v.* laq'akuy; **make trip and fall** laq'achiy
trip over *v.* misk'akuy
triumph *v.* llalliy
triumphantly *adv.* llalli llalli
true *adj.* chanin, cheqaq
tub: *n.* **wooden tub** wanpuru
tuber *(Andean varieties) n.* maswa, añu, oqa, ulluku, unkucha • *v.* **roast tubers** kusay
tumor *n.* ch'upu
tunic *n.* kusma, unku
turn over *v.* t'ikray; **help turn over** t'ikraysiy
turn slowly *v.* kutiriy
twilight *n.* arpha
twin *n.* wispa
twist *v.* q'ewiy, weqoy; **help twist** q'ewiysiy, weqoysiy; **make twist** q'ewichiy, weqochiy
twisted *adj.* q'ewisqa, weqo; **very twisted** q'ewi q'ewi • *v.* **become twisted** weqokuy
two *num.* iskay

U

ugly *adj.* millay
unbraid *v.* sinp'anay
uncle *(maternal) n.* kaka
uncover *v.* llat'ay, q'allpay
uncovered *adj.* llat'asqa
under *prep.* ura
undercooked *adj.* hanku hanku
underestimate *v.* pisichay
underwear *n.* ukhuna • *v.* **put on underwear** ukhunakuy
undo *v.* thullkiy
undone *adj.* thullkisqa
undress *v.* ch'utikuy, q'aray, q'alachay; **let oneself be undressed** q'alachikuy • *n.* **person who makes someone undress** q'alachiq
undress oneself *v.* q'alachakuy, q'arayay
unearth *v.* hallmay; **help unearth** hallmaysiy; **make unearth** hallmachiy • *n.* **person who unearths** hallmaq
unearthed *adj.* hallmasqa
unfermented juice *n.* upi
unforgettable *adj.* yuyaychana
unfriendly *adj.* salqa
unhappy *adj.* usuri
unified *adj.* hukllasqa
unify *v.* hukllay
uninhabited *adj.* purun
united *adj.* kuska
universe *n.* teqsimuyu
unmatched *adj.* ch'ullan
unorganized *(woman) adj.* waylaka
unpaired *adj.* ch'ullan, willu
unpleasant *adj.* millay
unripe *adj.* k'uku, qholla
unstitch *v.* llik'iy, siranay
untamed *adj.* k'ita
untidy *adj.* thamalanku

untie *v.* paskay; **make untie** paskachiy • *n.* **person who unties** paskaq
untied *adj.* paskasqa
uphold *v.* q'emiy
upper level *s.* hanaqpacha
uproot *v.* saphinay, t'iray; **help uproot** t'iraysiy
uprooted *adj.* t'irasqa
upset *adj.* llakisqa • *v.* **get upset continuously** llakipakuy
urinal *n.* hisp'ana
urinate *v.* hisp'ay; **have the urge to urinate** hisp'anayay; **make urinate** hisp'achiy
urinate constantly *v.* hisp'apakuy
urine *n.* hisp'ay
used *adj.* mawk'a
useless *adj.* akasapa, añaku
uselessly *adv.* yanqa
uterus *n.* kisma

V

vacate *v.* ch'usaqyachiy, qasichiy
vacillate *v.* iskayyay
vagina *n.* chupi
valley *n.* yunka
value *n.* chani • *v.* chaninchay
vampire *n.* masu
vapor *n.* waksi
vaporize *v.* waksichiy
vein *n.* sirk'a
vendor *n.* qhatuq
venerate *v.* apuchay
venerated *adj.* apuchasqa
venereal disease *n.* wanthi
venom *n.* miyu
venous *n.* sirk'ayoq
ventilate *v.* wayrachiy
verify *v.* cheqaqchay
vertical *adj.* sayanpa
vertically *adv.* sayanpamanta
very *adv.* anchata, sinchita • *adj.* askha, ancha, manchay
very new *adj.* mosoqllaña
very old *adj. (man)* machullaña, *(woman)* payallaña
victimized *adj.* wañuchisqa
victor *n.* atipaq, llalliq
vicuña *n.* wikuña
visible *adj.* rikunalla
visit *v.* watukuy
visitor *n.* watukuq
vixen *(animal) n.* unkaka
voice *n.* kunka
volcano *n.* areq
voluntarily *adv.* munay munaylla
vomit *v.* aqtoy, wikch'upakuy; **be about to vomit** aqtonayay; **have the urge to vomit** aqtonayay
vomit constantly *v.* aqtopayay

W

wait *v.* suyay • *n.* **person who waits** suyaq
wait anxiously *v.* suyapayay
wait for a long time *(standing) v.* takarayay
wake up *v.* rikch'ay; **be about to wake up** rikch'anayay
wake up every so often *v.* rikch'apakuy
wake up in the morning *v.* paqariy
walk *v.* puriy; **help walk** purichiy
walk around *v.* tumay
walk with small steps *v.* ichiy
walker *n.* puriq
wall *n.* perqa; **builder of walls** perqaq • *v.* **build a wall** perqay
walled *adj.* perqasqa
want *v.* munay
warm *adj.* q'oñi • *v.* **get warm** q'oñikuy; **make warm** q'oñichiy
warm up with body heat *v.* oqllay
warp *(threads) v.* allwiy, k'antiy; **help warp** allwiysiy; **make warp** allwichiy • *n.* **person who warps** allwiq
warped *(threads) adj.* allwisqa
wart *n.* tikti
wash *v.* maqchhiy, maylliy; **help wash** maqchhiysiy, maylliysiy; **make wash** maqchhichiy
wash again and again *v.* maqchhipayay
wash clothes *v.* t'aqsay; **command to wash clothes** t'aqsachiy; **help wash clothes** t'aqsaysiy
wash oneself *v.* maqchhikuy, mayllikuy
wash one's face *v.* uphakuy; **make wash one's face** uphachiy
washed *adj.* mayllisqa, *(clothes)* t'aqsasqa
wasp *n.* wayronqo
waste *v.* usuchiy
wasted *adj.* usuchisqa
water *n.* unu, yaku • *v.* qarpay; **action of water boiling** chhallchay; **help remove from water** llaphch'aysiy; **help water** qarpaysiy; **remove from water** llaphch'ay; **remove from water again and again** llaphch'apayay
water constantly *v.* qarpapayay

watered *adj.* qarpasqa
waterfall *n.* phaqcha
watery *adj.* unuy unuy
way *n.* ñan • *adv.* **in that way** chhayna
we *pron.* *(exclusive)* ñoqayku, *(inclusive)* ñoqanchis
weak *adj.* choqchi, llaphlla, llaphsa • *v.* **become weak** llaphllayay, llaphsayay, pisipay, tiwtiyay
weakened *adj.* pisipasqa
wean *v.* hanuk'ay; **make wean** hanuk'achiy
weaned *adj.* hanuk'asqa
wear out *(clothes)* *v.* thantay
wear out clothing until ragged *v.* chhachuy
wearily *adv.* sayk'uylla
weave *v.* away; **help weave** awaysiy; **make weave** awachiy
weave a plot *v.* allwiy
weaver *n.* awaq
weaving place *n.* awana
weaving tool *n.* awana
welcome *v.* chaskiy • *n.* **person who is welcomed** chaskichikuq
welcomed *adj.* chaskisqa
well *adv.* allinta
wet *adj.* api, ch'aqchusqa • *v.* apichay; **get wet** apiyay
wet the floor *v.* ch'aqchuy
what? *inter.* ima; **for what?** imapaq; **for what reason?** imamanta
what a pity! *interj.* akakallaw, kakallaw
what suffering! *interj.* ananay
when? *inter.* hayk'aq
where? *inter.* maypi; **from where?** maymanta; **to where?** mayman
which? *inter.* mayqen
whine *v.* ch'irchiykachay, waqapakuy
whip *n.* hasut'i, sikwana, soq'ana, waqtana; **person who whips** sikwaq, soq'aq, waqtaq • *v.* sikway, soq'ay, waqtay; **command to whip** sikwachiy, soq'achiy; **help whip** sikwaysiy, soq'aysiy, waqtaysiy; **let oneself be whipped** waqtachikuy; **make whip** waqtachiy
whip again and again *v.* soq'apayay, waqtapayay
whip constantly and disinterestedly *v.* sikwaykachay
whip one another *v.* sikwanakuy, soq'anakuy, waqtanakuy
whipped *adj.* sikwasqa, soq'asqa, waqtasqa
whisper *v.* siphsiy

whisperer *n.* siphsiq
whistle *n.* chilu, siwina • *v.* khuyuy, qoywiy, siwiy; **have the urge to whistle** siwinayay
whistler *n.* khuyuq
white *adj.* yuraq • *v.* **become white** yuraqyay; **become white like a lily** hamanq'ayay
whiten *v.* yuraqyachiy
who? *inter.* pi, pin
who knows! *interj.* yaqapaschá
why? *inter.* ima rayku
wide *adj.* phatu
widen *v.* phatuchay
widow *(woman) n.* ikma • *v.* **become widowed** ikmayay
wild *adj.* purun, salqa • *v.* **become wild** salqayay
win *v.* llalliy
wind *n.* wayra
window *n.* qhawana
wing *n.* pharpa, raphra; **sound of wings flapping at moment of flight** phar
wink *v.* ch'illmiy
wink repeatedly *v.* ch'illmipayay
winner *n.* llalliq
winnow grain *v.* eray • *n.* **place to winnow grain** era
wisdom *n.* yachay
witch *n.* layqa
witchcraft *n.* layqa
with difficulty *adv.* sasay sasay
woman *n.* warmi; **chosen woman in Inkan times** aklla; **manly woman** qharincha; **old woman** paya, *(affectionate)* mamaku; **small woman** t'ustu; **young woman** sipas, p'asña; **young woman in puberty** wachacha • *v.* **become a grown woman** warmiyay; **become a young woman** sipasyay
woman who gives birth *n.* wachakuq
woodcutter *n.* llant'aq
wooden platform *n.* kawitu
wooden post *(medium) n.* tanka
wooden splinter *n.* k'ullpi
wooden spoon *n.* wislla
wooden tub *n.* wanpuru
wool *n.* millma • *v.* **cover with wool** millmachay

wool thread *n.* q'aytu
wooly *adj.* millmasapa
work *n.* llank'ana • *v.* llank'ay; **help work** llank'aysiy; **make work** llank'achiy
work break *n.* hallpa
work temporarily *v.* llank'apakuy
worker *n.* llank'aq
worm *n.* kuru
worn down *adj.* ñañuyasqa
worn out *adj.* *(thing)* ñañu, *(clothes)* thanta
wound *n.* k'iri, nanaq; **stinging wound** k'araq
wounded *adj.* k'iri, k'irisqa
woven *adj.* awasqa
wrap *v.* wank'iy; **help wrap** wank'iysiy; **make wrap** wank'ichiy
wrap again and again *v.* wank'ipayay
wrap around *v.* ratay
wrapped *adj.* wank'isqa
wrapped around *adj.* ratasqa
wring out *v.* ch'arway; **help wring out** ch'arwaysiy
wrinkle *v.* ch'ipuy
wrinkled *adj.* ch'ipusqa
wrong way: *v.* **go the wrong way** pantay • *n.* **person who goes the wrong way** pantaq
wrung out *adj.* ch'arwasqa

Y/Z

yawn *v.* hanllariy
year *n.* wata • *adv.* **all year** watantin
yell *v.* qapariy; **make yell** qaparichiy
yell at one another *v.* qaparqachanakuy, seqachinakuy
yell continuously *v.* qaparqachay
yellow *adj.* q'ello, uwi • *v.* q'ellochay; **turn yellow** q'elloyay
yellowish *adj.* upichu
yes *adv.* arí; **clearly yes** riki
yesterday *n.* qayna p'unchay
you *pron.* *(singular)* qan, *(plural)* qankuna
young man *n.* maqt'a, wayna • *v.* **become a young man** waynayay
young offspring *n.* uña
young woman *n.* sipas, p'asña • *v.* **become a young woman** sipasyay
young woman in puberty *n.* wachacha
younger *adj.* sullk'a
yuca *n.* rumu

zigzag *n.* q'enqo

SPANISH QUECHUA

A

¿a causa de qué? *inter.* imamanta
a veces *adv.* mayninpi
abajo *prep.* uray
abandonado/a *adj.* qonqasqa, saqesqa, wikch'usqa
abandonar *v.* saqey, wikch'uy; **hacer abandonar** wikch'uchiy; **hacerse abandonar** saqechikuy; **hacerse dejar atrás** saqechikuy; **tener deseos de abandonar** wikch'unayay • *s.* **el/la que abandona** wikch'uq
abdomen *s.* wiksa
abeja *s.* wayronqo
abierto/a *adj.* kichasqa
abismo *s.* sankha
ablandar *v.* ñapuy
ablandarse *v.* ñapuyay
abofeteador/a *s.* ch'aqlaq
abofetear *v.* ch'aqlay; **dejarse abofetear** ch'aqlachikuy
abofetear reiteradamente *v.* ch'aqlapayay
abofetearse mutuamente *v.* ch'aqlanakuy
abollado/a *adj.* q'aphñisqa, q'aphñu q'aphñu
abollar *v.* q'aphñuy
abonado/a *adj.* wanuchasqa
abonar *v.* wanuchay
abono *s.* wanu
abortado/a *adj.* sullusqa
abortar *v.* sulluy; **hacer abortar** sulluchiy
abrazar *v.* mak'alliy
abrazarse mutuamente *v.* mak'allinakuy
abrigar *v.* p'istuy; **dejarse abrigar** p'istuchikuy; **hacer abrigar** p'istuchiy
abrigarse *v.* p'istukuy
abrigo *s.* p'istuna
abrir *v.* kichay
abrir la boca *v.* hanllay
abrir lentamente *v.* kichariy
abrir súbitamente *v.* kichariy

abrir un canal *v.* yarqhachay
abrir un forado *v.* wanphuy
abrir una salida *v.* punkuchay
abrir y cerrar la boca constantamente *v.* hanllaykachay
abrirse una flor *v.* phanchiy
abrojo *s.* qepu
absceso *s.* ch'upu
abstraerse *v.* hanrayay, upayay
abstraído/a *adj.* upa
abundar *v.* yalliy
acabarse *v.* tukukuy
acariciar *v.* wayllukuy, luluy
acariciarse mutuamente *v.* lulunakuy
ácaro *s.* itha
acaso *adv.* icha
acecinador/a *s.* ch'arkichiq
acecinar *v.* ch'arkichiy
acequia *s.* yarqha
acercar constantamente *v.* achhupayay
acercarse *v.* achhuykuy, sispay
achatado/a *adj.* t'asnu
achatar *v.* t'asnuy
acidez estomacal *s.* p'osqolli
acné *s.* khiki
acogedor/a *s.* chaskiq
acoger *v.* chaskiy
acogido/a *s.* chaskichikuq • *adj.* chaskisqa
acometer entre varios *v.* waykay
acompañar en el llanto *v.* waqaysiy
acordar *v.* hurk'ay
acostumbrarse *v.* yachakuy
adelgazado/a *(cosas) adj.* ñañuyasqa
adentrar *v.* ukhuchay
adentro *prep.* ukhu
adherido/a *adj.* ch'ipasqa, k'askasqa
adherir *v.* k'askay • *s.* **el/la que adhiere** k'askachiq
adinerado/a *adj.* qolqeyoq
adivinado/a *adj.* watusqa
adivinador/a *s.* watuq
adivinar *v.* watuy

adjuntado/a *adj.* k'intisqa
adjuntar *v.* k'intiy
adjunto *s.* k'inti
adoptar *v.* erqechay
adormecer *v.* utiy; **hacer adormecer** utichiy • *s.* **el/la/lo que causa adormecimiento** utichiq
adormecido/a *adj.* uti
adrede *adv.* yuyaypi
adulador/a *s.* llunk'u
adular *v.* llunk'uy
adulterio: *v.* **cometer adulterio** pantay
adúltero/a *s.* pantaq
aerolito *s.* aqochinchay
afligido/a *adj.* llakisqa
afligirse continuamente *v.* llakipakuy
afónico/a *adj.* ch'aka • *v.* **ocasionar afonía** ch'akayachiy
afuera *prep.* hawa
agacharse *v.* k'umuy; **hacer agachar** k'umuchiy
agarrar *v.* hap'iy
aglomerarse *v.* ch'unkunakuy, sisiykuy
aglutinado/a *adj.* ch'unku
agonizar *v.* wañunayay
agotado/a *adj.* sayk'usqa
agotarse *v.* sayk'uy
agradable *adj.* munay, sumaq
agrandar *v.* hatunchay
agregar *v.* yapay; **hacer agregar** yapachiy
agriarse *v.* p'osqoy
agrio *adj.* p'osqo
agrupador/a *s.* huñuq
agrupar *v.* huñuy; **ayudar a agrupar** huñuysiy
agrupar por cientos *v.* pachaqchay
agrupar por decenas *v.* chunkachay, chunkay
agua *s.* unu, yaku • *v.* **tener deseos de beber agua** ununayay; **acción del agua hirviendo** chhallchay
aguanoso/a *adj.* unuy unuy
águila *s.* anka
aguja grande *s.* yawri
aguja para coser *s.* sirana
agujereado/a *adj.* t'oqosqa

agujero *s.* t'oqo
ahijado/a de bautizo *s.* marq'asqa
ahombrada *s.* qharincha
ahora *adv.* kunan
ahora mismo *adv.* kunanpacha
ahuecado/a *adj.* t'oqosqa
airearse hasta secarse *v.* phaskichikuy; **hacer airear** phaskiyachiy
ajado/a *adj.* ch'awisqa
ajarse *v.* ch'awiy
ají *s.* uchu • *v.* **aliñar con ají** uchuchay
ají molido *s.* uchukuta
ajustar *v.* mat'iy
ajustar una y otra vez *v.* mat'ipayay
al revés *adv.* t'ikranpamanta
ala *s.* pharpa, raphra
alardear *v.* laqlay
alargado/a *adj.* suni
alargar *v.* suniy
alcanzar *v.* aypay; **ayudar a alcanzar** aypaysiy
alcanzar con las manos reiteradamente *v.* haywapayay; **intentar alcanzar con las manos** haywapakuy
alegrarse *v.* kusikuy
alegre *adj.* kusisqa
alegremente *adv.* q'ocho q'ocho
alegría *s.* kusi
alejamiento *s.* ch'usa
alejar *v.* karunchay
alejarse *v.* karunchakuy
aletear *v.* phalalalay, pharararay
alga marina *s.* qochayuyu
algunos/as *adj.* wakin
aliento *s.* samay
aligerar *v.* chhallayay
alimentar *v.* mihuchiy
alinear *v.* sinriy
aliñar con ají *v.* uchuchay
alistarse para viajar *v.* q'epichakuy
aliviado/a *adj.* thanisqa
aliviarse *v.* thaniy; **hacer aliviar** thanichiy • *s.* **el/la que se alivia** thaniq

allí *adv.* chaypi**; por allí** chayninta
alma *s.* nuna
almacenar productos *v.* taqey; **ayudar a almacenar productos** taqeysiy; **mandar a almacenar productos** taqechiy
almácigo *s.* wanpal
almohoda *s.* sawna
alocado/a *adj.* lamuku, waq'ayasqa • *s.* lamuku
alojar *v.* qorpachay
alojarse *v.* qorpachakuy
alpaca *s.* paqocha
alrededor *adv.* neqninta
alumbrar *v.* phallay
aluvión *s.* lloqlla
alzar *v.* hoqariy; **ayudar a alzar** hoqariysiy • *adj.* **fácil de alzar** hoqarinalla
amado/a *adj.* wayllusqa
amanecer *s.* illariy • *v.* illariy, paqariy
amante *s.* waylluq
amar *v.* waylluy
amargo/a *adj.* qhatqe
amargor en los dientes *s.* k'ipi
amarillear *v.* q'ellochay
amarillento/a *adj.* upichu
amarillo/a *adj.* q'ello, uwi • *v.* **tornarse amarillo/a** q'elloyay
amarse mutuamente *v.* wayllunakuy
amontonado/a *adj.* suntusqa
amontonar *v.* suntuy
amoretado/a *adj.* q'oyosqa
amputado/a *adj.* willusqa, wit'usqa
amputador/a *s.* wit'uq
amputar *v.* willuy, wit'uy; **ayudar a amputar** wit'uysiy; **hacer amputar** willuchiy, wit'uchiy
amputar la pierna *v.* chakannay
amuleto de piedra *s.* enqa, enqaychu
amurallado/a *adj.* perqasqa
anciana *(mujer) s.* paya
anciano *(hombre) s.* machu
anda *s.* wantu
andén florido *s.* inkillpata
anegarse *v.* unuyay

anémico/a *adj.* upichu
angosto: *adj.* **muy angosto** p'iti
ángulo *s.* huk'i
anhelo *s.* llachi
animal doméstico *s.* uywa
animal salvaje *s.* salqa uywa
anoche *adv.* ch'isi
anochecer *v.* ch'isinyay, rasphiyay, tutayay
anteayer *s.* qayninpa
anteceder *v.* ñawpariy
anterior *adj.* ñawpaq
anteriormente *adv.* ñawpaqta
anticipar *v.* uriy
anticiparse *v.* ñawpay
antiguo/a *adj.* *(cosa)* mawk'a, *(persona)* ñawpa
anudado/a *adj.* khipusqa
anudar *v.* khipuy; **ayudar a anudar** khipuysiy; **hacer anudar** khipuchiy • *s.* **nudo** khipu
anudar constantemente *v.* khipupayay
anverso *s.* uyanpa
año *s.* wata • *adv.* **todo el año** watantin
apagar el fuego con agua *v.* thasnuy; **ayudar a apagar el fuego con agua** thasnuysiy; **hacer apagar el fuego con agua** thasnuchiy
apalear *v.* p'anay, q'asuy; **ayudar a apalear** p'anaysiy, q'asuysiy; **mandar a apalear** p'anachiy, q'asuchiy
apalearse mutuamente *v.* p'ananakuy, q'asunakuy
aparearse *(aves)* *v.* chiway
aparecer *v.* rikhuriy; **hacer aparecer** rikhurichiy
aparecer en sueños *v.* mosqhoychay
aparecido/a *s.* kukuchi
apartar *v.* achhuchiy
apenas *adv.* ñak'ay
apestoso *adj.* asnaq
apilado *adj.* tawqa tawqa, tawqasqa
apilador/a *s.* tawqaq
apilar *v.* tawqay; **ayudar a apilar** tawqaysiy; **mandar a apilar** tawqachiy
apiñado/a *adj.* ch'unku
apiñarse *v.* ch'unkunakuy

aplanado/a *adj.* p'alta
aplanar *v.* mallmay, p'altachiy
aplaudir *v.* t'aqllay
apocar *v.* chikachay
apodar *v.* sutiyay
apolillado/a *adj.* thutasqa
apolillar *v.* thutay
aporcado/a *adj.* hallmasqa
aporcador/a *s.* hallmaq
aporcar *v.* hallmay; **ayudar a aporcar** hallmaysiy; **mandar a aporcar** hallmachiy
apoyarse en algo o alguien *v.* q'emipakuy
apreciado/a *adj.* qhapaq
aprender *v.* yachay; **tener deseos de aprender** yachanayay
apretadamente *adv.* mat'iy mat'iy
apretado/a *adj.* mat'i, mat'isqa
apretar *v.* mat'iy
apretar una y otra vez *v.* mat'ipayay
apretujado/a *adj.* qaqa
apretujar *v.* k'iskiy
apretujarse *v.* k'iskiyay
aprisa *adv.* phawaylla
aproximarse *v.* achhuykuy, sispay
apuntalado/a *adj.* q'emisqa, tusasqa
apuntalador/a *s.* tusaq
apuntalar *v.* q'emiy, tusay; **ayudar a apuntalar** tusaysiy; **hacer apuntalar** q'emichiy, tusachiy
aquel *adj.* haqhay
aquél *pron.* haqhay
aquella *adj.* haqhay
aquélla *pron.* haqhay
aquéllo *pron.* haqhay
aquí *adv.* kaypi; **por aquí** kayninta
arado andino *s.* taklla
araña *s.* apasanka, uru
árbol *(variedad andina) s.* lloqe
árbol frondoso *s.* sach'a
árbol medicinal *s.* tara
árbol pequeño *s.* mallki
árbol sin muchas ramas *s.* yura

arbusto ribereño *s.* totora
arco iris *s.* k'uychi
arder *v.* rawray, yawray; **hacer arder** rawrachiy, yawrachiy
arder con dificultad *v.* rawraykachay, yawraykachay
ardido/a *adj.* rawrasqa, yawrasqa
ardiente *adj.* k'anchaq, rawraq
arena *s.* aqo, t'iyu
arenoso/a *adj.* aqosapa
arisco/a *adj.* salqa
arqueado/a *adj.* weqru
arquear *v.* weqruy
arraigar *v.* takyay
arrancar un hilo *v.* p'itiy; **hacer arrancar un hilo** p'itichiy
arrastrar *v.* aysay; **ayudar a arrastrar** aysaysiy
arrear *v.* qatiy
arrebatar *v.* qechuy; **ayudar a arrebatar** qechuysiy
arrebatar constantemente *v.* qechuykachay
arreglado/a *adj.* allichasqa
arreglador/a *s.* allichaq
arreglar *v.* allichay; **hacer arreglar** *(algo)* allichachiy
arriba *adv.* hanan, wichay
arrinconar *v.* k'uchunay, k'uchunchay
arrodillarse *v.* qonqorikuy
arrogantemente *adv.* k'askiy k'askiy
arrogante *adj.* apusonqo, k'aski
arrojado/a *adj.* ch'aqesqa, chanqasqa
arrojado/a bruscamente *adj.* choqasqa
arrojador/a *s.* ch'aqeq
arrojar *v.* ch'aqey, chanqay; **ayudar a arrojar** ch'aqeysiy
arrojar bruscamente *v.* choqay
arrojar cosas sin freno *v.* chanqaykachay
arrumado/a *adj.* pirwasqa
arrumar *v.* pirway; **ayudar a arrumar** pirwaysiy
asa *s.* hap'ina
asar carne *v.* kankay
asar papas bajo tierra *v.* wathiyay
asar tubérculos *v.* kusay
ascender *v.* wichay; **ayudar a ascender** wichaysiy; **hacer ascender** wichachiy; **tener deseos de ascender** wichanayay
ascender con dificultad *v.* wichapakuy

ascender rápidamente *v.* wicharpariy
asco: *v.* **causar asco** millachiy; **tener asco** millakuy
asechar *(como un zorro) v.* atoqrayay
asediar *v.* achhupayay, muyuykachay
asentar la olla en el fogón *v.* churpuy
asentarse *v.* takyay, tiyay
asesinado/a *adj.* sipisqa
asesinar *v.* sipiy; **ayudar a asesinar** sipiysiy; **mandar a asesinar** sipichiy
asesino/a *s.* sipiq
asfixiado/a *adj.* mukisqa
asfixiar *v.* mukiy
así *adv.* akna, chayhina, chhayna, kayhina, khayna
asiento *s.* tiyana
asir prolongadamente *(algo) v.* hap'irayay
asomar *v.* achhuy
asperjado/a *(ritual) adj.* ch'allasqa
asperjador/a *(ritual) s.* ch'allaq
asperjar *(ritual) v.* ch'allay
asperjar repetidamente *(ritual) v.* ch'allapayay
áspero *adj.* qhasqa
asqueroso/a *adj.* millay • *v.* **causar asco** millachiy; **tener asco** millakuy
astilla de madera *s.* chhillpa, k'ullpi
astillar *v.* chhillpay, khallpay
asustadizo/a *adj.* manchali
asustado/a *adj.* mancharisqa
asustar *v.* manchachiy, manchay; **causar susto** mancharichiy
asustarse *v.* mancharikuy
atacar entre varios *v.* waykay
atado/a *adj.* watasqa
ataque en grupo contra uno *s.* waykilla
atar *v.* watay; **ayudar a atar** wataysiy; **hacer atar** watachiy
atar una y otra vez *v.* watapayay
atascarse *v.* chakarayay
atolondrarse *v.* hanllarayay
atormentar *v.* ñak'arichiy
atragantarse *v.* chakachikuy
atrapado/a con una red *adj.* llukusqa
atrapar a un animal vivo *v.* chakuy

atrapar con una red *v.* llukuy
atrás *prep.* qhepa
atravesar una valla *v.* wasapay
atropelladamente *adv.* tanqa tanqa
aturdido/a *adj.* thanpi • *v.* **estar aturdido/a** thanpiy
aumentar *v.* askhayachiy, yapay; **hacer aumentar** yapachiy
aumento *s.* yapa
aún más *adv.* astawan, aswanta
aún no *adv.* amaraq
ausencia *s.* ch'usa
ausentarse *v.* ch'usay • *s.* **el/la que se ausenta** ch'usaq
ave *(variedad andina) s.* hak'akllu, kukuli, tunki, urpi
avergonzado/a *adj.* p'enqali; p'enqasqa
avergonzarse *v.* p'enqakuy; **hacer avergonzar** p'enqachiy • *s.* **el/la que se averguenza** p'enqakuq
avisado/a *adj.* willasqa
avisador/a *s.* willaq
avisar *v.* willay; **mandar a avisar** willachiy; **tener deseos de avisar** willanayay
avisar reiteradamente *v.* willapayay
aviso *s.* willakuy
axila *s.* lluk'i
ayer *s.* qayna p'unchay
ayudante *s.* yanapaq
ayudar *v.* haymay, yanapay; **mandar a ayudar** yanapachiy
ayudarse mutuamente *v.* yanapanakuy
ayunar *v.* sasiy; **hacer ayunar** sasichiy
ayuno *s.* sasi
azotado/a *adj.* sikwasqa, soq'asqa
azotador/a *s.* sikwaq, soq'aq
azotar *v.* sikway, soq'ay; **ayudar a azotar** sikwaysiy, soq'aysiy; **mandar a azotar** sikwachiy, soq'achiy
azotar constante y desganadamente *v.* sikwaykachay
azotar una y otra vez *v.* soq'apayay
azotarse mutuamente *v.* sikwanakuy, soq'anakuy
azote *s.* sikwana, soq'ana
azul *adj.* anqas • *v.* **tornarse azul** anqasllay

B

baba *s.* llawsa
babeante *adj.* llawsasuru • *s.* llawsasuru
babear *v.* llawsay, thaltay
bailar *v.* tusuy; **acompañar a bailar** tusuysiy; **hacer bailar** tusuchiy; **tener deseos de bailar** tusunayay
bailarín *s.* tusuq
bajar *v.* uray; **ayudar a bajar** uraysiy; **tener deseos de bajar** uranayay
bajar con dificultad *v.* urapakuy
bajar de peso *v.* chhallayay
bajar rápidamente *v.* urarpariy
balbucir *v.* hanlluy
bambolearse *v.* wanlinyay
banderola *s.* laphara, wiphala
bañado/a *adj.* armasqa
bañar *v.* armay
bañarse *v.* armakuy
baño *s.* hisp'ana
barba *s.* sunkha
barbado *adj.* ch'apu, sunkhayoq
barbechado/a *adj.* yapusqa
barbechador/a *s.* yapuq
barbechar *v.* chaqmay, kuskiy, yapuy; **ayudar a barbechar** chaqmaysiy, yapuysiy; **hacer barbechar** chaqmachiy, yapuchiy
barranco *s.* qaqapana
barredor/a *s.* pichaq
barrer *v.* pichay; **ayudar a barrer** pichaysiy; **hacer barrer** pichachiy
barrer continuamente *v.* pichapayay
barrido/a *adj.* pichasqa
barrigón *adj.* phaksa • *s.* phaksa
barro *s.* t'uru
base *s.* siki, teqsi
bastante *adj.* askha, llasaq • *adv.* askhata
bastón *s.* tawna
basura *s.* q'opa

batea de madera *s.* wanpuru
bebé *s.* wawa
bebedor/a *s.* ukyaq
beber *v.* ukyay; **hacer beber** ukyachiy; **tener deseos de beber** ukyanayay; **tener deseos de beber agua** ununayay
beber a lengüetazos *v.* lapht'ay
beber a prisa *v.* ukyarpariy
bebida *s.* ukyana
bellamente *adv.* sumaqlla, sumaqta
besado/a *adj.* much'asqa
besador/a *s.* much'aq
besar *v.* much'ay; **dejarse besar** much'achikuy
besar indistintamente *v.* much'aykachay
besarse mutuamente *v.* much'anakuy
besuqueador/a *s.* much'apayaq
besuquear *v.* much'apayay
bien *adv.* allinta
bizcar *v.* wesq'oy
bizco *adj.* ch'oqo, lerq'o, wesq'o • *v.* **volverse bizco** lerq'oyay, wesq'oyay
bizquear *v.* lerq'oyay
blanco/a *adj.* yuraq • *v.* **ponerse blanco como el lirio** hamanq'ayay
blando/a *adj.* llank'i, ñapu • *v.* **ponerse blando/a** llank'iyay
blanquear *v.* yuraqyay
bobo/a *adj.* opa
boca *s.* simi
boca abajo *adv.* thallanpamanta • *s.* **el/la que está boca abajo** thallaq
boca arriba *adv.* hank'arpamanta
bocado masticado *s.* hach'u
bochorno *s.* p'enqay
bofetada *s.* ch'aqla
bolso *s.* ch'uspa
bonito/a *adj.* sumaq • *v.* **volverse bonito/a** sumaqyay
borde *s.* patan
borla de lana *s.* puyllu
borracho/a *adj.* machaq • *s.* machaq
bosque *s.* sach'a sach'a
bosta *s.* q'awa
bostezar *v.* hanllariy

botado/a *adj.* wikch'usqa
botador/a *s.* wikch'uq
botar *v.* wikch'uy; **ayudar a botar** wikch'uysiy; **hacer botar** wikch'uchiy; **tener deseos de botar** wikch'unayay
brasa *s.* sansa • *v.* **poner sobre las brasas** sansachay
brazo *s.* mak'a, marq'a • *adj.* **de un solo brazo** willu
brillar *v.* chipchiy, wach'iy; **hacer brillar** wach'ichiy
brillo *s.* chipchiy
brincotear *v.* p'itaykachay
brindar *v.* anqosay
brisa *s.* wayrari
brotado/a *adj.* phutusqa
brotado/a copiosamente *adj.* wakwasqa
brotar *v.* ch'ichiy, phutuy
brotar copiosamente *v.* wakway; **hacer brotar copiosamente** wakwachiy
brotar lentamente *v.* phuturiy
brote *s.* ch'ichi
brujería *s.* layqa
brujo/a *s.* layqa
bueno/a *adj.* allin
búho *s.* ch'oseq, tuku
bulto *s.* q'epi
burla *s.* laq'o
burlar *v.* laq'oy
buscado/a *adj.* maskhasqa
buscador/a *s.* maskhaq
buscar *v.* maskhay; **ayudar a buscar** maskhaysiy

C

cabecera *s.* umala
cabecera de la cama *s.* sawna
cabello *s.* chukcha; **persona con mucho cabello** chukchasapa • *adj.* **con mucho cabello** chukchasapa • *v.* **cortar el cabello** rutuy; **dejarse cortar el cabello** rutuchikuy; **hacer cortar el cabello** rutuchiy
cabeza *s.* uma • *v.* **poner la cabeza sobre la almohada** sawnakuy
cabezón *adj.* umasapa
cabizbajo *adj.* k'umu
cachorro *s.* t'ini
cada uno/a *adj.* sapanka
cadáver *s.* aya
cadera *s.* teqni
caderona *adj.* teqnisapa
caer *v.* urmay; **dejar caer** kachariy, urmachiy; **hacer caer** urmachiy
caer rodando *v.* soqyay
caerse una y otra vez *v.* urmaykachay
caído/a *adj.* urmasqa
calabaza *s.* lakawiti
calandria *s.* tuya
caldo sustancioso *s.* chupi
calentar *v.* q'oñichiy, q'oñiy
calentar con el calor del cuerpo *v.* oqllay
calentarse *v.* q'oñikuy
cálido/a *adj.* q'oñi
caliente *adj.* q'oñi, rupha
calladamente *adv.* upallaspa
callado/a *adj.* upallasqa
callar *v.* ch'inyay, upallay; **hacer callar** upallachiy
callejuela *s.* k'ikllu
calma: *adv.* **con calma** susigo
calor del sol *s.* ruphay
calvo/a *adj.* p'aqla • *v.* **volverse calvo/a** p'aqlayay
calzado tejido *s.* p'olqo
cama *s.* puñuna; **parte de la cama donde van los pies** hayt'a

caminante *s.* puriq
caminar *v.* puriy; **ayudar a caminar** purichiy
caminar alrededor de *v.* tumay
caminar con pasos cortos *v.* ichiy
caminar de puntillas *v.* hink'iy, kirkiy
camino *s.* ñan
camisón *s.* unku
campo *s.* panpa
cana *s.* soqo • *v.* **quitar las canas** soqonay
canal *s.* yarqha
canasta *s.* isanka, p'uktu
canción *s.* taki; *(variedad andina)* wayno
canilla *s.* chakisenqa
canoso/a *adj.* soqo
cansadamente *adv.* sayk'uylla
cansado/a *adj.* sayk'usqa
cansarse *v.* sayk'uy; **causar cansancio** sayk'uchiy
cantar *v.* takiy; **acompañar a cantar** takiysiy; **tener deseos de cantar** takinayay
cantar constantemente *v.* takipayay
cántaro *s.* chatu, p'uyñu
canto *(variedad andina) s.* haylli
canto del gallo *s.* wallpa waqay
cantor *s.* takiq
canturrear *v.* takiykachay
caña de maíz *s.* wiru
captura de animales entre muchas personas *(ritual) s.* chaku
capturar *v.* hap'iy; **dejarse capturar** hap'ichikuy • *adj.* **fácil de capturar** hap'inalla
cara *s.* uya
carbón *s.* k'illinsa
carcomer *v.* uthay
carcomerse *v.* mullphayay
carcomido/a *adj.* mullpha
carga *s.* q'epi
cargado/a *(en la espalda) adj.* q'episqa
cargador/a *s.* q'epiq
cargar en la espalda *v.* q'epiy; **ayudar a cargar en la espalda** q'epiysiy; **hacer cargar en la espalda** q'epichiy
carne *s.* aycha

carne asada *s.* kanka
carnoso/a *adj.* aychasapa
carrizo *s.* soqos
casa *s.* wasi • *v.* **construir una casa** wasichay
casada *(mujer) adj.* qosayoq
cascada *s.* phaqcha
cascajo: *v.* **cubrir con cascajo una vía** khallkachay; **quitar el cascajo de una vía** khallkanay
casi *adv.* yaqa
castaño *s.* k'ispa • *adj.* ch'unpi; **teñido/a de castaño** ch'unpichasqa • *v.* **teñir de castaño** ch'unpichay; **tornarse castaño/a** ch'unpiyay
caverna *s.* mach'ay
cavidad *s.* p'ukru
cecina *s.* ch'arki
ceja *s.* pullurki
celeste *adj.* qosi
cencerro *s.* chanrara
ceniza *s.* uspha • *v.* **cubrir con ceniza** usphachay; **empolvarse con ceniza** usphachakuy; **volverse ceniza** usphayay
centrar *v.* chawpinay • *s.* **el/la que centra** chawpichaq
centro *s.* chawpi, sonqo
cepillado/a *(madera) adj.* llaqllasqa
cepillar *(madera) v.* llaqllay; **ayudar a cepillar** llaqllaysiy; **hacer cepillar** llaqllachiy
cerámica *s.* k'akra
cerca *adj.* sispa
cerca de allí *adv.* chayneqpi
cerca de aquí *adv.* kayneqpi
cercenado/a *adj.* mut'u
cercenar *v.* mut'uy; **hacerse cercenar** mut'uchikuy
cerda *(pelo grueso) s.* suphu • *v.* **quitar las cerdas** suphunay
cerdo *s.* khuchi
cernícalo andino *s.* k'illichu
cernido/a *adj.* suysusqa
cernir *v.* suysuy; **ayudar a cernir** suysuysiy; **mandar a cernir** suysuchiy
cerrado/a *adj.* wesq'asqa • *v.* **mantenerse cerrado/a permanentemente** wesq'arayay
cerrar *v.* wesq'ay; **ayudar a cerrar** wesq'aysiy; **hacer cerrar** wesq'achiy • *s.* **el/la que cierra** wesq'aq

cerrarse difinitivamente *v.* wesq'akapuy
cerro de forma triangular *v.* pikchu
cesar *v.* tatiy
chal *s.* unkuña
chalina *s.* p'istuna
chamuscado/a *adj.* q'aspasqa
chamuscar *v.* q'aspay
chapotear *v.* wayt'aykachay
charco *s.* p'onqo
chicha *s.* akha
chicha no fermentada *s.* upi
chirrido *s.* k'ir
chisguetear *v.* ch'ikway, ch'iwkay
chismeador/a *s.* willapakuq
chismear *v.* willapakuy
choclo *s.* choqllo
chorrear *v.* ch'uychuy
choza *s.* ch'uklla; **constructor/a de chozas** ch'ukllaq • *v.* **construir una choza** ch'ukllay; **hacer construir una choza** ch'ukllachiy
chueco/a *adj.* weqru
chuño blanco *s.* moraya
chupar *v.* ch'onqay
chupar incesantemente *v.* ch'onqaykachay
ciego *adj.* ñawsa • *v.* **volverse ciego/a** ñawsayay
cielo *s.* hanaqpacha
cien *s.* pachaq • *v.* **agrupar por cientos** pachaqchay
cierto/a *adj.* cheqaq
cima de una montaña *s.* pikchu
cimarrón *adj.* ch'ita, k'ita
cinco *num.* pisqa
circular *adj.* suntur
círculo *s.* muyu
claro *adj.* sut'in
claro que sí *adv.* riki
clavado *adj.* sat'isqa
clavar *v.* ch'antiy, sat'iy, takay; **ayudar a clavar** takaysiy
clavar repetidas veces *v.* takapayay
coagularse *v.* tikayay
cobrar *v.* manuchay
coca *s.* kuka; **el/la que prepara las hojas de coca** k'intuq;

masticador/a de hoja de coca akulliq; **ramillete de hojas de coca** k'intu • *v.* **hacer masticar hoja de coca** akullichiy; **masticar hoja de coca** akulliy, chakchay, hallpay, pikchay; **preparar hojas de coca** *(ritual)* k'intuy
cocer *v.* chayay • *adj.* **a medio cocer** hanku hanku
cocer al vapor *v.* phasiy
cocido/a *adj.* wayk'usqa
cocido/a al vapor *adj.* phasi
cocinado/a *adj.* chayasqa, wayk'usqa
cocinar *v.* wayk'uy; **ayudar a cocinar** wayk'uysiy; **hacer cocinar** wayk'uchiy; **tener deseos de cocinar** wayk'unayay
cocinero/a *s.* wayk'uq
codiciar desesperadamente *v.* wañurqoy
coetáneo/a *adj.* wiñaqmasi
cola *s.* chupa
colaborar *v.* haymay
colaborar en desordenar *v.* rawiysiy
colado/a *adj.* ch'umasqa
colapsar *v.* chhullmiy; **hacer colapsar** chhullmichiy
colar *v.* ch'umay
colgado/a *adj.* warkusqa
colgador *s.* warkuna
colgar *v.* warkuy; **ayudar a colgar** warkuysiy; **hacer colgar** warkuchiy • *s.* **el/la que cuelga** *(algo)* warkuq; **lo que cuelga** warku
colina *s.* moqo
collar *s.* walqay
colmado/a *adj.* llinp'asqa
colmar *v.* llinp'ay
colmar un lugar *v.* sisiy
colmillo *s.* waqsa
colocado/a *adj.* churasqa
colocar *v.* churay
colocar al centro *(algo)* *v.* chawpichay, chawpinay
colocar al medio *(algo)* *v.* chawpichay, chawpinay
colocar en posición boca abajo *(algo)* *v.* thallachiy; **mandar a colocar en posición boca abajo** thallachiy
colocar en posición lateral *(algo)* *v.* k'achanpachiy
colocar soportes a las cosas *v.* chakichay
colonizar *v.* llaqtachakuy, mitmay

colono/a *s.* mitma
comenzado *adj.* qallarisqa
comenzar *v.* qallariy • *s.* **el/la que comienza** qallariq
comer *v.* mihuy; **tener deseos de comer** mihunayay • *s.* **el/la que come** mihuq
comer constantemente *v.* mihupayay
comida *s.* mihuna
comido *adj.* mihusqa
como *adv.* hina
compadecerse *v.* khuyapayay • *s.* **el/la que se compadece** khuyapayaq
competir *v.* atipanakuy
completado/a *adj.* hunt'asqa
completamente *adv.* llapanta, lluyta
completar *v.* hunt'ay
completo/a *adj.* hunt'a
comprado/a *adj.* rantisqa
comprador/a *s.* rantiq
comprar *v.* rantiy; **hacer comprar** rantichiy; **mandar a comprar** rantichiy; **tener deseos de comprar** rantinayay
comprimido/a *adj.* ñit'isqa, ñup'usqa
comprimir *v.* ñit'iy, ñup'uy; **ayudar a comprimir** ñit'iysiy; **hacer comprimir** ñit'ichiy
comprimir una y otra vez *v.* ñit'ipayay
comunidad *s.* ayllu
concha del molusco *s.* ch'uru
concha marina *s.* pututu
concluido/a *adj.* tukusqa
concluir *v.* tukukuy; **ayudar a concluir** tukuysiy; **hacer concluir** tukuchiy
concluir de prisa *v.* tukurpariy
condolerse *v.* llakipayay
cóndor *s.* kuntur
confluir *v.* tinkuy
confrontación *s.* tinku
confrontar *v.* tinkuy, uyanchay; **hacer confrontar** tinkuchiy
confrontarse *v.* tinkunakuy
confundir *v.* ch'arwiy
congregar *v.* tantay
congregarse *v.* tantanakuy

conjuntar *v.* tupachiy
conocer *v.* reqsiy; **hacer conocer** reqsichiy; **hacerse conocer** reqsichikuy; **tener deseos de conocer** reqsinayay
conocerse mutuamente *v.* reqsinakuy
conocido/a *adj.* reqsisqa, yachasqa • *s.* reqsisqa
conocimiento *s.* yachay
consanguíneo *s.* yawarmasi
conscientemente *adv.* yuyaypi
consejero/a *s.* uywaqe
consistente *adj.* ch'ila
conspirar *v.* allwiy, yachachinakuy
constelación *s.* warani
constructor/a de muros *s.* perqaq
constructor/a de chozas *s.* ch'ukllaq
construir una choza *v.* ch'ukllay; **hacer construir una choza** ch'ukllachiy
construir un fogón *v.* q'onchachay
construir un muro *v.* perqay
construir un nido *v.* q'esachakuy
construir una casa *v.* wasichay
consumido/a *adj.* t'antasqa
consumir *v.* t'antay
contable *(cantidades) adj.* yupa
contado/a *adj.* *(historias)* willasqa; *(cantidades)* yupasqa
contador/a *(cantidades) s.* yupaq
contar *v.* *(historias)* willay; *(cantidades)* yupay; **ayudar a contar** *(cantidades)* yupaysiy; **hacer contar** *(cantidades)* yupachiy; **mandar a contar** *(historias)* willachiy; **tener deseos de contar** *(historias)* willanayay
contar una y otra vez *(cantidades) v.* yupapayay
contar reiteradamente *(historias) v.* willapayay
contarse mutuamente *(historias) v.* willanakuy
contemporáneo/a *s.* wiñaqmasi
contrapesar *v.* turay
converger con *v.* tupay • *s.* **el/la que converge con** tupaq
convertir en harapos *v.* saphsachay
convertirse en tierra o polvo *v.* allpayapuy
conviviente *s.* kawsaqmasi
convocado/a para un trabajo comunal *adj.* mink'asqa
convocador/a para un trabajo comunal *v.* mink'akuq

convocar para un trabajo comunal *v.* mink'ay
coral *s.* mullu
corazón *s.* sonqo
corneado/a *adj.* waqrasqa
cornear *v.* waqray; **hacer cornear** waqrachiy; **tener deseos de cornear** waqranayay
cornearse mutuamente *v.* waqranakuy
corral *s.* kancha
correa *s.* mat'ina
correa tejida *s.* chunpi
corredor/a *s.* phawaq
correr *v.* phaway; **hacer correr** phawachiy; **tener deseos de correr** phawanayay • *s.* **el/la que hace correr** phawachiq
corretear *v.* phawakachay
corroer *v.* uthay
corroerse *(granos) v.* hut'uyay
cortar *v.* kuchuy
cortar el cabello *v.* rutuy; **dejarse cortar el cabello** rutuchikuy; **hacer cortar el cabello** rutuchiy
cortar los cuernos *v.* waqranay
cosechado/a *adj. (sobre la tierra)* pallasqa
cosechar *v.* aymuray, *(sobre la tierra)* pallay; **ayudar a cosechar** *(sobre la tierra)* pallaysiy; **mandar a cosechar** *(sobre la tierra)* pallachiy
cosedor/a *s.* siraq
coser *v.* siray; **ayudar a coser** siraysiy; **mandar a coser ropa para uno/a** sirachikuy
coser toscamente *v.* ch'ukay; **ayudar a coser toscamente** ch'ukaysiy
cosido/a *adj.* sirasqa
cosido/a toscamente *adj.* ch'ukasqa
cosquillas: *v.* **hacer cosquillas a alguien** kullachiy
costado *s.* kinra • *adv.* **de costado** *(posición)* k'achanpamanta • *v.* **poner de costado** *(algo)* k'achanpay
costilla *s.* waqta
costurero/a *s.* siraq
creado/a *adj.* kamasqa
creador/a *s.* kamaq, paqarichiq
crear *v.* kamay, paqarichiy
crecer *v.* hatunyay, wiñay; *(árbol)* yuray; **hacer crecer** wiñachiy

crecer la barba *v.* sunkhayay
crecido/a *adj.* wiñasqa
crespo/a *adj.* k'upa, k'uspa
cresta *s.* k'akara
cría de oveja *s.* chita
criado/a *adj.* uywasqa
criador/a *s.* uywaq
criar *v.* uyway
crío/a *s.* uña
cristal *s.* qespi
crudo/a *adj.* hanku
cruzar *v.* chinpay; **ayudar a cruzar** chinpachiy • *s.* **el/la que ayuda a cruzar** chinpachiq
cuadrúpedo *adj.* tawachaki
¿cuál? *inter.* mayqen
¿cuándo? *inter.* hayk'aq
¿cuánto/a? *inter.* hayk'a
¿cuántos/as? *inter.* hayk'a
cuatro *num.* tawa
cubierto/a con frazada *adj.* qatasqa
cubrir: *v.* **ayudar a cubrir** pakaysiy
cubrir con frazada *v.* qatay • *s.* **el/la que cubre con frazada** qataq
cubrir con cascajo una vía *v.* khallkachay; **quitar el cascajo de una vía** khallkanay
cubrir con ceniza *v.* usphachay
cubrir con lana *v.* millmachay
cubrir con tierra *v.* allpachay; **dejarse cubrir con tierra** *v.* p'anpachikuy
cubrirse con frazada *v.* qatakuy
cubrirse con hojarasca *v.* ch'aphrachakuy
cubrirse con plumas *v.* phurullikuy
cubrirse con ramas *v.* ch'aphrachakuy
cubrirse mutuamente con frazadas *v.* qatanakuy
cuchara de madera *s.* wislla
cucharón para sacar liquidos *s.* wisina
cuchicheador/a *s.* siphsiq
cuchichear *v.* siphsiy
cuchilla *(ritual) s.* tumi
cuchillo *s.* kuchuna

cuchillo desafilado *s.* morq'a
cuchillo para degollar *s.* nak'ana
cuello *s.* kunka
cuerda para atar *s.* watana
cuerno *s.* waqra
cuero *s.* qara
cuerpo *(persona) s.* ukhu
cueva *s.* mach'ay
cuidado: *adv.* **con mucho cuidado** allichallamanta
cuidado con ... *interj.* paqtataq
cuidado que ... *interj.* paqtataq
cuidar a alguien en su casa *v.* tiyaysiy
culebra *s.* mach'aqway
cuna *s.* k'iraw
curado/a *adj.* hanpisqa, qhaliyasqa
curador/a *s.* qhaliyachiq
curandero/a *s.* hanpiq
curar *v.* hanpiy, qhaliyachiy; **ayudar a curar** hanpiysiy; **hacer curar** hanpichiy; **hacerse curar** hanpichikuy
curarse *v.* hanpikuy
curva *s.* q'enqo
curvado/a *adj.* weqo
curvar *v.* weqoy; **ayudar a curvar** weqoysiy; **hacer curvar** weqochiy
curvarse *v.* weqokuy
cuy *s.* qowi
cuy macho *s.* kututu

D

dado/a *adj.* qosqa
dador/a *s.* qoq
danza andina de carnaval *s.* qhaswa
dañado/a *adj.* chirmasqa
dañar *v.* chirmay • *s.* **el/la/lo que causa daño** chirmaq
dar *v.* qoy
dar a luz *(persona) v.* wachakuy; **estar a punto de dar a luz** wachanayay • *s.* **persona que da a luz** wachakuq
dar a luz continuamente *(persona) v.* wachapakuy
dar alcance *v.* taripay
dar de comer de boca a boca *v.* umiy • *s.* **el/la que da de comer de boca a boca** umiq
dar de comer de boca a boca constantemente *v.* umipayay
dar leche de pecho *v.* ñuñuy
dar risotadas *v.* thintiy
dar risotadas una y otra vez *v.* thintipayay
dar un giro lentamente *v.* kutiriy
dar vueltas *v.* muyuy; **hacer dar vueltas** muyuchiy
dardo *s.* wach'i
de buena manera *adv.* allinta
de costado *(posición) adv.* k'achanpamanta • *v.* **poner de costado** *(algo)* k'achanpay
¿de dónde? *inter.* maymanta
de esa manera *adv.* chayhina, chhayna
de esta manera *adv.* akna, kayhina
de ninguna manera *adv.* amapuni, manapuni
de nuevo *adv.* hoqmanta, wakmanta, yapamanta
de vez en cuando *adv.* mayninpi
debajo *prep.* ura
debilitado/a *adj.* pisipasqa
debilitarse *v.* pisipay, tiwtiyay
decaído *adj. (salud)* machuyasqa, usphu
decapitar *v.* umanay
decir *v.* niy
decir incoherencias *v.* thawtiy • *s.* **el/la que dice incoherencias** thawtiq

decrépito/a *adj.* thultu • *v.* **devenir en decrépito/a** thultuyay
dedo pulgar *s.* mamaruk'ana
defecar *v.* akay, *(ganado)* uchhay; **hacer defecar** akachiy; **tener deseos de defecar** akanayay
defender a alguien *v.* sayapakuy
defenderse dando cornadas *v.* waqrapakuy
defenderse dando palazos *v.* p'anapakuy, q'asupakuy
degollado/a *adj.* nak'asqa
degollador/a *s.* nak'achu, nak'aq
degollar *v.* nak'ay; **hacer degollar** nak'achiy
degustar *v.* malliy; **hacer degustar** mallichiy
deidad andina *s.* apu, awki, waka
dejar *v.* saqey
dejar al cuidado de alguien *v.* saqekuy
dejarse ganar por las horas del día *v.* intiyay
delgado/a *(cosas) adj.* ñañu
delirante *adj.* musphaq
delirantemente *adv.* muspha muspha
delirar *v.* musphay
delirar constantemente *v.* musphapayay
demarcar *v.* suyunchay
demasiado/a *adj.* ñisu • *adv.* ñisuta
demorar: *v.* **hacer demorar** unayachiy
denso/a *adj.* thaka, pipu
dentelleado/a *adj.* khamusqa, p'atasqa
dentellear *v.* khamuy, p'atay; **hacer dentellear** khamuchiy
dentellearse mutuamente *v.* p'atanakuy
depósito provisional *s.* astana
depurar *v.* ch'uyayachiy
derecha *adj.* paña
derramado/a *adj.* hich'asqa
derramar *v.* hich'ay; **ayudar a derramar** hich'aysiy
derramar una y otra vez *v.* hich'apayay
derribado/a *adj.* kunpasqa, wikapasqa
derribar *v.* kunpay, wikapay; **hacer derribar** wikapachiy
derribar con o sin intención *v.* kunparpariy
derrumbado/a *adj.* thunisqa
derrumbar *v.* thuniy; **hacer derrumbar** thunichiy
desagradable *adj.* millay
desagradablemente *adv.* millay millay

desalentado/a *adj.* usphu, willpusqa
desalentarse *v.* usphuy; **hacer desalentar** usphuchiy
desaparecer *v.* ch'usaqyay; **hacer desaparecer** ch'usaqyachiy
desaparecer para siempre *v.* ch'usaqyapuy
desaparecido/a *adj.* ch'usaqyasqa
desarreglado/a *adj.* thamalanku
desarrollado/a *adj.* wiñasqa
desarrollar *v.* wiñay; **hacer desarrollar** wiñachiy
desarrollarse *v.* hatunyay
desastillar *v.* chhillpanay
desatado/a *adj.* paskasqa
desatador/a *s.* paskaq
desatar *v.* paskay; **hacer desatar** paskachiy
desbarrancarse *v.* qaqapay; **hacer desbarrancar** qaqapachiy
descansado/a *adj.* samasqa
descansar *v.* samay; **hacer descansar** samachiy; **tener deseos de descansar** samanayay • *s.* **lugar de descanso** samana
descarnar *v.* aycharay
descender *v.* urayay
descendido/a *adj.* urayasqa
descolorarse *v.* qhoqayay
descolorido/a *adj.* qhoqa
descomedida *(mujer) adj.* waylaka
descontento/a *adj.* waqati
descorrer *v.* llat'ay
descortés *adj.* haphlla
descortezado/a con los dientes *(un tallo) adj.* sinkhasqa
descortezar con los dientes *(un tallo) v.* sinkhay
descoser *v.* llik'iy, siranay
descubierto/a *adj.* llat'asqa
descubrir lo que está cubierto *v.* q'allpay
desde entonces *conj.* chaymantapacha
desdentado/a *adj.* hanllu, laqmu
desear *v.* munay
desecado/a *adj.* ch'akisqa
desechar *v.* yanqachay
desembarrar *v.* t'urunay
desenraizado/a *adj.* t'irasqa
desenraizar *v.* saphinay, t'iray; **ayudar a desenraizar** t'iraysiy
desestimar *v.* yanqachay

desgajar *v.* khakay
desgarrar *v.* llik'iy
desgastado/a *adj.* hallmu
desgastado/a por el uso *(ropa) adj.* thanta
desgastar *(ropa) v.* thantay
desgastar hasta deshilachar *(ropa) v.* chhachuy
desgracia *s.* aqoyraki
desgranado *(maíz) adj.* muchhasqa
desgranar *(maíz) v.* muchhay; **ayudar a desgranar** muchhaysiy
desgranarse *v.* chhallmay
desgreñado/a *adj.* t'anpa
desgreñarse *v.* t'anpachakuy
deshacer *v.* thullkiy
desharrapado/a *adj.* chhachu
deshecho/a *adj.* thullkisqa
deshidratado/a por el sol *adj.* qachasqa
deshojado *(mazorca de maíz) adj.* tipisqa
deshojar *(mazorca de maíz) v.* tipiy; **ayudar a deshojar** tipiysiy; **mandar a deshojar** tipichiy
desleal *adj.* iskayllu
desmoronado/a *adj.* thullkisqa
desmoronar *v.* thullkiy
desnudador/a *s.* q'alachiq
desnudar *v.* q'aray, q'alachay; **dejarse desnudar** q'alachikuy
desnudarse *v.* q'alachakuy, q'arayay
desnudo/a *adj.* q'ala, q'alalla, q'ara
desollado/a *adj.* lluch'isqa
desollar *v.* ch'utiy, lluch'iy, llust'iy; **mandar a desollar** ch'utichiy
desordenado/a *adj.* rawi, thamalanku
desordenar *v.* rawiy
desorejar *v.* rinrinay
desorganizada *(mujer) adj.* waylaka
despacio *adv.* susigo
desparramado/a *adj.* chhullmisqa, wisnisqa
desparramador/a *s.* wisniq
desparramar *v.* wisniy; **ayudar a desparramar** wisniysiy; **hacer desparramar** wisnichiy
desparramar por todas partes *v.* wisniykachay
despedazar *v.* k'iphtay
despedido/a de mala manera *adj.* qarqosqa

despedir de mala manera *v.* qarqoy; **ayudar a despedir de mala manera** qarqoysiy; **hacer despedir de mala manera** qarqochiy
despellejado/a *adj.* lluch'isqa
despellejar *v.* lluch'iy, llust'iy
despeñadero *s.* qaqapana
despeñarse *v.* qaqapay; **hacer despeñar** qaqapachiy
desperdiciado/a *adj.* usuchisqa
desperdiciar *v.* usuchiy
desperezarse *v.* chutarikuy
despertar *v.* rikch'ay; **estar a punto de despertar** rikch'anayay
despertarse a cada rato *v.* rikch'apakuy
despiojado/a *adj.* usasqa
despiojar *v.* usay; **dejarse despiojar** usachikuy; **hacer despiojar** usachiy
desplazarse *v.* kuyuriy
desplegar *v.* llat'ay
desplomado/a *adj.* thunisqa
desplomar *v.* thuniy; **hacer desplomar** thunichiy
desplumador/a *s.* phurunaq
desplumar *v.* phurunay
despojar *v.* ch'utiy, llat'anay; **mandar a despojar** ch'utichiy
despojar de las pertenencias *v.* q'alachay; **dejarse despojar de las pertenencias** chaskichikuy • *s.* **el/la que hace despojar de las pertenencias** q'alachiq; **persona que se deja despojar sus pertenencias** chaskichikuq
desportillado/a *adj.* k'aphtisqa, q'asasqa
desportillar *v.* k'aphtiy, khallpay, q'asay
desprender un fruto *v.* khakuy
después de eso *conj.* chaymanta
después de mucho tiempo *adv.* unaymanta
desteñido/a *adj.* qhoqa
desteñirse *v.* qhoqayay
destetado/a *adj.* hanuk'asqa
destetar *v.* hanuk'ay; **hacer destetar** hanuk'achiy
destrenzar *v.* sinp'anay
desunir *v.* hukllanay
desvariar *v.* thawtiy
desvestirse *v.* ch'utikuy
desviarse *v.* chinkay
desyerbar *v.* qoray

detener *v.* hark'ay, sayachiy; **ayudar a detener** hark'aysiy
deteriorar *v.* thantay
detestar *v.* cheqnikuy
deuda *s.* manu • *v.* **no pagar una deuda** ch'achuy
deudor/a *s.* ch'achu • *v.* **hacerse deudor** manuyay
devolver *v.* kutichiy
devorado/a *adj.* wap'usqa
devorar *v.* wap'uy; **tener deseos de devorar** wap'unayay
día *s.* p'unchay • *v.* **dejarse ganar por las horas del día** intiyay; **hacerse de día** p'unchayyay • *adv.* **todo el día** ch'isiyaq, p'unchaynintin
diáfano/a *adj.* ch'uya
diarrea *s.* q'echa, seqra • *v.* **estar con diarrea** q'echanayay; **tener diarrea** seqray
diente *s.* kiru
diez *num.* chunka
diferente *adj.* hoqniraq
diferentemente *adv.* hoqniraqta
difícil *adj.* sasa
difícilmente *adv.* sasay sasay
dificultar *v.* sasachay
difundir *v.* mast'ariy
diluido *adj.* unuyachisqa
diluirse *v.* unuyay
diminuto/a *adj.* ch'iñi
dinero *s.* qolqe
discutir *v.* seqachinakuy
disecar *v.* ch'alqey
diseminado/a *adj.* t'akasqa
diseminar *v.* t'akay
disminuido/a *adj.* waywasqa
disminuir *v.* asllayachiy, chikachay, wayway; **hacer disminuir** waywachiy
disolver *v.* chulluy, unuyachiy
disolver en la boca *v.* mullmuy
dispersado/a *adj.* ch'eqesqa
dispersado/a con la mano *adj.* qachisqa
dispersar *v.* ch'eqechiy
dispersar con la mano *v.* qachiy; **ayudar a dispersar con la mano** qachiysiy

dispersar con la mano una y otra vez *v.* qachipayay
disperso/a *adj.* ch'eqe
disputar *v.* atipanakuy
distinto/a *adj.* sapaq
distribuido/a *adj.* rakisqa
distribuidor/a *s.* rakiq
distribuir *v.* rakiy; **hacer distribuir** rakichiy
distribuirse mutuamente *v.* rakinakuy
disuelto/a *adj.* chullusqa, unuyachisqa
disuelto en la boca *adj.* mullmusqa
dividir en dos *v.* iskaychay
divulgar *v.* willaykachay
doblado/a *adj.* q'enpisqa
doblar *v.* pataray, q'enpiy; **hacer doblar** q'enpichiy
doler *v.* nanay
doler constantemente *v.* nanapayay
dolor *s.* nanay • *v.* **causar dolor** nanachiy
dominado/a *adj.* atipasqa
dominador/a *s.* atipaq
dominar *v.* atipay; **dejarse dominar** atipachikuy
¿dónde? *inter.* maypi
dorado/a *adj.* p'aqo, parusqa • *v.* **volverse dorado/a** p'aqoyay
dorar a fuego *v.* paruy; **hacer dorar a fuego** paruchiy
dormido/a *adj.* puñusqa
dormir *v.* puñuy; **acompañar a dormir** puñuysiy; **estar a punto de dormir** puñunayay; **tener deseos de dormir** puñunayay
dormir en casa ajena *v.* puñupakuy
dormitar *v.* puñupayay
dormitorio *s.* puñuna
dos *num.* iskay
dudar *v.* iskayyay, thukiy; **hacer dudar** thukichiy • *s.* **el/la que duda** thukiq
dudar a menudo *v.* thukiykachay
dueño/a *s.* kaqniyoq
dulce *adj.* misk'i; **muy dulce** misk'illaña
duplicar *v.* iskaychay
duro/a *adj.* anaq, ch'ila, chuchu • *v.* **ponerse duro** chuchuyay

E

¡eh! *interj.* yaw
él *pron.* pay
elegante *adj.* k'acha, qhapchi • *v.* **ponerse elegante** k'achayay
elegantemente *adv.* k'achay k'achay
ella *pron.* pay
ellas *pron.* paykuna
ellos *pron.* paykuna
embadurnar *v.* llunch'iy
embarazada *adj.* onqoq, wiksayoq • *v.* **estar embarazada** onqokuy
embarazarse *v.* wiksayay
embarrado/a *adj.* t'uruchasqa
emblanquecer *v.* yuraqyachiy
emborrachado/a *adj.* machasqa
emborracharse *v.* machay; **hacer emborrachar** machachiy
embriagado/a *adj.* machasqa
embriagarse *v.* machay; **acompañar a embriagarse** machaysiy; **hacer embriagar** machachiy
embrujado/a *adj.* layqasqa, umusqa
embrujar *v.* layqay, umuy; **hacer embrujar** layqachiy
empalagado/a *adj.* amisqa
empalagar *v.* amiy
empapado/a de agua *adj.* ch'uychu
emparejar *v.* yanachay
emparejarse con mujer *v.* warmichakuy
emparentarse *v.* aylluchakuy
empequeñecerse en la vejez *(mujer) v.* t'ustuyay
empezado *adj.* qallarisqa
empezar *v.* qallariy
emplastado/a *adj.* laq'asqa
emplastar *v.* laq'ay; **ayudar a emplastar** laq'aysiy
empobrecer *v.* q'alayay, wakchayay; **hacer empobrecer** wakchayachiy
embobrecido/a *adj.* q'alayasqa
empollar *v.* oqllay
empolvarse con ceniza *v.* usphachakuy

empozarse *v.* p'onqochakuy
empujar *v.* tanqay
empujarse mutuamente *v.* tanqanakuy
¿en dónde? *inter.* maypi
en vano *adv.* yanqa
enano *s.* ch'ukchu, umutu
encajar *v.* haykuchiy
encanecer *v.* soqoyay
encarar *v.* uyanchay
encargado/a *(cosas) adj.* suchisqa
encargador/a *s.* suchiq
encargar *v.* suchiy
encargo *s.* suchi
encender *v.* hap'ichiy
encender el fuego *v.* ninachay
encías *s.* lluch'a
encima *prep.* hanaq • *adv.* pata, wichay
enclenque *adj.* choqchi, k'arpi
encogerse *(cosas) v.* q'estiy
encogido/a *(cosas) adj.* q'estisqa
encontrado *adj.* tarisqa
encontrar *v.* tariy; **ayudar a encontrar** tariysiy
encontrarse con *v.* tupay • *s.* **el/la que se encuentra con** tupaq
encubierto/a *adj.* pakasqa
encubrir *v.* pakay
encubrirse mutuamente *v.* pakanakuy
endeble *adj.* tiwti, toqti
endulzar *v.* misk'ichiy
enemigo/a *s.* awqa • *v.* **hacer enemistar** awqanachiy
enfardado/a *adj.* wank'isqa
enfardar *v.* wank'iy; **ayudar a enfardar** wank'iysiy; **mandar a enfardar** wank'ichiy
enfardar una y otra vez *v.* wank'ipayay
enfermar *v.* onqoy
enfermarse frecuentemente *v.* onqopayay
enfermedad *s.* onqoy, machusqa
enfermedad venérea *s.* wanthi
enfermizo/a *adj.* onqoli
enfermo/a *adj.* onqoq
enflaquecer *v.* choqchiyay, tiwtiyay, tulluyay; **hacer enflaquecer** tulluyachiy

enflaquecer demasiado *v.* ch'arkiyay
enfrente de *adv.* chinpa
enfriado/a *adj.* chiriyasqa
enfriar *v.* chiriyay; **hacer enfriar** chiriyachiy
engalanado/a *adj.* siklla
engañado/a *adj.* q'otosqa, yukasqa
engañador/a *s.* yukaq
engañar *v.* laq'oy, q'otoy, qeqoy, yukay; **ayudar a engañar** yukaysiy; **dejarse engañar** q'otochikuy, qeqochikuy, yukachikuy
engañar constantemente *v.* yukapayay
engañarse mutuamente *v.* yukanakuy
engaño *s.* laq'o
engendrado/a *adj.* churiyasqa
engendrador/a *s.* churiyaq
engendrar *v.* churiyay, yumay
engordar *v.* wirayay; **hacer engordar** wirayachiy
engreído/a *adj.* apusonqo
engrosar *v.* phatuchay, rakhuyay
engullido/a *adj.* melq'osqa, millp'usqa, oqosqa, q'otosqa, wap'usqa
engullir *v.* melq'oy, millp'uy, oqoy, q'otoy, wap'uy; **hacer engullir** millp'uchiy, oqochiy; **tener deseos de engullir** wap'unayay
engullir una y otra vez *v.* millp'upayay, oqopayay
enjuagar *v.* ch'uyanay
enjuagarse la boca *v.* moqch'ikuy
enjuto/a *adj.* k'arpi, k'asu
enlazado/a *adj.* ch'atasqa
enlazar *v.* ch'atay; **ayudar a enlazar** ch'ataysiy
enlazar con una soga *v.* waskhay
enloquecer *v.* waq'ayay; **hacer enloquecer** waq'ayachiy
enloquecido/a *v.* waq'ayasqa
enlutado/a *adj.* yanallisqa
enlutarse *v.* yanallikuy • *s.* **el/la que se enluta** yanallikuq
enmudecer *v.* amuyay
enmugrecerse la piel *v.* kharkachakuy
ennegrecer *v.* yanayay
ennegrecerse *v.* yanachakuy
ennegrecido/a *adj.* yanachasqa
enojado/a *adj.* phiñasqa
enorme *adj.* hatunkaray
enracimado/a *adj.* khaka

enraízar *v.* saphiy
enredado/a *adj.* arwisqa, rank'usqa
enredar *v.* arwiy, ch'arwiy, rank'uy; **ayudar a enredar** arwiysiy, ch'arwiysiy; **hacer enredar** arwichiy, ch'arwichiy
enredar una y otra vez *v.* arwipayay, ch'arwipayay
enrojecer *v.* pukayay
enrollado/a *adj.* ratasqa
enrollado/a y liado/a *adj.* mayt'usqa
enrollar *v.* k'uyuy
enrollar y liar *v.* mayt'uy; **ayudar a enrollar y liar** mayt'uysiy
enrollar y liar una y otra vez *v.* mayt'uykachay
enrollarse *v.* ratay
enronquecer *v.* ch'akayay
enronquecer de por vida *v.* ch'akayapuy
ensalzado/a *adj.* sumaychasqa
ensalzar *v.* sumaychay
ensangrentado/a *adj.* yawarchasqa
ensangrentarse *v.* yawarchakuy
ensangrentarse mutuamente *v.* yawarchanakuy
enseñar *v.* yachachiy
ensordecer *v.* roqt'oyay
ensuciado/a *adj.* qhellichasqa
ensuciador/a *s.* qhellichaq
ensuciar *v.* map'ay, qhanray, qhellichay
ensuciarse *v.* qhellichakuy, wiswiyay
ensueño *s.* mosqhoy
ensurcado/a *adj.* wachu wachu
entenado *s.* hawaychuri
enterrador/a *s.* p'anpaq
enterrar *v.* p'anpay; **hacer enterrar** p'anpachiy
entonces *conj.* chayqa
entrada *s.* haykuna
entrar *v.* haykuy
entreabierto/a *adj.* kicharayaq
entremezclar *v.* mich'uy; **hacer entremezclar** mich'uchiy
entremezclarse *v.* taqrunakuy
entrepierna *s.* phaka
entretejido/a *adj.* allwisqa
entretener *v.* pullkachiy
entreverado/a *adj.* mich'usqa

entreverar *v.* mich'uy; **hacer entreverar** mich'uchiy
entristecerse *v.* llakikuy
entrometido/a *adj.* chakchaku
enturbiar *v.* q'atachay
enturbiarse *v.* q'atachakuy
envalentonarse *v.* qharichakuy
envejecer *v.* *(hombre)* machuyay; *(mujer)* payayay; **hacer envejecer** *(hombre)* machuyachiy; *(mujer)* payayachiy
envejecida *(mujer) adj.* payayasqa
envejecido *(hombre) adj.* machuyasqa
envenenado/a *adj.* miyusqa
envenenar *v.* miyuy; **mandar a envenenar** miyuchiy
enviar *v.* apachiy
enviudar *(mujer) v.* ikmayay
envoltorio *s.* khipu
envolver *v.* sonqonay
equivocadamente *adv.* pantaylla
equivocado/a *adj.* pantasqa, witisqa
equivocar *v.* witiy; **hacer equivocar** pantachiy, witichiy
erguido/a *adj.* sayarisqa
erigir *v.* hatarichiy; *(con barro)* llut'ay; **ayudar a erigir** *(con barro)* llut'aysiy; **hacer erigir** *(con barro)* llut'achiy
errado/a *adj.* witisqa
errar *v.* witiy; **hacer errar** witichiy
eructar *v.* khapay, khasay
ésa *pron.* chay; **esita** *(diminutivo)* chaycha
esa *adj.* chay
esa vez *adv.* chaypacha
escamarse *v.* phaspayay
escamoso/a *adj.* phaspa
escampar *v.* usariy
escapar: *v.* **dejar escapar** phawachiy; **hacer escapar** ayqechiy
escarabajo *s.* akatanqa, uti uti
escarbado/a *adj.* weq'asqa
escarbador/a *s.* hasp'iq, weq'aq, allaq
escarbar *v.* allay, hasp'iy, weq'ay; **ayudar a escarbar** allaysiy, hasp'iysiy, weq'aysiy; **hacer escarbar** allachiy, hasp'ichiy, weq'achiy • *s.* **instrumento para escarbar** weq'ana
escarbar una y otra vez *v.* allapayay
escarcha *s.* chhulla

escarchado/a *adj.* chhullasqa
escarchar *v.* chhullay
escarmentar *v.* wanay; **hacer escarmentar** wanachiy
escarmiento *s.* wana
escasear *v.* pisiy
escaso *adj.* aslla, pisi
esclarecer *v.* sut'inchay
esclarecido/a *adj.* sut'inchasqa
escoba *s.* pichana
escocer *v.* k'aray, seqsiy; **causar escozor** seqsichiy
escogedor/a *s.* akllaq
escoger *v.* akllay; **ayudar a escoger** akllaysiy; **hacer escoger** akllachiy
escoger para sí *v.* akllakuy
escogido/a *adj.* akllasqa
esconderse *v.* pakakuy; **mandar a esconder** pakachiy
escondido/a *adj.* pakasqa
escondite *s.* pakakuna
escuchador/a *s.* uyapakuq
escuchar *v.* uyariy; **hacer escuchar** uyarichiy; **hacerse escuchar** uyarichikuy • *s.* el/la que escucha
escuchar disimuladamente a otros *v.* uyapakuy
escucharse mutuamente *v.* uyarinakuy
escupido *adj.* thoqasqa
escupir *v.* thoqay; **mandar a escupir** thoqachiy; **tener deseos de escupir** thoqanayay
escupir constantamente *v.* thoqapayay
escupirse mutuamente *v.* thoqanakuy
escurrido/a *adj.* surusqa
escurrir *v.* llusp'iy, suruy
ése *pron.* chay; **esito** *(diminutivo)* chaycha
ese *adj.* chay
esfera *s.* lonq'o, lunp'u
esférico *adj.* lonq'o
esmirriado/a *adj.* eqo • *s.* sit'i
esmirriarse *v.* sit'iyay
éso *pron.* chay, chayta
eso *adj.* chay
esófago *s.* millp'uti
espalda *s.* wasa

esparcido/a *adj.* ch'eqe, ch'eqesqa
esparcido/a con la mano *adj.* qachisqa
esparcidor/a *s.* hach'iq
esparcir *v.* ch'eqechiy, hach'iy; **ayudar a esparcir** hach'iysiy
esparcir con la mano *v.* qachiy; **ayudar a esparcir con la mano** qachiysiy
esparcir con la mano una y otra vez *v.* qachipayay
esparcir por todos lados *v.* hach'iykachay
esparcir semillas *v.* husk'ay; **ayudar a esparcir semillas** husk'aysiy
esperado/a *adj.* suyasqa
esperar *v.* suyay • *s.* **el/la que espera** suyaq
esperar ansiosamente *v.* suyapayay
esperar por mucho tiempo *(parado) v.* takarayay
espesarse *(líquido) v.* thakayay; **hacer espesar** thakayachiy
espeso/a *adj.* thaka, pipu
espina *s.* k'aklla, kiska, qepu
espinoso/a *adj.* kiskasapa
espíritu *s.* nuna
esposo *s.* qosa • *adj.* **con esposo** qosayoq
espulgar *v.* pikiy
espuma *s.* phosoqo
espumajear *v.* ulthuy
esputar *v.* qhotoy
esputar el bocado masticado *v.* hach'uy
esputo *s.* qhoto
ésta *pron.* kay; **estita** *(diminutivo)* kaycha
esta *adj.* kay
estabilizar *v.* turay
estación *s.* mit'a
estafar *v.* ch'achuy
estallable *adj.* phataq
estallado/a *adj.* t'oqyasqa, t'ohasqa
estallar *v.* phatay, t'oqyay, t'ohay
estar sin hacer nada *v.* qasirayay
éste *pron.* kay; **estito** *(diminutivo)* kaycha
este *adj.* kay
estéril *adj.* urwa
esternón *s.* qhasqo tullu
estiércol *s.* isma, q'awa, uchha

estirado/a *adj.* chutasqa
estirar *v.* chutay; **hacer estirar** chutachiy • *s.* **el/la que estira** chutaq
estirar las piernas *v.* hayt'arikuy
estirarse *v.* chutarikuy
ésto *pron.* kay
estómago *s.* wiksa
estornudador/a *s.* achhiq, hach'iq
estornudar *v.* achhiy, hach'iy
estornudo *s.* achhi
estrangulado/a *adj.* seq'osqa
estrangulador/a *s.* seq'oq
estrangular *v.* seq'oy; **ayudar a estrangular** seq'oysiy; **mandar a estrangular** seq'ochiy
estrecho/a *adj.* k'ikllu, k'iski
estrella *s.* ch'aska, qoyllur
estremecerse *v.* chukchuy
estrujado/a *adj.* p'oqasqa, q'apisqa
estrujar *v.* p'oqay, q'apiy; **mandar a estrujar** q'apichiy
estrujar constantemente *v.* q'apiykachay
evacuar raudamente *v.* seqray
evadirse *v.* ch'itakuy, k'itakuy
evaporar *v.* waksiy • *s.* **lo que evapora** waksiq
evidente *adj.* sut'in
exactamente *adv.* k'apaklla
exacto/a *adj.* k'apak
excluido/a *adj.* sapanchasqa
excluir *v.* sapanchay
excluirse *v.* ch'ullachakuy
exclusivamente *adv.* ch'ullalla
excremento *s.* aka
exhalar buen olor *v.* q'apay
existencia *s.* kawsay
existir *v.* kawsay
expandir *v.* hatunchay
expeler aire con ruido seco *v.* chhasay
expendedor/a *s.* qhatuq
expender *v.* qhatuy; **ayudar a expender** qhatuysiy • *s.* **lugar donde se expende** qhatu
exponer al sol *v.* masay

exponer al sol continuamente *v.* masapayay
exponer al sol una y otra vez *v.* masaykachay
exprimido/a *adj.* ch'arwasqa
exprimir *(algo mojado) v.* ch'arway; **ayudar a exprimir** ch'arwaysiy
expuesto al sol *adj.* masasqa
expulsado/a *adj.* qarqosqa
expulsar *v.* qarqoy; **ayudar a expulsar** qarqoysiy; **hacer expulsar** qarqochiy
expulsar a alguien *v.* hat'ay
exquisitamente *adv.* sumaqlla, sumaqta
exquisito/a *adj.* sumaq • *v.* **volverse exquisito/a** sumaqyay
extender *v.* mast'ariy
extraer *v.* horqoy, k'isuy, sik'iy; **ayudar a extraer** sik'iysiy; **dejarse extraer** *(algo)* horqochikuy; **mandar a extraer** sik'ichiy • *s.* **el/la que extrae** horqoq
extraído/a *adj.* horqosqa, sik'isqa
extraviar *v.* chinkachiy
extraviarse *v.* chinkakuy
eyacular *v.* wawsay, yumay

F

factible *adj.* atinalla, atiylla
faja *s.* mat'ina
faja tejida *s.* chunpi
fajado/a *(bebé) adj.* walthasqa
fajador/a de un bebé *s.* walthaq
fajar un bebé *v.* chunpiy, walthay; **ayudar a fajar un bebé** walthaysiy
falda *s.* wali
falsamente *adv.* llullay llullay
familia *s.* ayllu
fantasma *s.* kukuchi
fatal *adj.* qhencha
fatalidad *s.* qhencha
fémur *s.* wich'un
fenecido/a *adj.* wañusqa
feo/a *v.* millay
fermentado/a *adj.* p'osqo, poqosqa
fermentar *v.* poqoy; **hacer fermentar** poqochiy
fermentarse *v.* p'osqoy
feto *s.* sullu
fiesta masiva *s.* raymi
fijado/a en forma de cruz *adj.* chakatasqa
fijar en forma de cruz *v.* chakatay
filetear la carne *v.* mat'ay
finalizar el día *v.* ch'isiyay
fingido/a *adj.* wakta
fino/a *adj.* qhapchi
flácido/a *adj.* ch'alqe, ch'olqe • *v.* **ponerse flácido/a** ch'alqeyay; **tornarse flácido/a** ch'olqeyay
flaco/a *adj.* tullu
flacuchento/a *adj.* q'awti
flamenco *(ave) s.* pariwana
flanco *s.* waqta
flaquísimo/a *adj.* harchi
flauta *s.* pinkuyllu, pitu, qena

flojo/a *adj.* qella
flor *s.* t'ika, *(variedades andinas)* phallcha, sirwana
florecer *v.* t'ikayay
flotador *s.* tuytuq
flotante *adj.* tuytuq
flotar *v.* tuytuy
fluir agua *v.* ch'uychuy
fogón *s.* q'oncha • *v.* **construir un fogón** q'onchachay
fontanela *s.* ñupu
formar pareja con una mujer *v.* warmichakuy
fornicador/a *s.* wachoq
fortalecer *v.* kallpachay
fortalecerse *v.* kallpachakuy
fracción *s.* phakmi
fraccionado/a *adj.* phakmisqa
fraccionar *v.* phakmiy
fragante *adj.* q'aparishaq
frágil *adj.* *(persona)* onqoli, *(cosa)* p'akina, *(cosa)* qhaphra
fragmentado/a *adj.* phakmisqa
fragmentar *v.* k'iphtay, phakmiy
fragmento *s.* k'iphta, phakmi
frazada *s.* qata • *v.* **cubrir con frazada** qatay; **cubrirse con frazada** qatakuy; **cubrirse mutuamente con frazadas** qatanakuy • *adj.* **cubierto/a con frazada** qatasqa
frecuente *adj.* pasaq
frecuentemente *adv.* pasaqlla
freír *v.* theqtichiy, t'eqtichiy
frente *s.* mat'i
frijol *(variedad andina)* *s.* chuwi, tarwi
frío/a *adj.* chiri • *v.* **hacer frío** chiriy
frito/a *adj.* theqtisqa, t'eqtisqa
fruncido/a *adj.* ch'ipusqa *(una tela)* sip'usqa
fruncir *v.* ch'ipuy *(una tela)* sip'uy
frutal *s.* muya
frutecer *v.* ruruy; **hacer frutecer** ruruchiy
frutecer abundantemente *v.* wayuy
fruto *s.* ruru
fuego *s.* nina
fuerte *adj.* kallpasapa
fuerza *s.* kallpa

fugitivo *s.* ayqeq
fumar *v.* pitay
fundar *v.* teqsiy

G

gallina *s.* wallpa
gallo *s.* k'anka, wallpa
gangoso/a *adj.* k'aku
ganso andino *s.* wallata
garganta *s.* tonqor
garra *s.* sillu
garrapata *s.* hamak'u
gateador/a *s.* lloqhaq
gatear *v.* lloqhay; **hacer gatear** lloqhachiy
gato *s.* michi
gato montés *s.* osqollo
gaviota *s.* qellwa
gélido/a *adj.* khutu • *v.* **ponerse gélido/a** khutuyay
gemelo *s.* wispa
generoso/a *adj.* sonqosapa
gestante *v.* onqokuq
gestar *(procreación)* *v.* chichuyay
girar *v.* muyuy
girar lentamente *v.* kutiriy
glotón *s.* rakrapu, rakraq
golosina *s.* hillu
golpeado/a con el puño *v.* saqmasqa
golpeador/a *s.* maqaq
golpear *v.* maqay, takay; **ayudar a golpear** maqaysiy, takaysiy; **dejarse golpear** maqachikuy
golpear constantemente *v.* maqapayay
golpear repetidas veces *v.* takapayay
gordo/a *adj.* wira, wirasapa
gorrión *s.* pichinku
gorro *s.* chuku • *v.* **ponerse el gorro** chukuchakuy
gorro andino *s.* ch'ullu
gota *(líquido)* *s.* sut'u
gotear *v.* sut'uy
gradería *s.* seqana
grande *adj.* hatun

granero *s.* taqe
graniento *(piel) adj.* khikisapa
granizar *v.* chikchiy
granizo *s.* chikchi
grano *s.* khiki
grano andino *s.* kinwa
grano seco *s.* k'ayu
grano tostado *s.* hank'a
granuloso/a *adj.* chhanqa
grasa *s.* wira
grillo *s.* ch'illiku
gripe *s.* chhulli
gris *adj.* oqe, oqhe • *v.* **tornarse gris** oqeyay, oqheyay
gritar *v.* qapariy; **hacer gritar** qaparichiy
gritar continuamente *v.* qaparqachay
gritarse mutuamente *v.* qaparqachanakuy
grueso/a *adj.* rakhu, phatu
grupo *s.* t'aqa
guardar *v.* waqaychay; **ayudar a guardar** waqaychaysiy; **hacer guardar** waqaychachiy
guía *s.* pusaq
guiar *v.* apay
guiar a alguien *v.* pusay; **hacer guiar a alguien** pusachiy
guiñar reiteradamente *v.* ch'illmipayay
guisar *v.* chupiy
gusano *s.* kuru

H

habas hervidas *s.* phuspu
hábil *adj.* ch'asti
habitante de la selva *s.* ch'unchu
habla *s.* simi
hablador/a *s.* laqla • *adj.* laqla
hablante *s.* rimaq
hablar *v.* rimay; **hacer hablar** rimachiy; **tener deseos de hablar** rimanayay
hablar constantemente *v.* rimapayay
hablar para sí *v.* rimapakuy
hablar por hablar *v.* rimakachay
hablarse mutuamente *v.* rimanakuy
hace un momento *adv.* ñaqha
hacer *v.* ruway; **ayudar a hacer** ruwaysiy; **mandar a hacer** ruwachiy; **tener deseos de hacer** ruwanayay
hacer de nuevo *v.* kutipay
hacerse tarde *v.* intiyay
hacia allí *adv.* chayman
hacia aquí *adv.* kayman
¿hacia dónde? *inter.* mayman
halcón *s.* waman
hambre *s.* yarqay • *v.* **tener hambre** yarqay
hambriento/a *adj.* yarqasqa
hambruna *s.* muchuy, yarqay
harapiento/a *adj.* chhachu, saphsa
harapo *s.* saphsa
harina *s.* hak'u
harinoso/a *adj.* hak'u; **muy harinoso/a** hak'uy hak'uy
harto/a *adj.* ancha
hastiado/a *adj.* amisqa
hastiar *v.* amiy
hecho *adj.* ruwasqa
hecho de tierra *adj.* allpamanta
heder *v.* asnay; **hacer heder** asnachiy • *s.* **el/la que hace heder** asnachiq; **el/la/lo que hiede** asnaq

hedor *s.* asnay
helada *s.* qasa • *adj.* qasasqa
helado/a *adj.* qasasqa
helar *adj.* khutuy, qasay • *v.* khutuy, qasay
hembra *s.* china
hender *v.* k'iñay
hendido/a *adj.* k'iñasqa
herida *s.* k'iri, nanaq
herida que escuece *s.* k'araq
herida que pica *s.* k'araq
herido/a *adj.* k'iri
herir *v.* k'iriy
hermana *s.* *(de mujer)* ñaña, *(de varón)* pana
hermano *s.* *(de mujer)* tura, *(de varón)* wayqe
herramienta andina de agricultura *s.* hallmana
herramienta de labranza *s.* chakitaklla
herramienta para cepillar madera *s.* llaqllana
herramienta para escarbar *s.* allachu, allana, hasp'ina
hervido/a *adj.* t'inpusqa
hervir *v.* t'inpuy
hervir habas *v.* phuspuy
hiel *s.* hayaqe
hierba *s.* qora
hierbas secadas *s.* qacha
hígado *s.* kukupin
hija *s.* *(del padre)* ususi, *(de la madre)* warmi wawa
hijo *s.* *(del padre)* churi, *(de la madre)* qhariwawa; **el menor de los hijos** chanaku • *adj.* **con muchos hijos varones** *(hombre)* churisapa
hijo adoptivo *s.* churichasqa
hilacha *s.* chhapu
hilado/a *adj.* puskasqa
hilandero/a *s.* puskaq
hilar *v.* puskay; **ayudar a hilar** puskaysiy
hilo de lana *s.* q'aytu
hincar *v.* t'urpuy
hinchado/a *adj.* p'unpu, punkisqa
hincharse *v.* p'unpuyay, punkiy
hipar *v.* hik'iy
hipo *s.* hik'i

hocico de ciertos animales *s.* suyt'u
hogar *s.* wasi
hoja *s.* raphi
hoja de quinua *s.* lliphch'a
hojarasca *s.* ch'aphra • *v.* **cubrirse con hojarasca** ch'aphrachakuy
hojas secas *s.* q'opa
holgado/a *adj.* waya; *(cosas)* p'olqo
hollar *v.* yupiy
hollín *s.* qhechincha, yanamanka
hombre *s.* qhari • *v.* **devenir en adulto** *(hombre)* qhariyay
hombre pequeño *s.* tanka, k'ichi
hombro *s.* rikra
honda *s.* warak'a
hondear *v.* warak'ay
hondo *adj.* p'onqo
hongo *s.* k'allanpa
honrado/a *adj.* apuchasqa, sumaychasqa
honrar *v.* apuchay, sumaychay
horizontal *adj.* hank'arpa
hormiga *s.* sisi
hormiga grande *s.* qollwi
hospedador/a *s.* qorpachaq
hospedar *v.* qorpachay
hospedarse *v.* qorpachakuy
hoy *adv.* kunan
hoyo *s.* p'ukru
hoyo profundo *s.* sankha
hozar *v.* uksiy
hueco *s.* t'oqo
huella *s.* yupi
huérfano/a *s.* wakcha, willullu • *v.* **devenir en huérfano/a** wakchayay
hueso *s.* tullu
huesudo/a *adj.* tullusapa
huevecillos de los peces *s.* kaw kaw
huevo *s.* runtu
huir *v.* ayqey; **ayudar a huir** ayqechiy
huir constantemente *v.* ayqepayay
humedecer *v.* ch'aranchay
humedecer el piso *v.* ch'aqchuy

humedecer hasta infestar *(granos) v.* hut'uy
humedecido/a *adj.* ch'aqchusqa
húmedo/a *adj.* api, ch'aran, hoq'o
humildemente *adv.* ullpu ullpu
humillado/a *adj.* saruchasqa
humillar *v.* alqochay, saruchay; **dejarse humillar** saruchikuy
humillarse *v.* k'umuykachay
humo *s.* q'osñi • *v.* **hacer humear** q'osñichiy
huraño/a *adj.* osqo • *v.* **volverse huraño/a** osqoyay
hurgador/a *s.* welq'aq
hurgar *v.* k'uskiy, welq'ay; **ayudar a hurgar** welq'aysiy; **hacer hurgar** welq'achiy • *s.* **instrumento para hurgar** welq'ana
huso *s.* puska

I

ida y vuelta *adj.* kutit'ikra • *adv.* kutit'ikra
idéntico/a *adj.* kikin
idiota *s.* opa • *v.* **causar idiotez** opayachiy; **devenir en idiota** opayay
iluminar *v.* k'anchay
ilusión *s.* llachi • *v.* **hacer ilusionar** llachichiy
ilusoriamente *adv.* llachi llachi
imitar al mono *v.* k'usillukuy
imitar con burla *v.* yachapayay
impar *adj.* willu, ch'ullan
implorar *v.* mañarikuy
implorar con las manos *v.* pituchakuy
impulsar *v.* tanqay
imputar *v.* manuchay
incapacitado/a *adj.* thultu • *v.* **devenir en incapacitado/a** thultuyay
inclinado/a *adj.* k'achanpa
inclinado/a a un costado *adj.* kinranpa • *adv.* kinranpamanta
inclinar *v.* t'iksuy
inclinarse *v.* k'achanpakuy, k'iray, t'iksuykachay
incrementar *v.* askhayachiy
inculpado/a *adj.* tunpasqa
inculpador/a *s.* tunpaq
inculpar *v.* tunpay
inculparse mutuamente *v.* tunpanakuy
incumplidor/a *s.* huchayoq
incumplimiento *s.* hucha
incumplir *v.* huchay • *s.* **el/la que incumple mucho** huchasapa
indagar *v.* tapuy
indagar una y otra vez *v.* tapukachay
indiscreto/a *adj.* llik'isimi
individuo *s.* runa
indolente *adj.* k'ullu • *v.* **volverse indolente** k'ulluyapuy
inepto/a *adj.* uti, wankhi
infeliz *adj.* usuri
infértil *adj.* urwa

infestado/a *(granos) adj.* hut'u
infestarse *(granos) v.* hut'uyay
ingeniosamente *adv.* ch'itilla
ingenioso/a *adj.* ch'iti
inhabitado/a *adj.* purun
inhalar por la nariz *v.* senq'ay
inicio *s.* umala
injuriarse *v.* millp'unakuy
injuriarse mutuamente *v.* lapht'anakuy
inmaduro *adj.* llullu, qholla**;** *(fruto)* k'uku
inmediatamente *adv.* kunachallan, kunanpacha
inolvidable *adj.* yuyaychana
insignia *s.* llawt'u
insinuado/a *adj.* siminchasqa
insinuar *v.* siminchay
insípido/a *adj.* q'ayma
insolado/a *adj.* q'ochasqa
insolar *v.* q'ochachiy
instructor/a *s.* yachachiq
instrumento para escarbar *s.* weq'ana
instrumento para hurgar *s.* welq'ana
instrumento para machucar *s.* saqtana
instrumento para remover *s.* weq'ana
instrumento para revolver *s.* qaywina
instrumento para tejer *s.* awana
insultador/a *s.* k'amiq
insultar *v.* k'amiy
insultar reiteradamente *v.* k'amipayay
insultarse mutuamente *v.* k'aminakuy
insulto *s.* k'ami
intelecto *s.* hamut'a, yuyay
intelectual *s.* hamut'aq
inteligente *adj.* ch'iti, yuyayniyoq
inteligentísimo/a *adj.* yuyaysapa
intercambiar *v.* haywanakuy, qonakuy
interceptar *v.* hark'ay; **ayudar a interceptar** hark'aysiy
interior *adj.* ukhu
internar *v.* ukhuchay
interponerse *v.* chawpinakuy, chawpinchakuy
interrumpir *v.* tatichiy

intestino *s.* ch'unchul
intrigar *v.* yachachinakuy
inútil *adj.* akasapa, añaku
inútilmente *adv.* yanqa
invidente *s.* ñawsa
invocar *v.* waqyarikuy
ir *v.* riy
ir en sentido equivocado *v.* pantay • *s.* **el/la que va en sentido equivocado** pantaq
ir hacia un costado *v.* kinray
iracundo *adj.* phiña
irrigado/a *adj.* qarpasqa
irrigar *v.* qarpay; **ayudar a irrigar** qarpaysiy
irrigar constantemente qarpapayay
irritación *s.* k'aray
irse *v.* ripuy
isla *s.* wat'a
izquierdo/a *adj.* lloq'e

J

jaguar *s.* uturunku
jalar *v.* aysay, chutay; **ayudar a jalar** aysaysiy, chutaysiy; **hacer jalar** chutachiy • *s.* **el/la que jala** chutaq
jalar esforzadamente *v.* chutapakuy
jardín *s.* inkill
jarro *s.* p'uyñu
jarrón grande de cerámica *s.* mak'as
jaspeado/a de blanco y negro *adj.* ch'eqchi • *v.* **jaspearse en blanco y negro** ch'eqchiyay
jilguero *s.* ch'ayña
jornalero *s.* llank'apakuq
joven[1] *(hombre) s.* wayna, maqt'a • *v.* **devenir en joven** *(el adolescente)* waynayay
joven[2] *(mujer) s.* sipas, p'asña • *v.* **devenir en joven** *(la adolescente)* sipasyay
juego *s.* pukllay
jugador/a *s.* pukllaq
jugar *v.* pukllay; **hacer jugar** pukllachiy; **tener deseos de jugar** pukllanayay
jugar constantemente *v.* pukllapayay
juguete *s.* pukllana
juguetón/a *adj.* pukllaq
juicioso/a *adj.* yuyayniyoq
juntado/a *adj.* t'inkisqa
juntamente *adv.* kuskalla
juntar *v.* t'inkiy; **ayudar a juntar** t'inkiysiy
juntar los sobrantes *v.* wakinchay
junto *adj.* kuska
justo/a *adj.* chanin

L

labio inferior *s.* werp'a
labios gruesos *s.* ch'utu
labrantío *s.* chakra
lactante *s.* ñuñuq
lactar *v.* tutuy
lactar la leche de madre ajena *v.* ñuñupakuy
ladeado/a *adj.* chinru, k'achanpa, phallu
ladearse *v.* k'achanpakuy, kinray
ladera *s.* qhata
lado *s.* kinra
ladrar *v.* waqway
ladrar una y otra vez *v.* waqwapayay
ladrón *s.* makiyoq, suwa
lagaña *s.* ch'oqñi
lagañoso/a *adj.* ch'oqñi • *v.* **tornarse lagañoso/a** ch'oqñiyay
lagarto *s.* qaraywa
lago *s.* qocha
lágrima *s.* weqe
lagrimear *v.* weqey; **hacer lagrimear** weqechiy
laguna *s.* qocha
lamedor/a *s.* llaqwaq, llunk'u
lamer *v.* llaqway, llunk'uy; **dejarse lamer** llaqwachikuy
lamerse *v.* llaqwakuy
lamerse mutuamente *v.* llaqwanakuy
lamido/a *adj.* llaqwasqa
laminar *v.* last'ay
lana *s.* millma; **borla de lana** puyllu; **hilo de lana** q'aytu • *v.* **cubrir con lana** millmachay
lánguido/a *adj.* unphu • *v.* **volverse lánguido/a** unphuyay
lanudo/a *adj.* millmasapa
lanzado/a *adj.* ch'aqesqa, chanqasqa
lanzado/a bruscamente *adj.* choqasqa
lanzador/a *s.* ch'aqeq
lanzar *v.* ch'aqey, chanqay; **ayudar a lanzar** ch'aqeysiy
lanzar bruscamente *v.* choqay

lanzar cosas sin freno *v.* chanqaykachay
lanzar por los aires *v.* wikapay
lapso de tiempo *s.* unay
largo/a *adj.* suni
látigo *s.* hasut'i, waqtana
latigueado/a *adj.* waqtasqa
latigueador/a *s.* waqtaq
latiguear *v.* waqtay; **ayudar a latiguear** waqtaysiy; **dejarse latiguear** waqtachikuy; **hacer latiguear** waqtachiy
latiguear una y otra vez *v.* waqtapayay
latiguearse mutuamante *v.* waqtanakuy
latir *(corazón)* *v.* phatatatay
lavado/a *adj.* mayllisqa; *(ropa)* t'aqsasqa
lavar *v.* maqchhiy, maylliy; *(ropa)* t'aqsay; **ayudar a lavar** maqchhiysiy, maylliysiy; *(ropa)* t'aqsaysiy; **hacer lavar** maqchhichiy; **mandar a lavar** *(ropa)* t'aqsachiy
lavar una y otra vez *v.* maqchhipayay
lavarse *v.* maqchhikuy, mayllikuy
lavarse la cara *v.* uphakuy; **hacer lavar la cara** uphachiy
leche *s.* ñukñu
lecho *s.* k'irana
lejano/a *adj.* karu
lejos *adv.* karu
lengua *(anatómico)* *s.* qallu
lengüetear *v.* lawq'ay
lentamente *adv.* ñuskhu ñuskhulla
lento/a *adj.* ñuskhu
leña *s.* llant'a; **hacer leña** llant'achay
leñador/a *s.* llant'aq
lerdo *adj.* p'anra • *v.* **ponerse lerdo/a** p'anrayay
letal *adj.* soq'a
levantado/a *adj.* sayarisqa
levantar la falda a una mujer *v.* q'allpay
levantar un muro *v.* perqay
levantarse *v.* hatariy, sayariy
liado/a *adj.* wank'usqa
liar *v.* wank'uy; **ayudar a liar** wank'uysiy; **mandar a liar** wank'uchiy
liar una y otra vez *v.* wank'upayay
libar *v.* upiy; **hacer libar** upichiy
líder *s.* umalli

liderar *v.* umalliy
liendre *s.* ch'iya; **sacador/a de liendres** ch'iyaq
liendroso/a *adj.* ch'iyasapa
lila *adj.* panti
limpiar la suciedad de la piel *v.* kharkannay
limpiarse *v.* pichakuy
limpio/a *adj.* ch'uya
lindo/a *adj.* munay
lirio blanco *s.* hamanq'ay • *v.* **ponerse blanco como el lirio** hamanq'ayay
litera *s.* wantu
liviano/a *adj.* llaphlla, llaphsa, chhaplla • *v.* **ponerse liviano/a** llaphllayay, llaphsayay
loco/a *adj.* waq'a
lograr *v.* aypay; **ayudar a lograr** aypaysiy
lombriz *s.* k'uyka
loro pequeño *s.* k'alla
luchar *v.* awqanakuy
luciérnaga *s.* pinchinkuru
lugar donde se pone momentáneamente *(algo) s.* churana
luminoso/a *adj.* k'anchaq; **muy luminoso/a** k'anchay k'anchay
luna *s.* killa
lunar *s.* ana
luz *s.* k'ancha

LL

llama *s.* llama
llamado/a *adj.* waqyasqa
llamar *v.* waqyay; **hacer llamar** waqyachiy
llamar una y otra vez *v.* waqyapayay
llamarse mutuamente *v.* waqyanakuy
llamero *s.* llamayoq
llegar *v.* chayay
llenado/a *adj.* hunt'asqa
llenar *v.* hunt'ay, llinp'ay
lleno/a *adj.* hunt'a
llevado/a *(en brazos) adj.* marq'asqa
llevado/a en hombros *adj.* wantusqa
llevar *v.* apay • *s.* **el/la que lleva** apaq
llevar a alguien *v.* pusay, ranpay; **ayudar a llevar a alguien** ranpaysiy; **hacer llevar a alguien** pusachiy
llevar de un lugar a otro *(algo) v.* apakachay
llevar en brazos *v.* marq'ay; **dejarse llevar en brazos** marq'achikuy • *s.* **el/la que lleva en brazos** marq'aq
llevar en el sobaco *v.* lluk'iy
llevar en hombros *v.* rikray, wantuy; **dejarse llevar en hombros** wantuchikuy; **llevar en hombros atropelladamente** wantuykachay • *s.* **el/la que lleva en hombros** rikraq
llorador/a *s.* waqaq
llorar *v.* waqay; **estar a punto de llorar** waqanayay; **hacer llorar** waqachiy; **tener deseos de llorar** waqanayay
llorar una y otra vez *v.* waqapayay
lloriquear *v.* ch'irchiykachay, waqapakuy
llorón/a *s.* waqati
llover *v.* paray; **estar a punto de llover** paranayay
llover constantemente *v.* paraykachay
llover persistentemente *v.* ch'allchay
llovizna *s.* siphsi, iphu
llovizna con sol *s.* chirapa
lloviznar *v.* iphuy, siphsiy
lloviznar mientras brilla el sol *v.* chirapay
lluvia *s.* para • *v.* **causar lluvia** parachiy
lluvioso/a *adj.* paraq

M

macho *s.* orqo
macho reproductor *s.* kututu
machucado/a *adj.* saqtasqa
machucar *v.* saqtay; **ayudar a machucar** saqtaysiy; **hacer machucar** saqtachiy • *s.* **instrumento para machucar** saqtana
madero *s.* k'ullu
madre *s.* mama
madre que da de lactar *s.* ñuñuq
madre tierra *s.* mamapacha
madrina de niño/a bautizado/a *s.* marq'aq
madrugada *s.* pacha illariy
madrugar *v.* tutapay
madurar *v.* poqoy; **hacer madurar** poqochiy
maduro/a *adj.* poqosqa
maestro/a *s.* yachachiq
maíz *s.* sara
maíz de grano pequeño *s.* ch'ullpi
maíz fresco *s.* choqllo
maíz hervido *s.* mot'e
mal *adj.* mana allin • *s.* onqoy, machusqa
mal causado por el influjo de un cádaver *s.* qhayqa
mal causado por el mal viento *s.* wayrasqa
mal transmitido por mosquitos *s.* utha
maldecido/a *adj.* ñakasqa
maldecidor/a *s.* ñakaq
maldecir *v.* ñakay
maldecir continuamente *v.* ñakapakuy
malgastado/a *adj.* usuchisqa
malgastar *v.* usuchiy
malgastarse *v.* usuy
malnutrido/a *adj.* eqosqa
mamar *v.* ñuñuy
manantial *s.* pukyu
manar *v.* phullpuy
mandar *v.* kamachiy

mandatario *s.* kamachiq
mandato *s.* kamachi
mandíbula *s.* qhaqllin
maní *s.* inchis
maniatar *v.* chaqnay, thunkuy; **ayudar a maniatar** thunkuysiy; **mandar a maniatar** thunkuchiy
mano *s.* maki
manoseado/a *adj.* mullkhusqa
manoseador/a *s.* mullkhuq
manosear *v.* llankhuy, mullkhuy
manso/a *adj.* sanp'a • *v.* **volverse manso/a** sanp'ayay
manta *s.* chusi, lliklla
mantecoso/a *adj.* llank'i • *v.* **ponerse mantecoso/a** llank'iyay
manto *s.* llaqolla, yaqolla
mañana *s.* *(día de mañana)* paqarin • *adv.* **por la mañana** tutamanta
mar *s.* mamaqocha
marcado/a *adj.* unanchasqa, irpasqa, tuyrusqa
marcar *v.* irpay, tuyruy, unanchay
mariposa *s.* pillpintu
mariposa nocturna *s.* taparaku
marrón *adj.* ch'unpi; **teñido/a de marrón** ch'unpichasqa • *v.* **teñir de marrón** ch'unpichay; **tornarse marrón** ch'unpiyay
más *adj.* aswan
más bien *adv.* aswan
máscara *s.* pukuchu, saynata
mascullar *v.* thutuy
masticado a medias *adj.* hach'u hach'u
masticador/a de hoja de coca *s.* akulliq
masticar hoja de coca *v.* akulliy, chakchay, hallpay, pikchay; **hacer masticar hoja de coca** akullichiy
matado/a *adj.* wañuchisqa
matador/a *s.* wañuchiq
matar *v.* wañuchiy
matarife *s.* nak'achu, nak'aq
matarse *v.* wañuchikuy
matarse mutuamente *v.* wañuchinakuy
mayor *(edad) adj.* kuraq
mazorca con hongo *s.* hat'upa
mecer *v.* kuyuchiy
mediano *(tamaño) adj.* malta

mediano casi pequeño *adj.* taksa
medicina *s.* hanpi
médico/a *s.* hanpiq
medidor/a *s.* tupuq
medio *s.* chawpi
medir *v.* tupuy; **mandar a medir** tupuchiy
médula *s.* toqton
mejorar *v.* allinchay
mejorarse *v.* allinyay, alliyay, thaniy • *s.* **persona que se mejora** alliyaq
memorable *adj.* yuyaychana
memoria *s.* yuyay
memorioso/a *adj.* yuyaysapa
menor *(edad) adj.* sullk'a
menospreciar *v.* alqochay, pisichay, saruchay
menstruación *s.* k'ikuy
menstruar *v.* k'ikuy
mentir *v.* llullakuy
mentira *s.* llulla
mentiroso/a *adj.* llulla
mentón *s.* k'aki
menudo/a *adj.* khullu, *(mujer)* t'usta, *(hombre)* tanka
mercado *s.* qhatu
mermado/a *adj.* waywasqa
mermar *v.* wayway; **hacer mermar** waywachiy
mes *s.* killa
meterse porfiadamente *v.* sat'ipakuy
mezclado/a *adj.* chaqrusqa, minusqa, taqrusqa
mezclado/a con agua *adj.* unuchasqa
mezclador/a *s.* taqruq
mezclar *v.* chaqruy, minuy, taqruy; **ayudar a mezclar** minuysiy, taqruysiy
mezclar con agua *v.* unuchay
mezclar una y otra vez *v.* taqruykachay
miel *s.* lachiwa
mil *num.* waranqa
mimado/a *adj.* wawachasqa
mimar *v.* erqechay, luluy, wawachay
mina de oro *s.* choqe
minúsculo/a *adj.* huch'uyllaña

mirador *s.* qhawana
mirar *v.* qhaway
mirar asiduamente *v.* qhawapayay
mirar como bizco *v.* wesq'oykachay
mirar indefinidamente *v.* qhawarayay
mirarse asiduamente *v.* qhawapayakuy
mirarse mutuamente *v.* qhawanakuy
mismo/a *adj.* kikin
mitad *s.* kuskan
moco *s.* qhoña
moco seco *s.* k'iski
mojado/a *adj.* api
mojar *v.* apichay
mojarse *v.* apiyay
moledor/a *s.* hak'uchiq
moler *v.* hak'uchiy, kutay, ñut'uy; **ayudar a moler** kutaysiy
molido/a *adj.* kutasqa, ñut'u
momificar *v.* ch'alqey
mono *s.* k'usillu
montador/a *s.* phakallikuq
montaña *s.* orqo
montar *v.* phakachakuy; **hacer montar** phakallichiy
montarse sobre algo *v.* phakallikuy
morado/a *adj.* kulli, sani • *v.* **volverse morado/a** saniyay
morder *v.* kaniy, khachuy
mordisqueado/a *adj.* khachusqa
mordisquear *v.* hanch'uy, khachuy
moretón *s.* q'oyo
moribundo/a *adj.* wañunayaq
morir *v.* wañuy; *(persona)* wañupuy
morir repentinamente *v.* wañurqoy
moroso/a *adj.* ch'achu
mortal *s.* wañuq
mortero *s.* mutk'a
mortero y piedra plana para moler *s.* kutana
mosca *s.* ch'uspi
moscardón *s.* wayronqo
mosquito *s.* uta
mosto *s.* upi
mostrar *v.* qhawachiy

mostrar la lengua *v.* qalluykachay
moverse *v.* kuyuy; **hacer mover** achhuchiy, kuyuchiy
muchacha *s.* sipas, p'asña
muchacha en edad de concebir *s.* wachacha
muchacho *s.* wayna, maqt'a
mucho[1] *adv.* anchata, askhata, ñisuta, sinchita
mucho/a[2] *adj.* ancha, askha, ñisu, sinchi, yupa
mucho tiempo *s.* unay
mudarse *v.* astakuy • *s.* **el/la que se muda** astakuq
mudo/a *adj.* amu, upa • *s.* upa • *v.* **volverse mudo/a** upayay
muerto/a *s.* wañusqa
mugre *s.* qhelli
mugriento/a *adj.* khanka
mujer *s.* warmi • *v.* **volverse mujer adulta** warmiyay
mujer escogida en tiempos del inka *s.* aklla
mujer pequeña *s.* t'ustu
muñeco para la buena suerte *s.* eqeqo
murciélago *s.* masu
murmurar *v.* thutuy
muro *s.* perqa; **constructor/a de muros** perqaq • *v.* **construir/levantar un muro** perqay
mutilado/a *adj.* mut'u, qhorusqa, willusqa
mutilar *v.* mut'uy, qhoruy, willuy; ; **ayudar a mutilar** willuysiy; **hacer mutilar** willuchiy; **hacerse mutilar** mut'uchikuy; **mandar a mutilar** qhoruchiy
mutilar el pie *v.* chakinnay
muy *adv.* anchata, sinchita • *adj.* manchay, askha, ancha

N

nacer *v.* paqariy
nada más *adv.* chaylla
nadador/a *s.* wayt'aq
nadar *v.* wayt'ay
nariz *s.* senqa
navegar *v.* wanp'uy; **mandar a navegar** wanp'uchiy
neblina *s.* pacha phuyu
negar *v.* mananchay
negrísimo/a *adj.* ch'illu; **teñido/a de negrísimo** ch'illuyasqa • *v.* **teñir de negrísimo** ch'illuchay; **tornarse negrísimo/a** ch'illuyay
negro/a *adj.* yana
nervio *s.* hank'u
nevar *v.* rit'iy
nido *s.* q'esa • *v.* **construir un nido** q'esachakuy
nieto/a *s.* haway
nieve *s.* rit'i
niño/a *s.* erqe, warma
niño/a llorón/ona *s.* ch'irchi
nivel superior *s.* hanaqpacha
nivelar *v.* panpachay
no *adv.* mana; *(prohibitivo)* ama • *interj.* **¡no!** manakaw
noche *s.* ch'isi, tuta • *adv.* **toda la noche** tutantin
nombrar *v.* sutichay
nombre *s.* suti
nosotros *pron. (exclusivo)* ñoqayku, *(inclusivo)* ñoqanchis
nube *s.* phuyu
nublado/a *adj.* phuyu
nublar *v.* phuyuy
nuca *s.* much'u
nudo *s.* khipu • *adj.* **anudado/a** khipusqa • *v.* **anudar** khipuy; **anudar constantemente** khipupayay; **ayudar a anudar** khipuysiy; **hacer anudar** khipuchiy
nuera *s.* qhachun
nueve *num.* isqon
nuevo/a *(cosas) adj.* mosoq; **muy nuevo/a** mosoqllaña

numerado/a *adj.* yupasqa
numerador/a *s.* yupaq
numerar *v.* yupay; **ayudar a numerar** yupaysiy; **hacer numerar** yupachiy

O

o *conj.* icha, otaq
obedecer *v.* kasuy
obediente *adj.* kasukuq
objetar *v.* kutipakuy
objeto para apuntalar *s.* q'emina
objeto punzante *s.* sat'ina
observador/a *s.* qhawaq
observar *v.* qhaway
observar asiduamente *v.* qhawapayay
observar indefinidamente *v.* qhawarayay
observarse asiduamente *v.* qhawapayakuy
observarse mutuamente *v.* qhawanakuy
obstruir *v.* hark'apayay
obstinado/a *adj.* umasapa
obstrucción *s.* hark'ana
océano *s.* mamaqocha
ocho *num.* pusaq
ocultamente *adv.* pakalla
ocultar *v.* pakay; **ayudar a ocultar** pakaysiy
ocupante *s.* mitma
ocupar un lugar ajeno *v.* q'esachakuy
ocupar un territorio *v.* llaqtachakuy, mitmay
odiado/a *adj.* cheqnisqa
odiar *v.* cheqniy
odiarse mutuamente *v.* cheqninakuy
oferente *s.* arpaq
ofrendar *v.* arpay, haywarikuy • *s.* **lugar de ofrendas** arpana
oír *v.* uyariy; **hacer oír** uyarichiy; **hacerse oír** uyarichikuy
oírse mutuamente *v.* uyarinakuy
ojo *s.* ñawi
oler *v.* muskhiy; **hacer oler** muskhichiy
olfatear a distancia *v.* muskhipakuy
olfatear constantemente *v.* muskhipayay
olfatearse mutuamente *v.* muskhinakuy
olla *s.* manka • *v.* **asentar la olla en el fogón** churpuy

olla pequeña *s.* ch'amillku
olvidable *adj.* qonqana
olvidado/a *adj.* qonqasqa
olvidar *v.* qonqay; **hacer olvidar** qonqachiy
ombligo *s.* puputi
ondear *v.* laphapay
ordenar a hacer algo *v.* kachay
ordeñado/a *adj.* ch'awasqa
ordeñador/a *s.* ch'awaq
ordeñar *v.* ch'away, ñukñuy; **ayudar a ordeñar** ch'awaysiy
oreable *adj.* phaskiq
oreado/a *adj.* phaski
orear *v.* phaskiy
oreja *s.* rinri • *adj.* **de oreja mutilada** chunu; **de oreja pequeña** chunu
orilla *s.* patan
orina *s.* hisp'ay
orinar *v.* hisp'ay; **hacer orinar** hisp'achiy; **tener deseos de orinar** hisp'anayay
orinar constantemente *v.* hisp'apakuy
oro *s.* qori
ortiga *s.* kisa
oruga *s.* utuskuru
oscurecer *v.* laqhayay, tutayay, yanachay; **tornarse oscuro/a** arphayay
oscuridad *s.* tutayaq
oscuro/a *adj.* laqha
oso *s.* ukuku
otorgado/a *adj.* qosqa
otra vez *adv.* hoqmanta, wakmanta
otro/a *adj.* hoq
ovalado *adj.* suyt'u
oyente *s.* uyariq

P

padecer *v.* ñak'ariy; **hacer padecer** ñak'arichiy
padecimiento *s.* ñak'a
padre *s.* tayta • *v.* **hacerse de un padre ajeno** taytachakuy
padrino de niño/a bautizado/a *s.* marq'aq
país *s.* llaqta
paisano *s.* llaqtamasi
paja *s.* ichhu
pájaro *(variedad andina) s.* hak'akllu, kukuli, tunki, urpi
pajonal *s.* ichhupanpa
palanquear *v.* wanqhay
palmada en la espalda *s.* k'unu
palmear *v.* t'aqllay
palmear en la espalda *v.* k'unuy
palmear reiteradamente *v.* t'aqllapayay
palo *s.* k'aspi
palo para golpear *s.* p'anana, q'asuna
paloma *s.* urpi
palpable *adv.* llaminalla
palpar *v.* llamiy
palpar levemente *v.* tupaykuy
palpar reiteradamente *v.* llamipayay
palpar suavamente *v.* llamiykuy
palparse *v.* llamikuy
palparse mutuamente *v.* llaminakuy
pan *s.* t'anta
panal *s.* lachiwana
páncreas *s.* k'ayrapin
pantalones *s.* wara
pantorrilla *s.* ch'upa
pañuelo *s.* piskita
papa *s.* papa
papa deshidratada *s.* ch'uñu, tunta
¿para qué? *inter.* imapaq
para siempre *adv.* wiñaypaq
paradero *s.* sayana

parcela *s.* ch'eqta
parecerse a alguien *v.* rikch'akuy
pared *s.* perqa
pareja *s.* yana
paria *adj.* k'ita
parir *v.* wachay; phallay **ayudar en el parto o a parir** wachachiy; **estar a punto de parir** wachanayay • *s.* **el/la que ayuda en el parto o a parir** wachachiq
parpadear *v.* ch'illmiy, k'inllay
párpado *s.* ñawi qara
parte alta *s.* pata
participar en una conversación sin ser invitado/a *v.* rimaysikuy
particular *adj.* sapaq
pasado mañana *s.* minchha
pasar con la mano *v.* hayway
pasar el tiempo con alguien en su casa *v.* tiyapayay
pasear *v.* purikuy
pasmarse *v.* utiy
paso entre dos montañas *s.* q'asa
pastizal *s.* waylla
pasto *s.* q'achu
pastor *(de animales)* *s.* michiq
pastorear *v.* michiy; **ayudar a pastorear** michiysiy
pastorear el ganado ajeno *v.* michipakuy
pastura *s.* michina
pata *s.* chaki
patada *s.* hayt'a
patalear *v.* hayt'aykachay
pateado/a *adj.* hayt'asqa
patear *v.* hayt'ay; **ayudar a patear** hayt'aysiy; **hacer patear** hayt'achiy
patearse mutuamente *v.* hayt'anakuy
patio de juegos *s.* pukllana
pato macho *s.* khaka
patriarca *s.* tayta, yaya
pausa en el trabajo *s.* hallpa
pecado *s.* hucha
pecador/a *s.* huchasapa, huchayoq
pecar *v.* huchallikuy
pecho *s.* qhasqo

pedazo *s.* k'iphta
pedazos rotos de tiestos *s.* k'arpa
pedir *v.* mañakuy, qochikuy
pedregoso/a *adj.* khallka
pegado/a *adj.* k'askasqa
pegar *v.* k'askay • *s.* k'askachiq
peinado/a *v.* ñaqch'asqa
peinar *v.* ñaqch'ay; **ayudar a peinar** ñaqch'aysiy
peinar una y otra vez *v.* ñaqch'apayay
peinarse *v.* ñaqch'akuy
peinarse una y otra vez *v.* ñaqch'apakuy
peine *s.* ñaqch'a
pelado/a *adj.* llust'i, p'aqla, q'ara • *v.* **volverse pelado/a** p'aqlayay
pelar *v.* q'aray
pelarse *v.* q'arayay
pelearse *v.* maqanakuy
pellejo *s.* qara
pellizcar *v.* llipch'iy, t'ipiy; **dejarse pellizcar** t'ipichikuy
pellizcar constantemente *v.* t'ipipayay
pellizcarse mutuamente *v.* t'ipinakuy
pena *s.* llaki • *v.* **causar pena** llakichiy
penacho *s.* k'akara
pender *v.* walqay; **hacer pender** walqachiy
pene *s.* ullu
penosamente *adv.* ñak'ayllaña
pensado/a *adj.* yuyasqa
pensador/a *s.* yuyaq
pensar *v.* yuyay
penumbra *s.* arpha
penuria *s.* ñak'a
pepino *s.* kachun
pequeño/a *adj.* huch'uy, khullu; **más o menos pequeño** huch'uyniraq
perderse *v.* chinkakuy, chinkay; **hacer perder** chinkachiy
perdido/a *adj.* chinkasqa
perdiz *s.* lluthu, p'isaqa
perdonar *v.* panpachay
perecer *v.* wañuy; *(persona)* wañupuy
perezoso/a *adj.* qella
perforado/a *adj.* khapusqa, wanphusqa

perforar *v.* khapuy, wanphuy; **ayudar a perforar** khapuysiy, wanphuysiy; **hacer perforar** khapuchiy
perfumado/a *adj.* q'apachisqa
perfumar *v.* q'apachiy
perfumarse *v.* q'apachikuy
perímetro *s.* marka
periodo de cosecha *s.* aymura
periodo de tiempo *s.* mit'a
permanecer *v.* qhepay
permanecer parado/a *v.* sayarayay
permanecer sin salir *v.* sat'irayay
permitir entrar *v.* haykuchiy
pernil *s.* chakan
pero *conj.* ichaqa
perro *s.* alqo
perro peludo *s.* ch'aku
perseguir *v.* qatikachay
perseguir continuamente *v.* qatipayay
perseguirse mutuamente *v.* qatinakuy
persistente *adj.* atipakuq
persistir *v.* atipakuy
persona *s.* runa
pesadilla *s.* llap'i
pesado/a *adj.* llasa; **muy pesado/a** llasallaña • *v.* **hacer más pesado/a** llasayachiy
pesante *adj.* llasa; **muy pesante** llasallaña
pescado *s.* challwa
pescador/a *s.* challwaq
pescar *v.* challway
pestaña *s.* qhechiphra
pestañear *v.* ch'illmiy
pez *s.* challwa
pezón *s.* ñuñu
pezuña *s.* phapallu
picaflor *s.* q'ente
picante *adj.* haya, uchusapa
picar *(una herida) v.* k'aray
pichón de ave *s.* chiwchi, malqo • *v.* **devenir en pichón de ave** chiwchiyay
picor *s.* k'aray

pie *s.* chaki • *adj.* **de pie** sayanpa, sayanpamanta; **de pies grandes** chakisapa • *v.* **estar de pie** sayay; **poner de pie** sayachiy; **tener deseos de estar parado/a** sayanayay
piedra *s.* rumi
piedra plana para moler *s.* maran
piedra preciosa *s.* umiña
pierna *s.* chaka
pinchar *v.* ch'antiy
pinchar con abrojo *v.* qepuchiy
piojo *s.* usa
piojoso/a *adj.* usasapa
pisado/a *adj.* sarusqa
pisar *v.* saruy; **hacerse pisar** saruchikuy • *s.* **el/la que pisa** saruq
pisotear *v.* saruykachay
pisotearse mutuamente *v.* sarunakuy
planicie *s.* panpa
planta de tabaco *s.* sayri
plata *(mineral) s.* qolqe
plato *s.* p'uku
playa *s.* aqopampa, qochapata
plegado/a *adj.* ch'ipusqa, q'empisqa, taparasqa
plegar *v.* ch'ipuy, pataray, q'empiy, taparay; **ayudar a plegar** taparaysiy; **hacer plegar** q'empichiy
plomo *s.* titi
pluma *s.* phuru; **desplumador/a** phurunaq • *adj.* **sin plumas** hallaka • *v.* **cubrirse con plumas** phurullikuy; **desplumar** phurunay
pobre *adj.* wakcha
pocillo *s.* p'uku
poco/a *adj.* as, pisi • *adv.* **poco** asta
poco a poco *adv.* allillamanta, asllallamanta, pisi pisimanta
poder *v.* atiy
poderoso/a *adj.* qhapaq
podrido/a *adj.* ismu, ismusqa; *(huevo)* lloqllo
poema *s.* harawi, haylli
polen *s.* sisa
polilla *s.* thuta
pollo *s.* wallpa
polvoreado/a con harina *adj.* hak'usqa
polvoreador/a con harina *s.* hak'uchaq

polvorear con harina *v.* hak'uchay
pómulo *s.* k'aklla
poner *v.* churay
ponerse *v.* churakuy
ponerse de mal humor *v.* akanayay, enqhey
ponerse de mal humor constantemente *v.* enqhepakuy
¿por qué razón? *inter.* ima rayku
por supuesto *adv.* riki
porfiado/a *adj.* atipakuq
porfiar *v.* atipakuy, kutipakuy
portarse como un/a niño/a *v.* erqekachay
posada *s.* sayana, tanpu
poseedor/a de tierras *s.* chakrayoq
posible de ser cargado/a *(en la espalda) adj.* q'epina
posponer *v.* qhepanchay
poste de madera *(mediano) s.* tanka
preciso/a *adj.* k'apak
predecir *v.* umulliy
pregunta *s.* tapuna
preguntar *v.* tapuy; **mandar a preguntar** tapuchiy
preguntar sobre una y otra cosa *v.* tapukachay
preguntarse a sí mismo *v.* tapukuy
preguntarse mutuamente *v.* tapunakuy
preguntón/a *s.* tapupakuq
prematuramente *adv.* urilla
prenda para envolver un bebé *s.* waltha
prendedor *s.* tupu
preñar *v.* wiksayachiy
preparar barro *v.* t'uruchay
preparar hojas de coca *(ritual) v.* k'intuy • *s.* **el/la que prepara las hojas de coca** k'intuq
preparar la carga *v.* q'epichay
presagiador/a *s.* watupakuq
presagiar *v.* umulliy, watupakuy
prescindir *v.* haqey
presentarse *v.* reqsichikuy
preservar *v.* waqaychay; **ayudar a preservar** waqaychaysiy; **mandar a preservar** waqaychachiy
prestado/a *adj.* mañasqa
prestamista *s.* manuq • *adj.* manuq

prestar *v.* mañay
prestar dinero *v.* manuy
prestarse dinero *v.* manukuy
presuntuoso/a *adj.* qhaphchiykachaq
pretender *v.* munapayay
previamente *adv.* ñawpaqta
previo *adj.* ñawpaq
primera cosecha *s.* *(maíz)* miskha; *(papa)* maway
primo/a *s.* qayri
primogénito/a *s.* phiwi
princesa inka *s.* ñust'a
principiante *s.* qallariq
privarse *v.* muchuy; **causar privación** muchuchiy; **padecer privación** ch'achay • *s.* **el/la que padece privación** ch'achaq
procrear *v.* churiyay, wawachay
prolongadamente *adv.* unay unay
propalar *v.* willaykachay
propietario/a *s.* kaqniyoq
proteger entre las piernas *(algo)* *v.* phakallikuy
provocarse risa unos a otros *v.* asichinakuy
próximo *adj.* sispa
púber *s.* warma
pudrir *v.* ismuy
pueblo *s.* llaqta
puede ser que *adv.* ichapas
puente *s.* chaka
puerta *s.* punku
puesto/a *adj.* churasqa
pulga *s.* piki
pulmón *s.* sorq'an
pulsar *v.* phatatatay
pulverizar *v.* allpayachiy
punzado *adj.* sat'isqa
punzar *v.* sat'iy, t'urpuy
punzón *s.* t'urpuna
puñado *s.* hapht'a
puñetear *v.* saqmay; **dejarse puñetear** saqmachikuy; **hacer golpear con el puño** saqmachiy; **dar puñetazos repetidamente** saqmaykachay
puñetear constantemente *v.* saqmapayay

puñetearse mutuamente *v.* saqmanakuy
puño *s.* ch'oqmi, saqma
pupila *s.* ñawi ruru
pureza *s.* llunp'a
purificar *v.* ch'uyayachiy
puro/a *adj.* llunp'a
pus *s.* q'ea
pusilánime *adj.* unphu, wañu wañu • *v.* **volverse pusilánime** unphuyay

Q

¿qué? *inter.* ima
¡qué bueno/a! *interj.* kusa
¡qué desagradable! *interj.* atataw
¡qué dolor! *interj.* achakaw
¡qué frío! *interj.* alalaw
¡qué hermoso/a! *interj.* añañaw, achalaw
¡qué miedo! *interj.* atakaw
¡qué pena! *interj.* akakallaw, kakallaw
¡qué problema! *interj.* achachaw
¡qué sufrimiento! *interj.* ananay
quebradizo/a *adj.* qhaphra
quebrantado/a *adj.* chhallusqa
quebrantar *v.* chhalluy
quedarse *v.* qhepay, qhepakuy
quemado/a *adj.* kanasqa, ruphasqa
quemar *v.* kanay, ruphay; **hacer quemar** ruphachiy
querer *v.* munay; *(afecto)* munakuy
quererse mutuamente *v.* munanakuy
querido/a *adj.* munasqa
¿quién? *inter.* pi, pin
¡quién sabe! *interj.* yaqapaschá
quietamente *adv.* qasi qasilla
quijada *s.* k'aki, waqo
quinua *s.* kinwa
quitar el cascajo de una vía *v.* khallkanay; **cubrir con cascajo una vía** khallkachay
quitarle a alguien *(algo) v.* qochiy
quitasol *s.* llanthuna
quizás *adv.* chaychá, paqta

R

ración *s.* achura
racionador/a *s.* achuraq
racionar *v.* achuray
radiante *adj.* ch'ak, illaq • *v.* **ponerse radiante** ch'askayay
raicilla *s.* chhapu
raído/a *adj.* thanta
raíz *s.* saphi
rajado/a *adj.* raqra
rajadura *s.* raqra
rajarse *v.* raqray
rallado/a *adj.* thupasqa
rallar *v.* thupay; **ayudar a rallar** thupaysiy
rallar una y otra vez *v.* thupaykachay
rama *s.* ch'aphra • *v.* **cubrirse con ramas** ch'aphrachakuy
ramillete de hojas de coca *s.* k'intu
ramilletes: *v.* **hacer ramilletes** ch'antay • *s.* **el/la que hace ramilletes** ch'antaq
ramo *s.* wayta
rana *s.* ch'eqlla, k'ayra
rancio/a *adj.* maq'a • *v.* **ponerse rancio/a** maq'ayay
rápidamente *adv.* q'osti, usqhay, usqhaylla, usqhayta
rápido/a *adj.* q'osti • *adv.* usqhay, usqhaylla, usqhayta
raposa *n.* unkaka
rascar *v.* rachiy; **tener deseos de rascarse** rachinayakuy
rascar una y otra vez *v.* rachipayay
rascarse mutuamente *v.* rachinakuy
rasgado/a *adj.* eqhasqa
rasgar *v.* eqhay
rasguñador/a *s.* hallp'iq
rasguñar *v.* hallp'iy, sillkuy
raspado/a *adj.* thupasqa
raspar *v.* qhetuy, thupay; **ayudar a raspar** thupaysiy
raspar insistentemente *v.* qhetuykachay
raspar una y otra vez *v.* qhetupayay, thupaykachay
rastrillo *s.* allachu, allana
rastro *s.* yupi

ratón *s.* huk'ucha
reanimar *v.* kawsarichiy
rebanado/a *adj.* q'allasqa
rebanar *v.* q'allay; **hacer rebanar** q'allachiy
rebasado/a *adj.* lleqmasqa
rebasar *v.* lleqmay, yalliy
rebelde *s.* ankalli • *adj.* ankalli
rebuscador/a *s.* t'aqwiq
rebuscar *v.* k'uskiy, maskhaykachay, t'aqwiy; **ayudar a rebuscar** t'aqwiysiy; **mandar a rebuscar** t'aqwichiy
rechoncho *adj.* oqocho
recibido/a *adj.* chaskisqa
recibiente *s.* chaskiq
recibir *v.* chaskiy • *s.* **el/la que recibe para sí** chaskikuq
recién *adv.* chayraq
recientemente *adv.* kunanllaraq
recipiente tejido *s.* taqe
reciprocidad en el trabajo *s.* ayni
recogedor/a de frutos *s.* *(de debajo de la tierra)* allaq, *(sobre la tierra)* pallaq
recoger *v.* hoqariy, *(sobre la tierra)* pallay; **ayudar a recoger** hoqariysiy, *(sobre la tierra)* pallaysiy; **mandar a recoger frutos** *(sobre la tierra)* pallachiy • *adj.* **fácil de recoger** hoqarinalla
recoger en puñados *v.* hapht'ay; **ayudar a recoger en puñados** hapht'aysiy
recoger en puñados constantemente *v.* hapht'aykachay
recoger frutos *(de debajo de la tierra)* *v.* allay; **ayudar a recoger frutos** allaysiy; **hacer recoger frutos** allachiy
recoger frutos una y otra vez *(de debajo de la tierra)* *v.* allapayay
recoger la basura *v.* q'opanay
recoger las hojas secas *v.* q'opanay
recogido/a *adj.* *(sobre la tierra)* pallasqa, *(de debajo de la tierra)* allasqa
recolector/a de restos *s.* pallapakuq
recolectar bosta *v.* q'away; **ayudar a recolectar bosta** q'awaysiy; **mandar a recolectar bosta** q'awachiy
recolectar los tallos resecos de maíz *v.* chhallakuy
recolectar restos *v.* pallapay
reconciliar: *v.* **reconciliarse mutuamente** allipunakuy; **hacer que dos personas se reconcilien** allipunachiy • *s.* **el/la que hace reconciliar** allipunachiq

reconocer *v.* reqsikuy
recordado/a *adj.* yuyasqa
recordar *v.* yuyay; **hacer recordar** yuyachiy • *s.* **el/la que recuerda** yuyaq
recordar súbitamente *v.* yuyariy
recostado/a *adj.* k'irasqa
recostar *v.* k'iray; **hacer recostar** k'irachiy
recriminarse continuamente *v.* ñakapakuy
recuperar uno sus pertenencias y llevárselas *v.* apakapuy
redondeado/a *adj.* muyuchasqa
redondo/a *adj.* muyu
reducido/a a polvo *adj.* allpayasqa
reducir *v.* huch'uyyachiy, pisichay, taksayachiy; **hacer reducir** pisichiy
reemplazar *v.* rantiy
reflejar *v.* lirpuy
refresco *s.* ch'akipa
refresco dulce de maíz *s.* teqte
regado/a *adj.* ch'aqchusqa, qarpasqa
regañador/a *s.* anyaq
regañar *v.* anyay; **hacer regañar** anyachiy • *s.* **el/la que hace regañar** anyachiq
regañar continuamente *v.* anyapayay
regañarse *v.* anyakuy
regañarse insistentemente *v.* anyapakuy
regañarse mutuamente *v.* anyanakuy
regar *v.* qarpay; **ayudar a regar** qarpaysiy
regar constantemente *v.* qarpapayay
región *s.* suyu
regresar *v.* kutiy
regurgitar *v.* kutirpay
reidor/a *s.* asiq
reina *s.* qoya
reír *v.* asiy; **hacer reír** asichiy
reírse *v.* asikuy
reírse continuamente *v.* asiykachay
reírse del dolor de otro *v.* asipayay
rejuvenecer *v.* *(el hombre viejo)* waynayay, *(la mujer vieja)* sipasyay
relamer *v.* llaqwapayay
relamerse *v.* llaqwapakuy

relámpago *s.* illapa
relampaguear *v.* illapay
relato *s.* willakuy
relator/a *s.* willaq
relumbrar *v.* lliphlliy, wach'iy; **ponerse relumbrante** lliphlliyay
remanente *s.* puchu
remar *v.* t'uyuy, tuyuy; **ayudar a remar** t'uyuysiy
remedar con burla *v.* yachapayay • *s.* **el/la que remeda con burla** yachaphuku, yachapayaq
remedio *s.* hanpi
rememorar *v.* yuyapay
remesa *s.* suchi
remesante *s.* suchiq
remesar *v.* suchiy
remezclar *v.* minupayay
remojado/a *adj.* chapusqa, chullusqa
remojar *v.* chapuy, chulluy
remojar una y otra vez *v.* chapuykachay
removedor/a *s.* weq'aq
remover *v.* weq'ay; **ayudar a remover** weq'aysiy; **hacer remover** weq'achiy • *s.* **instrumento para remover** weq'ana
removido/a *adj.* weq'asqa
renacuajo *s.* hoq'oyllo
renovador *s.* mosoqchaq
renovar *v.* mosoqchay
reparado/a *adj.* allichasqa
repartir *v.* achuray; **ayudar a repartir** achuraysiy, rakiysiy; **hacer repartir** achurachiy • *s.* **el/la que hace repartir** achurachiq
repentinamente *adv.* qonqaylla
repetidamente *adv.* kuti kuti, yapa yapa
replicarse mutuamente *v.* ninakuy
reprendedor/a *s.* phiñaq
reprender *v.* phiñay
reprochador/a *s.* anyaq
reprochar *v.* anyay; **hacer reprochar** anyachiy • *s.* **el/la que hace reprochar** anyachiq
reprochar continuamente *v.* anyapayay
reprocharse *v.* anyakuy
reprocharse insistentemente *v.* anyapakuy
reprocharse mutuamente *v.* anyanakuy

reproducirse *v.* miray; **hacer reproducir** mirachiy • *s.* **el/la que hace reproducir** mirachiq
reptador/a *s.* lloqhaq
reptar *v.* chhuchuy, lloqhay
resbalar *v.* suskhay, lluskhay; **hacer resbalar** lluskhachiy
resbaloso/a *adj.* lluskha, suskha
resecado/a *(carne) adj.* ch'arkisqa
resecarse *(carne) v.* ch'arkiyay
reseco/a *adj.* k'irku
resistente *adj.* anaq
resonar *(el cencerro) v.* chanrararay
resonar por la nariz al respirar *v.* ñusñuy
resoplar *v.* phukupakuy
respirar *v.* samay
resplandecer *v.* lliphlliy
resplandeciente *adj.* k'anchay k'anchay • *v.* **ponerse resplandeciente** lliphlliyay
resplandor *s.* ch'ak
responder *v.* kutichiy
restablecerse *(salud) v.* runayay
restaurador/a *s.* mosoqchaq
restaurar *v.* mosoqchay
retener *v.* qhepachiy
retirarse *v.* kuyuriy
retoñar *v.* ch'ichiy, llanllariy
retoño *s.* ch'ichi
retorcido/a *adj.* q'ewi q'ewi
retornar *v.* hampuy
retroceder *v.* kutiriy
reunir *v.* tantay
reunirse *v.* huñunakuy, tantanakuy
reventado *(maíz o trigo) adj.* phatasqa
reventar *v.* phatay; **hacer reventar** phatachiy
reverdecer *v.* llanllay, q'omeryay
reverdecido/a *adj.* llanllasqa
reverenciar *v.* saminchay
revitalizador/a *s.* qespichiq
revitalizar *v.* qespiy; **hacer revitalizar** qespichiy
revivir *v.* kawsariy
revolcarse *v.* qhospay

revolvedor/a *s.* harwiq
revolver *v.* chaqruy, maywiy; **ayudar a revolver** maywiysiy; **hacer revolver** qaywichiy • *s.* **instrumento para revolver** qaywina
revolver fluidos *v.* qaywiy; **ayudar a revolver fluidos** qaywiysiy
revolver fluidos con indiferencia *v.* qaywiykachay
revolver fluidos con mucha voluntad *v.* qaywiyuy
revolver granos *v.* harwiy
revuelto *adj.* chaqrusqa, maywisqa, *(fluidos)* qaywisqa, *(granos)* harwisqa
rezumar *v.* llilliy
rincón *s.* k'uchu
río *s.* mayu
risible *adj.* asina
risotada: *v.* **dar risotadas** thintiy; **dar risotadas una y otra vez** thintipayay
rival *s.* awqa
robado/a *adj.* suwasqa
robar *v.* suway; **ayudar a robar** suwaysiy; **mandar a robar** suwachiy
roca *s.* qaqa, wanka
rocoso/a *adj.* wanka wanka
rodear *v.* tumay
rodeo *s.* tuma
rodilla *s.* moqo, qonqor
roedor/a *s.* khaskaq
roer *v.* khaskay, khastuy
roído/a *adj.* khaskasqa
rojo *adj.* puka
rombo *s.* puytu
romo *adj.* hallmu
romper *v.* p'akiy, *(tela)* qhasuy; **ayudar a romper** p'akiysiy; **mandar a romper** p'akichiy
romper una y otra vez *(tela)* *v.* qhasuykachay
roncador/a *s.* qhorqoq
roncar *v.* qhorqoy
ronco/a *adj.* ch'aka
rondar *v.* muyupayay
ropa *s.* p'acha • *v.* **mandar a coser ropa para uno/a** sirachikuy
ropa interior *s.* ukhuna • *v.* **ponerse la ropa interior** ukhunakuy
roquedal *s.* wanka

roto/a *adj.* llik'i, p'akisqa; *(tela)* qhasusqa
rozar la frente de una mujer con la barbilla *v.* sunkhay
rubio/a *adj.* p'aqo • *v.* **tornarse rubio/a** p'aqoyay
ruiseñor *s.* ch'eqollo

S

sábana *s.* llanp'una
sabedor/a *s.* yachaq
sabelotodo *s.* yachaysapa
saber *v.* yachay • *s.* yachay; **persona con sabiduría** yachaq
sabido *adj.* yachasqa
sabihondo/a *s.* yachaykachaq
sacador/a *s.* horqoq
sacador/a de liendres *s.* ch'iyaq
sacador/a de terrones *s.* ch'anpaq
sacar *v.* horqoy
sacar del agua *(algo) v.* llaphch'ay; **ayudar a sacar del agua** llaphch'aysiy
sacar del agua una y otra vez *(algo) v.* llaphch'apayay
sacar pus *v.* q'eanay
sacar líquido con cucharón *v.* wisiy; **ayudar a sacar líquidos con cucharón** wisiysiy
sacar terrones *v.* ch'anpay
saciado/a *adj.* saksasqa
saciarse *v.* saksay
sacrificado/a *(animal) adj.* nak'asqa
sacrificar *(animal) v.* nak'ay
sacudidor/a *s.* chhaphchiq
sacudir *v.* chhaphchiy, chukchuchiy; **ayudar a sacudir** chhaphchiysiy
sacudir constantemente *v.* chhaphchiykachay
sagrado/a *adj.* willka
sajado/a *adj.* khallasqa
sajador/a *s.* khallaq
sajar *v.* khallay; **ayudar a sajar** khallaysiy; **hacer sajar** khallachiy
sal *s.* kachi
salado/a *adj.* kachisapa, qollpa
salar *v.* kachiyay
salida *s.* punku
salir *v.* lloqsiy; **hacer salir** lloqsichiy
salir una y otra *vez* *v.* lloqsipayay
saliva *s.* thoqay

saltador/a *s.* p'itaq
saltar *v.* p'itay
saltar hacia abajo *v.* p'itayuy
saltarín *s.* p'itakachaq
saludar *v.* napaykuy
saludarse mutuamente *v.* napaykunakuy
salvaje *adj.* salqa • *v.* **volverse salvaje** salqayay • *s.* **animal salvaje** salqa uywa
sanar *v.* allinyay, alliyay; **hacer sanar** alliyachiy, qhaliyachiy
sanar poco a poco *v.* qhaliyay
sandalia *s.* lanq'e, usuta, husut'a
sangrar *v.* sirk'ay
sangre *s.* yawar
sano/a *adj.* qhali
sapo *s.* hanp'atu
satisfacerse *v.* saksay
satisfecho/a *adj.* saksasqa
sazonar *v.* uchuchay • *adj.* **muy sazonado/a** uchusapa
secar *v.* ch'akiy
secar hierbas al sol *v.* qachay
seco/a *adj.* ch'aki
sed *s.* ch'akiy • *v.* **tener sed** ch'akiy
sedimento *s.* t'iyu
segadera *s.* ichhuna
segar *v.* rutuy; **ayudar a segar** rutuysiy; **hacer segar** rutuchiy
segar la paja *v.* ichhuy
segar maíz *v.* kallchay
seguir *v.* qatiy
seguir las huellas *v.* yupichay
seis *num.* soqta
seleccionado/a *adj.* akllasqa, chiklluscqa
seleccionador/a de semillas *s.* muhuchaq
seleccionar *v.* akllay, chiklluy; **ayudar a seleccionar** akllaysiy
seleccionar las semillas *v.* muhuchay
selva *s.* yunka; **habitante de la selva** ch'unchu
sembrado/a *adj.* tarpusqa
sembrador/a *s.* tarpuq
sembrar *v.* tarpuy; **ayudar a sembrar** tarpuysiy; **hacer sembrar** tarpuchiy
sembrío *s.* chakra

semen *s.* wawsa, yuma
semilla *s.* muhu, ruru
señalador/a con el dedo *s.* t'oqsiq
señalar con el dedo *v.* t'oqsiy
señalizar *v.* tuyruy
seno *s.* ñuñu
sentado/a *adj.* tiyasqa
sentarse *v.* tiyay, *(expresión coloquial para niño/as)* pachiy; **hacer sentar** tiyachiy; **mantenerse sentado/a por largo tiempo** tiyarayay; **tener deseos de sentarse** tiyanayay
sentarse una y otra vez *v.* tiyakachay
sentirse como un/a niño/a *v.* erqeyay
separado/a *adj.* t'aqasqa
separar *v.* t'aqay; **ayudar a separar** t'aqaysiy; **mandar a separar** t'aqachiy
separar una y otra vez *v.* t'aqapayay
sepulcro *s.* p'anpana
ser *v.* kay
ser pillado/a *v.* hap'ichikuy
serpiente *(ritual) s.* amaru
servidor/a *s.* yanapaq
servir *v.* yanapay; **mandar a servir** yanapachiy
servir los alimentos *v.* qaray; **ayudar a servir los alimentos** qaraysiy; **mandar a servir los alimentos** qarachiy
servirse mutuamente *v.* yanapanakuy
sesgado/a *adj.* phallu
seso *s.* ñosqhon
sí *adv.* arí
si *conj.* sichus
siega de maíz *s.* kallchay
siete *num.* qanchis
silbador/a *s.* khuyuq
silbar *v.* khuyuy, qoywiy, siwiy; **tener deseos de silbar** siwinayay
silbato *s.* chilu, siwina
silencio *s.* ch'in
silenciosamente *adv.* ch'inlla
silencioso/a *adj.* ch'in
silla *s.* tiyana
silvestre *adj.* purun
sin par *adj.* ch'ullan

sin plumas *adj.* hallaka
sin recursos *adj.* q'alalla
sirena *s.* challwawanka
sirviente *s.* k'umillu
sistema de ayuda mutua *s.* mink'a
sistema de trabajo comunal *s.* mink'a
situarse *v.* churakuy
sobaco *s.* wallwak'u
sobrante *s.* puchu • *adj.* wakin
sobrar *v.* puchuy
sobrecargado/a *adj.* paltasqa
sobrecargar *v.* paltay
sobrepesar *v.* llasay
sobrino *s.* mulla
sobrio/a *(no ebrio/a) adj.* ch'akisonqo
sofocado/a *adj.* mukisqa
sofocar *v.* mukiy
sofocarse de calor *v.* ruphapakuy
soga *s.* q'eswa, waskha
sol *s.* inti; **calor del sol** ruphay
solamente uno/a *adv.* ch'ullalla, huklla • *v.* **reducirse a uno/a** ch'ullayay
soldado *(hombre) s.* wisa, wamink'a
solear *v.* ruphayay
solicitado/a *adj.* maskhasqa
solicitar *(algo) v.* qochikuy
sollozante *s.* anchhiq
sollozar *v.* anchhiy, hik'ipakuy, uyuy, waqapakuy
sollozar constantemente *v.* anchhiykachay
solo uno/a *adj.* ch'ullalla • *v.* **reducirse a uno/a** ch'ullayay
soltar *v.* kachariy, paskay
soltar repentinamente *v.* kacharpariy
sombra *s.* llanthu, supa • *v.* **hacerse sombra mutuamente** llanthunakuy; **ponerse en la sombra** llanthurikuy
sombrear *v.* llanthuy, supay
sombrero *s.* chuku • *v.* **ponerse el sombrero** chukuchakuy
sombrilla *s.* llanthuna
sonido de alas al momento de emprender vuelo *s.* phar
sonido emitido por los loros *s.* k'allallallay
sonreír *v.* asiriy

sonreírse *v.* asirikuy
soñar *v.* mosqhokuy
soñar y sobresaltarse *v.* mosqhopakuy
sopa *(densa) s.* lawa
soplado/a *adj.* phukusqa
soplador/a *s.* phukuq
soplar *v.* phukuy; **ayudar a soplar** phukuysiy; **hacer soplar** phukuchiy
soplar el viento *v.* wayray
soplar una y otra vez *v.* phukupayay
sorber *v.* loqloy, upiy; **hacer sorber** upichiy
sorber por la nariz *v.* senq'ay
sordo/a *adj.* roqt'o, loqt'o, wanq'o • *s.* roqt'o • *v.* **causar sordera** wanq'oyachiy; **volverse sordo/a** wanq'oyay
sospechar *v.* watupakuy • *s.* **el/la que sospecha** watupakuq
sostenedor/a *s.* tusaq
sostener *v.* q'emiy, tusay; **ayudar a sostener** tusaysiy; **hacer sostener** tusachiy
sostener con un palo *v.* tankachay
sostenido/a *adj.* tusasqa
suave *adj.* llanp'u, manti • *v.* **ponerse suave** llanp'uyariy
suavísimo *adj.* llanp'ullaña
subir *v.* seqay, wichay; **ayudar a subir** seqaysiy, wichaysiy; **hacer subir** seqachiy, wichachiy; **intentar subir** seqapakuy; **tener deseos de subir** seqanayay, wichanayay
subir con dificultad *v.* wichapakuy
subir rápidamente *v.* wicharpariy
subir una y otra vez *v.* seqapayay
succionar *v.* ch'onqay
sucesivamente *adv.* qayllalla
suciedad *s.* qhanra, wiswi
sucio/a *adj.* map'a, khacha, qhanra qhanra, qhelli, wiswi; *(piel)* kharka
sudado/a *adj.* hunp'isqa
sudador/a *s.* hunp'iq
sudar *v.* hunp'iy; **hacer sudar** hunp'ichiy
sudor *s.* hunp'i
suelo *s.* allpa
suelto/a *adj.* ch'olqe, waya • *v.* **tornarse suelto/a** ch'olqeyay
sueño *s.* mosqhoy • *v.* **aparecer en sueños** mosqhoychay; **velar el sueño de otro/a** puñuysiy

sufrir *v.* ñak'ariy
sufrir un robo *v.* suwachikuy
suicidarse *v.* wañuchikuy
sujetar la ropa con un prendedor *v.* tupuchay
sumarse a una libación *v.* ukyaysiy
sumergido/a *adj.* challpusqa
sumergir *v.* challpuy • *s.* **el/la que sumerge** challpuq
sumergir una y otra vez *v.* challpuykachay
sumisamente *adv.* ullpu ullpu
supremo/a *adj.* yaya
surco *(tierra)* *s.* wachu • *v.* **ayudar a hacer surcos** wachuysiy; **hacer surcos** wachuy
surgir: *v.* **hacer surgir** paqarichiy • *s.* **el/la que hace surgir** paqarichiq
suspirante *s.* anchhiq
suspirar *v.* anchhiy
suspirar constantemente *v.* anchhiykachay
sustraedor/a *s.* ch'aspaq
sustraer *v.* ch'aspay; **ayudar a sustraer** ch'aspaysiy
sustraído/a *adj.* ch'aspasqa
susto *s.* manchay • *v.* **causar susto** mancharichiy

T

tábano *s.* tankayllu
tacaño/a *adj.* maqlla, akakutirpa, mich'a
tal vez *adv.* chaychá, paqta
tal vez no *adv.* manapaschá
tal vez sí *adv.* yaqapaschá
talado/a *adj.* wit'usqa
talador/a *s.* wit'uq
talar *v.* ch'eqtay, wit'uy; **ayudar a talar** ch'eqtaysiy, wit'uysiy; **hacer talar** wit'uchiy; **mandar a talar** ch'eqtachiy
talego *s.* kutama
tallos resecos de maíz *s.* chhalla
talón *s.* takillpa
tamaño *s.* sayay
tambor *s.* wankar
tamborcillo *s.* tinya
tañer el tambor *s.* tinyay
tapa *s.* kirpa
tapar *v.* kirpay
tarea *s.* llank'ana, ruwana
tarima *s.* kawitu
tartamudear *v.* haklluykachay
tartamudo/a *adj.* hakllu
tejedor/a *s.* awaq
tejer *v.* away; **ayudar a tejer** awaysiy; **hacer tejer** awachiy • *s.* **instrumento para tejer** awana; **lugar donde se teje** awana
tejido/a *adj.* awasqa
tela para cargar *(en la espalda)* *s.* q'eperina
telar *s.* allwina
temblar *v.* chukchuy, khatatay; **hacer temblar** chukchuchiy, khatatachiy • *s.* **el/la/lo que tiembla** chukchuq
temer *v.* manchakuy
temible *adj.* manchana
tender *v.* mant'ay, mast'ay; **ayudar a tender** mant'aysiy, mast'aysiy; **hacer tender** mant'achiy, mast'achiy
tender una y otra vez *v.* mast'apayay, mant'apayay

tender un puente *v.* chakachay
tendido/a *adj.* mant'asqa, mast'asqa
tendón *s.* hank'u
tener *v.* kay
tenue *adj.* llaphlla, llaphsa • *v.* **ponerse tenue** llaphllayay, llaphsayay
teñido/a *adj.* tullpusqa
teñido/a de castaño *adj.* ch'unpichasqa
teñido/a de marrón *adj.* ch'unpichasqa
teñido/a de negrísimo *adj.* ch'illuyasqa
teñidor/a *s.* tullpuq
teñir *v.* tullpuy; **ayudar a teñir** tullpuysiy; **mandar a teñir** tullpuchiy
teñir de castaño *v.* ch'unpichay
teñir de marrón *v.* ch'unpichay
teñir de negrísimo *v.* ch'illuchay
terminado/a *adj.* tukusqa
terminar *v.* tukuy; **ayudar a terminar** tukuysiy; **hacer terminar** tukuchiy
terminar de prisa *v.* tukurpariy
terminar desnudo/a *v.* q'alayay
terminar lo que se dejó inconcluso *v.* tukupay
ternero *s.* phuchu
terrateniente *s.* allpayoq
terremoto *s.* pachakuyuy
terreno *s.* allpa
territorio *s.* marka
terrón *s.* k'urpa • *s.* **sacador/a de terrones** ch'anpaq
terrón con césped *s.* ch'anpa
terroso con mucho polvo *adj.* allpasapa
tía paterna *s.* ipa
tibia *s.* wamantullu
tiempo-espacio *s.* pacha
tierno *adj.* qholla
tierra *s.* allpa; **el/la que posee tierras** allpayoq • *v.* **dejarse cubrir con tierra** p'anpachikuy; **quitar la tierra** allpanay
Tierra *(planeta) s.* Pacha
tierra madre *s.* mamapacha
tiesto *s.* k'akra
tímido/a *adj.* p'enqali, manchali, osqo; • *v.* **volverse tímido/a** osqoyay

tío materno *s.* kaka
tiritar *v.* khatatay; **hacer tiritar** khatatachiy
tiznado/a *adj.* yanachasqa
tiznarse *v.* yanachakuy
tizne *s.* yanamanka
tocar *v.* llamiy
tocar reiteradamente *v.* llamipayay
tocar suavamente *v.* llamiykuy
tocarse mutuamente *v.* llaminakuy
toda la noche *adv.* tutantin
todavía no *adv.* amaraq, manaraq
todo/a *adj.* llapa, llapan, lliw, lluy, tukuy • *adv.* llapanta, lluyta
todo el año *adv.* watantin
todo el día *adv.* ch'isiyaq, p'unchaynintin
todos/as *adj.* llapa, llapan, lliw, lluy, tukuy
tomar uno/a su ración *v.* achurakuy
tomar y llevárselo *(algo)* *v.* apakamuy
tontear *v.* oqarayay
tonto/a *adj.* opa
torcer *v.* q'ewiy, weqoy; **ayudar a torcer** q'ewiysiy, weqoysiy; **hacer torcer** q'ewichiy, weqochiy
torcerse *v.* weqokuy
torcido/a *adj.* q'ewisqa, weqo
torpe *adj.* hat'upa, ñuskhu; *(al andar)* khitu
torpemente *adv.* ñuskhu ñuskhulla
tos *s.* uhu
toser *v.* uhuy; **hacer toser** uhuchiy; **tener deseos de toser** uhunayay • *s.* **el/la que tose** uhuq
toser constantemente *v.* uhupakuy
tostar granos *v.* hank'ay • *s.* **el/la que tuesta granos** hank'aq
totalmente *adv.* q'ala
trabajador/a *s.* llank'aq
trabajar *v.* llank'ay; **ayudar a trabajar** llank'aysiy; **hacer trabajar** llank'achiy
trabajar temporalmente *v.* llank'apakuy
trabajo *s.* llank'ana
traducir *v.* t'ikray
tragado/a *adj.* millp'usqa, oqosqa, rakrasqa
tragar *v.* millp'uy, oqoy, rakray; **hacer tragar** millp'uchiy, oqochiy
tragar saliva *v.* millp'upakuy

tragar una y otra vez *v.* millp'upayay, oqopayay
traicionado/a *adj.* sirpasqa
traicionar *v.* sirpay
traicioneramente *adv.* sirpaylla
traidor/a *s.* sirpaq
tranquilamente *adv.* qasi qasilla, thak
tranquilo *adj.* qasi, thak
tras *adv.* qhepa
trasero *s.* siki
trasladar *v.* astay; **ayudar a trasladar** astaysiy; **hacer trasladar** astachiy • *s.* **el/la que traslada** astaq
trasladar constantemente *v.* astapayay
trasladarse *v.* astakuy
trastornado/a *adj.* loqhe
tratar a alguien como hermano *(mujer) v.* turachakuy
tratar a alguien como hijo/a *v.* wawachakuy
travesaño *s.* chakapa • *v.* **colocar travesaños** chakanay
travieso/a *adj.* saqra; **hacer travesuras** saqraykachay • *v.* **volverse travieso/a** saqrayay
trenza *s.* sinp'a
trenzado/a *adj.* rank'usqa, sinp'asqa
trenzador/a *s.* sinp'aq
trenzar *v.* rank'uy, sinp'ay; **ayudar a trenzar** sinp'aysiy; **dejarse trenzar** sinp'achikuy; **mandar a trenzar** sinp'achiy
tres *num.* kinsa
triste *adj.* llakisqa
tristemente *adv.* khuyay khuyay, llakilla
tristeza *s.* llaki
triturado/a *adj.* ñut'u
triturar *v.* ñut'uy
triturar con los dientes *v.* k'utuy
triunfador/a *s.* llalliq
triunfantemente *adv.* llalli llalli
triunfar *v.* llalliy
trompo *s.* p'esqoyllo
tronado/a *adj.* t'oqyasqa, t'ohasqa
tronar *v.* t'oqyay, t'ohay
tronco de árbol *s.* kurku
tropezarse *v.* misk'akuy
tropezarse y caerse *v.* laq'akuy; **hacer tropezar y caer** laq'achiy

trotar con brincos *v.* chakchay
trueno *s.* qhaqya
tú *pron.* qan
tubérculo *(variedades andinas) s.* añu, maswa, oqa, ulluku, unkucha
tuerto/a *adj.* churchu • *v.* **devenir tuerto/a** churchuyay
tullido/a *adj.* such'u • *v.* **volverse tullido/a** such'uyay
tumba prehispánica *s.* ch'ullpa, p'uytu
tumor *s.* ch'upu
túnica *s.* kusma, unku
tupido/a *adj.* k'iki
turbio/a *adj.* q'ata • *v.* **volverse turbio poco a poco** q'atayay

U

un *art. indet.* huk
una *art. indet.* huk
ungido/a *adj.* hawisqa
ungir *v.* hawiy, llunch'iy
único/a *adj.* sapa
unido/a *adj.* kuska
unificado/a *adj.* hukllasqa
unificar *v.* hukllay
universo *s.* teqsimuyu
uno/a *num.* huk • *v.* **reducirse a uno/a** ch'ullayay
uno tras otro *adv.* qati qati
untado/a *adj.* llusisqa
untar *v.* llusiy; **ayudar a untar** llusiysiy
untar una y otra vez *v.* llusipayay
untarse *v.* llusikuy
untarse mutuamente *v.* llusinakuy
uña *s.* sillu
urdido/a *(hilos) adj.* allwisqa
urdir *(hilos) v.* allwiy, k'antiy; **ayudar a urdir** allwiysiy; **hacer urdir** allwichiy • *s.* **persona que urde** allwiq
urinario *s.* hisp'ana
usado/a *adj.* mawk'a
útero *s.* kisma

V

vaciado/a *adj.* tallisqa, ch'usaqyasqa
vaciar *v.* ch'usaqyachiy, qasichiy
vaciar un líquido totalmente *v.* ch'uymay
vaciar un recipiente *v.* talliy; **ayudar a vaciar un recipiente** talliysiy
vacilar *v.* iskayyay
vacío/a *adj.* ch'usaq
vadear *v.* chinpay
vado de un río *s.* ch'aqcha
vagar *v.* usuy
vagina *s.* chupi
valle *s.* yunka
valoración *s.* chani
valorador/a *s.* chaninchaq
valorar *v.* chaninchay
¡vamos! *interj.* haku, hakuchis
vampiro *s.* masu
vapor *s.* waksi
vaporizar *v.* waksichiy
varón *s.* qhari
vasija *s.* k'akra
vasija grande *s.* urpu
vasija andina para tostar *s.* hank'ana, k'analla
vaso *s.* q'ero
vecino/a *s.* wasimasi
velar el sueño de otro/a *v.* puñuysiy
vena *s.* sirk'a
venado *s.* luychu, taruka
vencedor/a *s.* llalliq, atipaq
vencer *v.* atipay, llalliy; **dejarse vencer** atipachikuy
vencer categóricamente *v.* akachiy
vencido/a *adj.* atipasqa
vendedor/a *s.* qhatuq
vender *v.* qhatuy; **ayudar a vender** qhatuysiy
veneno *s.* miyu

venerado/a *adj.* apuchasqa
venerar *v.* apuchay
venoso/a *s.* sirk'ayoq
ventana *s.* qhawana
ventear *v.* wayray
ventear los granos *v.* eray • *s.* **lugar donde se ventean los granos** era
ventilar *v.* wayrachiy
ventosear *v.* chhakchay
ver *v.* rikuy; **dejarse ver** rikuchikuy; **hacer ver** rikuchiy
verdadero/a *adj.* chanin, cheqaq
verde *adj.* q'omer • *v.* **tornarse verde** q'omerchay
vergüenza *s.* p'enqay
verificar *v.* cheqaqchay
verruga *s.* tikti
verse mutuamente *v.* rikunakuy
vertical *adj.* sayanpa
verticalmente *adv.* sayanpamanta
vestido/a *adj.* p'achasqa
vestir *v.* p'achay; **ayudar a vestir** p'achachiy
vestirse *v.* p'achakuy
vestirse bien *v.* k'achallikuy
vez *(frecuencia) s.* kuti
vía *s.* ñan
viajar *v.* ch'usay, puriy
viajero/a *s.* puriq
victimado/a *adj.* wañuchisqa
vicuña *s.* wikuña
vida *s.* kawsay
vieja *(mujer) s.* paya; • *adj.* **muy vieja** payallaña
viejita *(mujer) s.* mamaku
viejito *(hombre) s.* machula
viejo *(hombre) s.* machu • *adj.* **muy viejo** machullaña
viento *s.* wayra
viga *s.* chakapa • *v.* **colocar una viga** chakapay
visible *adj.* rikunalla
visitante *s.* watukuq
visitar *v.* watukuy
visto *adj.* rikusqa
viuda *s.* ikma

vivero *s.* wanpal
viviente *adj.* kawsaq
vivir temporalmente en casa ajena *v.* tiyapakuy
vociferar *v.* waqway
volar *v.* phaway
volcán *s.* areq
voltear *v.* t'ikray; **ayudar a voltear** t'ikraysiy
voluntariamente *adv.* munay munaylla
volver *v.* hampuy
volver a abonar *v.* wanupay
vomitar *v.* aqtoy, wikch'upakuy; **estar a punto de vomitar** aqtonayay; **tener deseos de vomitar** aqtonayay
vomitar constantemente *v.* aqtopayay
voz *s.* kunka
vuelta *s.* tuma • *v.* **dar vueltas** muyuy; **hacer dar vueltas** muyuchiy

Y/Z

y *conj.* ima
y entonces *conj.* chayqa, hinaspa
¿y entonces? *inter.* chayrí?
ya no *adv.* amaña
yacer *v.* chutarayay
yerno *s.* qatay, tullka
yeso *s.* pachas
yo *pron.* ñoqa
yuca *s.* rumu

zampoña *s.* antara
zancudo *s.* wanwa
zarigüeya *n.* unkaka
zigzag *s.* q'enqo
zorrillo *s.* añas
zorrino *s.* añas
zorro *s.* atoq
zumbar *v.* wanway
zurdo/a *adj.* lloq'e, lloq'enchu • *v.* **devenir en zurdo/a** lloq'eyay

ABOUT THE AUTHORS

Odi Gonzales is a native Quechua speaker, researcher, translator, and poet. He has published several scholarly books in the field of Latin American literature, and many multilingual collections of poetry. He has led the Quechua language program at New York University since 2008. He currently lives in New York City and travels frequently to Peru.

Christine Mladic Janney is a PhD candidate in Anthropology at New York University. She received a Fulbright Grant for research in Peru, a Public Humanities Fellowship to develop digital Quechua language resources, and Foreign Language and Area Studies Fellowships to study Quechua in New York and Peru. She currently resides in Brooklyn, New York.

Emily Fjaellen Thompson earned her BA from Vassar College, where she was awarded the Burnam Fellowship and the Cornelisen Fellowship for Language and Cultural Study. She received her MA from New York University, where she was granted Foreign Language and Area Studies Fellowships for Quechua language study in New York and Peru. She currently lives in Oakland, California.

www.ingramcontent.com/pod-product-compliance
Lightning Source LLC
Jackson TN
JSHW071700170426
101040JS00022B/442

* 9 7 8 0 7 8 1 8 1 3 5 4 9 *